DATA ANALYTICS

Principles, Tools and Practices

DATA ANALYTICS

Principles, Tools and Practices

Ramesh Kait

Pooja Mittal

Supreet Thapar

The Readers Paradise

New Delhi - 110002

Data Analytics - Principles,Tools and Practices
Ramesh Kait, Pooja Mittal, Supreet Thapar

Ist Edition

ISBN - 978-93-5977-023-9

Published by
THE READERS PARADISE
103, 4787/23, Ansari Road, Daryaganj,
New Delhi - 110002
Phone - 9654444181
thereadersparadisesales@gmail.com
www.thereadersparadise.com

Pages - 454 | Paper - 80gsm | Size - 7.5x9.5

Typesetting by
Shri Sai Printographers, Mukherjee Nagar, Delhi

Cover Design by
Kamini Bijoria, Daryaganj, New Delhi - 110002

Printed in India
Trident Enterprises, Noida, Delhi

Preface

In an age where data is hailed as the new oil, the importance of data analytics has surged across various industries, transforming decision-making processes and strategic directions. This comprehensive guide aims to illuminate the multifaceted world of data analytics, providing both foundational knowledge and practical insights for aspiring data professionals, business leaders, and anyone intrigued by the power of data.

Data analytics is not merely a tool for processing information; it is a crucial driver of innovation and efficiency. From healthcare to finance, marketing to logistics, organizations leverage data to gain insights that foster competitive advantage, optimize operations, and enhance customer experiences. As we navigate this guide, we will explore how data analytics has evolved, its key applications across sectors, and the pivotal role it plays in shaping modern enterprises.

The landscape of data analytics has experienced significant evolution. In the early days, data analysis was often limited to basic statistical methods and manual processes. However, with advancements in technology and the exponential growth of data, analytics has transformed into a sophisticated discipline encompassing various methodologies, tools, and technologies. We will delve into emerging trends such as big data analytics, artificial intelligence (AI), and machine learning (ML), which are redefining how organizations harness data. The journey begins with an understanding of the foundational elements of data analytics.

Chapter 1: Foundations of Data Analytics

Part I of this guide introduces the core concepts, starting with the definition of data analytics and its importance across industries. We will explore the different types of data—structured, semi-structured, and unstructured alongside the various storage formats such as relational databases and data lakes. Understanding data acquisition methods and ethical considerations surrounding data collection is also paramount, as these elements set the stage for effective analysis.

Data cleaning and preparation, crucial for ensuring high data quality, will also be examined. Techniques for handling missing values, duplicates, and outliers are essential for transforming raw data into reliable information. Exploratory Data Analysis (EDA) will further be discussed, showcasing how descriptive statistics and visualization techniques can reveal patterns and insights that drive decision-making.

Chapter 2: Core Principles of Data Analytics

As we progress into Part II, we will delve into the core principles that underpin data analytics. This section provides a statistical foundation, essential for interpreting data accurately. Probability theory, hypothesis testing, and the distinction between correlation and causation will be explored, alongside key statistical tools like R and Python libraries.

Data mining techniques, machine learning fundamentals, and predictive analytics are also pivotal topics that will be covered. Understanding these concepts is vital for developing models that not only analyze past trends but also forecast future outcomes. We will discuss algorithms, model evaluation techniques, and the emergence of deep learning, equipping readers with the knowledge to navigate this rapidly evolving field.

Chapter 3: Tools and Technologies

In Part III, we will shift our focus to the tools and technologies that enable data analytics. A comparison of popular tools such as R, Python, Excel, and SQL will be provided, along with insights into data visualization platforms like Tableau and Power BI. The rise of cloud-based analytics platforms, including AWS and Azure, will also be discussed, as they offer scalable solutions for processing large datasets.

Big data technologies, including the Hadoop ecosystem and real-time processing tools like Spark and Kafka, represent a significant leap forward in the ability to handle vast amounts of data efficiently. Additionally, we will examine business intelligence frameworks, text analytics, natural language processing (NLP), and data privacy considerations, ensuring that readers are equipped to tackle the challenges of modern data analytics.

Chapter 4: Applications and Case Studies

Understanding theoretical concepts is crucial, but applying these principles in real-world scenarios is where the true value of data analytics emerges. Part IV presents a collection of applications across various domains marketing, finance, healthcare, supply chain, and human resources. Each chapter will highlight case studies that demonstrate how organizations have successfully implemented data analytics to drive performance and achieve strategic goals.

From customer segmentation in marketing to predictive modeling in healthcare, these case studies will illustrate the transformative impact of data analytics and inspire readers to envision its potential within their own organizations.

Chapter 5: Future Trends and Challenges

Finally, in Part V, we will explore the future of data analytics, examining emerging technologies such as AI and quantum computing. As analytics continues to evolve, ethical considerations will also take center stage. We will address the challenges of bias in algorithms and the importance of developing ethical guidelines that govern data analytics practices. Preparing for the future of data analytics means not only embracing new technologies but also fostering skills and competencies that align with evolving industry needs.

This guide aims to serve as both a comprehensive introduction and a practical resource for navigating the complex world of data analytics. Whether you are a novice seeking to understand the basics or a seasoned professional looking to deepen your expertise, this text provides the knowledge and tools necessary to thrive in the data-driven landscape. As we embark on this journey through the chapters, let us explore the vast potential of data analytics and its capacity to transform insights into impactful actions.

Author

Contents

1

Foundations of Data Analytics

Data analytics is a crucial discipline that enables organizations to extract meaningful insights from vast amounts of data. At its core, data analytics involves a systematic approach to examining data sets, employing statistical tools and techniques to identify trends, patterns, and relationships. This process typically encompasses several stages, including data collection, data cleaning, data analysis, and data interpretation. The rise of big data has exponentially increased the importance of data analytics, as organizations are now inundated with information from various sources, including social media, customer interactions, and transactional databases.

The foundation of data analytics lies in its methodologies, which can be broadly categorized into descriptive, diagnostic, predictive, and prescriptive analytics. Descriptive analytics focuses on summarizing historical data to understand what has happened in the past. Diagnostic analytics delves deeper to determine the causes of past outcomes. Predictive analytics uses statistical models and machine learning techniques to forecast future events based on historical data. Finally, prescriptive analytics provides recommendations on possible actions to optimize outcomes. By leveraging these methodologies, organizations can make data-driven decisions that enhance operational efficiency, improve customer satisfaction, and drive business growth.

In addition to methodologies, a strong foundation in data analytics requires proficiency in tools and technologies. Commonly used software includes Excel for basic data manipulation, SQL for database management, and programming languages like Python and R for advanced statistical analysis. Furthermore, data visualization tools such as Tableau and Power BI play a pivotal role in communicating insights effectively. As organizations continue to recognize the strategic value of data, cultivating a data-literate workforce and fostering a data-driven culture will be essential for harnessing the full potential of analytics to navigate the complexities of the modern business landscape.

1. Introduction to Data Analytics

Data analytics is a critical field that involves examining and interpreting complex data to derive actionable insights. At its core, data analytics transforms raw data into meaningful information through various techniques and processes. This includes descriptive analytics, which summarizes historical data to provide insights into past performance; diagnostic analytics, which explores data to understand why certain events occurred; predictive analytics, which uses statistical models to forecast future outcomes; and prescriptive analytics, which offers actionable recommendations based on data-driven insights. Each type of analysis serves a distinct purpose, from summarizing past events to recommending specific actions, and plays a vital role in strategic decision-making.

The process of data analytics involves several key steps: data collection, cleaning, exploration, analysis, interpretation, and visualization. First, data is gathered from diverse sources, including databases, surveys, and sensors. This data is then cleaned to address inaccuracies and inconsistencies. Exploratory techniques are used to understand the data's structure, followed by analytical methods to extract insights. The results are interpreted and presented through visualizations like charts and dashboards to make them accessible and understandable. Across various sectors such as business, healthcare, finance, and government data analytics help optimize operations, enhance decision-making, and drive innovation. However, challenges like ensuring data quality and maintaining privacy must be addressed to fully leverage the potential of data analytics.

Data analytics is the science of analyzing raw data to make conclusions about that information. It encompasses a variety of techniques and methods to inspect, clean, transform, and model data, aiming to uncover useful information, inform conclusions, and support decision-making. The field of data analytics can be broadly divided into several types, including descriptive, diagnostic, predictive, and prescriptive analytics.

1. **Descriptive Analytics:** This type of analysis focuses on summarizing historical data to understand what has happened. It uses statistical techniques to describe the past and can include generating reports, dashboards, and data visualizations. For example, a retail company might use descriptive analytics to report monthly sales figures or customer demographics.

2. **Diagnostic Analytics:** This type examines data to understand why something happened. It goes beyond mere descriptions to identify patterns or anomalies and determine their causes. For example, if a company's sales dropped in a particular quarter, diagnostic analytics would investigate potential reasons, such as changes in market conditions or consumer behavior.

3. **Predictive Analytics:** Predictive analytics uses historical data and statistical algorithms to forecast future events. By identifying trends and patterns, it can predict future outcomes with a degree of certainty. For instance, predictive analytics might be used to forecast customer churn or sales growth.

4. **Prescriptive Analytics:** This type of analysis provides recommendations for actions based on data insights. It goes beyond predicting future events to suggest specific strategies or actions. For example, prescriptive analytics might advise a marketing team on the best strategies to increase customer engagement based on predictive models.

Defining Data Analytics

Data analytics is the process of systematically examining data to extract meaningful insights and inform decision-making. It involves several stages, starting with data collection, where raw data is gathered from various sources such as databases, sensors, or surveys. This data is then subjected to data cleaning to correct inaccuracies and ensure consistency.

Once cleaned, the data undergoes data exploration, which involves summarizing and visualizing it to understand its structure and identify initial patterns or anomalies. The core of data analytics is data analysis, where advanced techniques such as statistical methods, machine learning algorithms, and data mining are applied to uncover deeper insights and relationships within the data.

After analysis, the findings are interpreted to draw actionable conclusions. These insights are then presented through data visualization, using tools like charts, graphs, and dashboards to make complex results more accessible and understandable to stakeholders.

Data analytics helps organizations and individuals make informed decisions by transforming raw data into actionable insights. It is crucial in various fields including business, where it aids in optimizing operations and enhancing customer experience; healthcare, for improving patient outcomes and predicting disease trends; and finance, for risk management and investment strategies. By leveraging data analytics, entities can make evidence-based decisions, optimize processes, and uncover new opportunities for growth and improvement.

Data analytics is used in a wide array of applications across different industries, each benefiting from its ability to transform raw data into actionable insights. Here are some key ways in which data analytics is employed:

Data Analytics Process: The data analytics process is shown in fig.1.1, it typically involves several key steps:

1. **Data Requirements Specification:** The data required for analysis is based on a question or an experiment. Based on the requirements of those directing the analysis, the data necessary as inputs to the analysis is identified (e.g., Population of people). Specific variables regarding a population (e.g., Age and Income) may be specified and obtained. Data may be numerical or categorical.
2. **Data Collection:** Data Collection is the process of gathering information on targeted variables identified as data requirements. The emphasis is on ensuring accurate and honest collection of data. Data Collection ensures that data

gathered is accurate such that the related decisions are valid. Data Collection provides both a baseline to measure and a target to improve.

Data is collected from various sources ranging from organizational databases to the information in web pages. The data thus obtained, may not be structured and may contain irrelevant information. Hence, the collected data is required to be subjected to data processing and data cleaning.

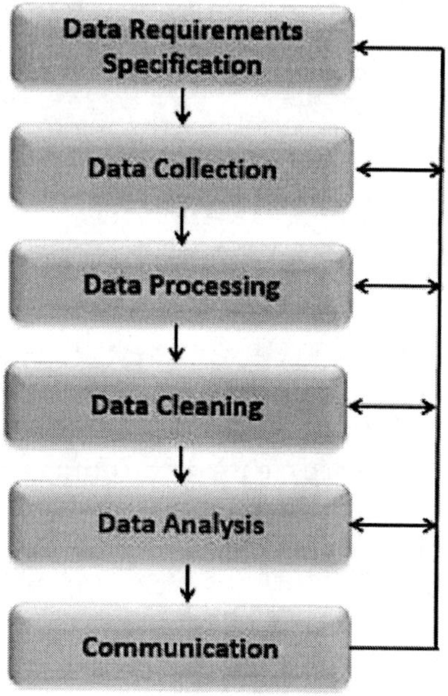

Fig. 1.1

3. **Data Processing:** The data that is collected must be processed or organized for analysis. This includes structuring the data as required for the relevant Analysis Tools. For example, the data might have to be placed into rows and columns in a table within a Spreadsheet or Statistical Application. A data model might have to be created.
4. **Data Cleaning:** The processed and organized data may be incomplete, contain duplicates, or contain errors. Data cleaning is the process of preventing and correcting these errors. There are several types of data cleaning that depend on the type of data. For example, while cleaning the financial data, certain totals might be compared against reliable published numbers or defined thresholds. Likewise, quantitative data methods can be used for outlier detection that would be subsequently excluded in analysis.
5. **Data Analysis:** Data that is processed, organized and cleaned would be ready for the analysis. Various data analysis techniques are available to understand, interpret, and derive conclusions based on the requirements. Data visualization may also be used to examine the data in graphical format, to obtain additional insight regarding the messages within the data.

   Statistical data models such as correlation, regression analysis can be used to identify the relations among the data variables. These models that are descriptive of the data are helpful in simplifying analysis and communicate results.

   The process might require additional data cleaning or additional data collection, and hence these activities are iterative in nature.
6. **Communication:** The results of the data analysis are to be reported in a format as required by the users to support their decisions and further action. The feedback from the users might result in additional analysis.

The data analysts can choose data visualization techniques, such as tables and charts, which help in communicating the message clearly and efficiently to the users. The analysis tools provide facility to highlight the required information with color codes and formatting in tables and charts.

Importance and Applications Across Industries

Data analytics is vital for transforming raw data into actionable insights, enabling informed decision-making, operational efficiency, and predictive capabilities. Across industries, its applications are extensive: businesses leverage it for customer segmentation and sales optimization; healthcare uses it for personalized medicine and operational management; finance employs it for fraud detection and credit scoring; governments utilize it for policy formulation and resource management; retail applies it to inventory management and customer experience; sports teams analyze performance and fan engagement; and educational institutions track student achievement and improve administrative efficiency. Overall, data analytics drives innovation, enhances performance, and provides a competitive edge.

Importance of Data Analytics: Data analytics has become indispensable across industries due to its ability to transform raw data into actionable insights. Its importance lies in several key areas:

1. **Informed Decision-Making:** By analyzing data, organizations can make decisions based on empirical evidence rather than intuition or guesswork. This leads to more accurate and effective strategies.
2. **Operational Efficiency:** Data analytics identifies inefficiencies and optimizes processes, helping organizations streamline operations and reduce costs.
3. **Predictive Capabilities:** It enables forecasting of future trends and behaviors, allowing organizations to anticipate challenges and opportunities.
4. **Enhanced Customer Understanding:** Analytics provides deep insights into customer preferences and behaviors, enabling more personalized and targeted approaches.
5. **Risk Management:** By identifying potential risks and anomalies, data analytics helps in mitigating risks and avoiding potential pitfalls.
6. **Innovation and Competitive Advantage:** Data-driven insights can lead to new product developments, improved services, and innovative business models, providing a competitive edge.

Applications Across Industries: The applications of data analysis across industries are as follows:

1. **Business and Marketing**
   - **Customer Segmentation:** Businesses use analytics to segment customers based on demographics, behavior, and preferences, leading to more effective marketing strategies and personalized experiences.

- **Sales Optimization:** By analyzing sales data, companies can identify high-performing products, understand market demand, and develop strategies to boost sales.
- **Churn Analysis:** Predictive analytics helps identify customers at risk of leaving, allowing businesses to implement retention strategies.

2. **Healthcare**
   - **Personalized Medicine:** Data analytics helps in tailoring treatment plans based on individual patient data, improving outcomes and efficiency in care delivery.
   - **Predictive Analytics for Health:** By analyzing patient data, healthcare providers can predict disease outbreaks, manage chronic conditions, and improve preventive care.
   - **Operational Efficiency:** Hospitals use analytics to manage resources effectively, optimize staffing, and improve patient flow.
3. **Finance**
   - **Fraud Detection:** Financial institutions use data analytics to detect unusual patterns and transactions, preventing fraudulent activities.
   - **Credit Scoring:** Analytics models assess creditworthiness by analyzing financial behavior and transaction history, improving lending decisions.
   - **Market Analysis:** Investment firms analyze market trends and economic indicators to make informed investment decisions and develop strategies.
4. **Government**
   - **Policy Formulation:** Governments use data analytics to evaluate the impact of policies, understand demographic trends, and design evidence-based policies.
   - **Resource Management:** Analytics helps in allocating resources efficiently, managing public services, and planning infrastructure projects.
   - **Public Safety:** Crime data analysis supports law enforcement in predicting crime patterns, optimizing patrol routes, and enhancing community safety.
5. **Retail**
   - **Inventory Management:** Retailers use analytics to forecast demand, manage stock levels, and reduce inventory costs.
   - **Customer Experience:** Analyzing shopping behavior helps in personalizing recommendations, optimizing store layouts, and improving customer satisfaction.
   - **Pricing Strategies:** Data-driven insights help retailers adjust pricing strategies based on market conditions, competition, and consumer behavior.

6. **Sports**
   - **Player Performance Analysis:** Teams and coaches use analytics to assess player performance, design training programs, and develop game strategies.
   - **Fan Engagement:** Sports organizations analyze fan data to create targeted marketing campaigns, enhance game experiences, and increase fan loyalty.
   - **Injury Prevention:** Data analytics helps monitor player health and performance to prevent injuries and optimize recovery.
7. **Education**
   - **Student Achievement:** Analytics helps in tracking student performance, identifying learning gaps, and implementing personalized educational interventions.
   - **Administrative Efficiency:** Schools and universities use data to optimize scheduling, manage resources, and improve operational processes.
   - **Curriculum Development:** Insights from student performance data inform curriculum design and instructional methods.

Evolution and Trends in Data Analytics

The field of data analytics has evolved significantly over the past few decades, adapting to advancements in technology and shifts in data complexity. Here's an overview of its evolution and current trends:

Evolution of Data Analytics: The evolution of data analytics is as under:

1. **Early Data Processing (1950s-1980s):**
   - **Manual Analysis:** Initially, data analysis involved manual calculations and simple statistical methods. Computers began to automate these processes in the 1960s and 1970s.
   - **Business Intelligence (BI):** In the 1980s, BI tools emerged, focusing on reporting and querying data from relational databases. These tools helped in generating reports and performing basic analyses.
2. **Advanced Analytics and Big Data (1990s-2000s):**
   - **Data Warehousing:** The 1990s saw the development of data warehousing technologies, allowing organizations to consolidate large volumes of data from various sources for more comprehensive analysis.
   - **Data Mining:** In the late 1990s and early 2000s, data mining techniques emerged to discover patterns and relationships in large datasets using algorithms and statistical methods.
   - **Big Data:** The explosion of data in the 2000s led to the advent of big data technologies like Hadoop and Spark, which allowed for the processing and analysis of massive datasets beyond the capabilities of traditional databases.

3. **Real-time and Predictive Analytics (2010s-Present):**
   - **Real-time Analytics:** With advancements in technology, real-time analytics became feasible, enabling organizations to analyze and respond to data as it is generated.
   - **Predictive and Prescriptive Analytics:** Predictive analytics, leveraging statistical models and machine learning to forecast future trends, and prescriptive analytics, providing actionable recommendations, have become integral to decision-making.

Current Trends in Data Analytics: The current trends in data analytics are as follows:

1. **Artificial Intelligence (AI) and Machine Learning (ML):** AI and ML are increasingly being integrated into data analytics for more sophisticated modeling, automation, and pattern recognition. These technologies enable predictive analytics and enhance the accuracy of data-driven insights.
2. **Augmented Analytics:** Augmented analytics leverages AI to automate data preparation, insight generation, and analytics processes. It aims to make data analysis more accessible to non-technical users by simplifying complex tasks and enhancing data-driven decision-making.
3. **Data Privacy and Security:** With growing concerns about data privacy, regulations such as GDPR and CCPA are shaping data analytics practices. Ensuring data security and compliance has become a critical focus, leading to the development of advanced data protection technologies.
4. **Cloud Computing:** Cloud-based analytics solutions offer scalability, flexibility, and cost-efficiency. They enable organizations to store and analyze large volumes of data without investing in extensive on-premises infrastructure.
5. **Real-time Data Processing:** The ability to process and analyze data in real-time is becoming increasingly important for industries that require immediate insights, such as finance, retail, and healthcare.
6. **Data Democratization:** There is a growing emphasis on making data and analytics tools accessible to a broader audience within organizations. Self-service analytics platforms empower users across various departments to perform their own analyses and make data-driven decisions.
7. **Edge Analytics:** With the rise of IoT devices, edge analytics processes data at the source rather than sending it to a centralized data center. This reduces latency and bandwidth use, providing faster insights for real-time applications.

In summary, data analytics has evolved from manual and basic reporting methods to sophisticated, real-time, and AI-driven techniques. The current trends reflect a focus on enhancing accessibility, ensuring security, and leveraging advanced technologies to derive actionable insights from ever-increasing volumes of data.

Characteristics of Data Analysis: Data analysis involves a set of practices and techniques aimed at interpreting, transforming, and drawing insights from data. Here are some key characteristics of data analysis:

1. **Objective-oriented:** Data analysis is driven by specific goals or questions. Whether it's to identify trends, make predictions, or test hypotheses, the analysis is directed toward achieving particular objectives.
2. **Systematic Process:** It follows a structured approach which often includes data collection, cleaning, exploration, modeling, and interpretation. This systematic process helps ensure thorough and reliable results.
3. **Quantitative and Qualitative:** Data analysis can involve both numerical (quantitative) data and non-numerical (qualitative) data. Quantitative analysis includes statistical methods and mathematical modeling, while qualitative analysis might involve thematic coding and pattern recognition.
4. **Exploratory and Confirmatory:** Exploratory data analysis (EDA) is used to uncover patterns, spot anomalies, and test assumptions without preconceived notions. Confirmatory data analysis (CDA) is aimed at testing specific hypotheses or theories.
5. **Data Cleaning and Preparation:** Before analysis can begin, data often needs to be cleaned and pre-processed. This involves handling missing values, removing duplicates, and correcting errors to ensure the accuracy and quality of the analysis.
6. **Statistical Methods:** Data analysis frequently employs statistical techniques to summarize data, identify correlations, and make inferences. This includes descriptive statistics, inferential statistics, regression analysis, and more.
7. **Visualization:** Effective data analysis often involves visualizing data through charts, graphs, and plots. Visualization helps to present findings clearly, making complex data more understandable and actionable.
8. **Predictive and Prescriptive:** Predictive analysis involves forecasting future trends based on historical data, while prescriptive analysis provides recommendations for actions based on data insights.
9. **Nature:** Data analysis is often iterative, meaning the process can involve revisiting and refining analysis based on new insights or feedback. This iterative approach helps to continually improve and adjust findings.
10. **Contextual Understanding:** To interpret data accurately, analysts need to understand the context in which the data was collected. This includes considering the source of the data, its relevance, and any external factors that might influence the results.

These characteristics help ensure that data analysis is thorough, reliable, and meaningful, ultimately leading to more informed decision-making and insights.

Future of Data Analytics

The field of data analytics is continuously evolving with advancements in technology. Emerging trends include the increasing use of artificial intelligence (AI) and machine learning for more sophisticated analyses, real-time data processing, and the integration of data from various sources for more comprehensive insights.

In conclusion, data analytics is a powerful tool that helps organizations and individuals make informed decisions by transforming raw data into actionable insights. As data continues to grow in volume and complexity, mastering data analytics will become even more crucial for success across all sectors. Embracing this field not only enhances decision-making but also opens up new opportunities for innovation and growth.

2. Data Types and Structures

Data types like integers, floats, strings, booleans define data values, while data structures loke data frames, tables, trees, graphs organize data. Proper selection ensures effective data manipulation, exploration, and modeling, impacting accuracy and performance in generating insights and making decisions. Data types and structures are crucial as they determine how data is stored, accessed, and processed.

Data Types: The types of data types is shown in fig.1.2.

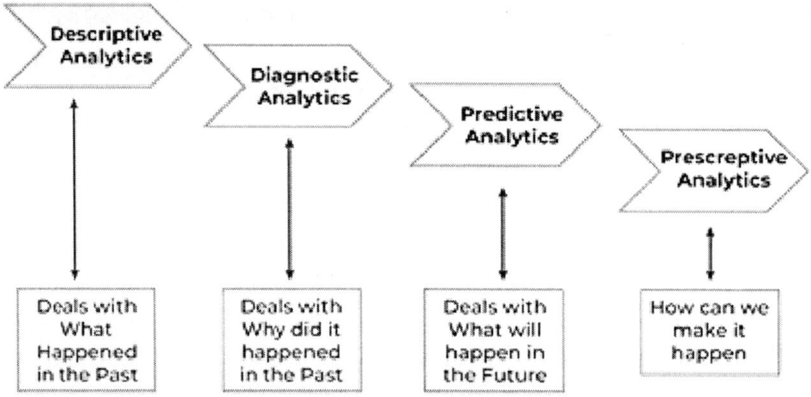

Fig. 1.2

1. **Predictive Analytics:** Predictive analytics turn the data into valuable, actionable information. predictive analytics uses data to determine the probable outcome of an event or a likelihood of a situation occurring. Predictive analytics holds a variety of statistical techniques from modeling, machine learning , data mining , and game theory that analyze current and historical facts to make predictions about a future event. Techniques that are used for predictive analytics are linear regression, time series analysis and forecasting, data mining.

2. **Descriptive Analysis:** Descriptive analytics looks at data and analyze past event for insight as to how to approach future events. It looks at past performance and understands the performance by mining historical data to understand the cause of success or failure in the past. Almost all management reporting such as sales, marketing, operations, and finance uses this type of analysis. The descriptive model quantifies relationships in data in a way that is often used to classify customers or prospects into groups. Unlike a predictive model that focuses on predicting the behavior of a single customer, Descriptive analytics identifies many different relationships between customer and product. Common examples of Descriptive analytics are company reports that provide historic reviews like data queries, reports, descriptive statistics and data dashboard.

3. **Prescriptive Analytics:** Prescriptive Analytics automatically synthesize big data, mathematical science, business rule, and machine learning to make a prediction and then suggests a decision option to take advantage of the prediction. Prescriptive analytics goes beyond predicting future outcomes by also suggesting action benefits from the predictions and showing the decision maker the implication of each decision option. Prescriptive Analytics not only anticipates what will happen and when to happen but also why it will happen. Further, Prescriptive Analytics can suggest decision options on how to take advantage of a future opportunity or mitigate a future risk and illustrate the implication of each decision option. For example, Prescriptive Analytics can benefit healthcare strategic planning by using analytics to leverage operational and usage data combined with data of external factors such as economic data, population demography, etc.

4. **Diagnostic Analytics:** We generally use historical data over other data to answer any question or for the solution of any problem. We try to find any dependency and pattern in the historical data of the particular problem. For example, companies go for this analysis because it gives a great insight into a problem, and they also keep detailed information about their disposal otherwise data collection may turn out individual for every problem and it will be very time-consuming. Common techniques used for Diagnostic Analytics are data discovery, data mining and correlations.

Data Structure: Data structures are essential tools used to organize, manage, and store data efficiently. They help in processing, retrieving, and analyzing large datasets effectively. Here are some key types of data structures commonly used in data analysis:

1. **Arrays:** Arrays are collections of elements, typically of the same type, stored in contiguous memory locations. They allow for efficient indexing, making it easy to access elements using their positions. Arrays are particularly useful for storing and accessing data in a structured manner, such as numerical data in statistical analysis or pixel values in image processing.

Example: In a dataset of daily temperatures for a month, an array can store the temperature values: [30, 32, 31, 29, 28, 30, 31, ...]. Each element can be accessed using its index, making it easy to perform operations like calculating the average temperature.

2. **Linked Lists:** Linked lists consist of nodes, where each node contains data and a reference (or link) to the next node in the sequence. Unlike arrays, linked lists do not require contiguous memory locations, making them more flexible for dynamic data structures. They are useful when the size of the data set is unknown or when frequent insertions and deletions are required, such as in managing a list of tasks or events.

   Example: A linked list can be used to manage a playlist of songs. Each node contains the song details and a reference to the next song in the list. This allows for easy insertion and deletion of songs without reorganizing the entire list.

3. **Stacks:** Stacks follow the Last In, First Out (LIFO) principle, meaning the last element added is the first one to be removed. Elements are added (pushed) and removed (popped) from the top of the stack. Stacks are used in scenarios where data needs to be processed in reverse order, such as in undo mechanisms in software applications or in parsing expressions in compilers.

   Example: In a web browser, the back button uses a stack to keep track of visited pages. The most recently visited page is at the top, and pressing the back button pops the current page off the stack to return to the previous one.

4. **Queues:** Queues follow the First In, First Out (FIFO) principle, where the first element added is the first one to be removed. Elements are added at the rear and removed from the front. Queues are essential in scenarios like task scheduling, where tasks are processed in the order they arrive, or in buffering data streams.

   Example: A queue can be used in a print job management system. Print jobs are added to the queue, and the printer processes them in the order they were received.

5. **Trees:** Trees are hierarchical structures with a root node and child nodes forming a tree-like structure. Each node can have multiple children, but only one parent. Trees are used to represent hierarchical data, such as organizational structures, file systems, or decision trees in machine learning. Binary trees, a specific type of tree where each node has at most two children, are particularly useful in searching and sorting algorithms.

   Example: A binary search tree can be used to store a sorted list of numbers. Each node contains a number, and the left child contains a smaller number while the right child contains a larger number. This structure allows for efficient searching, insertion, and deletion operations.

6. **Graphs:** Graphs consist of nodes (vertices) and edges connecting them. They

are used to represent relationships between entities, such as social networks, transportation networks, or web page links. Graphs can be directed or undirected, weighted or unweighted, and are essential in network analysis, shortest path algorithms, and clustering.

Example: A social network can be represented as a graph where each node is a user and each edge represents a friendship. This structure allows for analysis of relationships and connections between users.

7. **Hash Tables:** Hash tables use a hash function to map keys to values, allowing for efficient data retrieval. They are particularly useful for implementing associative arrays, database indexing, and caching. Hash tables provide average-case constant time complexity for search, insert, and delete operations, making them highly efficient for large datasets.

   Example: A hash table can be used to implement a dictionary where words are keys and their definitions are values. The hash function maps each word to a unique index, enabling quick lookups.

Understanding Data: Structured, Semi-structured, and Unstructured

Structured Data: Structured data refers to information that is highly organized and easily searchable in traditional databases. It is often stored in tabular formats, such as relational databases, spreadsheets, or data warehouses, where each piece of data is neatly arranged into rows and columns. This organization allows for straightforward querying and analysis using structured query language (SQL) or similar tools. Common examples include customer names, addresses, and transaction records.

The main advantage of structured data is its ease of access and manipulation. It is highly standardized, which facilitates efficient storage, retrieval, and analysis. This data type benefits from predefined data models, which enforce data integrity and consistency. For instance, in a relational database, tables are defined with specific schemas that dictate the type of data that can be stored in each column, such as integers, text, or dates.

Structured data is ideal for tasks that require precise and repeatable queries, such as generating financial reports, managing inventory, or analyzing sales performance. Its rigid format and organization make it highly compatible with various analytical tools and software, leading to quick insights and decision-making capabilities. However, structured data has limitations. Its rigidity can be a drawback when dealing with dynamic or rapidly changing information. Additionally, it does not easily accommodate complex or unstructured data types, such as multimedia files or textual data with varied formats.

Semi-structured Data: Semi-structured data occupies a middle ground between structured and unstructured data. It does not conform to the strict schema of structured data but still contains organizational properties that make it easier to analyze than unstructured data. Semi-structured data often includes tags or markers that help to identify and separate different data elements.

Common examples of semi-structured data include XML files, JSON files, and emails. For instance, XML files contain data in a tagged format, which provides a hierarchical structure and metadata that indicate relationships between data elements. JSON files, often used in web applications, present data in a key-value pair format that is flexible and easily interpretable by programming languages.

The primary advantage of semi-structured data is its flexibility. It allows for the inclusion of diverse data types and structures without requiring a predefined schema. This flexibility makes it suitable for scenarios where data formats may change over time or where different data sources need to be integrated.

However, while semi-structured data offers more flexibility than structured data, it still requires some level of parsing and transformation to be fully utilized. Analyzing semi-structured data often requires specialized tools or frameworks to interpret and convert the data into a format that can be used effectively.

Unstructured Data: Unstructured data is the most complex and least organized type of data. It does not fit neatly into traditional database schemas or tables and often lacks a predefined format. Examples of unstructured data include text documents, social media posts, videos, images, and audio recordings.

This data type is characterized by its variability and richness. For instance, an email may contain a mix of text, attachments, and metadata, while a video file may include visual and auditory information. The challenge with unstructured data lies in its diverse formats and the difficulty in extracting meaningful insights without advanced processing techniques.

Despite these challenges, unstructured data holds significant value. It often contains nuanced information that can reveal insights about consumer behavior, trends, or sentiment. Technologies such as natural language processing (NLP), machine learning, and big data analytics are increasingly used to analyze and derive insights from unstructured data. These tools can identify patterns, perform sentiment analysis, and extract relevant information from large volumes of text, images, or audio.

The main disadvantage of unstructured data is the complexity involved in its analysis. Traditional data processing tools and techniques are often inadequate for handling the vast and varied nature of unstructured data. As a result, organizations may need to invest in specialized technologies and expertise to unlock the value of unstructured data effectively.

Conclusion

In summary, structured data is highly organized and easily searchable, semi-structured data offers some degree of organization with greater flexibility, and unstructured data is complex and varied, requiring advanced techniques for analysis. Each data type plays a unique role in information management and decision-making, and understanding their characteristics is crucial for leveraging data effectively in various applications.

Differences Between Structured, Semi-structured, and Unstructured Data

Table 1.1

S.No.	Aspect	Structured Data	Semi-structured Data	Unstructured Data
1.	Organization	Highly organized; follows a strict schema. Stored in tables with rows and columns.	Partially organized; includes tags or metadata but lacks a strict schema.	Lacks predefined format or organization; free-form and varied.
2.	Storage	Relational databases, spreadsheets.	XML, JSON files, NoSQL databases.	Text documents, emails, multimedia files, social media posts.
3.	Flexibility	Less flexible; changes in data format require schema adjustments.	More flexible; accommodates variations in format and structure.	Highly flexible and diverse; supports a wide range of data types and formats.
4.	Use Cases	Financial transactions, customer databases, inventory management.	Data integration from various sources, document repositories, web services.	Gaining insights from social media, multimedia content, and customer feedback.
5.	Examples	Customer names, addresses, transaction records.	XML configuration files, JSON data in APIs.	Emails, social media posts, videos, images.

Data Storage Formats: Relational Databases, NoSQL, Data Lakes

Data storage formats refer to the methods and structures used to save and organize data within a storage system. They define how data is encoded, stored, and accessed, impacting the efficiency, flexibility, and scalability of data management. Different data storage formats are designed to meet various needs based on the nature of the data, the volume, and the requirements for querying and processing.

Relational Databases

Relational databases, or RDBMS (Relational Database Management Systems), are a foundational technology in data management, characterized by their use of structured tables to organize and store data. Each table in a relational database consists of rows and columns, where rows represent individual records and columns represent attributes of these records. The structure of these tables is defined by a schema, which specifies the columns, data types, and constraints, ensuring data integrity and consistency. Relationships between tables are managed through keys primary keys uniquely identify records within a table, while foreign keys establish connections between tables, allowing for complex queries and relational data operations. SQL (Structured Query Language) is the standard language used to interact with relational databases, enabling users to perform a wide range of operations, from simple queries to complex data manipulations and aggregations.

Despite their robust data management capabilities, relational databases face limitations in scalability and flexibility. They are well-suited for environments requiring transactional consistency and data integrity, such as financial systems, customer relationship management (CRM), and enterprise resource planning (ERP) systems. However, their rigid schema can make it challenging to adapt to evolving data requirements, and scaling a relational database typically involves vertical scaling upgrading the hardware of a single server rather than horizontal scaling, which distributes data across multiple servers. As a result, while relational databases offer powerful querying and data integrity features, they may be less adaptable to dynamic or large-scale data environments compared to modern NoSQL databases or data lakes.

Applications of Relational Databases in Data Analysis

1. **Business Intelligence and Reporting:** Relational databases are central to business intelligence (BI) applications. Analysts use SQL to query data and generate reports that provide insights into business performance. For example, a retail company might analyze sales data to identify trends, forecast demand, and optimize inventory.

2. **Customer Relationship Management (CRM):** CRM systems rely on relational databases to store and manage customer information. Analysts use these databases to track customer interactions, analyze customer behavior, and develop targeted marketing strategies. By linking customer data with sales and support records, businesses can improve customer satisfaction and drive growth.

3. **Financial Analysis:** In the financial sector, relational databases are used to manage and analyze transaction data, track investments, and generate financial reports. Analysts can use SQL to perform calculations, such as profit margins and return on investment, and create financial models to support decision-making.

4. **Healthcare Analytics:** Relational databases play a crucial role in healthcare analytics by managing patient records, treatment histories, and clinical data. Analysts can query these databases to track patient outcomes, evaluate treatment effectiveness, and support clinical research. Data from different tables, such as patient demographics and medical histories, can be combined to identify patterns and improve patient care.

5. **E-commerce:** E-commerce platforms use relational databases to manage product catalogs, customer information, and order histories. Analysts can query these databases to analyze purchasing behavior, track inventory levels, and optimize pricing strategies. By understanding customer preferences and trends, e-commerce businesses can enhance their offerings and increase sales.

Relational databases are indispensable tools in data analysis, offering a structured and efficient way to manage and query data. Their support for data integrity, complex relationships, and powerful querying capabilities makes them suitable for a wide range of applications, from business intelligence to healthcare analytics. While challenges exist, ongoing advancements and best practices continue to enhance the effectiveness of relational databases in data analysis. As data grows in volume and complexity, relational databases will remain a cornerstone of data management and analysis, driving informed decision-making and business success.

NoSQL

NoSQL is a type of database management system (DBMS) that is designed to handle and store large volumes of unstructured and semi-structured data. Unlike traditional relational databases that use tables with pre-defined schemas to store data, NoSQL databases use flexible data models that can adapt to changes in data structures and are capable of scaling horizontally to handle growing amounts of data.

The term NoSQL originally referred to "non-SQL" or "non-relational" databases, but the term has since evolved to mean "not only SQL," as NoSQL databases have expanded to include a wide range of different database architectures and data models.

NoSQL databases are generally classified into four main categories:

1. **Document Databases:** These databases store data as semi-structured documents, such as JSON or XML, and can be queried using document-oriented query languages.
2. **Key-value Stores:** These databases store data as key-value pairs, and are optimized for simple and fast read/write operations.
3. **Column-family Stores:** These databases store data as column families, which are sets of columns that are treated as a single entity. They are optimized for fast and efficient querying of large amounts of data.
4. **Graph Databases:** These databases store data as nodes and edges, and are designed to handle complex relationships between data.

NoSQL databases are often used in applications where there is a high volume of data that needs to be processed and analyzed in real-time, such as social media analytics, e-commerce, and gaming. They can also be used for other applications, such as content management systems, document management, and customer relationship management.

However, NoSQL databases may not be suitable for all applications, as they may not provide the same level of data consistency and transactional guarantees as traditional relational databases. It is important to carefully evaluate the specific needs of an application when choosing a database management system.

NoSQL originally referring to non-SQL or non-relational is a database that provides a mechanism for storage and retrieval of data. This data is modelled in means other than the tabular relations used in relational databases. Such databases came into existence in the late 1960s, but did not obtain the NoSQL moniker until a surge of popularity in the early twenty-first century. NoSQL databases are used in real-time web applications and big data and their use are increasing over time.

Advantages of NoSQL: There are many advantages of working with NoSQL databases such as MongoDB and Cassandra. The main advantages are high scalability and high availability.

1. **High scalability:** NoSQL databases use sharding for horizontal scaling. Partitioning of data and placing it on multiple machines in such a way that the order of the data is preserved is sharding. Vertical scaling means adding more resources to the existing machine whereas horizontal scaling means adding more machines to handle the data. Vertical scaling is not that easy to implement but horizontal scaling is easy to implement. Examples of horizontal scaling databases are MongoDB, Cassandra, etc. NoSQL can handle a huge amount of data because of scalability, as the data grows NoSQL.
2. **Flexibility:** NoSQL databases are designed to handle unstructured or semi-structured data, which means that they can accommodate dynamic changes to the data model. This makes NoSQL databases a good fit for applications that need to handle changing data requirements.
3. **High availability:** The auto, replication feature in NoSQL databases makes it highly available because in case of any failure data replicates itself to the previous consistent state.
4. **Scalability:** NoSQL databases are highly scalable, which means that they can handle large amounts of data and traffic with ease. This makes them a good fit for applications that need to handle large amounts of data or traffic
5. **Performance:** NoSQL databases are designed to handle large amounts of data and traffic, which means that they can offer improved performance compared to traditional relational databases.

Disadvantages of NoSQL: NoSQL has the following disadvantages.

1. **Lack of standardization:** There are many different types of NoSQL databases, each with its own unique strengths and weaknesses. This lack of standardization can make it difficult to choose the right database for a specific application
2. **Lack of ACID compliance:** NoSQL databases are not fully ACID-compliant, which means that they do not guarantee the consistency, integrity, and durability of data. This can be a drawback for applications that require strong data consistency guarantees.
3. **Narrow focus:** NoSQL databases have a very narrow focus as it is mainly designed for storage but it provides very little functionality. Relational databases are a better choice in the field of Transaction Management than NoSQL.
4. **Open-source:** NoSQL is an open-source database. There is no reliable standard for NoSQL yet. In other words, two database systems are likely to be unequal.
5. **Lack of support for complex queries:** NoSQL databases are not designed to

handle complex queries, which means that they are not a good fit for applications that require complex data analysis or reporting.

When should NoSQL be used:

1. When a huge amount of data needs to be stored and retrieved.
2. The relationship between the data you store is not that important
3. The data changes over time and is not structured.
4. Support of Constraints and Joins is not required at the database level
5. The data is growing continuously and you need to scale the database regularly to handle the data.

Data Lakes

A Data Lake is a storage system that can store structured and unstructured data at any scale. It differs from traditional databases by allowing data to be stored in its raw, unprocessed form. Data lakes have emerged as a critical component in modern data architecture, particularly for organizations dealing with large volumes of diverse and unstructured data. Unlike traditional relational databases, which structure data into tables and enforce schemas, data lakes offer a more flexible approach to storing and analyzing data.

Data Lake Architecture

A data lake is a centralized depository that allows associations to store all their structured and unshaped data at any scale. Unlike traditional data storage systems, a data lake enables the storage of raw, granular data without the need for a predefined schema. The architecture of a data lake is designed to handle massive volumes of data from various sources and allows for flexible processing and analysis.

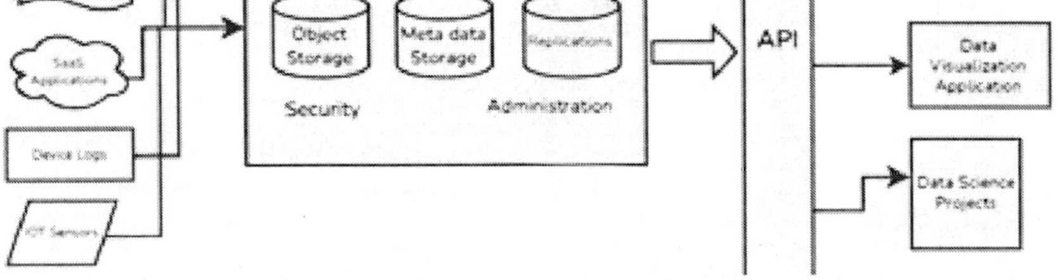

Fig.1.3 Data Lake Architecture

Essential Elements of a Data Lake and Analytics Solution

1. **Storage Layer:** The core of a data lake is its storage layer, which can accommodate structured, semi-structured, and unstructured data. It is typically built on scalable and distributed file systems or object storage solutions.
2. **Ingestion Layer:** This layer involves mechanisms for collecting and loading data into the data lake. Various tools and technologies, such as ETL (Extract, Transform, Load) processes, streaming data pipelines, and connectors, are used for efficient data ingestion.
3. **Metadata Store:** Metadata management is crucial for a data lake. A metadata store keeps track of information about the data stored in the lake, including its origin, structure, lineage, and usage.
4. **Security and Governance:** As data lakes hold diverse and sensitive information, robust security measures and governance policies are essential. Access controls, encryption, and auditing mechanisms help ensure data integrity and compliance with regulations.
5. **Processing and Analytics Layer:** This layer involves tools and frameworks for processing and analyzing the data stored in the lake. Technologies like Apache Spark, Apache Flink, and machine learning frameworks can be integrated for diverse analytics workloads.
6. **Data Catalog:** A data catalog provides a searchable inventory of available data assets within the data lake.

Applications of Data Lakes in Data Analysis

1. **Big Data Analytics:** Data lakes are well-suited for big data analytics, where the volume, variety, and velocity of data exceed the capabilities of traditional data processing systems. For example, organizations can analyze social media data, sensor data, and transaction logs to derive insights into customer behavior and operational efficiency.
2. **Data Science and Machine Learning:** Data lakes provide the raw data necessary for data scientists to build and train machine learning models. By accessing diverse data sources and integrating them into a unified repository, data scientists can develop more accurate models and conduct sophisticated analyses.
3. **Real-time Analytics:** With support for real-time data processing, data lakes can facilitate real-time analytics applications. For instance, companies can analyze streaming data from IoT devices or online transactions to make immediate decisions and respond to emerging trends or issues.
4. **Customer Insights:** Organizations use data lakes to gather and analyze customer data from various touchpoints, such as websites, mobile apps, and

social media. By integrating this data, businesses can gain deeper insights into customer preferences, behaviors, and interactions, leading to more personalized marketing and improved customer experiences.

5. **Operational Analytics:** Data lakes support operational analytics by providing a comprehensive view of business operations. For example, manufacturers can analyze data from production lines, supply chains, and quality control processes to optimize operations and reduce downtime.

Differences Between Relational Databases, NoSQL and Data Lakes

Table 1.2

S.No.	Aspect	Relational Databases	NoSQL	Data Lakes
1.	Data Model	Structured, tables with rows and columns	Flexible, can be document, key-value, column-family, or graph-based	Unstructured or semi-structured data; raw format
2.	Schema	Fixed schema, requires schema definition	Schema-less or dynamic schema	Schema-on-read; schema applied at query time
3.	Scalability	Vertical scaling (scale-up)	Horizontal scaling (scale-out)	Horizontal scaling (scale-out)
4.	Transaction Support	ACID (Atomicity, Consistency, Isolation, Durability)	Varies; some support ACID, others do not	Typically limited; focus on scalability and flexibility
5.	Query Language	SQL (Structured Query Language)	Varies (e.g., MongoDB uses BSON, Couchbase uses N1QL)	Varies; often uses SQL-like queries, or custom tools for querying
6.	Use Cases	Transactional applications, structured data	Big data, real-time web apps, unstructured data	Big data storage, data warehousing, data integration

Data Warehousing and Data Marts

Data warehousing is a system used for reporting and data analysis, and is considered a core component of business intelligence. It involves collecting and managing data from various sources into a centralized repository designed to support decision-making processes. Whereas, data mart is a subset of a data warehouse tailored to the needs of a specific business unit or department. It focuses on a particular area of the business, such as marketing, finance, or sales, and provides more specialized data and insights relevant to that area.

3. Data Collection and Acquisition

Data collection and acquisition involve gathering and obtaining information from various sources for analysis, research, or decision-making.

Data Collection

Data collection is the systematic process of gathering information from various

Table 1.3

S.No.	Aspects	Data Warehousing	Data Marts
1.	Definition	A centralized repository for storing and managing large volumes of data from multiple sources for analysis and reporting.	A subset of a data warehouse, designed for a specific department or business unit.
2.	Scope	Enterprise-wide; integrates data across the entire organization.	Departmental or business unit-specific; focuses on a particular area or function.
3.	Data integration	Integrates data from various sources including operational systems, external sources, and other data warehouses.	Typically integrates data from a subset of sources relevant to its specific function.
4.	Complexity	Generally, more complex; involves extensive data transformation, cleansing, and integration processes.	Less complex; involves a smaller scope of data and may have simpler data transformation processes.
5.	Performance	Optimized for querying large datasets and complex analytical queries across the organization.	Optimized for specific queries and reporting needs of the particular department or function, often leading to faster performance for those queries.
6.	User Base	Used by enterprise-wide users, including business analysts, data scientists, and decision-makers across the organization.	Used by specific departmental users or business unit analysts who need access to relevant data for their specific needs.

sources to address a specific research question or problem. It is fundamental to research and decision-making across various fields, including business, healthcare, social sciences, and more. The purpose of data collection is to obtain accurate and relevant information that can be analyzed to draw conclusions, make decisions, or support hypotheses.

Types of Data Collection: There are two types of data collection which are as follows:

1. **Primary Data Collection:** This involves gathering data directly from original sources. It is usually tailored to specific research questions and often yields highly relevant and accurate data. The methods of primary data collection are as under:

    - **Surveys and Questionnaires:** These are structured tools used to collect data from a large number of respondents. They can be distributed in person, by mail, online, or through phone interviews. For example, a company might use an online survey to gather customer feedback on a new product.
    - **Interviews:** These involve direct interaction between the interviewer and the interviewee. They can be structured (with a predefined set of questions), semi-structured (with a general guideline but allowing for open-ended

responses), or unstructured (more like a conversation). For instance, a researcher conducting a study on job satisfaction might interview employees to gain in-depth insights.

- **Observations:** This method involves systematically watching and recording behaviors or events. For example, an ethnographer might observe interactions in a cultural setting to understand social practices.
- **Experiments**: These involve manipulating variables to observe their effects. For instance, a clinical trial testing a new drug would collect data on its effectiveness and side effects.

2. **Secondary Data Collection:** This involves using existing data that was collected by others for purposes other than the current research. It is often used to complement primary data or when primary data collection is impractical. The source of secondary data collection is as under:

- **Databases:** Academic, government, or commercial databases provide access to a wealth of previously collected data. For example, a researcher might use census data to analyze demographic trends.
- **Published Research:** Academic journals, books, and reports often contain data that can be reanalysed or used to support new research. For example, a literature review on climate change might draw on existing studies to identify gaps and trends.
- **Government Reports:** Many governments publish statistical data on various aspects like economic performance, health metrics, and social indicators. For example, the Bureau of Labor Statistics provides data on employment and wage trends.

Steps in Data Collection

1. **Define Objectives:** Clearly outline what you want to achieve with your data collection. This will guide your choice of methods and tools.
2. **Select Methods:** Choose appropriate methods based on your objectives, resources, and the nature of the data required.
3. **Design Tools:** Develop surveys, questionnaires, or observation checklists, ensuring they are clear and unbiased.
4. **Pilot Testing:** Test your data collection tools on a small sample to identify any issues.
5. **Collect Data:** Implement your data collection methods and gather information.

Fig. 1.4

6. **Monitor and Adjust:** Ensure the data collection process is running smoothly and make adjustments as needed.

Example:

Imagine a company wants to improve its customer service. It decides to collect data to understand customer satisfaction better. The company uses multiple methods:

- **Surveys:** An online survey is sent to customers asking about their recent service experience, covering aspects like wait time, staff friendliness, and overall satisfaction.
- **Interviews:** A few customers are selected for in-depth interviews to explore their experiences and gather detailed feedback.
- **Observations:** Staff interactions with customers are observed in-store to identify areas for improvement.

The collected data is analyzed to identify trends and areas needing improvement, helping the company enhance its customer service strategies.

Data Acquisition

Data acquisition refers to the process of obtaining and integrating data from various sources into a usable format for analysis or operational purposes. It often involves transferring data from multiple systems, sensors, or databases into a centralized location for processing. Data acquisition ensures that data is collected efficiently, accurately, and in a format suitable for analysis. Types of data acquisition are as under:

1. **Manual Data Acquisition**: Involves human effort to gather and input data into systems. This might include entering data from paper forms into digital databases or manually extracting information from reports. **Examples:**
   - **Manual Entry:** Inputting survey responses into a spreadsheet or database.
   - **Data Extraction:** Manually extracting data from paper records or PDFs.
2. **Automated Data Acquisition:** Utilizes technology and software to gather data with minimal human intervention. This often involves sensors, software applications, or automated systems that continuously collect and transmit data. **Examples:**
   - **Sensors:** Environmental sensors that collect data on temperature, humidity, or air quality and transmit it to a central system.
   - **Web Scraping:** Automated tools that extract data from websites. For instance, a company might use web scraping to gather product prices from competitors' websites.
   - **APIs (Application Programming Interfaces):** Allow software applications to interact and exchange data. For example, a financial application might use an API to retrieve real-time stock market data.

3. **Real-time Data Acquisition:** Involves collecting data as it is generated, allowing for immediate analysis and decision-making. This is crucial in scenarios where timely information is essential. **Examples:**
   - **IoT Devices**: Internet of Things devices that collect and send data in real-time, such as smart thermostats that report temperature data to a central system.
   - **Transaction Systems**: Financial systems that process and report transactions in real-time, such as point-of-sale systems in retail.
4. **Batch Data Acquisition:** Involves collecting data at scheduled intervals rather than continuously. This method is often used when real-time data is not necessary. **Examples:**
   - **Daily Data Uploads:** A company might collect and upload daily sales data from various stores into a central database.
   - **Periodic Reports:** Data collected and aggregated from various sources periodically, such as monthly performance reports.

Steps in Data Acquisition

1. **Identify Sources:** Determine where and how data will be obtained, including physical sensors, databases, or external data sources.
2. **Select Tools and Technologies:** Choose appropriate software, sensors, or systems for data acquisition based on the nature of the data and requirements.
3. **Set Up Data Collection:** Configure tools and systems to collect data according to predefined parameters and intervals.
4. **Data Integration:** Combine data from different sources into a centralized system or database for processing and analysis.
5. **Monitor Data Quality:** Ensure that data is accurate, complete, and consistent. Address any issues that arise during the acquisition process.

Fig. 1.5

Example:

Consider a smart city project that aims to monitor and manage traffic flow. The project involves several steps:

- **Identify Sources:** Traffic cameras, GPS data from vehicles, and sensors embedded in roads.
- **Select Tools:** Install cameras and sensors, and use software to aggregate and analyze data.

- **Set Up Data Collection:** Configure sensors to collect data on vehicle count, speed, and traffic congestion at different times of day.
- **Data Integration:** Aggregate data from various sensors and cameras into a central traffic management system.
- **Monitor Data Quality:** Regularly check the data for accuracy and address any discrepancies or sensor malfunctions.

The acquired data is analyzed to optimize traffic signals, reduce congestion, and improve overall traffic management in the city.

Conclusion

Both data collection and acquisition are crucial components of the research and data management processes. Data collection involves gathering new information directly or from existing sources, while data acquisition focuses on obtaining and integrating data from various systems and sources into a usable format. Each process has its methods and best practices, and they often overlap, especially in complex data-driven projects. Understanding and effectively implementing both processes ensure that valuable insights can be derived from data, leading to informed decisions and advancements in various fields.

Differences Between Data Collection and Acquisition

Table 1.4

S.No.	Aspect	Data Collection	Data Acquisition
1.	Definition	The process of gathering data directly from sources through methods such as surveys, interviews, or observations.	The process of obtaining and integrating data from various sources into a usable format, often using technology or automated systems. Definition
2.	Primary Methods	Surveys, interviews, observations, experiments	Sensors, APIs, web scraping, manual data entry
3.	Purpose	To collect new, relevant data tailored to specific research questions or objectives.	To obtain and integrate data from existing systems or sources, often for analysis or operational use.
4.	Data Source	New or original data gathered directly from participants or experiments.	Existing data from databases, sensors, or other automated systems.
5.	Timing of Collection	Can be done in real-time, periodically, or as needed, depending on the method.	Often involves real-time data collection or scheduled batch updates, depending on the system.

Data Sources Internal vs. External

Internal Data Sources: Data generated and maintained within an organization, reflecting its operations and activities, such as sales records, employee performance data, and financial reports. It is directly relevant, under organizational control, and readily accessible to authorized personnel.

Example:

1. **Sales Data Analysis:** Analyzing sales data from a company's internal CRM (Customer Relationship Management) system to identify trends, customer preferences, and sales performance. This might involve examining sales volumes, customer acquisition costs, and seasonal sales patterns to optimize marketing strategies and sales forecasts.
2. **Customer Feedback Analysis:** Analyzing feedback from customer surveys and service interactions stored in the company's customer support database. This analysis could uncover recurring issues, assess customer satisfaction, and inform improvements in product features or customer service processes.

External Data Sources: Data obtained from outside the organization, including market research reports, government statistics, and social media data. It provides insights into external factors, often requiring evaluation for relevance and may involve costs or permissions for access.

Example:

1. **Market Research Analysis:** Using external market research reports from firms like Nielsen or Gartner to understand market trends and consumer behavior. This might involve analyzing data on industry growth rates, competitive landscape, and customer demographics to guide strategic planning and product development.
2. **Economic Data Analysis:** Analyzing government economic statistics, such as GDP growth rates or unemployment figures, to understand macroeconomic conditions that might impact business operations. For instance, a company might use economic data to adjust its investment strategy or sales forecasts in response to economic downturns.

Table 1.5

S.No.	Aspect	Internal Data Sources	External Data Sources
1.	Origin	Data generated within the organization through its own operations and activities.	Data obtained from outside the organization, produced by external entities.
2.	Control	The organization has significant control over data quality, collection methods, and access.	Limited control over the data's quality, format, and update frequency, as it is managed by external sources.
3.	Relevance	Directly relevant to the organization's specific internal operations and strategic goals.	Relevance must be assessed; data may need adaptation to fit the organization's needs.
4.	Access	Generally, readily accessible to authorized personnel within the organization.	May require additional costs, subscriptions, or permissions to access; availability can be subject to external terms.
5.	Cost	Typically involves lower costs, mainly related to internal management and storage.	Often involves higher costs for purchasing data, subscriptions, or acquiring access rights.

Data Collection Techniques: Surveys, Web Scraping, Sensors

Data collection techniques like surveys, web scraping, and sensors are methods used to gather information from various sources for analysis. Each technique has its unique advantages and applications. Here's a detailed overview of these three data collection methods:

Surveys

Surveys are structured tools used to gather information from respondents. They can be distributed through various channels such as online forms, telephone interviews, or face-to-face interactions. Surveys are used to collect both quantitative and qualitative data, often for research, feedback, or decision-making purposes.

Techniques: The techniques of surveys are:

1. **Questionnaires:** Sets of predefined questions with fixed response options, such as multiple-choice or Likert scales.
2. **Interviews:** Direct interactions with respondents, which can be structured (fixed questions), semi-structured (guided conversation), or unstructured (open-ended discussion).
3. **Focus Groups:** Group discussions guided by a facilitator to explore opinions and attitudes on specific topics.

Advantages: The advantages of surveys are:

1. **Direct Feedback:** Provides firsthand responses from participants on specific issues.
2. **Customizable:** Surveys can be tailored to address particular research questions or gather targeted data.
3. **Quantifiable Data:** Enables the collection of numerical data that can be statistically analyzed.

Disadvantages: The disadvantages of surveys are:

1. **Response Bias:** Participants may provide socially desirable responses or misunderstand questions.
2. **Low Response Rates:** Surveys, especially online ones, may suffer from low participation rates.
3. **Limited Depth:** While surveys can gather a broad range of data, they may not capture the depth of responses that qualitative methods can provide.

Example: A company wants to assess customer satisfaction with a new product. It sends out an online survey with questions about product features, ease of use, and overall satisfaction to a sample of its customers.

Web Scraping

Web scraping involves extracting data from websites using automated tools or scripts. This technique is used to collect information available on the web, such as product prices, user reviews, or social media content.

Techniques: The techniques of web scraping are:

1. **HTML Parsing:** Extracting data from the HTML structure of web pages using libraries like BeautifulSoup or lxml.
2. **API Integration:** Using web APIs provided by websites to retrieve data in a structured format.
3. **Automated Crawlers:** Employing bots or scripts to navigate websites and collect data programmatically.

Advantages: The advantages of web scraping are:

1. **Large-scale Data:** Allows for the collection of large amounts of data from numerous web sources quickly.
2. **Up-to-date Information:** Provides access to real-time or frequently updated data from websites.
3. **Cost-effective:** Often more affordable than purchasing data from commercial sources.

Disadvantages: The disadvantages of web scraping are:

1. **Legal and Ethical Issues:** Web scraping may violate terms of service of websites or copyright laws.
2. **Data Quality:** Data extracted from the web may be inconsistent or unstructured.
3. **Maintenance:** Websites often change their structure, requiring regular updates to scraping scripts.

Example: A market analyst uses web scraping to gather pricing information from various e-commerce websites to compare prices and track trends for a specific product category.

Sensors

Sensors are devices that collect data through physical or environmental measurements. They are used in various fields, including industrial monitoring, environmental science, and healthcare.

Techniques: The techniques of sensors are:

1. **Environmental Sensors:** Measure physical properties like temperature, humidity, or air quality. Examples include weather stations and air pollution monitors.
2. **Wearable Sensors:** Track physiological metrics such as heart rate, steps, or activity levels. Examples include fitness trackers and smartwatches.
3. **Industrial Sensors:** Monitor machinery and production processes for parameters like pressure, flow, or vibration. Examples include sensors in manufacturing equipment and industrial IoT devices.

Advantages: The advantages of sensors are:

1. **Real-time Data:** Provides continuous, real-time measurements and monitoring.

2. **High Precision:** Offers accurate data for specific environmental or operational conditions.
3. **Automation:** Enables automated data collection without manual intervention.

Disadvantages: The disadvantages of sensors are:

1. **Cost:** High-quality sensors and their deployment can be expensive.
2. **Maintenance:** Sensors require regular calibration and maintenance to ensure accuracy.
3. **Data Volume:** Sensors can generate large amounts of data, which requires efficient storage and analysis systems.

Example: A smart city initiative uses environmental sensors to monitor air quality across different urban areas. The collected data helps in assessing pollution levels and informing public health policies.

All the above three technique has its specific use cases and can be chosen based on the type of data required and the context of the analysis.

Differences Between Surveys, Web Scraping and Sensors

Table 1.6

S.No.	Aspect	Surveys	Web Scraping	Sensors
1.	Purpose	To gather information directly from individuals through structured questions.	To extract data from websites and online sources.	To measure physical or environmental parameters automatically.
2.	Data Type	Qualitative and quantitative data from human respondents.	Structured data such as text, images, or prices from web pages.	Quantitative data from environmental or physical measurements.
3.	Method of Collection	Direct interaction with participants via questionnaires, interviews, or focus groups.	Automated extraction using scripts or web crawlers.	Continuous monitoring using physical devices or instruments.
4.	Data Accessibility	Requires respondent participation; accessible through various channels (online, phone, in-person).	Requires access to web pages; data can be extracted programmatically.	Data is captured directly by sensors; requires deployment and setup.
5.	Advantages and Challenges	**Advantages**: Direct feedback, customizable questions, detailed responses. **Challenges**: Response bias, low response rates, limited depth.	**Advantages**: Large-scale data collection, real-time updates, cost-effective. **Challenges**: Legal and ethical issues, inconsistent data, maintenance of scraping scripts.	**Advantages**: Real-time, precise data collection, automation. **Challenges**: High cost, maintenance, large data volume.

Data Ingestion Methods and Tools

Data ingestion is the process of collecting and importing data from various sources into a data storage system where it can be analyzed and processed. This is a crucial step in data management, enabling organizations to integrate disparate data sources into a cohesive system for analytics and reporting. There are several methods and tools for data ingestion, each with its own strengths and use cases.

Data Ingestion Methods

Data ingestion is a fundamental process in data management, involving the collection and integration of data from various sources into a central repository for processing and analysis. Different methods of data ingestion are used based on the nature of data, requirements for timeliness, and the volume of data. Below are the primary data ingestion methods:

1. **Batch Ingestion:** Batch ingestion involves collecting and processing data in bulk at scheduled intervals. The data is accumulated over a period and then ingested into the target system all at once, usually during off-peak hours or during a pre-defined window. Batch ingestion is a data processing method where data is collected and processed in bulk at scheduled intervals rather than continuously. This approach involves accumulating data over a specific period, such as daily or weekly, and then processing it all at once during off-peak hours. Batch ingestion is efficient for handling large volumes of data, allowing for optimized resource use and cost-effective processing by leveraging scheduled processing windows. However, it introduces latency, meaning there is a delay between data generation and its availability for analysis, which may not be suitable for applications requiring real-time or near-real-time data. While batch ingestion simplifies infrastructure and is often less expensive than real-time systems, it requires careful management of errors, as issues in batch processing can impact large datasets. Commonly used in scenarios such as data warehousing and end-of-day processing, batch ingestion enables comprehensive reporting and trend analysis by aggregating historical data, making it ideal for applications where timely updates are less critical.

Characteristics:

- **Frequency:** Data is collected and processed periodically (e.g., hourly, daily, weekly).
- **Latency:** There is a delay between data generation and its availability for analysis, depending on the batch interval.
- **Volume:** Well-suited for handling large volumes of data in one go.
- **Complexity:** Generally simpler to manage as it deals with data in chunks rather than continuously.

Advantages:

- **Efficiency:** Processes large datasets effectively and can be optimized for performance.

- **Resource Management:** Allows for better utilization of computing resources by scheduling jobs during non-peak hours.
- **Cost-effective:** Often less expensive to implement and maintain compared to real-time systems.

Disadvantages:

- **Data Freshness:** Not suitable for scenarios requiring real-time or near real-time data.
- **Error Handling:** Errors or issues in batch jobs can affect large volumes of data, necessitating robust error handling and recovery mechanisms.

Use Cases:

- **Data Warehousing:** Loading large volumes of historical data into a data warehouse for reporting and analytics.
- **End-of-day Processing:** Aggregating and analyzing daily transactional data from financial systems.

Example:

A retail chain collects sales data from all its stores throughout the day and ingests this data into a central data warehouse every night. This allows the company to generate daily sales reports and perform trend analysis.

2. **Real-time Ingestion:** Real-time ingestion involves continuously streaming data into the target system as it is generated. This method ensures that data is available almost instantaneously for analysis and decision-making. Real-time ingestion is a data processing method that continuously streams data into a system as it is generated, ensuring that the data is available almost immediately for analysis and decision-making. This approach involves ingesting and processing data in real-time or at very short intervals, often every second or millisecond, to provide up-to-the-minute information. Real-time ingestion is ideal for applications that require immediate data updates, such as financial trading platforms, monitoring systems, or live analytics dashboards. It enables prompt responses to emerging trends, events, or anomalies, enhancing the ability to make timely decisions based on the latest data. However, real-time ingestion can be more complex and expensive to implement compared to batch processing due to the need for high-performance infrastructure and continuous data flow management. It requires robust systems for handling high-velocity data streams, ensuring low latency, and maintaining data integrity. While it offers significant advantages in terms of immediacy and responsiveness, it demands substantial computing resources and sophisticated management to handle continuous data ingestion and real-time analytics effectively.

Characteristics:

- **Frequency:** Data is ingested continuously or at very short intervals (e.g., every second or millisecond).

- **Latency:** Minimal delay between data generation and its availability in the target system.
- **Volume:** Capable of handling high-velocity data streams with the need for low-latency processing.
- **Complexity:** More complex to implement and manage due to the need for continuous data processing and real-time analytics.

Advantages:

- **Immediate Insights:** Provides up-to-the-minute data, enabling timely analysis and decision-making.
- **Enhanced User Experience:** Suitable for applications that require live updates, such as monitoring systems and live dashboards.
- **Responsiveness:** Enables prompt responses to changes or events as they occur.

Disadvantages:

- **Cost:** Can be more expensive due to the need for high-performance infrastructure and real-time processing capabilities.
- **Resource Intensive:** Requires significant computing resources for handling and processing continuous data streams.
- **Complexity:** Requires sophisticated infrastructure for managing data flow, fault tolerance, and scaling.

Use Cases:

- **Real-time Analytics:** Financial trading platforms that need to process and act on market data as it is received.
- **Monitoring Systems:** Social media monitoring tools that track and analyze user sentiment in real-time.

Example:

A stock trading platform uses real-time ingestion to process and analyze stock prices as they change, allowing traders to make instant decisions based on the latest market data.

3. **Micro-batch Ingestion:** Micro-batch ingestion is a hybrid approach where data is collected and processed in small, frequent batches. This method strikes a balance between traditional batch processing and real-time streaming.

Characteristics:

- **Frequency:** Data is processed in small batches at frequent intervals (e.g., every few minutes).
- **Latency:** Provides more timely updates compared to traditional batch processing but with higher latency than real-time ingestion.
- **Volume:** Handles moderate to high volumes of data efficiently.

- **Complexity:** Intermediate complexity, offering a middle ground between the simplicity of batch processing and the immediacy of real-time processing.

Advantages:

- **Timeliness:** Provides frequent updates, making it suitable for scenarios where near real-time data is valuable.
- **Scalability:** Can handle varying data loads and is generally easier to scale than real-time systems.
- **Flexibility:** Useful for applications that do not require continuous real-time data but need more frequent updates than traditional batch processing.

Disadvantages:

- **Resource Utilization:** More frequent processing can lead to increased resource consumption compared to traditional batch jobs.
- **Complexity in Management**: Requires efficient management of data pipelines and scheduling to ensure timely processing.

Use Cases:

- **E-Commerce:** Collecting and processing user activity data in micro-batches to update product recommendations and personalization features.
- **IoT Systems:** Processing sensor data in small, frequent batches for real-time analytics and monitoring.

Example:

An online video streaming service ingests user interaction data (such as watch history and search queries) in micro-batches every 5 minutes to update recommendations and personalize user experiences.

Data Ingestion Tools: Data ingestion tools offer diverse solutions to cater to various needs and technical expertise.

1. **Open-source Tools:** Tools that provide free access to the software's source code, giving users complete control and the ability to customize the tool.
2. **Proprietary Tools:** Solutions that are developed and licensed by software vendors, they offer prebuilt functions and varied pricing plans but might come with vendor lock-in and ongoing licensing costs.
3. **Cloud-based Tools:** Ingestion tools that are housed within a cloud environment, simplifying deployment and maintenance and offering scalability without the need for upfront infrastructure investment.
4. **On-premises Tools:** These tools are installed and managed on a local or private cloud network, providing greater control over data security but requiring investment in hardware and ongoing IT support.

Ethical Considerations in Data Collection

Ethical considerations in data collection are crucial for ensuring the integrity, respect, and rights of participants.

1. **Informed Consent:** Informed consent is a foundational principle in ethical data collection, ensuring that participants understand the nature, purpose, and potential risks of the research before agreeing to participate. Researchers must provide clear and comprehensive information, allowing participants to make an informed decision without coercion. This includes details about the study's objectives, what participation entails, and any foreseeable consequences. Consent should be documented, and participants should have the right to withdraw at any time without penalty. Special care must be taken when working with vulnerable populations, such as children or individuals with cognitive impairments, to ensure that consent is obtained appropriately and ethically. By prioritizing informed consent, researchers foster trust and respect, creating a collaborative environment that values the autonomy and dignity of participants.

Fig.1.6

2. **Privacy and Confidentiality:** Privacy and confidentiality are critical ethical considerations in data collection, aiming to protect participants' personal information from unauthorized access and misuse. Researchers must implement robust data protection measures to ensure that sensitive information remains confidential. This can include anonymizing data, encrypting digital files, and securely storing physical records. Participants should be informed about how their data will be used, shared, and stored, and they should be assured that their identities will not be disclosed without their explicit permission. Upholding confidentiality not only protects participants but also enhances the overall integrity of the research. Researchers must also remain vigilant about potential breaches of confidentiality, ensuring that data sharing

practices comply with legal and ethical standards. By prioritizing privacy, researchers foster a culture of respect and accountability in their work.

3. **Minimizing Harm:** Minimizing harm is an ethical imperative that requires researchers to carefully consider the potential risks their study may pose to participants. This involves conducting a thorough risk assessment to identify any physical, emotional, or psychological harms that could arise from participation. Researchers should implement strategies to mitigate these risks, such as providing support resources or designing studies that avoid sensitive topics if possible. Furthermore, the potential benefits of the research should outweigh any risks involved. Participants should also be informed about any risks they may encounter during the study. By prioritizing the well-being of participants, researchers demonstrate a commitment to ethical practices that uphold the dignity and safety of individuals involved in their studies. This not only protects participants but also enhances the credibility and ethical standing of the research itself.

4. **Fairness and Equity:** Fairness and equity in data collection involve ensuring that all participants are treated justly and that diverse populations are represented in research. Researchers should strive for inclusive sampling methods that account for various demographic factors, such as age, gender, race, and socioeconomic status. Special attention should be paid to vulnerable groups, ensuring they are not exploited or subjected to additional risks. Researchers should be aware of power dynamics that may influence participation and take steps to empower marginalized communities. This can include engaging with community leaders and ensuring that the benefits of the research are shared equitably. By committing to fairness and equity, researchers promote social justice and inclusivity, enhancing the generalizability of their findings while fostering trust and collaboration with the communities involved.

5. **Integrity of Data:** Integrity of data is crucial for maintaining the credibility and reliability of research findings. Researchers must adhere to rigorous standards of accuracy and honesty throughout the data collection and analysis process. This includes avoiding fabrication, falsification, and plagiarism, as well as ensuring that results are reported transparently. Researchers should also be diligent in maintaining the integrity of their methodologies, using appropriate techniques for data collection and analysis. It is essential to address any conflicts of interest that may arise and to disclose these openly. Upholding data integrity not only strengthens the validity of the research but also builds trust with participants, stakeholders, and the wider community. By prioritizing ethical practices in data integrity, researchers contribute to the advancement of knowledge while safeguarding the trust placed in scientific inquiry.

6. **Compliance with Regulations:** Compliance with regulations is a fundamental ethical consideration in data collection, ensuring that researchers adhere to

established legal and institutional standards governing research practices. This includes understanding and following relevant laws, such as the General Data Protection Regulation (GDPR) in Europe or the Health Insurance Portability and Accountability Act (HIPAA) in the United States, which dictate how personal data should be handled and protected. Researchers are often required to seek approval from Institutional Review Boards (IRBs) or ethics committees, which review research proposals to ensure they meet ethical standards. Compliance not only protects participants but also enhances the overall quality and credibility of the research. By staying informed about applicable regulations and seeking necessary approvals, researchers demonstrate their commitment to ethical responsibility and accountability in their work.

7. **Cultural Sensitivity:** Cultural sensitivity is an essential ethical consideration in data collection, particularly in diverse or cross-cultural research contexts. Researchers must recognize and respect the cultural norms, values, and practices of the populations they study. This involves adapting research methodologies to align with local customs and traditions, ensuring that participants feel valued and understood. Engaging with community leaders and stakeholders can help researchers navigate cultural dynamics and build trust. Researchers should also be aware of potential biases in their own perspectives that may affect the interpretation of data. By prioritizing cultural sensitivity, researchers not only enhance the quality of their findings but also promote inclusivity and respect within the research process. This commitment fosters positive relationships with participants and communities, ultimately leading to more ethical and meaningful research outcomes.
8. **Transparency in Reporting:** Transparency in reporting is a vital ethical consideration that emphasizes the need for researchers to communicate their methods, findings, and potential conflicts of interest clearly and openly. By sharing comprehensive details about how data was collected, analyzed, and interpreted, researchers enable others to understand and replicate their work, fostering a culture of accountability and credibility in the scientific community. Transparency also involves disclosing any funding sources or affiliations that may influence the research. Additionally, researchers should aim to publish both positive and negative findings to provide a more complete picture of the research landscape. This commitment to openness enhances trust among participants, stakeholders, and the public, reinforcing the integrity of the research process. By prioritizing transparency, researchers contribute to the advancement of knowledge and promote ethical standards within their field.

4. Data Cleaning and Preparation

Data cleaning and preparation are crucial steps in the data analysis process, aimed at ensuring that datasets are accurate, consistent, and ready for analysis. This process involves identifying and rectifying errors, inconsistencies, and missing values within the data. It sets the stage for meaningful insights and reliable decision-making. Key components:

1. **Data Cleaning:** This involves correcting inaccuracies, removing duplicates, and addressing missing values. It ensures that the data is trustworthy and usable.
2. **Data Preparation:** This includes transforming and structuring the data for analysis. It may involve standardizing formats, encoding categorical variables, and normalizing numerical values to ensure compatibility with analytical tools.

Steps to Perform Data Cleanliness

Performing data cleaning involves a systematic process to identify and rectify errors, inconsistencies, and inaccuracies in a dataset. The following are essential steps to perform data cleaning.

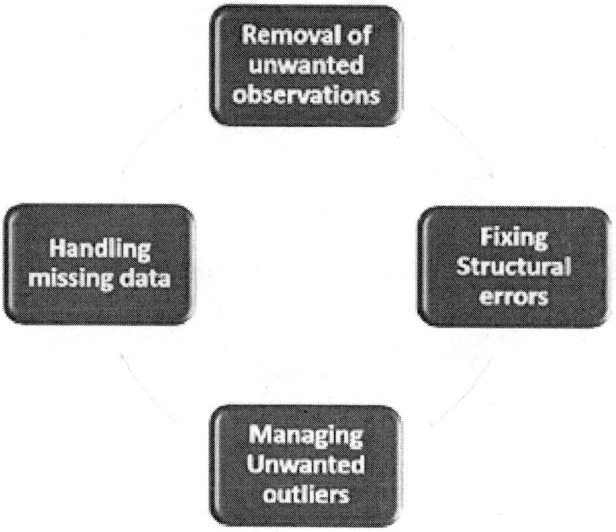

Fig.1.7

1. **Removal of Unwanted Observations:** Identify and eliminate irrelevant or redundant observations from the dataset. The step involves scrutinizing data entries for duplicate records, irrelevant information, or data points that do not contribute meaningfully to the analysis. Removing unwanted observations streamlines the dataset, reducing noise and improving the overall quality.
2. **Fixing Structure Errors:** Address structural issues in the dataset, such as inconsistencies in data formats, naming conventions, or variable types. Standardize formats, correct naming discrepancies, and ensure uniformity in data representation. Fixing structure errors enhances data consistency and facilitates accurate analysis and interpretation.
3. **Managing Unwanted Outliers:** Identify and manage outliers, which are data points significantly deviating from the norm. Depending on the context, decide whether to remove outliers or transform them to minimize their impact on

analysis. Managing outliers is crucial for obtaining more accurate and reliable insights from the data.

4. **Handling Missing Data:** Devise strategies to handle missing data effectively. This may involve imputing missing values based on statistical methods, removing records with missing values, or employing advanced imputation techniques. Handling missing data ensures a more complete dataset, preventing biases and maintaining the integrity of analyses.

Importance of Data Cleaning and Preparation

1. **Enhances Data Quality:** High-quality data is essential for reliable analysis. Cleaning data helps identify and rectify inaccuracies, inconsistencies, and errors.
2. **Improves Decision-Making:** Organizations rely on accurate data to make informed decisions. Clean data provides a strong foundation for strategic planning and operational improvements.
3. **Facilitates Data Integration:** When combining multiple datasets, ensuring that they are cleaned and standardized reduces discrepancies and enhances data coherence.
4. **Saves Time and Resources:** Investing time in the cleaning phase minimizes the risk of errors during analysis, saving time and resources in the long run.
5. **Increases Credibility:** High-quality, well-prepared data enhances the credibility of research and analysis, building trust with stakeholders.

Data Quality Issues: Missing Values, Duplicates, Outliers

Data quality issues can significantly impact the results of data analysis. Among the most common problems are missing values, duplicates, and outliers. Understanding and addressing these issues is crucial for ensuring the integrity of the dataset and the reliability of the insights derived from it.

Missing Values

Missing values occur when data entries are incomplete or absent for certain observations. This can happen due to various reasons, such as errors in data collection, non-responses in surveys, or system malfunctions. Missing values occur when data entries are absent for specific observations in a dataset.

Types of Missing Values: The types of missing values are as follows:

1. **Missing Completely at Random (MCAR):** The probability of a value being missing is unrelated to any other observed or unobserved data. If data is MCAR, analyses can be conducted without bias, as the missingness does not affect the overall dataset.
2. **Missing at Random (MAR):** The missingness is related to observed data but not to the missing data itself. For example, respondents with certain

characteristics (e.g., age) may be less likely to answer specific questions, but other observed variables can help predict missingness.

3. **Missing Not at Random (MNAR):** The missingness is related to the unobserved data itself. For instance, individuals with high incomes may not disclose their income level, leading to missing data that is directly tied to the variable of interest.

Impact of Missing Values: The impact of missing values are as follows:

1. **Bias:** If missing values are not random, they can introduce bias into analyses, potentially skewing results and leading to inaccurate conclusions. For example, if survey participants with specific demographics are less likely to respond, the resulting data may misrepresent the broader population.
2. **Loss of Information:** Removing rows or columns with missing values can significantly reduce the dataset size and may eliminate valuable information. This loss can lead to an incomplete picture of the data and obscure important trends.
3. **Reduced Statistical Power:** Smaller datasets resulting from the removal of missing values can decrease the power of statistical tests, making it more challenging to detect true effects or relationships.

Best Practices: The best practices of missing values are as follows:

1. **Understand the Pattern of Missingness:** Analyze the reasons and patterns behind missing values to choose the most appropriate handling strategy.
2. **Documentation:** Clearly document any methods used to address missing values for transparency and reproducibility in analyses.
3. **Sensitivity Analysis:** Conduct sensitivity analyses to determine how different methods of handling missing values affect the results, helping to understand the potential impact of missing data.

Missing values present significant challenges in data analysis, impacting the reliability and accuracy of results. By understanding the types of missingness and employing appropriate strategies for handling them, analysts can mitigate the negative effects on data quality. This ensures that analyses are robust, leading to more reliable insights and informed decision-making. Prioritizing the management of missing values is essential in maintaining the integrity of datasets in any analytical endeavour.

Duplicates

Duplicates occur when identical records are present multiple times in a dataset. This issue can arise from various sources, including data entry errors, merging datasets without proper checks, or system redundancies. Duplicates can distort the integrity of the data and lead to misleading results.

Impact: The impact of duplicates are as follows:

1. **Inflated Metrics:** Duplicates can result in overestimated counts, averages, or totals. For example, in a customer database, duplicate entries may inflate customer counts and misrepresent sales figures.
2. **Obscured Insights:** The presence of duplicates can mask underlying trends and patterns, making it difficult to extract accurate insights from the data.
3. **Compromised Analysis:** Statistical analyses can be adversely affected, leading to incorrect conclusions and potentially misguided decisions based on faulty data.

Strategies for Handling Duplicates: The strategies for handling duplicates:

1. **Identification:** Use tools and techniques to identify duplicates based on key identifiers (e.g., names, email addresses, or IDs). Data manipulation tools like SQL or Python libraries (e.g., Pandas) can facilitate this process.
2. **Retention Criteria:** Once duplicates are identified, determine which records to retain based on criteria such as recency, completeness, or relevance.
3. **Removal:** After establishing retention criteria, remove unnecessary duplicates to clean the dataset while documenting the process for transparency.

Best Practices: The best practices of duplicates are as follows:

1. Regularly audit datasets to identify and resolve duplicates.
2. Maintain strict data entry protocols to minimize duplicate occurrences.
3. Educate team members on the importance of data quality to prevent errors.

Addressing duplicates is essential for maintaining data quality. By implementing effective identification and removal strategies, analysts can enhance the reliability of datasets, leading to more accurate insights and informed decision-making. Prioritizing duplicate management ensures that analyses are based on clean and trustworthy data.

Outliers

Outliers are data points that significantly deviate from other observations in a dataset. They can occur due to various reasons, including measurement errors, data entry mistakes, or genuine variability in the data. Identifying and addressing outliers is crucial for maintaining data quality.

Impact: The impact of outliers are as follows:

1. **Skewed Analysis:** Outliers can disproportionately influence statistical measures, particularly the mean, which can misrepresent the overall data trends. For example, a few extremely high values can inflate the average, leading to misleading conclusions.
2. **Distorted Relationships:** In regression analyses, outliers can affect the slope and intercept, skewing predictions and undermining the model's accuracy.
3. **Obscured Patterns:** The presence of outliers can mask underlying trends and relationships within the data, making it difficult to derive actionable insights.

Strategies for Handling Outliers: The strategies for handling outliers are as follows:

1. **Identification:** Use statistical methods such as Z-scores, the Interquartile Range (IQR), or visualizations like box plots to detect outliers.
2. **Assessment:** Evaluate whether outliers are genuine observations or errors. Consider the context to decide on their relevance.
3. **Treatment Options:**
   - Removal: Exclude outliers if they are determined to be errors or irrelevant.
   - Transformation: Apply techniques such as logarithmic transformation to reduce the influence of outliers.
   - Capping: Set thresholds to limit the effect of extreme values while preserving them in the dataset.

Effectively managing outliers is essential for ensuring data quality. By employing proper identification and treatment strategies, analysts can enhance the reliability of their datasets, leading to more accurate analyses and informed decision-making. Addressing outliers helps maintain the integrity of data insights, ultimately contributing to better outcomes across various fields.

Difference Between Data Quality Issues: Missing Values, Duplicates, Outliers

Table 1.7

S.No.	Impact	Missing Values	Duplicates	Outliers
1.	Definition	Absence of data entries for specific observations.	Identical records appearing multiple times in a dataset.	Data points that significantly deviate from other observations.
2.	Causes	Errors in data collection, non-responses, or entry mistakes.	Data entry errors, merging datasets without checks.	Measurement errors, genuine variability, or data entry mistakes.
3.	Impact on Analysis	Can lead to biased results and loss of information	Inflates metrics, leading to misrepresentation of data.	Skews statistical measures and obscures true data trends.
4.	Handling Strategies	Deletion, imputation, or flagging for missing data.	Identification, retention criteria, and removal of duplicates.	Identification, assessment, removal, transformation, or capping.
5.	Types of Issues	Deletion, imputation, or flagging for missing data.	Primarily involves exact matches based on key identifiers.	Typically involves extreme values that can vary in direction.
6.	Effect on Data Size	May reduce the dataset size if rows/columns are deleted.	Can lead to an inflated number of records if not managed.	Often does not change the size significantly unless removed.

Data Transformation Techniques: Normalization, Encoding, Aggregation

Data transformation techniques are essential processes in data preparation that enhance the quality and usability of data for analysis and machine learning. Here's an overview of key data transformation techniques:

1. **Normalization:** Normalization is a data preprocessing technique used to scale numeric values to a common range, typically between 0 and 1, or -1 and 1. This technique is crucial in many machine learning algorithms, especially those that rely on distance metrics, such as k-nearest neighbors (KNN) and support vector machines (SVM). If the features of a dataset are measured in different scales (e.g., age in years and income in thousands), normalization ensures that no single feature disproportionately influences the model's predictions. The techniques of normalization are as:

   - **Min-Max Scaling:** This is the most common normalization technique. It rescales each feature to a fixed range, usually [0, 1]. The formula used is:

     $$X' = \frac{X - X_{\min}}{X_{\max} - X_{\min}}$$

     Here, X' is the normalized value, X is the original value, X_{min} is the minimum value of the feature, and X_{max} is the maximum value. This method preserves the relationships between values, ensuring they remain proportionate.

   - **Z-Score Normalization (Standardization):** This method transforms data to have a mean of 0 and a standard deviation of 1, making it suitable for algorithms that assume a Gaussian distribution. The formula is:

     $$X' = \frac{X - \mu}{\sigma}$$

     where μ is the mean and σ is the standard deviation. This transformation is particularly useful when the data contains outliers, as it reduces their influence.

     Use Cases: Normalization is commonly employed in machine learning workflows, particularly for gradient-based optimization algorithms, where consistent data scaling can significantly improve convergence speed and model accuracy. It is also useful in data visualization, ensuring that different features can be compared directly on the same graph.

     Challenges: While normalization is beneficial, it can also introduce challenges. For instance, min-max scaling can be sensitive to outliers since they can dramatically affect the minimum and maximum values. In such cases, Z-score normalization might be preferable. Additionally, when applying normalization, it's essential to fit the scaling parameters (mean, min, max) only on the training data to prevent data leakage.

2. **Encoding:** Encoding is a critical data transformation technique that converts

categorical variables into a numerical format, enabling machine learning algorithms to process them effectively. Many algorithms require numerical input, making encoding a necessary step in data preprocessing. Proper encoding ensures that the model can interpret categorical data without introducing biases or incorrect interpretations. The techniques are as:

- **One-Hot Encoding:** This technique transforms categorical variables into binary columns. For example, a feature "Color" with categories [Red, Green, Blue] is converted into three new binary features: "Color_Red," "Color_Green," and "Color_Blue." Each category is represented by a 1 (presence) or 0 (absence). One-hot encoding prevents the introduction of ordinal relationships among categories, which is crucial when categories have no inherent order.
- **Label Encoding:** This method assigns a unique integer to each category. For instance, "Red" might be encoded as 0, "Green" as 1, and "Blue" as 2. While this method is simple and effective, it can create an unintended ordinal relationship among the categories, which could mislead certain algorithms that assume a ranking exists.
- **Target Encoding:** In this method, categories are replaced with the mean of the target variable for each category. This approach can capture the relationship between the categorical variable and the target variable but runs the risk of overfitting, particularly in small datasets.

  Use Cases: Encoding is vital in various machine learning applications, such as predicting customer behavior based on demographic information or classifying products based on attributes. By transforming categorical data, models like decision trees, neural networks, and regression algorithms can effectively learn patterns from the data.

  Challenges: While encoding is essential, it can also introduce challenges. One-hot encoding can lead to a significant increase in dimensionality, especially when dealing with high-cardinality categorical variables (those with many unique categories). This situation can lead to the "curse of dimensionality," making the model more complex and harder to interpret. Thus, it's crucial to choose the appropriate encoding method based on the specific dataset and model requirements.

3. **Aggregation:** Aggregation is the process of summarizing data to provide insights and facilitate analysis. It reduces data volume by combining multiple data points into a single representative value, such as sums, averages, or counts. This technique is commonly used in data analysis and reporting to condense large datasets into manageable and informative summaries. The techniques are as:

   Group By: This technique groups data based on one or more keys, allowing for the calculation of summary statistics for each group. For example, in a sales dataset, you could group by "Product Category" and calculate total sales or average sales price for each category.

Window Functions: These functions perform calculations across a set of rows related to the current row, allowing for moving averages, cumulative sums, and other complex aggregations. For instance, a moving average can provide insights into trends over time without the influence of extreme values.

Use Cases: Aggregation is widely used in business intelligence for generating reports and dashboards. It helps organizations analyze trends, performance metrics, and other key indicators over time or across different categories. For instance, sales teams can aggregate data by month to visualize sales trends, while finance departments can summarize expenses by category to monitor budget adherence.

These transformation techniques are fundamental for preparing data for effective analysis and ensuring high-quality input for machine learning models. Each technique plays a crucial role in enhancing the data's interpretability and usability.

Difference Between Normalization, Encoding, Aggregation

Table 1.8

S.No.	Aspects	Normalization	Encoding	Aggregation
1.	Purpose	Scale numerical data to a common range	Convert categorical variables into numerical format	Summarize and condense data into representative values
2.	Types of Data Handled	Primarily continuous numerical data	Categorical data	Both categorical and numerical data
3.	Techniques Used	Min-Max Scaling, Z-Score Normalization	One-Hot Encoding, Label Encoding, Target Encoding	Group By operations, summation, averages, window functions
4.	Impact on Data Structure	Changes the scale without altering relationships	Alters the structure by creating new numerical columns	Reduces data points by summarizing them
5.	Application Context	Preprocessing for machine learning models	Preparing categorical data for algorithms	Data analysis, reporting, and visualization

Tools for Data Cleaning: OpenRefine, Trifacta, Python Libraries

1. **OpenRefine:** OpenRefine is an open-source tool designed for cleaning and transforming messy data. It provides a user-friendly interface that allows users to explore and analyze datasets through filtering and faceting. Ideal for data wrangling, OpenRefine helps users efficiently prepare data for analysis, ensuring accuracy and consistency in their datasets. Its extensibility and community support further enhance its usability for data scientists and analysts. Support for multiple data formats such as CSV, Excel, and JSON make OpenRefine versatile for various data sources. Additionally, its capability to connect to external APIs allows users to enrich their datasets with supplementary information.

Key Features:

- **Data Exploration:** Users can easily explore and analyze data with filtering and faceting options, helping identify inconsistencies.
- **Clustering Algorithms:** OpenRefine provides built-in clustering algorithms to detect and merge similar values, such as duplicate names or variations in text.
- **Transformation Language:** It includes a flexible transformation language called GREL (General Refine Expression Language) for data manipulation.
- **Data Format Support:** Supports a wide range of data formats, including CSV, Excel, and JSON, making it versatile for various data sources.

Use Cases: Ideal for cleaning messy datasets, reconciling data from multiple sources, and preparing data for analysis or further processing.

2. **Trifacta:** Trifacta is a powerful data preparation tool designed to streamline the process of cleaning, transforming, and enriching data for analysis. Featuring an intuitive, interactive interface, Trifacta allows users to visualize their data and see the impact of transformations in real-time. This user-friendly approach makes it accessible to both technical and non-technical users.

One of Trifacta's key strengths is its smart recommendations, powered by machine learning algorithms that suggest data cleaning and transformation steps based on the patterns identified in the data. This feature accelerates the data wrangling process, enabling users to focus on insights rather than manual data manipulation.

Trifacta supports a wide array of data sources, including cloud storage, databases, and flat files, facilitating seamless data ingestion. Its built-in data profiling capabilities automatically assess data quality, identifying outliers and trends to inform cleaning decisions.

Key Features:

- **Interactive Interface:** Offers a visual interface that allows users to see the effects of transformations in real-time.
- **Smart Recommendations:** Utilizes machine learning to suggest data cleaning and transformation steps based on the user's actions.
- **Data Profiling:** Automatically profiles data to identify data quality issues, outliers, and trends, helping users make informed decisions.
- **Integration:** Seamlessly integrates with various data sources and platforms, including cloud storage and databases, facilitating data ingestion.

Use Cases: Well-suited for organizations needing to prepare large volumes of data quickly and efficiently, particularly in analytics and business intelligence contexts.

3. **Python Libraries:** Python libraries are essential tools for data cleaning and manipulation, widely used by data scientists and analysts for their versatility and efficiency.

Key Libraries:

- **Pandas:** A widely used library that provides data structures and functions to manipulate structured data. It supports operations like filtering, merging, and grouping. Pandas, which offers data structures like DataFrames, allowing for powerful operations such as filtering, merging, and aggregating datasets. Its intuitive syntax makes complex data manipulations straightforward, making it a staple in data preparation workflows.
- **NumPy:** While primarily focused on numerical data processing, NumPy is often used alongside Pandas for efficient array operations and handling missing data. NumPy complements Pandas by providing support for numerical operations and efficient handling of arrays, which is particularly useful for mathematical computations and handling missing data. Together, these libraries facilitate comprehensive data manipulation tasks.
- **Dask:** Dask offers capabilities to scale computations beyond memory limitations, enabling efficient data handling without sacrificing performance.
- **Beautiful Soup and Scrapy:** Beautiful soup and scrapy are excellent for web scraping, allowing users to extract and clean data directly from web pages.

Key Features:

- **Flexibility:** Offers extensive capabilities for data manipulation, enabling users to write custom cleaning scripts.
- **Integration:** Easily integrates with other data science tools and frameworks, facilitating end-to-end data workflows.
- **Community Support:** Strong community support and extensive documentation make it easy to find resources and solutions for specific cleaning challenges.
- **Use Cases:** Ideal for custom data cleaning tasks, automating repetitive cleaning processes, and integrating data cleaning into broader data analysis and machine learning pipelines.

These tools each offer unique features and capabilities for data cleaning, catering to different user needs and workflows. OpenRefine and Trifacta provide user-friendly interfaces for non-programmers, while Python libraries offer flexibility and power for those comfortable with coding.

5. Exploratory Data Analysis (EDA)

Exploratory Data Analysis (EDA) is a crucial initial step in data science projects. It involves analyzing and visualizing data to understand its key characteristics, uncover patterns, and identify relationships between variables refers to the method of studying and exploring record sets to apprehend their predominant traits, discover patterns, locate outliers, and identify relationships between variables. EDA is normally carried out as a preliminary step before undertaking extra formal statistical analyses or modeling. Key aspects of EDA include:

1. **Distribution of Data:** Examining the distribution of data points to understand their range, central tendencies (mean, median), and dispersion (variance, standard deviation).
2. **Graphical Representations:** Utilizing charts such as histograms, box plots, scatter plots, and bar charts to visualize relationships within the data and distributions of variables.
3. **Outlier Detection:** Identifying unusual values that deviate from other data points. Outliers can influence statistical analyses and might indicate data entry errors or unique cases.
4. **Correlation Analysis:** Checking the relationships between variables to understand how they might affect each other. This includes computing correlation coefficients and creating correlation matrices.
5. **Handling Missing Values:** Detecting and deciding how to address missing data points, whether by imputation or removal, depending on their impact and the amount of missing data.
6. **Summary Statistics:** Calculating key statistics that provide insight into data trends and nuances.
7. **Testing Assumptions:** Many statistical tests and models assume the data meet certain conditions (like normality or homoscedasticity). EDA helps verify these assumptions.

Types of Exploratory Data Analysis

There are various sorts of EDA strategies that can be hired relying on the nature of the records and the desires of the evaluation. Depending on the number of columns we are analyzing we can divide EDA into three types:

1. **Univariate Analysis:** Univariate analysis focuses on a single variable to understand its internal structure. It is primarily concerned with describing the data and finding patterns existing in a single feature. This sort of evaluation makes a speciality of analyzing character variables inside the records set. It involves summarizing and visualizing an unmarried variable at a time to understand its distribution, relevant tendency, unfold, and different applicable records. Common techniques include:
   - **Histograms:** Used to visualize the distribution of a variable.
   - **Box plots:** Useful for detecting outliers and understanding the spread and skewness of the data.
   - **Bar charts:** Employed for categorical data to show the frequency of each category.
   - **Summary statistics:** Calculations like mean, median, mode, variance, and standard deviation that describe the central tendency and dispersion of the data.

2. **Bivariate Analysis:** Bivariate evaluation involves exploring the connection between variables. It enables find associations, correlations, and dependencies between pairs of variables. Bivariate analysis is a crucial form of exploratory data analysis that examines the relationship between two variables. Some key techniques used in bivariate analysis:
   - **Scatter Plots:** These are one of the most common tools used in bivariate analysis. A scatter plot helps visualize the relationship between two continuous variables.
   - **Correlation Coefficient:** This statistical measure (often Pearson's correlation coefficient for linear relationships) quantifies the degree to which two variables are related.
   - **Cross-tabulation:** Also known as contingency tables, cross-tabulation is used to analyze the relationship between two categorical variables. It shows the frequency distribution of categories of one variable in rows and the other in columns, which helps in understanding the relationship between the two variables.
   - **Line Graphs:** In the context of time series data, line graphs can be used to compare two variables over time. This helps in identifying trends, cycles, or patterns that emerge in the interaction of the variables over the specified period.
   - **Covariance:** Covariance is a measure used to determine how much two random variables change together. However, it is sensitive to the scale of the variables, so it's often supplemented by the correlation coefficient for a more standardized assessment of the relationship.
3. **Multivariate Analysis:** Multivariate analysis examines the relationships between two or more variables in the dataset. It aims to understand how variables interact with one another, which is crucial for most statistical modeling techniques. Techniques include:
   - **Pair plots:** Visualize relationships across several variables simultaneously to capture a comprehensive view of potential interactions.
   - **Principal Component Analysis (PCA):** A dimensionality reduction technique used to reduce the dimensionality of large datasets, while preserving as much variance as possible.

Descriptive Statistics and Summary Measures

Descriptive statistics and summary measures are essential components of data analysis that help summarize and interpret large datasets.

Descriptive Statistics

Descriptive statistics provide simple summaries about the sample and the measures. They allow analysts to describe and understand the basic features of the data without making inferences about a larger population. Descriptive statistics help describe and explain the features of a specific data set by giving short summaries about the sample and measures of the data. The most recognized types of descriptive statistics are measures of center. For example, the mean, median, and mode, which are used at almost all levels of math and statistics, are used to define and describe a data set. The mean, or the average, is calculated by adding all the figures within the data set and then dividing by the number of figures within the set.

For example, the sum of the following data set is 20: (2, 3, 4, 5, 6). The mean is 4 (20/5). The mode of a data set is the value appearing most often, and the median is the figure situated in the middle of the data set. It is the figure separating the higher figures from the lower figures within a data set. However, there are fewer common types of descriptive statistics that are still very important.

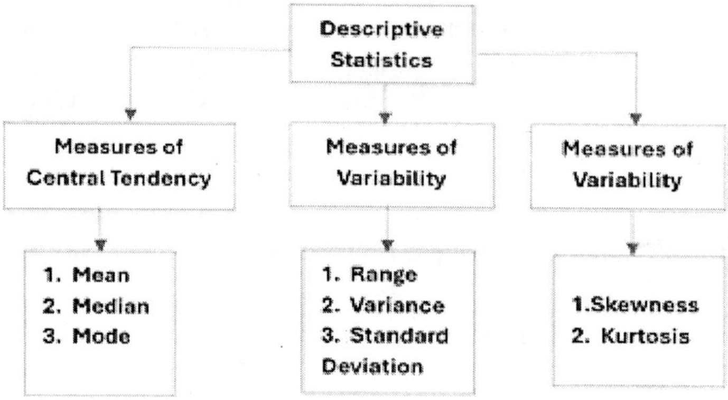

Fig.1.8

Descriptive statistics can be divided into as follows:

1. **Measures of Central Tendency:** These statistics summarize a dataset with a single value that represents the center of its distribution:
   - **Mean:** The arithmetic average of a set of values, calculated by summing all values and dividing by the number of observations. It is sensitive to outliers.
   - **Median:** The middle value when the data is sorted in ascending or descending order. It is less affected by outliers and provides a better measure of central tendency for skewed distributions.
   - **Mode:** The most frequently occurring value(s) in the dataset. A dataset can be unimodal (one mode), bimodal (two modes), or multimodal (multiple modes).
2. **Measures of Variability:** These statistics describe the spread or dispersion of the data:
   - **Range:** The difference between the maximum and minimum values in the dataset, providing a simple measure of spread.

- **Variance:** Measures the average squared deviation of each number from the mean. A higher variance indicates greater dispersion.
- **Standard Deviation:** The square root of the variance, indicating how much individual data points typically deviate from the mean. It is expressed in the same units as the data.

3. **Measures of Distribution:** These statistics provide insights into the shape of the data distribution:
   - **Skewness:** A measure of the asymmetry of the data distribution. Positive skewness indicates a longer tail on the right, while negative skewness indicates a longer tail on the left.
   - **Kurtosis:** Measures the "tailedness" of the distribution. High kurtosis indicates a distribution with heavy tails and a sharp peak, while low kurtosis indicates a flatter distribution.

Summary Measures

Summary measures combine various descriptive statistics to provide a comprehensive overview of the dataset. Common summary measures include:

- **Five-Number Summary:** Consists of the minimum, first quartile (Q1), median (Q2), third quartile (Q3), and maximum. This summary is useful for visualizing the distribution of the data and identifying outliers.
- **Interquartile Range (IQR):** The difference between Q3 and Q1, representing the range of the middle 50% of the data. It is a robust measure of variability that is less influenced by outliers.

Importance of Descriptive Statistics and Summary Measures

Descriptive statistics and summary measures are crucial for:

1. **Data Understanding:** They provide a clear and concise summary of the dataset, helping analysts quickly grasp its main characteristics.
2. **Data Quality Assessment:** They help identify data entry errors, outliers, and missing values, which are essential for ensuring data integrity.
3. **Decision Making:** By summarizing key aspects of the data, these measures assist in informed decision-making and guide further analysis, including inferential statistics and predictive modeling.

Conclusion

Descriptive statistics and summary measures are foundational tools in data analysis that facilitate a clear understanding of data characteristics. By summarizing large datasets, they enable analysts to make informed decisions and drive deeper insights into the data.

Data Visualization Techniques: Histograms, Box Plots, Scatter Plots

Data visualization is crucial for understanding and communicating complex information. Histograms, box plots, and scatter plots are powerful tools that reveal patterns, distributions, and relationships in data. These techniques help analysts explore datasets visually, uncovering insights that might be missed in raw numbers.

Each visualization method serves a specific purpose. Histograms show frequency distributions, box plots highlight outliers and compare groups, and scatter plots reveal relationships between variables. Mastering these techniques empowers data analysts to tell compelling stories and make informed decisions based on visual evidence.

Data visualization techniques are essential for understanding and communicating data insights effectively. Here's an overview of three key visualization techniques:

1. **Histograms:** Histograms are a powerful data visualization technique used to represent the distribution of numerical data by dividing it into bins (intervals). Each bin corresponds to a range of values, and the height of the bar indicates the number of observations within that range. This allows analysts to quickly assess the frequency distribution of a dataset.

It looks somewhat like a bar chart, but with key differences that make it suitable for showing how data is distributed across continuous intervals or specific categories that are considered "bins". Unlike bar graphs, which are used for categorical data, histograms are designed for continuous data, grouping it into logical ranges or "bins."

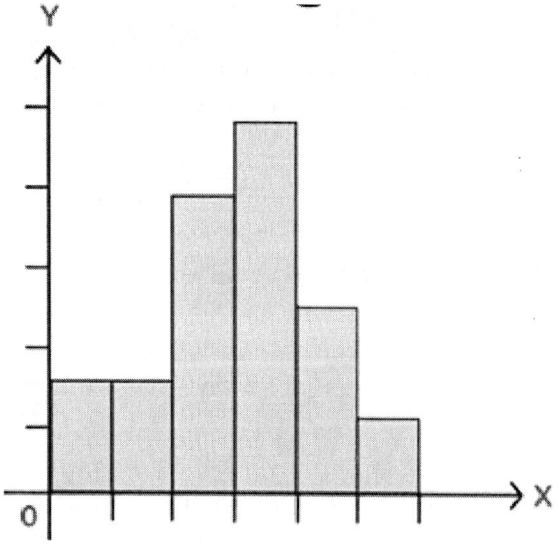

Fig.1.9

A histogram is similar to a bar graph. The basic difference between the two is that bar charts correlate a value with a single category or discrete variable, whereas histograms visualize frequencies for continuous variables.

The following are some typical forms of histograms and their characteristics:

- **Uniform Histogram:** A Uniform Histogram shows uniform distribution means that the data is uniformly distributed among the classes, with each having a same number of elements. It may display many peaks, suggesting varying degrees of incidence.
- **Bimodal Histogram:** A histogram is called bimodal if it has two distinct peaks. This implies that the data consists of observations from two distinct groups or categories, with notable variations between them.
- **Symmetric Histogram:** Symmetric Histogram is also known as a bell-shaped histogram, it has perfect symmetry when divided vertically down the centre, with both sides matching each other in size and shape. The balance reflects a steady distribution pattern.

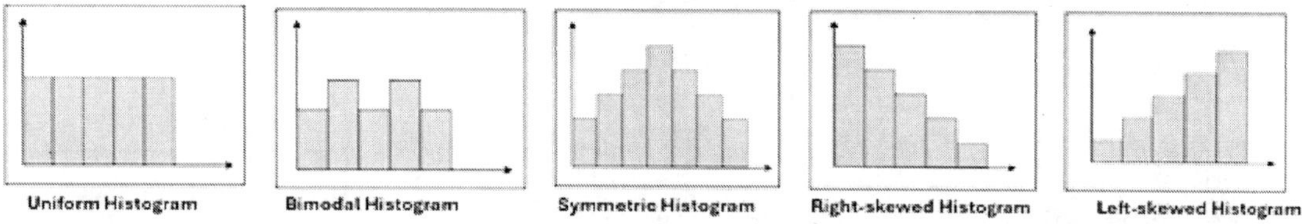

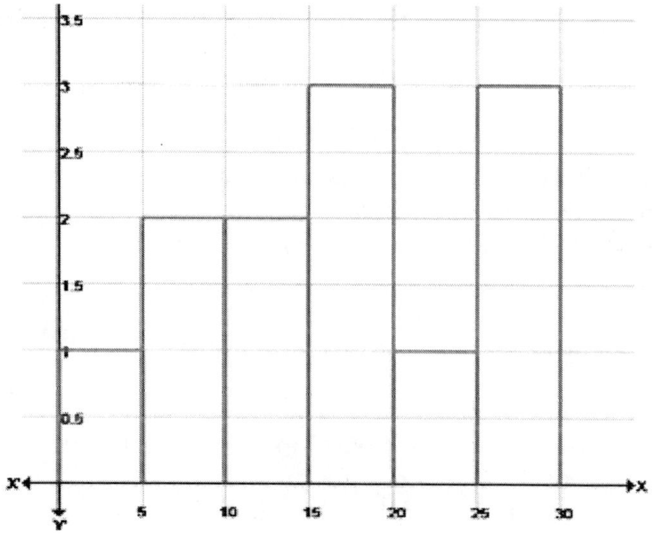

Fig.1.10

- **Right-skewed Histogram:** A right-skewed histogram shows bars leaning towards the right side. This signifies that the majority of the data points are on the left side, with a few outliers reaching to the right. Consider a histogram showing the distribution of family earnings. A right-skewed histogram occurs when the majority of families are in lower income groups, but a small number of highly rich households skew the average income.
- **Left-skewed Histogram:** A left-skewed histogram shows bars that lean

towards the left side. This means that the majority of the data points are on the right side, with a few exceptionally low values extending to the left. Consider a histogram reflecting the distribution of test scores in a classroom. A left-skewed histogram occurs when the majority of students receive excellent grades but a few do badly, resulting in an average that is dragged to the left.

Steps to Draw Histogram: Histogram is the basic toll of representing data and we can easily draw histogram by following the steps added below:

Step 1: Collect the data you wish to display in the histogram. This might range from test results to population distribution. For example: Assume we get the following test scores: 14, 20, 12, 26, 8, 7, 2, 28, 30, 16, 18, 23. First arrange it in ascending order. Exam results: 2, 7, 8, 12, 14, 16, 18, 19, 23, 26, 28 and 30.

Step 2: Determine the number of intervals, or "bins," you wish to split your data into. This is determined by the scope and distribution of your data, as well as the amount of information you choose to display. Assume we wish to divide the scores into 5 bins.

Step 3: Determine the limits of each bin. These bounds should encompass the complete range of your data and be regularly spaced. 0-5. 5-10, 10-15, 15-20, 20-25, 25-30.

Class Interval	Frequency
0-5	1
5-10	2
10-15	2
15-20	3
20-25	1
25-30	3

Fig.1.11

Step 4: Count the number of data points that belong in each bin.

Step 5: On a graph, show the bin borders on the x-axis and the frequency of data points in each bin on the y-axis. Create bars for each bin, with the height of each bar representing the frequency of data points in that bin.

In this histogram, the x-axis depicts the bins, while the y-axis indicates the frequency of data points falling within each bin. The bars represent the sample data's distribution across the given bins.

Advantages:

- Histograms provide an easy-to-understand visual representation, allowing for fast estimate of key statistical measures such as the mean and median based solely on the shape and central tendency of the graph.
- Histograms can give insights into probable future data events by highlighting patterns and trends in the current dataset, which can help with forecasting and decision-making.
- Histograms are a simple way to exhibit data of variable frequencies and kinds, allowing for clear communication and analysis across several domains and disciplines.
- Statisticians respect histograms for their consistency since they organize data into intervals with uniform distribution, guaranteeing precision and dependability when showing data distributions.

Disadvantages:

- While histograms provide a simple visual representation, they might oversimplify complicated data patterns, potentially leading to misconceptions or missing subtleties in the information.
- Histogram interpretation can be subjective since people perceive patterns differently, resulting in various judgements regarding the data.
- The bin sizes and intervals used in a histogram can influence the visual look and perception of the data. Poorly designed bins might hide key details or generate fake patterns.
- In rare situations, histograms can be visually deceiving, particularly if the scale or axes are modified to emphasize some traits or downplay others, resulting in inaccurate data interpretation.
- While histograms are useful for visualizing a single dataset, they may not allow for straightforward comparison of many datasets, particularly those with differing sizes or distributions.

2. **Box Plots:** Box Plot is a graphical method to visualize data distribution for gaining insights and making informed decisions. Box plot is a type of chart that depicts a group of numerical data through their quartiles. Let us take a sample data to understand how to create a box plot.

Here are the runs scored by a cricket team in a league of 12 matches – 100, 120, 110, 150, 110, 140, 130, 170, 120, 220, 140, 110.

To draw a box plot for the given data first we need to arrange the data in ascending order and then find the minimum, first quartile, median, third quartile and the maximum.

Ascending Order – 100, 110, 110, 120, 120, 130, 140, 150, 170, 220

Median (Q2) = (120 + 130) / 2 = 125 Since, there were even values

To find the First Quartile we take the first six values and find their median.

Q1 = (110 +110) / 2 = 110

For the Third Quartile, we take the next six and find their median.

Q3 = (140 + 150) / 2 = 145

Note: If the total number of values is odd then we exclude the Median while calculating Q1 and Q3. Here since there were two central values, we included them. Now, we need to calculate the Inter Quartile Range.

IQR = Q3 – Q1 = 145 – 110 = 35

We can now calculate the Upper and Lower Limits to find the minimum and maximum values and also the outliers if any.

Lower Limit = Q1 – 1.5 * IQR = 110 – 1.5 * 35 = 57.5

Upper Limit = Q3 + 1.5 * IQR = 145 + 1.5 * 35 = 197.5

So, the minimum and maximum between the range [57.5,197.5] for our given data are –

Minimum = 100 and Maximum = 170

The outliers which are outside this range are –

Outliers = 220

Now we have all the information, so we can draw the box plot shown in fig.1.12.

We can see from the diagram that the Median is not exactly at the center of the box and one whisker is longer than the other. We also have one Outliers.

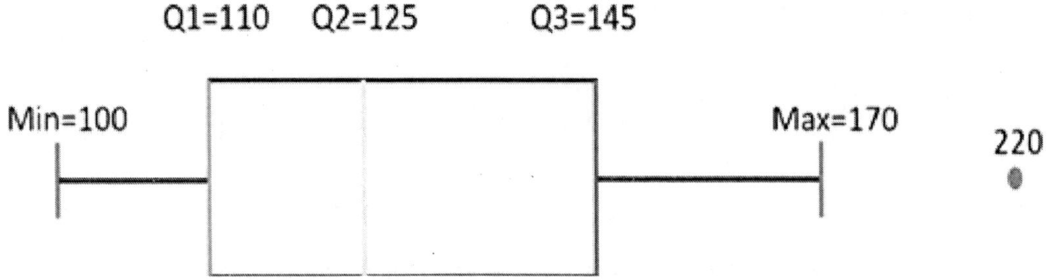

Fig.1.12

3. **Scatter Plots:** Scatter plot is one of the most important data visualization techniques and it is considered one of the Seven Basic Tools of Quality. A scatter plot is used to plot the relationship between two variables, on a two-dimensional graph that is known as Cartesian Plane on mathematical grounds.

It is generally used to plot the relationship between one independent variable and one dependent variable, where an independent variable is plotted on the x-axis and a dependent variable is plotted on the y-axis so that you can visualize the effect of the independent variable on the dependent variable. These plots are known as Scatter Plot Graph or Scatter Diagram.

How to Construct a Scatter Plot: To construct a scatter plot, we have to follow the given steps.

Step 1: Identify the independent and dependent variables

Step 2: Plot the independent variable on x-axis

Step 3: Plot the dependent variable on y-axis

Step 4: Extract the meaningful relationship between the given variables.

Example: Let's understand the process through an example. In the following table, a data set of two variables is given. Now in this data set there are two variables, first is the number of matches played by a certain player and second is the number of goals scored by that player. Suppose, we aim to find out the relationship between the number of matches played by a certain player and the number of goals scored by him/her. For now, let us discard our obvious intuitive understanding that the number of goals scored is directly proportional to the number of matches played. For now, let us assume that we just have the given dataset and we have to extract out relationship between given data pair.

As you can see in the given Scatter Plot, there is some kind of relationship between number of matches played and number of goals scored by a certain player.

Matches Played	2	5	7	1	12	15	18
Goals Scored	1	4	5	2	7	12	11

Differences Between Data Visualization Techniques: Histograms, Box Plots, Scatter Plots

Table 1.9

S.No.	Aspects	Histograms	Box Plots	Scatter Plots
1.	Purpose	Shows frequency distribution of a single variable	Summarizes data through five-number summary	Displays relationship between two variables
2.	Data Type	Univariate (one variable)	Univariate or bivariate (one or two variables)	Bivariate (two variables)
3.	Representation	Bars representing frequency in intervals	Box and whiskers representing quartiles and outliers	Points plotted on a Cartesian plane
4.	Outlier Detection	Not explicitly; focuses on distribution	Explicitly shows outliers	Can indicate outliers as distant points
5.	Shape/Structure	Provides insight into the shape of the distribution (e.g., normal, skewed)	Visualizes spread and central tendency	Reveals correlation and patterns (linear, nonlinear)
6.	Interpretation	Useful for understanding data distribution	Helpful for comparing distributions across groups	Effective for exploring relationships and trends

Identifying Patterns and Trends

Identifying patterns and trends is crucial for deriving meaningful insights and making informed decisions. This process involves examining data to understand its structure, relationships, and variations over time or across different groups. In this discussion, we will explore various methods and techniques to identify patterns and trends, focusing on three common visualization tools: histograms, box plots, and scatter plots.

Understanding Patterns and Trends: Before diving into specific tools, it's important to clarify the concepts of patterns and trends:

1. **Patterns** refer to recurring characteristics or arrangements within the data. They can be visual, numerical, or conceptual, highlighting regularities that may indicate deeper insights.
2. **Trends** signify a general direction in which data is moving over time. They

can show growth, decline, stability, or volatility in a dataset, providing context for understanding changes.

Both patterns and trends can help identify relationships, outliers, and anomalies, enabling better predictions and strategies.

Visualization Tools for Identifying Patterns and Trends

1. **Histograms:** A histogram is a graphical representation of the distribution of numerical data. It organizes data into bins (intervals) and displays the frequency of data points within each bin using bars.

Identifying Patterns:

- **Distribution Shape:** Histograms reveal the overall shape of the data distribution—whether it is normal, skewed (left or right), uniform, or bimodal. For instance, a normal distribution exhibits a bell curve, while a right-skewed distribution has a longer tail on the right side.
- **Peaks and Modes:** The number of peaks indicates modes in the dataset. A unimodal histogram has one peak, while a bimodal histogram has two. Multiple modes can suggest subpopulations within the data.
- **Gaps and Outliers:** Gaps between bars may indicate areas where data points are missing, while isolated bars can highlight potential outliers.

Identifying Trends:

- **Temporal Analysis**: When histograms are created for different time periods, they can show how distributions change over time. For example, comparing monthly sales data can reveal seasonal patterns.
- **Comparative Analysis:** Overlaying histograms for different groups (e.g., male vs. female income) can help identify trends in disparities or similarities across demographics.

2. **Box Plots:** A box plot (or whisker plot) summarizes data through its quartiles, illustrating the spread and central tendency. It displays the median, lower and upper quartiles, and potential outliers.

Identifying Patterns:

- **Five-Number Summary:** Box plots provide a concise summary of the data distribution through five key statistics: minimum, first quartile (Q1), median (Q2), third quartile (Q3), and maximum. This summary helps to quickly identify the central tendency and variability.
- **Spread and Skewness:** The length of the box and whiskers indicates the spread of the data. A longer box or whisker on one side suggests skewness in the distribution.
- **Outlier Detection:** Points outside the whiskers are marked as outliers, helping analysts identify unusual data points that may require further investigation.

Identifying Trends:

- **Comparing Groups:** Box plots are particularly effective for comparing distributions across multiple groups. For example, comparing test scores of students from different schools can reveal trends in educational performance.
- **Changes Over Time:** Creating box plots for different time periods can help visualize shifts in central tendency and variability, indicating trends in the data.

3. **Scatter Plots:** A scatter plot displays values for two variables as points in a Cartesian plane, allowing for a visual examination of the relationship between them.

Identifying Patterns:

- **Correlation:** Scatter plots can reveal correlations between two variables. A positive correlation is indicated by points trending upwards, while a negative correlation shows a downward trend. No clear trend suggests a lack of correlation.
- **Clusters:** Data points may form distinct clusters, suggesting subgroups within the dataset. Identifying these clusters can lead to valuable insights about different segments of data.
- **Outliers:** Distant points from the main cluster can indicate outliers, which may warrant further examination.

Identifying Trends:

- **Trend Lines:** Adding a trend line (linear or nonlinear) to a scatter plot helps visualize the overall direction and strength of the relationship. This can provide a predictive element, suggesting how one variable may affect another.
- **Temporal Changes:** When time is one of the variables, scatter plots can show how relationships evolve. For instance, plotting years on the x-axis and sales figures on the y-axis can reveal growth trends over time.

EDA Tools: Pandas, Tableau, Power BI

1. **Pandas:** Pandas is a powerful Python library essential for exploratory data analysis (EDA), providing flexible data structures such as Series and DataFrames that facilitate efficient handling and manipulation of structured data. With its intuitive functions, users can easily load data from various formats (e.g., CSV, Excel), explore datasets using summary statistics, and visualize distributions and relationships through basic plotting. Pandas excels in data cleaning, enabling the handling of missing values and duplicates while offering tools for filtering, grouping, and aggregating data to derive insights. Its seamless integration with other libraries like NumPy and Matplotlib enhances its capabilities for statistical analysis and advanced visualizations. The typical EDA workflow involves importing data, conducting initial

explorations, cleaning and transforming data, and finally visualizing patterns and trends, making Pandas a cornerstone for data scientists and analysts. By leveraging these features, users can gain a comprehensive understanding of their data, identify key insights, and prepare datasets for further analysis or modeling.

Features: Pandas offers a wide range of features that enhance data visualization and analysis. Here are some key features:

- **Data Structures:** Pandas provides two primary data structures - Series (one-dimensional) and DataFrame (two-dimensional). These structures are efficient and flexible for handling and exploring data.
- **Handling Missing Data:** Pandas has built-in functions to handle missing data, which is crucial for maintaining the integrity of your analysis.
- **Indexing and Alignment:** It offers robust methods for indexing and aligning data, making it easier to organize and label your datasets.
- **Input and Output Tools:** Pandas supports a variety of file formats, including CSV, Excel, JSON, and SQL databases, making it easy to read from and write to different data sources.
- **Data Cleaning:** The library provides tools for cleaning and preparing data, which is essential for accurate analysis.
- **Data Wrangling:** Pandas excels at data wrangling tasks such as merging, sorting, grouping, and reshaping data.
- **Descriptive Statistics:** It includes functions to calculate descriptive statistics like mean, standard deviation, and quartiles.
- **Integration with Other Libraries:** Pandas integrates seamlessly with other data science libraries like NumPy, Matplotlib, and Scikit-learn, enhancing its functionality.

2. **Tableau:** Tableau is a powerful data visualization tool that enables users to transform raw data into interactive and shareable dashboards. With its user-friendly interface, Tableau allows individuals to connect to various data sources, including spreadsheets, databases, and cloud services, making it versatile for different industries. Users can easily drag and drop elements to create compelling visual representations, such as charts, graphs, and maps, facilitating better insights and data storytelling. Its features, like real-time data analysis and collaborative capabilities, enhance decision-making processes, allowing teams to explore data together and derive actionable insights. Tableau's ability to handle large datasets efficiently and its robust community support further contribute to its popularity among data professionals. Additionally, the tool offers various deployment options, including on-premises and cloud-based solutions, catering to diverse organizational needs. Overall, Tableau empowers users to visualize complex data patterns, fostering

a data-driven culture and enabling organizations to leverage their data for strategic advantages.

Features: Tableau offers a wide range of features that enhance data visualization and analysis. Here are some key features:

- **User-friendly Interface:** Intuitive drag-and-drop functionality allows users to create visualizations easily without extensive coding knowledge.
- **Data Connectivity:** Connects to various data sources, including spreadsheets, databases, and cloud services, enabling seamless integration.
- **Interactive Dashboards:** Users can create interactive dashboards that allow viewers to explore data through filters, parameters, and tooltips.
- **Real-time Data Analysis:** Provides real-time data updates, allowing users to make timely decisions based on the latest information.
- **Advanced Analytics:** Features such as trend lines, forecasting, and statistical modeling support deeper data analysis.
- **Collaboration Tools:** Enables sharing of dashboards and reports with team members, promoting collaboration and data-driven discussions.
- **Mobile Compatibility:** Dashboards are optimized for mobile devices, ensuring accessibility on-the-go.
- **Customizable Visualizations:** Offers a variety of chart types and customization options to suit specific data storytelling needs.
- **Security Features:** Provides robust security measures, including user permissions and data encryption.

? **Community and Resources:** A strong user community and extensive online resources, including tutorials and forums, support users in maximizing their use of the tool.

These features make Tableau a comprehensive solution for data visualization and business intelligence.

3. **Power BI:** Power BI is a business analytics tool developed by Microsoft that enables users to visualize and share insights from their data in real-time. With its intuitive interface, Power BI allows individuals to connect to a wide array of data sources, including Excel spreadsheets, cloud services, and on-premises databases. Users can create interactive reports and dashboards through a simple drag-and-drop process, making data exploration accessible even for those without a technical background. Power BI's advanced features include natural language queries, AI-driven insights, and customizable visuals, which enhance the storytelling aspect of data. It supports collaboration through shared dashboards and integrates seamlessly with other Microsoft products, such as Azure and Office 365, ensuring a cohesive ecosystem for data management. Additionally, Power BI offers robust security features, including

row-level security and data encryption, to protect sensitive information. With its ability to handle large datasets and provide real-time analytics, Power BI empowers organizations to make data-driven decisions quickly and effectively, fostering a culture of analytical thinking across teams. Overall, Power BI serves as a powerful tool for transforming raw data into meaningful insights that drive strategic initiatives.

Features: Power BI is a powerful business analytics tool from Microsoft that provides a wide range of features for data visualization and reporting. Here are some of its key features:

- **Data Connectivity:** Power BI can connect to a variety of data sources, including Excel, SQL Server, cloud services (like Azure, Google Analytics), and many more.
- **Data Transformation:** With Power Query, users can clean, transform, and manipulate data to prepare it for analysis.
- **Interactive Dashboards:** Users can create interactive dashboards that allow stakeholders to visualize data through various charts, graphs, and maps.
- **Custom Visuals:** Power BI supports custom visuals, enabling users to create unique representations of their data or import visuals from the Power BI Marketplace.
- **Natural Language Querying:** The Q&A feature allows users to ask questions in natural language and get answers in the form of visualizations.
- **Real-time Data Access:** Users can access real-time data and create dashboards that update automatically with live data feeds.
- **Collaboration:** Power BI facilitates sharing and collaboration among team members through the Power BI service, enabling them to work together on reports and dashboards.
- **Mobile Access:** Power BI offers mobile apps for iOS and Android, allowing users to view reports and dashboards on the go.
- **Data Security:** Power BI includes features like row-level security and data encryption to ensure sensitive data is protected.
- **Integration with Other Microsoft Services:** Power BI integrates seamlessly with other Microsoft products like Excel, SharePoint, and Teams.
- **Scheduled Data Refresh:** Users can schedule automatic data refreshes to ensure they always have the latest information.
- **Custom Calculations with DAX:** Data Analysis Expressions (DAX) allow users to create custom calculations and aggregations for more complex data analysis.
- **AI Features:** Power BI incorporates AI capabilities, such as anomaly detection and automated insights, to help users gain deeper insights from their data.

These features make Power BI a versatile tool for businesses looking to leverage data for better decision-making and insights.

Differences Between Pandas, Tableau and Power BI

Table 1.10

S.No.	Aspects	Pandas	Tableau	Power BI
1.	Purpose	Data manipulation and analysis	Data visualization and reporting	Business intelligence and analytics
2.	Programming Language	Python	Primarily drag-and-drop (GUI)	Primarily drag-and-drop (GUI), with DAX for calculations
3.	Ease of Use	Requires programming knowledge	User-friendly, intuitive interface	User-friendly, intuitive interface
4.	Data Handling	Excellent for large datasets, data cleaning, and transformation	Great for visualization but less flexible for data transformation	Good data transformation and modeling capabilities
5.	Visualizations	Limited to basic plotting with libraries (like Matplotlib)	Extensive range of advanced visualizations	Wide variety of visualizations with custom options
6.	Deployment	Requires code deployment, usually within a Python environment	Desktop and online versions; easy sharing via Tableau Server	Desktop and online versions; integrates well within Microsoft ecosystem

CASE STUDIES OF FOUNDATIONS OF DATA ANALYTICS

Case Study 1: Retail Sales Optimization

Background

In the fast-paced retail environment, understanding customer behavior and optimizing inventory are crucial for success. A national retail chain, "RetailCo," faced challenges with excess inventory, stockouts, and declining customer satisfaction. The management realized that data analytics could provide insights to drive better decision-making.

Objective: RetailCo aimed to enhance sales performance by leveraging data analytics to identify sales trends, customer preferences, and inventory needs. The goals were to reduce excess inventory, minimize stockouts, and improve targeted marketing efforts.

Approach

1. **Data Collection:** RetailCo collected data from various sources, including:
   - Point-of-sale (POS) systems to track sales transactions.
   - Customer loyalty programs to gather demographic information and purchasing history.
   - Social media platforms to analyze customer sentiment and engagement.
   - External market data to assess competitive positioning.

2. **Data Preparation:** The data was cleaned and transformed using Python and Pandas. Data wrangling processes included handling missing values, normalizing data formats, and merging datasets to create a comprehensive view of customer behavior and sales trends.
3. **Data Analysis**: Using statistical analysis and visualization tools like Tableau, the analytics team explored the data. They identified key metrics such as:
   - Sales trends by product category and region.
   - Customer purchasing patterns over time.
   - Seasonal effects on product demand.
4. **Insights Generation:** The analysis revealed several critical insights:
   - Certain products, like seasonal apparel, showed peak sales during specific months, while other items had consistent year-round demand.
   - Geographic trends indicated that some products sold significantly better in certain regions due to local preferences and cultural factors.
   - Customers engaged more with targeted promotions, leading to higher conversion rates.
5. **Actionable Strategies:** Based on the insights, Retai-\lCo implemented several strategies:
   - **Inventory Optimization:** Adjusted inventory levels based on regional demand forecasts, which reduced stockouts by 30%.
   - **Targeted Marketing Campaigns:** Launched region-specific promotions tailored to customer preferences, increasing sales by 15% during peak seasons.
   - **Dynamic Pricing:** Implemented a dynamic pricing strategy that adjusted prices based on demand and competition, further enhancing sales.

Outcome: Over the course of a year, RetailCo experienced significant improvements:

- **Sales Growth:** Total sales increased by 12%, with targeted campaigns proving particularly effective in driving customer engagement.
- **Inventory Efficiency:** The company reduced excess inventory by 25%, leading to lower holding costs and improved cash flow.
- **Customer Satisfaction:** Enhanced inventory management reduced stockouts, leading to a noticeable increase in customer satisfaction scores.

RetailCo's leadership recognized the value of data analytics as a strategic asset. The company committed to ongoing analytics initiatives, establishing a dedicated team to continually analyze data and refine strategies.

Case Study 2: Healthcare Patient Readmission Reduction

Background

In the healthcare sector, patient readmissions are a significant concern, leading to increased costs and poor patient outcomes. A regional healthcare organization, "HealthOrg," faced challenges with high readmission rates for patients with chronic conditions, impacting both patient care and operational efficiency.

Objective: HealthOrg aimed to reduce patient readmissions by leveraging data analytics to identify the factors contributing to readmissions and implement targeted interventions to improve patient care.

Approach

1. **Data Collection:** HealthOrg gathered data from multiple sources, including:
   - Electronic health records (EHR) for patient demographics, diagnoses, treatments, and readmission histories.
   - Follow-up appointment data to analyze post-discharge care.
   - Patient surveys to capture feedback on their care experience and adherence to treatment plans.
2. **Data Preparation:** The data was cleaned and organized using R and SQL. This involved:
   - Standardizing patient records.
   - Identifying and addressing missing or inconsistent data.
   - Creating a comprehensive dataset that included demographic information, medical history, and readmission outcomes.
3. **Data Analysis:** HealthOrg employed statistical analysis and machine learning techniques to uncover patterns associated with readmissions. Key methods included:
   - Logistic regression to identify risk factors for readmission.
   - Decision trees to classify patients based on their likelihood of readmission.
   - Clustering techniques to segment patients into risk categories.
4. **Insights Generation**: The analysis yielded critical insights:
   - Patients with chronic conditions (e.g., heart failure, diabetes) and those lacking adequate follow-up care had significantly higher readmission rates.
   - Social determinants of health, such as socioeconomic status and access to transportation, were correlated with readmission risks.
   - Patients who received clear discharge instructions and follow-up calls were less likely to be readmitted.
5. **Actionable Strategies:** HealthOrg developed targeted interventions based on the insights:

- **Follow-up Programs:** Established a post-discharge follow-up program where nurses contacted patients to reinforce care plans and address concerns.
- **Patient Education:** Created educational materials to help patients understand their conditions and the importance of follow-up care.
- **Community Resource Connections:** Partnered with local organizations to assist high-risk patients with transportation and social support.

Outcome: Over the next year, HealthOrg achieved substantial improvements:

Readmission Reduction: The organization reduced overall readmission rates by 20%, with specific chronic conditions showing even greater declines.

Improved Patient Outcomes: Patient satisfaction scores increased as follow-up care enhanced their understanding of treatment plans.

Cost Savings: Reduced readmissions led to significant cost savings for the organization, allowing funds to be redirected toward further patient care improvements.

HealthOrg's commitment to leveraging data analytics transformed its approach to patient care. The organization recognized the importance of ongoing analytics efforts and planned to integrate predictive analytics for future initiatives.

Conclusion

These case studies highlight how data analytics can drive strategic decisions and lead to improved outcomes across various industries. By leveraging data effectively, organizations can enhance operational efficiency, optimize resources, and ultimately deliver better services to their customers and patients.

SUMMARY OF FOUNDATIONS OF DATA ANALYTICS

1. Introduction to Data Analytics

Data analytics involves systematically examining and interpreting data to uncover patterns, trends, and insights. By utilizing statistical methods and advanced tools, organizations can make informed decisions, optimize processes, and enhance customer experiences, ultimately driving growth and improving overall performance in an increasingly data-driven world.

Defining Data Analytics

Data analytics is the systematic computational analysis of data, aimed at extracting meaningful insights and facilitating informed decision-making. It encompasses a variety of techniques and tools designed to process and interpret large volumes of data. At its core, data analytics transforms raw data into useful information that can guide business strategies and enhance operational efficiency.

Importance and Applications Across Industries

The significance of data analytics is evident across numerous industries. In healthcare, it enables improved patient outcomes through predictive modeling and analysis of treatment effectiveness. In finance, analytics drives risk assessment, fraud detection, and portfolio management. Retailers leverage data to understand consumer behavior, optimize inventory, and tailor marketing efforts. Furthermore, sectors like transportation and logistics use analytics to enhance route efficiency and reduce costs. As organizations increasingly rely on data-driven decisions, the demand for skilled data analysts continues to grow.

Evolution and Trends in Data Analytics

Data analytics has evolved significantly over the past few decades. Initially, analytics focused on basic descriptive statistics. Today, the field has expanded to include advanced methodologies like predictive and prescriptive analytics, driven by developments in machine learning and artificial intelligence. Key trends include the rise of real-time analytics, the increasing integration of AI in data analysis, and the growing importance of data governance and ethical considerations. These trends reflect a shift towards more sophisticated, responsive, and responsible analytics practices.

2. Data Types and Structures

Data types refer to the categorization of data, including numerical, categorical, ordinal, and textual formats. Data structures, such as arrays, lists, and data frames, organize this data efficiently for analysis. Understanding these types and structures is essential for effective data manipulation and interpretation in analytics and programming tasks.

Understanding Data: Structured, Semi-Structured, and Unstructured

Data can be classified into three main types:

1. **Structured Data:** Highly organized and easily searchable, typically found in relational databases. Examples include tables with defined rows and columns.
2. **Semi-Structured Data:** Contains organizational properties but does not adhere strictly to a schema. Common formats include JSON and XML, which are used in web applications and APIs.
3. **Unstructured Data:** Lacks a predefined format, making it more challenging to analyze. Examples include text documents, images, and videos. Unstructured data accounts for a significant portion of the data generated today.

Data Storage Formats: Relational Databases, NoSQL, Data Lakes

Data storage options vary based on data types and usage:

1. **Relational Databases:** Use structured data models and SQL for queries. Ideal for transactions and structured data management.
2. **NoSQL Databases:** Designed for flexibility, scalability, and handling unstructured or semi-structured data. Common types include document stores, key-value stores, and column-family stores.

3. **Data Lakes:** Store vast amounts of raw data in its native format until needed. They support big data analytics and allow for a more exploratory approach to data analysis.

Data Warehousing and Data Marts

Data warehousing involves consolidating data from various sources into a central repository for analysis and reporting. It supports historical data analysis and complex queries. Data marts are subsets of data warehouses, focused on specific business lines or departments, facilitating faster access to relevant data for analysis.

3. Data Collection and Acquisition

Data collection and acquisition involve gathering information from various sources, including surveys, databases, sensors, and web scraping. This process ensures the data is relevant, accurate, and timely, forming the foundation for analysis. Effective data collection methods are crucial for generating reliable insights and driving informed decision-making in organizations.

Data Sources: Internal vs. External

Data can be sourced from internal systems (such as CRM and ERP systems) or external sources (like social media, market research, and third-party data providers). Internal data provides insights specific to an organization, while external data can enhance analysis by incorporating broader market trends.

Data Collection Techniques: Surveys, Web Scraping, Sensors

Effective data collection methods are crucial for gathering relevant information:

1. **Surveys:** Used to collect qualitative and quantitative data directly from participants, providing insights into customer preferences and behaviors.
2. **Web Scraping:** Automates the extraction of data from websites, useful for gathering information on market trends, competitor analysis, and more.
3. **Sensors:** Collect real-time data from physical environments, such as IoT devices, enabling applications in logistics, healthcare, and smart cities.

Data Ingestion Methods and Tools

Data ingestion involves importing data into analytics systems. Common methods include batch processing (transferring large volumes of data at scheduled intervals) and stream processing (real-time data ingestion). Tools like Apache Kafka and AWS Glue facilitate efficient data ingestion, ensuring timely access to data for analysis.

Ethical Considerations in Data Collection

Ethics play a critical role in data collection. Organizations must ensure data privacy, obtain informed consent from participants, and comply with regulations like GDPR. Ethical data practices foster trust and transparency, which are essential for maintaining customer relationships and organizational integrity.

4. Data Cleaning and Preparation

Data cleaning and preparation involve identifying and correcting errors, inconsistencies, and missing values in datasets. This process ensures data quality and accuracy, making it suitable for analysis. Techniques include removing duplicates, standardizing formats, and handling outliers, ultimately enhancing the reliability of insights derived from the data.

Data Quality Issues: Missing Values, Duplicates, Outliers

Data cleaning is a crucial step in the analytics process. Common data quality issues include:

1. **Missing Values:** Gaps in data that can lead to inaccurate analysis. Techniques to handle missing data include imputation and removal.
2. **Duplicates:** Redundant records that skew results. Identifying and eliminating duplicates is essential for data integrity.
3. **Outliers:** Extreme values that may indicate errors or variability in data. Analyzing outliers helps determine whether to exclude them or investigate further.

Data Transformation Techniques: Normalization, Encoding, Aggregation

Data transformation prepares data for analysis:

1. **Normalization:** Adjusts data to a common scale, improving comparability.
2. **Encoding:** Converts categorical data into numerical formats for analytical algorithms.
3. **Aggregation:** Summarizes data, providing insights at higher levels (e.g., daily sales totals vs. individual transactions).

Tools for Data Cleaning: OpenRefine, Trifacta, Python Libraries

Several tools facilitate data cleaning and preparation:

OpenRefine: An open-source tool for cleaning messy data, offering powerful transformation capabilities.

Trifacta: A data wrangling tool that simplifies the process of data preparation through an intuitive interface.

Python Libraries: Libraries like Pandas and NumPy provide extensive functionalities for data manipulation and cleaning, enabling analysts to efficiently prepare datasets for analysis.

5. Exploratory Data Analysis (EDA)

Exploratory Data Analysis (EDA) is a crucial step in the data analysis process, where analysts visually and statistically examine data to uncover patterns, trends, and anomalies. EDA techniques, such as summary statistics, data visualization, and correlation analysis, help in understanding data distributions, guiding further analysis and hypothesis formation.

Descriptive Statistics and Summary Measures

EDA is the initial step in analyzing data, focusing on summarizing and visualizing datasets. Key techniques include calculating descriptive statistics (mean, median, mode, standard deviation) to understand data distributions and variability. Summary measures provide a high-level overview of trends and patterns within the data.

Data Visualization Techniques: Histograms, Box Plots, Sc atter Plots

Visualization is crucial for EDA, allowing analysts to identify patterns and outliers visually. Common techniques include:

1. **Histograms:** Display the frequency distribution of a dataset, helping identify the shape and spread of data.
2. **Box Plots:** Summarize data through quartiles, highlighting outliers and central tendencies.
3. **Scatter Plots:** Illustrate relationships between two variables, revealing correlations and trends.

Identifying Patterns and Trends

EDA aims to uncover insights that inform further analysis and decision-making. By identifying patterns, such as seasonality or correlations, analysts can generate hypotheses for deeper statistical testing and predictive modeling.

EDA Tools: Pandas, Tableau, Power BI

Several tools facilitate EDA:

1. **Pandas:** A powerful Python library for data manipulation, offering functions for data cleaning, analysis, and visualization.
2. **Tableau:** A visualization tool that allows users to create interactive dashboards, making data exploration intuitive and accessible.
3. **Power BI:** A business analytics tool from Microsoft that provides robust data visualization capabilities, enabling organizations to create insightful reports and dashboards.

Conclusion

Part I of the Foundations of Data Analytics lays the groundwork for understanding the significance of data in today's data-driven landscape. From defining data analytics and exploring various data types and structures to discussing data collection techniques and the importance of data cleaning, this section highlights the critical components of the analytics process. It emphasizes the importance of exploratory data analysis in uncovering insights and trends, setting the stage for more advanced analytical techniques and methodologies in subsequent parts. As organizations continue to harness the power of data, a solid foundation in these principles is essential for driving informed decision-making and achieving strategic objectives.

2

Core Principles of Data Analytics

The core principles of data analytics revolve around clarity, accuracy, and actionable insights. First, understanding the objectives of the analysis is crucial. Clearly defining questions and goals helps to focus the data collection and analysis processes. This principle ensures that the analytics effort aligns with business needs, making the insights relevant and useful.

Second, data quality is paramount. Accurate, complete, and consistent data forms the backbone of effective analytics. This requires diligent data cleaning and preparation to eliminate errors and inconsistencies, ensuring that the results of any analysis are trustworthy. Third, employing appropriate analytical techniques is vital; selecting the right methods whether descriptive, diagnostic, predictive, or prescriptive enables analysts to draw meaningful conclusions.

Another essential principle is the importance of data visualization. Presenting data through visual formats like charts and graphs makes complex information more accessible, facilitating easier interpretation and communication of insights. Finally, fostering a culture of data-driven decision-making within an organization encourages stakeholders to trust and act on analytical findings, leading to more informed strategic choices. By adhering to these core principles, organizations can maximize the value of their data, enhancing decision-making processes and driving sustainable growth.

1. Statistical Foundations

Statistical foundations are crucial for analyzing data and making informed decisions across various fields, including healthcare, finance, and social sciences. At its core, statistics involves two main branches: descriptive statistics and inferential statistics. Descriptive statistics summarize the characteristics of a dataset using measures of central tendency, such as the mean, median, and mode, which provide insights into the "center" of the data. Measures of dispersion, including range, variance, and standard deviation, help to understand the spread and variability within the dataset. In contrast, inferential statistics allows researchers to make predictions or generalizations about a larger population based on a sample. This involves hypothesis testing, where assumptions about population parameters are tested using sample data, and the construction of confidence intervals that estimate the range within which a population parameter likely falls.

Understanding probability is fundamental to the statistical framework, as it quantifies the likelihood of events and underpins many statistical methods. Key concepts include random variables, which can be discrete or continuous, and probability distributions, such as the normal and binomial distributions. Additionally, techniques like correlation and regression analysis assess relationships between variables, with correlation measuring the strength and direction of these relationships, while regression models predict outcomes based on independent variables. Effective data visualization techniques, such as histograms and scatter plots, are essential for presenting insights clearly, enabling analysts to identify trends, patterns, and outliers. Overall, a solid grasp of these statistical principles empowers professionals to navigate data-driven environments effectively, leading to informed decision-making and improved outcomes.

Key Concepts in Statistics

1. **Descriptive Statistics:** This branch summarizes and describes the main features of a dataset. Key measures include:

   - **Measures of Central Tendency:** These include the mean (average), median (middle value), and mode (most frequent value). They provide a sense of the "center" of the data.

   - **Measures of Dispersion:** These include range (difference between the maximum and minimum), variance (average of the squared differences from the mean), and standard deviation (the square root of variance). They help understand the spread or variability of the data.

2. **Inferential Statistics:** While descriptive statistics summarize data, inferential statistics allow us to make generalizations or predictions about a population based on a sample. Key components include:

   - **Hypothesis Testing:** This involves making assumptions (hypotheses) about a population parameter and using sample data to test these assumptions. Common tests include t-tests, chi-square tests, and ANOVA.

   - **Confidence Intervals:** These provide a range of values within which a population parameter is likely to fall, offering a measure of uncertainty around a sample estimate.

3. **Probability:** Understanding probability is fundamental to statistics. It quantifies the likelihood of events occurring and forms the basis for many statistical methods. Key concepts include:

   - **Random Variables:** These are variables whose values result from random phenomena. They can be discrete (specific values) or continuous (any value within a range).

- **Probability Distributions:** These describe how probabilities are distributed over the values of a random variable. Common distributions include the normal distribution, binomial distribution, and Poisson distribution.

4. **Correlation and Regression:** These techniques assess relationships between variables:
   - **Correlation** measures the strength and direction of the relationship between two variables, typically using the Pearson correlation coefficient.
   - **Regression Analysis** estimates the relationships among variables, often used for prediction. Linear regression models the relationship between a dependent variable and one or more independent variables.
5. **Data Visualization**: Effective data visualization techniques, such as histograms, scatter plots, and box plots, are crucial for presenting data insights clearly. Visualization aids in identifying trends, patterns, and outliers, making it easier to communicate findings.

Conclusion

Statistical foundations provide a critical framework for data analysis, enabling analysts to draw meaningful conclusions from data. By understanding key concepts like descriptive and inferential statistics, probability, correlation, regression, and data visualization, professionals can make informed decisions that drive strategy and improve outcomes across various domains. As data continues to grow in importance, strong statistical knowledge will be an invaluable asset in navigating the complexities of data-driven environments.

Probability Theory and Distributions

Probability theory is a mathematical framework that quantifies uncertainty and provides tools for modeling random phenomena. It serves as the foundation for statistical analysis, enabling researchers to draw inferences and make predictions based on incomplete information. Probability is defined as a measure of the likelihood of an event occurring, ranging from 0 (impossible event) to 1 (certain event).

Key Concepts in Probability

1. **Sample Space and Events:**
   - The sample space (S) is the set of all possible outcomes of a random experiment. For instance, in a coin toss, the sample space is {Heads, Tails}.
   - An event is a subset of the sample space. For example, getting Heads in a coin toss is an event.
2. **Probability of Events:** The probability of an event A is defined as the ratio of the number of favourable outcomes to the total number of outcomes in the sample space. Mathematically, this is expressed as:

$$P(A) = \frac{\text{Number of favorable outcomes}}{\text{Total number of outcomes}}$$

3. **Complementary Events:** The complement of an event A, denoted as A', is the event that A does not occur. The probability of the complement can be calculated as:

$$P(A') = 1 - P(A)$$

4. **Independent and Dependent Events:**
   - Two events are independent if the occurrence of one does not affect the occurrence of the other. For independent events A and B, the joint probability is given by:

$$P(A \cap B) = P(A) \cdot P(B)$$

   - Conversely, events are dependent if the occurrence of one event affects the probability of the other.

5. **Conditional Probability:** The probability of an event A given that event B has occurred is known as conditional probability, denoted as $P(A|B)$. It is calculated as:

$$P(A|B) = \frac{P(A \cap B)}{P(B)}$$

Probability Distributions

Probability distributions describe how probabilities are assigned to different possible outcomes of a random variable. There are two main types of probability distributions:

1. **Discrete Probability Distributions:** A discrete probability distribution applies to random variables that can take on a countable number of values. The probability mass function (PMF) defines the probabilities of these values.
   - **Binomial Distribution:** This distribution models the number of successes in a fixed number of independent Bernoulli trials (e.g., coin flips). The PMF is given by:

$$P(X = k) = \binom{n}{k} p^k (1 - p)^{n-k}$$

     where n is the number of trials, k is the number of successes, and p is the probability of success on each trial.
   - **Poisson Distribution:** This distribution models the number of events occurring within a fixed interval of time or space, given a known average rate of occurrence. The PMF is defined as:

$$P(X = k) = \frac{\lambda^k e^{-\lambda}}{k!}$$

where λ is the average rate of occurrence, and e is Euler's number (approximately 2.71828).

2. **Continuous Probability Distributions:** Continuous probability distributions apply to random variables that can take on an infinite number of values within a given range. The probability density function (PDF) describes these distributions.

   - **Normal Distribution:** Also known as the Gaussian distribution, it is characterized by its bell-shaped curve and is defined by two parameters i.e., mean (μ) and standard deviation(σ) The PDF is given by:

     $$f(x) = \frac{1}{\sigma\sqrt{2\pi}} e^{-\frac{(x-\mu)^2}{2\sigma^2}}$$

     The normal distribution is significant in statistics due to the Central Limit Theorem, which states that the sum of a large number of independent random variables will approximate a normal distribution, regardless of the original distributions.

   - **Exponential Distribution:** This distribution models the time until an event occurs, such as the time until a radioactive particle decays. The PDF is defined as:

     $$f(x; \lambda) = \lambda e^{-\lambda x} \quad (x \geq 0)$$

     where λ is the rate parameter, indicating how often events occur.

3. **Uniform Distribution:** This distribution indicates that all outcomes are equally likely within a specified range. The PDF for a uniform distribution between a and b is:

   $$f(x) = \frac{1}{b - a} \quad (a \leq x \leq b)$$

Applications of Probability Theory: Probability theory is widely used across various domains:

1. **Finance:** To model market risks and returns, evaluate investment strategies, and assess insurance policies.
2. **Healthcare:** In clinical trials to analyze treatment efficacy, assess patient risks, and make predictions based on patient data.
3. **Engineering:** For reliability testing, quality control, and risk assessment in manufacturing processes.
4. **Machine Learning:** To develop algorithms that can learn from data, make predictions, and enhance decision-making processes.

Conclusion

Probability theory and distributions are fundamental components of statistics, providing the tools to quantify uncertainty and model real-world phenomena. Understanding key concepts such as sample spaces, events, and types of distributions is essential for effective data analysis and decision-making. As we continue to generate vast amounts of data, the principles of probability will remain critical in interpreting information and guiding actions across diverse fields. By mastering probability theory, individuals and organizations can make more informed decisions and improve outcomes based on data-driven insights.

Hypothesis Testing and Confidence Intervals

Hypothesis testing and confidence intervals are fundamental concepts in statistics that allow researchers to make inferences about populations based on sample data. Both methods are essential for decision-making in various fields, including medicine, social sciences, marketing, and quality control. While they serve different purposes, they are interconnected and often used together to draw conclusions from data.

Hypothesis Testing

Hypothesis testing is a statistical method used to determine whether there is enough evidence in a sample to support a specific claim (hypothesis) about a population parameter. It involves formulating two competing hypotheses:

1. **Null Hypothesis (H_o):** This hypothesis states that there is no effect or no difference. It is the hypothesis that researchers aim to test against. For example, (H_o) The mean height of a certain species of plant is 50 cm.
2. **Alternative Hypothesis (H_o or H_1) :** This hypothesis represents the claim that researchers want to support. It states that there is an effect or a difference. For example, (H_o or H_1) The mean height of the species of plant is not equal to 50 cm.

Steps in Hypothesis Testing

1. **Formulate the Hypotheses:** Define the null and alternative hypotheses clearly.
2. **Select a Significance Level (α \alpha):** The significance level is the threshold for rejecting the null hypothesis, commonly set at 0.05 (5%) or 0.01 (1%). This level indicates the probability of committing a Type I error, which occurs when the null hypothesis is incorrectly rejected.
3. **Collect Data:** Obtain a sample from the population and calculate the necessary statistics.
4. **Choose the Appropriate Test:** Depending on the data type and the hypotheses, select a statistical test (e.g., t-test, chi-square test, ANOVA).
5. **Calculate the Test Statistic:** Use the sample data to compute a test statistic that measures how far the sample statistic is from the null hypothesis.
6. **Determine the p-value:** The p-value indicates the probability of observing

the test statistic, or something more extreme, under the null hypothesis. A low p-value (typically less than α) suggests that the null hypothesis may be rejected.

7. **Make a Decision:** If the p-value is less than or equal to α, reject the null hypothesis; otherwise, fail to reject it.
8. **Draw Conclusions:** Interpret the results in the context of the research question.

Example of Hypothesis Testing: Suppose a researcher wants to determine if a new drug affects blood pressure. The null hypothesis is that the drug has no effect on blood pressure, while the alternative hypothesis is that it does. After conducting a study, the researcher collects data, performs a t-test, and obtains a p-value of 0.03. Since 0.03 is less than the significance level of 0.05, the researcher rejects the null hypothesis, concluding that the drug likely affects blood pressure.

Confidence Intervals

A confidence interval (CI) is a range of values that is used to estimate a population parameter. It provides an interval estimate, along with a degree of certainty about that estimate. For example, a 95% confidence interval suggests that if we were to take many samples and construct a confidence interval from each, approximately 95% of those intervals would contain the true population parameter.

Components of Confidence Intervals

1. **Point Estimate**: This is a single value that serves as the best estimate of the population parameter (e.g., sample mean).
2. **Margin of Error**: This represents the amount of uncertainty associated with the point estimate. It is calculated as the product of a critical value (based on the desired confidence level) and the standard error of the estimate.
3. **Confidence Level**: This indicates the degree of certainty associated with the interval. Common levels include 90%, 95%, and 99%.

Formula for Confidence Intervals

For a population mean, the confidence interval can be calculated as follows:

$$\text{CI} = \text{Point Estimate} \pm \text{Margin of Error}$$

Where the margin of error is determined using:

$$\text{Margin of Error} = z^* \times \frac{\sigma}{\sqrt{n}} \quad \text{(for large samples)}$$

or

$$\text{Margin of Error} = t^* \times \frac{s}{\sqrt{n}} \quad \text{(for small samples)}$$

where,

- z^* is the critical value from the standard normal distribution.
- t^* is the critical value from the t-distribution.
- σ is the population standard deviation (if known).
- s is the sample standard deviation.
- n is the sample size.

Example of a Confidence Interval

If a researcher calculates a sample mean blood pressure of 120 mmHg from a sample of 30 patients, with a sample standard deviation of 10 mmHg, they can construct a 95% confidence interval. The critical value t^* for 29 degrees of freedom at 95% confidence is approximately 2.045. The standard error is:

The margin of error is:

$$\text{SE} = \frac{s}{\sqrt{n}} = \frac{10}{\sqrt{30}} \approx 1.83$$

Thus, the 95% confidence interval for the mean blood pressure is:

$$\text{Margin of Error} = t^* \times \text{SE} \approx 2.045 \times 1.83 \approx 3.74$$

This interval suggests that the researcher can be 95% confident that the true mean blood pressure of the population falls between 116.26 mmHg and 123.74 mmHg.

$$120 \pm 3.74 \Rightarrow (116.26, 123.74)$$

Relationship Between Hypothesis Testing and Confidence Intervals

Hypothesis testing and confidence intervals are closely related. When a null hypothesis is tested, the results can often be interpreted using confidence intervals. For example, if a 95% confidence interval for a parameter does not include the null hypothesis value (often 0 for differences or 1 for ratios), it suggests that the null hypothesis can be rejected at the 0.05 significance level.

Example:

Continuing the previous example, if the null hypothesis was that the mean blood pressure is 125 mmHg, we can see that since 125 mmHg falls outside the confidence interval (116.26, 123.74), we would reject the null hypothesis at the 0.05 significance level.

Conclusion

Hypothesis testing and confidence intervals are powerful statistical tools that enable researchers to make informed decisions based on sample data. By understanding the processes and principles behind these methods, analysts can derive meaningful insights, validate research claims, and ultimately contribute to evidence-based practices across various disciplines. As data continues to play a critical role in decision-making, proficiency in hypothesis testing and confidence intervals will remain invaluable for researchers and practitioners alike.

Correlation and Causation

Correlation and causation are fundamental concepts in statistics and research methodology that are often discussed in the context of data analysis. Understanding the difference between these two concepts is crucial for accurately interpreting data and making informed decisions based on that data. While correlation can indicate a relationship between two variables, it does not imply that one variable causes changes in the other. This distinction is vital across various fields, including healthcare, economics, social sciences, and environmental studies.

Correlation

Correlation refers to a statistical measure that describes the extent to which two variables move in relation to each other. It quantifies the strength and direction of a linear relationship between the variables. The correlation coefficient, typically denoted as r, ranges from -1 to +1:

- **r = +1:** Perfect positive correlation, indicating that as one variable increases, the other variable also increases.
- **r = –1:** Perfect negative correlation, indicating that as one variable increases, the other variable decreases.
- **r = 0:** No correlation, indicating no linear relationship between the variables.

Types of Correlation: The types of correlation are as follows:

1. **Positive Correlation:** Both variables increase or decrease together. For example, there is often a positive correlation between education level and income; as education level increases, income tends to increase as well.
2. **Negative Correlation:** One variable increase while the other decreases. For instance, there is generally a negative correlation between smoking and lung function; as smoking increases, lung function typically decreases.
3. **Zero Correlation:** There is no discernible relationship between the two variables. For example, there might be no correlation between shoe size and intelligence.

Measuring Correlation

Correlation is commonly measured using Pearson's correlation coefficient for linear relationships, but other methods exist, such as Spearman's rank correlation coefficient, which is suitable for non-parametric data.

Limitations of Correlation: While correlation is useful for identifying relationships between variables, it has several limitations:

1. **Does Not Imply Causation:** Correlation alone cannot establish a cause-and-effect relationship. For example, a strong correlation between ice cream sales and drowning incidents does not mean that ice cream sales cause drowning.
2. **Influence of Outliers:** Correlation can be significantly affected by outliers, which may distort the perceived relationship between the variables.

3. **Confounding Variables:** A third variable may influence both correlated variables, leading to a spurious relationship. For example, an observed correlation between exercise and weight loss could be influenced by dietary habits.

Causation

Causation, or causal relationship, indicates that changes in one variable (the cause) directly produce changes in another variable (the effect). Establishing causation requires more than just observing a correlation; it involves demonstrating that one variable directly influences the other.

Criteria for Establishing Causation

To establish a causal relationship, researchers typically use several criteria:

1. **Temporal Precedence**: The cause must precede the effect in time. For instance, to claim that smoking causes lung cancer, smoking behavior must occur before the onset of cancer.
2. **Covariation**: There must be a demonstrated relationship between the cause and effect. This can be shown through correlation.
3. **Elimination of Alternative Explanations**: Researchers must rule out other potential causes that could explain the observed effect. This often involves controlling for confounding variables.

Experimental Design: Experimental designs, such as randomized controlled trials (RCTs), are the gold standard for establishing causation. In an RCT, participants are randomly assigned to treatment or control groups, which helps control for confounding variables. This allows researchers to isolate the effect of the treatment and make stronger causal inferences.

Observational Studies: In cases where experimental designs are not feasible, researchers may rely on observational studies. While these can provide valuable insights, they are more susceptible to confounding factors and cannot definitively establish causation. Techniques like statistical controls and causal inference methods, such as propensity score matching, can help strengthen causal claims in observational research.

The Relationship Between Correlation and Causation: Understanding the relationship between correlation and causation is essential for accurate data interpretation:

1. **Correlation Does Not Equal Causation:** This phrase encapsulates the primary distinction between the two concepts. A strong correlation between two variables does not imply that one causes the other. For example, a correlation between increased screen time and lower academic performance does not mean that screen time directly causes poor performance; other factors, such as time management skills or parental involvement, may be at play.

2. **Causation Implies Correlation:** If one variable cause another, there must be a correlation between them. However, the reverse is not true correlation does not imply that one variable causes the other.
3. **Spurious Correlations:** Sometimes, two variables may be correlated due to a third variable influencing both. For example, an increase in the number of fire trucks at a fire might correlate with the amount of damage caused, but this does not mean that fire trucks cause damage. Instead, both are influenced by the severity of the fire.

Differences Between Correlation and Causation

Table 2.1

S.No.	Aspect	Correlation	Causation
1.	Definition	A statistical measure of the relationship between two variables.	Indicates that one variable directly affects another.
2.	Nature	Observational; can be seen in data.	Involves a cause-and-effect relationship.
3.	Direction	Can be positive, negative, or zero.	Directional; one variable causes a change in another.
4.	Establishment	Can be determined through statistical analysis.	Requires experimental design or rigorous methods to establish.
5.	Implication	Does not imply one variable affects the other.	Implies that a change in the cause results in a change in the effect.
6.	Confounding Variables	Does not account for other influencing factors.	Must control for confounding factors to establish true causation.
7.	Examples	Ice-cream sales and drowning incidents.	Smoking causing lung cancer.

Statistical Tools: R, SAS, Python Libraries

Statistical analysis is crucial in various fields, including academia, finance, healthcare, and data science. The tools used for statistical analysis vary widely, with each offering distinct features, capabilities, and advantages. In this overview, we will explore three of the most prominent statistical tools: R, SAS, and Python libraries.

R

R is a powerful programming language and environment specifically designed for statistical computing and data analysis. Originally developed by statisticians, R has become a cornerstone in data science, academia, and various industries for its extensive capabilities in statistical modeling, data visualization, and data manipulation.

One of R's key features is its ability to handle large datasets and perform complex calculations efficiently. It supports various statistical techniques, from basic descriptive statistics to advanced modeling approaches like linear regression, time series analysis, and clustering. The language's syntax is designed to facilitate exploratory data analysis, allowing users to quickly generate insights. R also benefits from a strong community that contributes to its growing ecosystem of packages. This makes it easy to find tools for specific tasks, from bioinformatics to finance. Furthermore, R integrates well with other programming languages and software, enhancing its utility in diverse applications.

Overall, R's flexibility, comprehensive statistical capabilities, and robust visualization options make it an essential tool for anyone working with data. Whether for academic research or industry applications, R empowers users to uncover patterns and communicate findings effectively.

Key Features of R

1. **Open Source:** R is free to use, making it accessible to anyone interested in statistical analysis. Its open-source nature encourages collaboration and the continuous development of packages.
2. **Comprehensive Package Ecosystem:** R boasts thousands of packages that extend its capabilities. CRAN (Comprehensive R Archive Network) is the primary repository, offering packages for various statistical techniques, data manipulation, and visualization.
3. **Data Visualization:** R excels in creating high-quality graphics. The **ggplot2** package, based on the Grammar of Graphics, allows users to create complex, multi-layered visualizations with minimal code.
4. **Data Manipulation:** The **dplyr** and **tidyr** packages streamline data manipulation tasks, enabling users to filter, summarize, and reshape data effortlessly.
5. **Statistical Modeling:** R provides a wide array of statistical models, including linear regression, generalized linear models, time series analysis, and machine learning algorithms, making it suitable for various analytical tasks.
6. **Reproducibility:** R facilitates reproducible research through R Markdown, which allows users to combine code, output, and narrative in a single document. This is crucial for sharing findings and maintaining transparency in research.

Statistical Techniques in R

1. **Descriptive Statistics:** Functions such as mean(), median(), sd(), and summary() provide quick insights into data characteristics.
2. **Inferential Statistics:** R supports hypothesis testing and confidence intervals. Functions for ANOVA, chi-squared tests, and regression analyses are integral for inferential statistics.
3. **Time Series Analysis:** R has specialized packages like forecast and zoo that cater to time series data, allowing users to model trends, seasonality, and perform forecasting.
4. **Machine Learning:** With packages like caret, randomForest, and xgboost, R

offers robust tools for machine learning. Users can implement supervised and unsupervised learning algorithms easily.

5. **Bayesian Statistics:** R facilitates Bayesian analysis through packages like rstan and brms, making it accessible for users familiar with Bayesian concepts.

Basic Statistical Operations in R

1. **Descriptive Statistics:** R provides functions like mean(), median(), sd(), and summary() to compute basic descriptive statistics. For example:

```
data <- c(1, 2, 3, 4, 5)
mean_value <- mean(data)
sd_value <- sd(data)
summary(data)
```

2. **Data Visualization:** Creating visualizations is straightforward in R. Using ggplot2, one can generate a scatter plot as follows:

```
library(ggplot2)

df <- data.frame(x = rnorm(100), y = rnorm(100))
ggplot(df, aes(x = x, y = y)) +
  geom_point() +
  labs(title = "Scatter Plot", x = "X-axis", y = "Y-axis")
```

3. **Inferential Statistics:** R can perform various inferential statistical tests, such as t-tests and ANOVA. For example, a t-test can be conducted as follows:

```
group1 <- c(5, 6, 7, 8, 9)
group2 <- c(1, 2, 3, 4, 5)
t.test(group1, group2)
```

Advanced Statistical Techniques

1. **Regression Analysis:** R supports linear regression through the lm() function. For instance:

```
model <- lm(y ~ x, data = df)
summary(model)
```

2. **Time Series Analysis:** R is equipped for time series analysis with packages like forecast and ts. Users can model and forecast time series data effectively.

3. **Machine Learning:** The caret package simplifies the process of creating predictive models, enabling users to train and evaluate multiple algorithms easily.

Applications of R: The application of R is as:

1. **Academia and Research:** R is extensively used in academic research for statistical analysis and data visualization. Its ability to handle complex datasets and perform advanced statistical tests makes it an ideal choice for researchers across disciplines.
2. **Healthcare:** In the healthcare sector, R is employed for analyzing clinical trial data, epidemiological studies, and bioinformatics. Its visualization capabilities help in understanding patterns in patient data, leading to better decision-making.
3. **Finance:** R is widely used in finance for risk assessment, portfolio optimization, and time series forecasting. Financial analysts leverage R's statistical capabilities to model market behavior and analyze financial data.
4. **Marketing and Social Sciences:** R is useful for market research, survey analysis, and social science studies. Researchers analyze consumer behavior and social trends, making data-driven decisions.

SAS (Statistical Analysis System)

SAS (Statistical Analysis System) is a powerful software suite developed by SAS Institute for advanced analytics, business intelligence, data management, and predictive analytics. Since its inception in the 1970s, SAS has become a leading tool in the fields of data analysis and statistical modeling, widely used across various industries, including healthcare, finance, and marketing.

Key Features of SAS

1. **Comprehensive Analytics:** SAS provides a wide range of analytical tools, including descriptive statistics, inferential statistics, regression analysis, time series analysis, and machine learning algorithms.
2. **User-friendly Interface:** SAS offers both a graphical user interface (SAS Enterprise Guide) and a programming environment (SAS Base), allowing users to choose their preferred method of interaction.
3. **Data Management:** SAS excels in data manipulation and preparation, offering robust tools for data cleaning, merging, and transformation.
4. **Reporting and Visualization:** With powerful reporting features and graphical capabilities, SAS enables users to create informative reports and visualizations to communicate results effectively.
5. **Security and Compliance:** SAS provides strong security features, making it

suitable for industries that require strict data governance and compliance with regulations.

Basic Statistical Operations in SAS

1. **Descriptive Statistics:** SAS provides procedures like PROC MEANS and PROC FREQ for calculating basic descriptive statistics and frequency distributions. For example:

```
data sample;
   input value;
   datalines;
1
2
3
4
5
;
run;

proc means data=sample;
run;

proc freq data=sample;
   tables value;
run;
```

2. **Data Visualization**: SAS has various options for data visualization, such as the SAS/GRAPH module. For instance, creating a simple scatter plot can be done with:

```
proc sgplot data=sample;
   scatter x=value y=value;
run;
```

3. **Inferential Statistics:** SAS can conduct a variety of inferential statistical tests. For a t-test, you would use:

```
data group1;
   input score @@;
   datalines;
5 6 7 8 9
;
run;

data group2;
   input score @@;
   datalines;
1 2 3 4 5
;
run;

proc ttest data=group1;
   class group;
   var score;
run;
```

Advanced Statistical Techniques

1. **Regression Analysis:** SAS supports various regression models using PROC REG for linear regression and PROC GLM for general linear models. For example:

```
proc reg data=sample;
   model value = x;
run;
```

2. **Time Series Analysis:** The PROC TIMESERIES and PROC ARIMA procedures allow users to analyze and forecast time series data effectively.

3. **Machine Learning:** SAS includes machine learning capabilities in SAS Viya, offering procedures like PROC FOREST and PROC SVM for building decision trees and support vector machines.

Applications of SAS

1. **Healthcare:** SAS is extensively used in healthcare for clinical trial analysis, patient data management, and epidemiological studies. Its robust statistical capabilities help in ensuring regulatory compliance and improving patient outcomes.
2. **Finance:** In finance, SAS is employed for risk analysis, fraud detection, and portfolio management. Analysts leverage its powerful modeling tools to interpret financial data and develop predictive models.
3. **Marketing:** SAS aids in customer segmentation, campaign analysis, and market research. Marketers use SAS to analyze consumer behavior and optimize marketing strategies based on data-driven insights.
4. **Government and Academia:** SAS is also prevalent in government agencies and academic institutions for statistical research, public health analysis, and educational purposes.

Python Libraries

Python has become a prominent language in data science and statistical analysis due to its simplicity, versatility, and the availability of a rich ecosystem of libraries. This article explores some of the most widely used Python libraries for statistical analysis and their applications.

1. **NumPy:** NumPy (Numerical Python) is a foundational library for numerical computing in Python. It provides support for large, multi-dimensional arrays and matrices, along with a collection of mathematical functions to operate on these data structures. Key Features:
   - Efficient array operations and mathematical functions.
   - Support for linear algebra, Fourier transforms, and random number generation.

   Example:

```
import numpy as np

data = np.array([1, 2, 3, 4, 5])
mean = np.mean(data)
std_dev = np.std(data)
```

2. **Pandas:** Pandas is a powerful library for data manipulation and analysis. It offers data structures like DataFrames and Series, making it easy to work with structured data. Key Features:

- Data cleaning and preparation.
- Time series analysis and data visualization.
- Grouping, merging, and reshaping datasets.

Example:

```
data = pd.DataFrame({'value': [1, 2, 3, 4, 5]})
mean_value = data['value'].mean()
summary = data.describe()
```

3. **SciPy:** SciPy is built on NumPy and provides additional functionality for scientific and technical computing. It includes modules for optimization, integration, interpolation, eigenvalue problems, and more. Key Features:
   - Advanced mathematical functions and algorithms.
   - Statistical distributions and tests.

   Example:

```
from scipy import stats

data = [1, 2, 3, 4, 5]
t_stat, p_value = stats.ttest_1samp(data, 3)  # One-sample t-test
```

4. **Statsmodels:** Statsmodels is a library specifically designed for statistical modeling. It provides classes and functions for estimating and testing statistical models, including regression, time series analysis, and more. Key Features:
   - Comprehensive statistical tests and data exploration tools.
   - Support for linear models, generalized linear models, and mixed models.

   Example:

```
import statsmodels.api as sm

X = sm.add_constant(data['value'])  # Add constant for intercept
model = sm.OLS(data['value'], X).fit()  # Ordinary Least Squares regression
summary = model.summary()
```

5. **scikit-learn:** Scikit-learn is a powerful library for machine learning and predictive analytics. While not exclusively a statistical library, it includes various statistical techniques and methods for classification, regression, clustering, and model evaluation. Key Features:

- Extensive collection of algorithms for supervised and unsupervised learning.
- Tools for model selection and evaluation.

Example:

```
from sklearn.linear_model import LinearRegression

model = LinearRegression()
model.fit(X, y)  # Fit a linear model
predictions = model.predict(X)
```

6. **Matplotlib:** Matplotlib is a plotting library for creating static, interactive, and animated visualizations in Python. It works seamlessly with NumPy and Pandas, making it easy to visualize data. Key Features:

- Flexible plotting functions for creating a variety of plots.
- Customizable visualizations with detailed control over plot elements.

Example:

```
import matplotlib.pyplot as plt

plt.hist(data['value'], bins=5)
plt.title('Histogram of Values')
plt.xlabel('Value')
plt.ylabel('Frequency')
plt.show()
```

7. **Seaborn:** Seaborn is built on top of Matplotlib and provides a high-level interface for drawing attractive statistical graphics. It simplifies complex visualizations and supports statistical functions. Key Features:

- Built-in themes for styling Matplotlib graphics.
- Functions for visualizing distributions and relationships in datasets.

Example:

```
import seaborn as sns

sns.boxplot(x=data['value'])
plt.title('Box Plot of Values')
plt.show()
```

8. **PyMC3 / PyMC4:** PyMC3 and its successor PyMC4 are libraries for probabilistic programming, allowing users to build Bayesian models. They are particularly useful for complex statistical modeling and inference. Key Features:
   - Support for Markov Chain Monte Carlo (MCMC) and variational inference.
   - Ability to define custom probabilistic models.

   Example:

```
import pymc3 as pm

with pm.Model() as model:
    mu = pm.Normal('mu', mu=0, sigma=1)
    sigma = pm.HalfNormal('sigma', sigma=1)
    y = pm.Normal('y', mu=mu, sigma=sigma, observed=data['value'])

    trace = pm.sample(1000)
```

Conclusion

Python's rich ecosystem of libraries makes it a powerful tool for statistical analysis and data science. Libraries like NumPy, Pandas, and SciPy provide foundational support for numerical computations, while statsmodels and scikit-learn enable advanced statistical modeling and machine learning. Visualization libraries such as Matplotlib and Seaborn enhance the ability to present data insights effectively. Whether you are conducting basic statistical analyses or building complex models, these libraries provide the necessary tools to turn data into actionable insights.

Differences Between Statistical Tools: R, SAS, Python Libraries

Table 2.2

S.No.	Aspect	R	SAS	Python Libraries
1.	Accessibility and Cost	Open-source and free	Commercial, requires a license	Open-source and free
2.	User Interface	Primarily command-line, RStudio available	GUI and scripting options	Scripting, enhanced by IDEs (e.g., Jupyter, PyCharm)
3.	Statistical Modeling	Extensive packages for complex modeling	Strong procedures for analytics	Versatile libraries (e.g., scikit-learn, statsmodels)
4.	Data Manipulation	Intuitive with dplyr, tidyr	Extensive capabilities in native language	Flexible with Pandas
5.	Visualization Capabilities	Exceptional with ggplot2	Strong reporting tools, less flexible	Robust libraries (Matplotlib, Seaborn)
6.	Community and Support	Strong academic and research community	Dedicated support from SAS Institute	Large, diverse community across multiple domains

2. Data Mining and Knowledge Discovery

Data mining and knowledge discovery are crucial processes in the field of data science, enabling organizations to extract valuable insights from large datasets. As data generation continues to increase exponentially, these processes become essential for effective decision-making across various sectors, including business, healthcare, finance, and social sciences. This article explores the concepts, techniques, tools, and applications of data mining and knowledge discovery.

Data Mining

Data mining is the process of discovering patterns and extracting valuable insights from large datasets. By employing various techniques from statistics, machine learning, and database systems, data mining enables organizations to identify trends, make predictions, and inform decision-making. It involves several stages, including data collection, cleaning, and analysis, often utilizing algorithms to recognize hidden relationships and anomalies. Applications span multiple industries, from finance to healthcare, where data-driven insights can enhance efficiency and customer satisfaction.

The importance of data mining has surged with the exponential growth of data in the digital age. Businesses leverage data mining to personalize marketing strategies, optimize supply chains, and improve customer service. Furthermore, it plays a crucial role in risk management by detecting fraud and forecasting potential risks. As technology evolves, the tools and methodologies for data mining continue to advance, making it an essential component of data analytics and business intelligence strategies. Ultimately, effective data mining can transform raw data into actionable knowledge, driving innovation and competitive advantage.

Key Objectives of Data Mining

1. **Classification:** Assigning data into predefined categories. For example, classifying emails as spam or not spam.
2. **Clustering:** Grouping a set of objects in such a way that objects in the same group (cluster) are more similar to each other than to those in other groups. This is useful for market segmentation.
3. **Association Rule Learning:** Finding interesting relationships between variables in large databases. A classic example is market basket analysis, which identifies items frequently bought together.
4. **Anomaly Detection:** Identifying rare items or events that differ significantly from the majority of the data. This is crucial in fraud detection.
5. **Regression:** Predicting a continuous outcome variable based on one or more predictor variables, such as forecasting sales or stock prices.

Applications of Data Mining: Data mining is applied across various industries, showcasing its versatility and importance in data analysis:

1. **Retail:** In retail, data mining is used for market basket analysis, customer segmentation, and inventory management. For instance, retailers analyze purchasing patterns to recommend products to customers, thereby increasing sales.
2. **Healthcare:** Healthcare organizations utilize data mining to analyze patient records for disease prediction, treatment efficacy, and patient behavior analysis. Predictive models can improve patient outcomes by enabling early diagnosis and targeted interventions.
3. **Finance:** In finance, data mining helps in credit scoring, fraud detection, and risk assessment. Financial institutions analyze transaction patterns to identify fraudulent activities and assess the creditworthiness of loan applicants.
4. **Telecommunications:** Telecom companies use data mining for customer retention, network optimization, and service usage analysis. By identifying patterns in customer behavior, companies can develop targeted marketing strategies and reduce churn rates.
5. **Social-media:** Data mining techniques analyze social media interactions to gauge public sentiment, identify trending topics, and understand user behavior. Brands leverage these insights to enhance customer engagement and refine marketing strategies.

Data Knowledge Discovery

Data Knowledge Discovery, often referred to as Knowledge Discovery in Databases (KDD), is a comprehensive process that involves extracting useful knowledge from vast amounts of data. As organizations increasingly rely on data-driven decision-making, understanding the KDD process and its methodologies has become essential.

Data Mining" can be referred to as knowledge mining from data, knowledge extraction, data/pattern analysis, data archaeology, and data dredging. Data Mining also known as Knowledge Discovery in Databases, refers to the nontrivial extraction of implicit, previously unknown and potentially useful information from data stored in databases.

The need of data mining is to extract useful information from large datasets and use it to make predictions or better decision-making. Nowadays, data mining is used in almost all places where a large amount of data is stored and processed. **For examples:** Banking sector, Market Basket Analysis, Network Intrusion Detection.

KDD Process: KDD (Knowledge Discovery in Databases) is a process that involves the extraction of useful, previously unknown, and potentially valuable information from large datasets. The KDD process is an iterative process and it requires multiple iterations of the above steps to extract accurate knowledge from the data. The steps which are included in KDD process is shown in fig.2.1, each step is as follows:

1. **Data Cleaning:** Data cleaning is defined as removal of noisy and irrelevant data from collection.
   - Cleaning in case of Missing values.
   - Cleaning noisy data, where noise is a random or variance error.
   - Cleaning with Data discrepancy detection and Data transformation tools.
2. **Data Integration:** Data integration is defined as heterogeneous data from multiple sources combined in a common source (DataWarehouse). Data integration using Data Migration tools, Data Synchronization tools and ETL(Extract-Load-Transformation) process.
3. **Data Selection:** Data selection is defined as the process where data relevant to the analysis is decided and retrieved from the data collection. For this we can use Neural network, Decision Trees, Naive bayes, Clustering, and Regression methods.
4. **Data Transformation:** Data Transformation is defined as the process of transforming data into appropriate form required by mining procedure. Data Transformation is a two-step process:
   - **Data Mapping:** Assigning elements from source base to destination to capture transformations.
   - **Code generation:** Creation of the actual transformation program.
5. **Data Mining:** Data mining is defined as techniques that are applied to extract

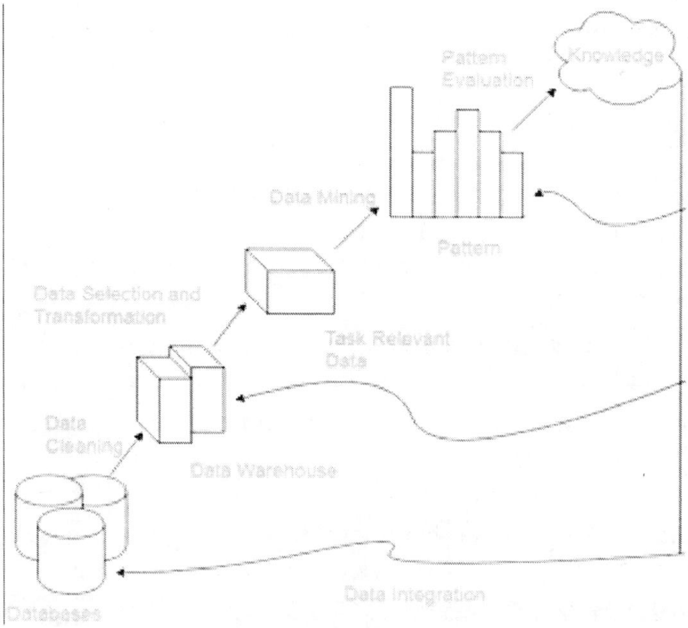

Fig.2.1

patterns potentially useful. It transforms task relevant data into patterns, and decides purpose of model using classification or characterization.

6. **Pattern Evaluation:** Pattern Evaluation is defined as identifying strictly increasing patterns representing knowledge based on given measures. It finds interestingness score of each pattern, and uses summarization and Visualization to make data understandable by user.
7. **Knowledge Representation:** This involves presenting the results in a way that is meaningful and can be used to make decisions.

Conclusion

KDD is an iterative process where evaluation measures can be enhanced, mining can be refined, new data can be integrated and transformed in order to get different and more appropriate results. Preprocessing of databases consists of Data cleaning and Data Integration.

Advantages of KDD:

1. **Improves Decision-making:** KDD provides valuable insights and knowledge that can help organizations make better decisions.
2. **Increased Efficiency:** KDD automates repetitive and time-consuming tasks and makes the data ready for analysis, which saves time and money.
3. **Better Customer Service:** KDD helps organizations gain a better understanding of their customers' needs and preferences, which can help them provide better customer service.
4. **Fraud Detection:** KDD can be used to detect fraudulent activities by identifying patterns and anomalies in the data that may indicate fraud.
5. **Predictive Modeling:** KDD can be used to build predictive models that can forecast future trends and patterns.

Disadvantages of KDD

1. **Privacy Concerns:** KDD can raise privacy concerns as it involves collecting and analyzing large amounts of data, which can include sensitive information about individuals.
2. **Complexity:** KDD can be a complex process that requires specialized skills and knowledge to implement and interpret the results.
3. **Unintended Consequences:** KDD can lead to unintended consequences, such as bias or discrimination, if the data or models are not properly understood or used.
4. **Data Quality:** KDD process heavily depends on the quality of data, if data is not accurate or consistent, the results can be misleading
5. **High Cost:** KDD can be an expensive process, requiring significant investments in hardware, software, and personnel.

6. **Overfitting:** KDD process can lead to overfitting, which is a common problem in machine learning where a model learns the detail and noise in the training data to the extent that it negatively impacts the performance of the model on new unseen data.

Differences Between Data Mining and Data Knowledge Discovery

Table 2.3

S.No.	Aspect	Data Mining	Data Knowledge Discovery
1.	Definition	The process of extracting patterns and insights from large datasets using algorithms and statistical techniques.	A broader process that encompasses the entire workflow of transforming raw data into useful knowledge, including data mining as a core component. Encompasses data selection, preprocessing, mining, evaluation, and presentation of knowledge.
2.	Scope	Focused primarily on the application of specific algorithms and techniques to analyze data.	Encompasses data selection, preprocessing, mining, evaluation, and presentation of knowledge.
3.	Objectives	Aims to discover patterns, correlations, and anomalies within	Aims to generate valid, novel, and useful knowledge from data, making it actionable and understandable.
4.	Process Stages	Involves specific stages like applying algorithms and models to data.	Involves multiple stages, including data selection, preprocessing, mining, evaluation, and knowledge presentation.
5.	Outcome	Produces specific patterns or models, such as classification rules or clusters.	Produces actionable knowledge and insights that can inform decision-making and strategy.
6.	Tools and Techniques	Utilizes specific algorithms (e.g., clustering, classification, involves specific stages like applying algorithms and models to data. regression) for analysis.	Employs a range of techniques, including data mining, statistical analysis, and visualization tools, to present the knowledge derived from data.

Introduction to Data Mining Techniques

Data Mining Techniques: The data mining techniques is shown in fig.2.2, the explanation of each is as follows:

1. **Association Rules:** Association analysis is the finding of association rules showing attribute-value conditions that occur frequently together in a given set of data. Association analysis is widely used for a market basket or transaction data analysis. Association rule mining is a significant and exceptionally dynamic area of data mining research. One method of association-based classification, called associative classification, consists of two steps. In the main step, association instructions are generated using a modified version of the standard association rule mining algorithm known as Apriori.

The second step constructs a classifier based on the association rules discovered.

Applications: Market basket analysis, cross-selling strategies, recommendation systems.

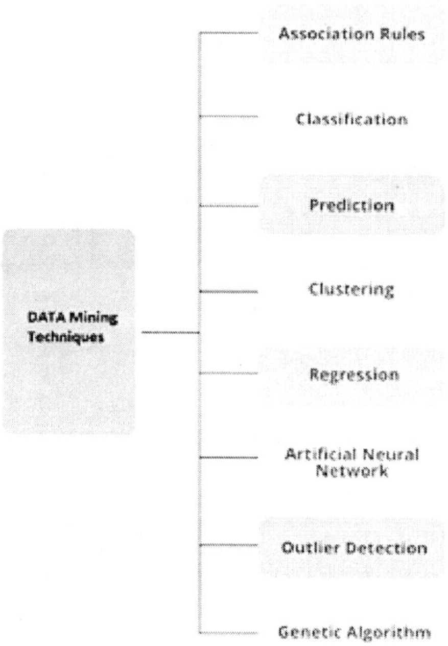

Fig.2.2

2. **Classification:** Classification is the processing of finding a set of models (or functions) that describe and distinguish data classes or concepts, for the purpose of being able to use the model to predict the class of objects whose class label is unknown. The determined model depends on the investigation of a set of training data information (i.e. data objects whose class label is known). The derived model may be represented in various forms, such as classification (if – then) rules, decision trees, and neural networks. Data Mining has a different type of classifier are Decision Tree, SVM (Support Vector Machine), Generalized Linear Models, Bayesian, Fuzzy Logic.

   Applications: Spam detection, credit scoring, disease diagnosis.

3. **Prediction:** Data Prediction is a two-step process, similar to that of data classification. Although, for prediction, we do not utilize the phrasing of "Class label attribute" because the attribute for which values are being predicted is consistently valued(ordered) instead of categorical (discrete-esteemed and unordered). The attribute can be referred to simply as the predicted attribute. Prediction can be viewed as the construction and use of a model to assess the

class of an unlabeled object, or to assess the value or value ranges of an attribute that a given object is likely to have.

4. **Clustering:** Unlike classification and prediction, which analyze class-labeled data objects or attributes, clustering analyzes data objects without consulting an identified class label. In general, the class labels do not exist in the training data simply because they are not known to begin with. Clustering can be used to generate these labels. The objects are clustered based on the principle of maximizing the intra-class similarity and minimizing the interclass similarity. That is, clusters of objects are created so that objects inside a cluster have high similarity in contrast with each other, but are different objects in other clusters. Each Cluster that is generated can be seen as a class of objects, from which rules can be inferred. Clustering can also facilitate classification formation, that is, the organization of observations into a hierarchy of classes that group similar events together.

   Applications: Customer segmentation, social network analysis, image segmentation.

5. **Regression:** Regression can be defined as a statistical modeling method in which previously obtained data is used to predicting a continuous quantity for new observations. This classifier is also known as the Continuous Value Classifier. There are two types of regression models: Linear regression and multiple linear regression models.

   Applications: Sales forecasting, risk assessment, financial modeling.

6. **Artificial Neural network (ANN) Classifier Method:** An artificial neural network (ANN) also referred to as simply a "Neural Network" (NN), could be a process model supported by biological neural networks. It consists of an interconnected collection of artificial neurons. A neural network is a set of connected input/output units where each connection has a weight associated with it. During the knowledge phase, the network acquires by adjusting the weights to be able to predict the correct class label of the input samples. Neural network learning is also denoted as connectionist learning due to the connections between units. Neural networks involve long training times and are therefore more appropriate for applications where this is feasible. They require a number of parameters that are typically best determined empirically, such as the network topology or "structure". Neural networks have been criticized for their poor interpretability since it is difficult for humans to take the symbolic meaning behind the learned weights. These features firstly made neural networks less desirable for data mining.

   Applications: Image recognition, speech recognition, and natural language processing tasks.

7. **Outlier Detection:** A database may contain data objects that do not comply with the general behavior or model of the data. These data objects are Outliers.

The investigation of OUTLIER data is known as OUTLIER MINING. An outlier may be detected using statistical tests which assume a distribution or probability model for the data, or using distance measures where objects having a small fraction of "close" neighbors in space are considered outliers. Rather than utilizing factual or distance measures, deviation-based techniques distinguish exceptions/outlier by inspecting differences in the principle attributes of items in a group.

8. **Genetic Algorithm:** Genetic algorithms are adaptive heuristic search algorithms that belong to the larger part of evolutionary algorithms. Genetic algorithms are based on the ideas of natural selection and genetics. These are intelligent exploitation of random search provided with historical data to direct the search into the region of better performance in solution space. They are commonly used to generate high-quality solutions for optimization problems and search problems. Genetic algorithms simulate the process of natural selection which means those species who can adapt to changes in their environment are able to survive and reproduce and go to the next generation. In simple words, they simulate "survival of the fittest" among individuals of consecutive generations for solving a problem. Each generation consist of a population of individuals and each individual represents a point in search space and possible solution. Each individual is represented as a string of character/integer/float/bits. This string is analogous to the Chromosome.

Dimensionality Reduction: PCA and LDA

Dimensionality reduction is a vital technique in machine learning and data analysis, allowing us to simplify complex datasets while retaining their essential features. Two of the most prominent methods for dimensionality reduction are Principal Component Analysis (PCA) and Linear Discriminant Analysis (LDA). Both techniques serve different purposes and are based on distinct principles. This article delves into the mechanics, applications, and differences between PCA and LDA.

Dimensionality Reduction

Dimensionality reduction refers to the process of reducing the number of random variables under consideration by obtaining a set of principal variables. High-dimensional datasets can be challenging to visualize, analyze, and process. Techniques such as PCA and LDA aim to reduce dimensions while preserving as much information as possible, making it easier to interpret and work with the data.

Principal Component Analysis (PCA)

PCA is an unsupervised linear transformation technique that converts a set of correlated variables into a set of uncorrelated variables called principal components. The first principal component captures the most variance in the data, followed by the second, which captures the second most variance, and so on. This process helps identify patterns and structure in the data. Principal Component Analysis(PCA) technique was introduced by the mathematician Karl Pearson in 1901. It works on the condition that while the data in a higher dimensional space is mapped to data in a lower dimension space, the variance of the data in the lower dimensional space should be maximum.

1. Principal Component Analysis (PCA) is a statistical procedure that uses an orthogonal transformation that converts a set of correlated variables to a set of uncorrelated variables. PCA is the most widely used tool in exploratory data analysis and in machine learning for predictive models. Moreover,
2. Principal Component Analysis (PCA) is an unsupervised learning algorithm technique used to examine the interrelations among a set of variables. It is also known as a general factor analysis where regression determines a line of best fit.
3. The main goal of Principal Component Analysis (PCA) is to reduce the dimensionality of a dataset while preserving the most important patterns or relationships between the variables without any prior knowledge of the target variables.

Mathematical Foundation

1. **Standardization:** PCA begins with standardizing the dataset to have a mean of zero and a standard deviation of one for each feature.
2. **Covariance Matrix:** Calculate the covariance matrix of the standardized data, which shows how variables vary together.

$$\text{Cov}(X) = \frac{1}{n-1}(X^T X)$$

3. **Eigenvalues and Eigenvectors:** The next step is to compute the eigenvalues and eigenvectors of the covariance matrix. The eigenvectors represent the directions of maximum variance, while the eigenvalues indicate the magnitude of variance in those directions.
4. **Sorting:** Sort the eigenvalues in descending order and select the top k eigenvectors, forming a new matrix w.
5. **Projection:** Finally, the original data is projected onto the new subspace using:

$$Y = XW$$

where Y is the transformed dataset.

Applications of PCA

1. **Data Visualization:** PCA is commonly used to reduce dimensions for visualization, allowing us to plot high-dimensional data in 2D or 3D.
2. **Noise Reduction:** By eliminating components with low variance, PCA can help reduce noise in the data.
3. **Preprocessing for Machine Learning:** PCA is often used as a preprocessing

step to enhance the performance of machine learning models by reducing computational complexity and improving model interpretability.

Linear Discriminant Analysis (LDA)

Linear Discriminant Analysis (LDA) is a powerful statistical technique widely used in machine learning and pattern recognition for classification and dimensionality reduction. It focuses on finding a linear combination of features that best separates two or more classes of data. Unlike unsupervised methods such as Principal Component Analysis (PCA), LDA takes class labels into account, making it a supervised learning algorithm. This article explores the theory, mathematical foundation, applications, advantages, and limitations of LDA.

The primary goal of LDA is to maximize the separation between multiple classes while minimizing the variance within each class. This is particularly useful in classification tasks, where we want to predict the category of new observations based on their features. By projecting the data onto a lower-dimensional space defined by the linear discriminants, LDA enhances the model's discriminative power.

Mathematical Foundation

LDA involves several key steps, rooted in linear algebra and statistics. The process can be summarized as follows:

1. **Class Mean Vectors:** For each class C_k in the dataset, calculate the mean vector μ_k:

$$\mu_k = \frac{1}{N_k} \sum_{x_i \in C_k} x_i$$

Where, N_k is the number of samples in class C_k and X_i represents individual data points.

2. **Overall Mean Vector:** Compute the overall mean vector μ of the entire dataset:

$$\mu = \frac{1}{N} \sum_{k=1}^{K} N_k \mu_k$$

Where, N is the total number of samples across all classes.

3. **Scatter Matrices:** LDA uses two scatter matrices to analyze data variance:
   - **Within-Class Scatter Matrix (S_w) :** This measures the variability within each class:

$$S_W = \sum_{k=1}^{K} \sum_{x_i \in C_k} (x_i - \mu_k)(x_i - \mu_k)^T$$

   - **Between-Class Scatter Matrix (S_B) :** This measures the variability between different classes:

$$S_B = \sum_{k=1}^{K} N_k(\mu_k - \mu)(\mu_k - \mu)^T$$

4. **Maximizing the Discriminative Criterion:** The main goal of LDA is to maximize the ratio of the determinant of the between-class scatter matrix to the determinant of the within-class scatter matrix:

$$J(w) = \frac{|S_B|}{|S_W|}$$

To achieve this, LDA solves the generalized eigenvalue problem:

$$S_W^{-1} S_B v = \lambda v$$

Here, ν are the eigenvectors, and λ are the corresponding eigenvalues.

5. **Selecting Eigenvectors:** The eigenvectors associated with the largest eigenvalues are selected to construct a new feature space. For a classification problem with K classes, at most K-1 linear discriminants can be used.

6. **Projection:** Finally, the original data is projected onto this new subspace defined by the selected eigenvectors:

$$Y = XW$$

Where, Y is the transformed dataset and is the matrix of selected eigenvectors.

Applications of LDA: LDA is employed in various fields due to its effectiveness in classification tasks:

1. **Face Recognition:** LDA is commonly used in face recognition systems to distinguish between different individuals based on facial features. By projecting images into a space that maximizes class separability, LDA improves recognition accuracy.

2. **Medical Diagnosis:** In healthcare, LDA helps classify patients based on symptoms, lab results, or imaging data, aiding in diagnoses such as identifying diseases from medical scans.

3. **Financial Analysis:** In finance, LDA can classify investment opportunities based on historical performance and market indicators, helping analysts make informed decisions.

4. **Speech Recognition:** LDA is used in speech recognition systems to classify spoken words or phrases, enhancing the accuracy of automatic transcription.

5. **Customer Segmentation:** Businesses utilize LDA to segment customers based on purchasing behavior and demographics, allowing for targeted marketing strategies.

Differences Between PCA and LDA

Table 2.4

S.No.	Aspect	PCA	LDA
1.	Feature	Dimensionality reduction, capturing variance	Class separation, maximizing between-class variance
2.	Input Data	Unsupervised, does not consider class labels	Supervised, requires class labels
3.	Output Components	Orthogonal components (principal components)	Linear combinations that best separate classes
4.	Optimization Goal	Maximize variance in the projected space	Maximize the ratio of between-class variance to within-class variance
5.	Usage Context	Exploratory data analysis, noise reduction	Classification, pattern recognition
6.	Assumptions	Assumes linearity and captures maximum variance	Assumes normal distribution of classes and equal covariance among classes

Case Studies in Data Mining

Data mining is a powerful tool that involves extracting valuable insights from vast amounts of data. By employing various techniques such as classification, clustering, regression, and association rule mining, organizations can make informed decisions that enhance their operations. Here, we explore several case studies from diverse industries to illustrate the practical applications and benefits of data mining.

1. **Retail Industry: Customer Segmentation**

   Company: Target

   Objective: Enhance marketing strategies through targeted promotions.

   Approach: Target used data mining techniques to analyze purchasing behavior and demographic data. By employing clustering algorithms, they identified distinct customer segments based on shopping habits and preferences.

   Outcome: The company developed personalized marketing campaigns that significantly improved customer engagement. For example, Target could predict pregnancy-related purchases and send tailored coupons to expecting parents. This targeted approach not only increased sales but also fostered customer loyalty, as shoppers appreciated receiving relevant offers.

2. **Healthcare: Predictive Analytics for Patient Care**

   Company: Mount Sinai Health System

   Objective: Reduce hospital readmission rates.

   Approach: Mount Sinai employed predictive modeling to analyze patient data, including medical histories, demographics, and treatment plans. Using classification techniques, they identified patients at high risk of readmission.

Outcome: The health system implemented targeted interventions for high-risk patients, such as follow-up care and personalized health plans. As a result, they achieved a 20% reduction in readmissions within a year, leading to improved patient outcomes and significant cost savings.

3. **Finance: Fraud Detection**

   Company: PayPal

   Objective: Minimize fraudulent transactions.

   Approach: PayPal utilized data mining techniques such as anomaly detection and classification to identify patterns indicative of fraudulent activity. By analyzing transaction data in real-time, they could flag suspicious transactions for further review.

   Outcome: The implementation of these techniques led to a significant reduction in fraud-related losses. PayPal's fraud detection system became more sophisticated over time, leveraging machine learning to adapt to new fraud patterns, which enhanced the security of their transactions and instilled greater trust among users.

4. **Telecommunications: Churn Prediction**

   Company: Vodafone

   Objective: Decrease customer churn rates.

   Approach: Vodafone applied data mining techniques to analyze customer behavior data, billing information, and service usage patterns. By utilizing classification algorithms like decision trees, they developed models to predict which customers were likely to churn.

   Outcome: Armed with insights from the predictive model, Vodafone implemented retention strategies such as targeted promotions and enhanced customer support for at-risk customers. These efforts led to a reduction in churn rates by approximately 15%, resulting in substantial revenue preservation.

5. **E-commerce: Recommendation Systems**

   Company: Amazon

   Objective: Increase sales through personalized recommendations.

   Approach: Amazon employs collaborative filtering and content-based filtering techniques to analyze customer behavior, purchase history, and product attributes. By leveraging large datasets, they generate personalized recommendations for each user.

   Outcome: The recommendation engine significantly boosts sales, accounting for a substantial portion of Amazon's revenue. Customers are more likely to purchase items that are recommended based on their preferences and previous purchases, enhancing user experience and increasing overall customer satisfaction.

6. **Manufacturing: Predictive Maintenance**

   Company: General Electric (GE)

   Objective: Improve equipment reliability and reduce downtime.

   Approach: GE applied data mining techniques to analyze sensor data from industrial machinery. By using predictive analytics, they identified patterns that indicated potential equipment failures before they occurred.

   Outcome: This proactive approach to maintenance resulted in reduced unplanned downtime and maintenance costs. GE's predictive maintenance model enabled them to schedule maintenance activities during non-peak hours, improving overall operational efficiency.

7. **Transportation: Route Optimization**

   Company: Uber

   Objective: Enhance driver efficiency and reduce wait times.

   Approach: Uber utilizes data mining to analyze traffic patterns, rider demand, and historical data to optimize driver routes. By applying clustering and regression analysis, they can predict high-demand areas and recommend optimal pickup routes for drivers.

   Outcome: The implementation of these techniques has led to improved service quality, shorter wait times for riders, and increased earnings for drivers. This data-driven approach allows Uber to dynamically adjust to changing conditions in real-time, enhancing the overall efficiency of their service.

Conclusion

These case studies illustrate the diverse applications of data mining across various sectors. By leveraging data mining techniques, organizations can uncover hidden patterns, enhance decision-making, and drive significant business value. Whether it's through targeted marketing, improved customer retention, or operational efficiency, the impact of data mining is profound and transformative. As technology continues to evolve, the potential for data mining to influence strategic initiatives will only expand, making it an essential component of modern business strategy.

3. Machine Learning Fundamentals

Machine learning (ML) is a subset of artificial intelligence that enables systems to learn from data and make predictions or decisions without explicit programming. It encompasses three main types: supervised learning, which uses labeled datasets to train models; unsupervised learning, which identifies patterns in unlabeled data; and reinforcement learning, where agents learn optimal actions through trial and error by interacting with an environment. Key concepts include features (input variables), labels (output targets), model training, and evaluation metrics such as accuracy, precision, recall, and F1 score. The machine learning workflow involves several steps: data collection, preprocessing, model selection, training, evaluation, hyperparameter tuning, deployment, and ongoing monitoring. Applications of ML span various fields, including healthcare for predicting patient outcomes, finance for fraud detection, retail for customer segmentation, and natural language processing for sentiment analysis. By leveraging algorithms that can adapt and improve over time, machine learning plays a pivotal role in transforming industries and enhancing decision-making processes. As data generation accelerates, the significance of machine learning in driving innovation and operational efficiency will continue to expand, making it an essential area of study and application in technology and business.

Supervised Learning

Supervised learning is a type of machine learning algorithm that learns from labeled data. Labeled data is data that has been tagged with a correct answer or classification.

Supervised learning, as the name indicates, has the presence of a supervisor as a teacher. Supervised learning is when we teach or train the machine using data that is well-labelled. Which means some data is already tagged with the correct answer. After that, the machine is provided with a new set of examples(data) so that the supervised learning algorithm analyses the training data (set of training examples) and produces a correct outcome from labeled data. Some Key Points are as:

- Supervised learning involves training a machine from labeled data.
- Labeled data consists of examples with the correct answer or classification.
- The machine learns the relationship between inputs (fruit images) and outputs (fruit labels).
- The trained machine can then make predictions on new, unlabeled data.

For example, a labeled dataset of images of Elephant, Camel and Cow would have each image tagged with either "Elephant", "Camel" or "Cow."

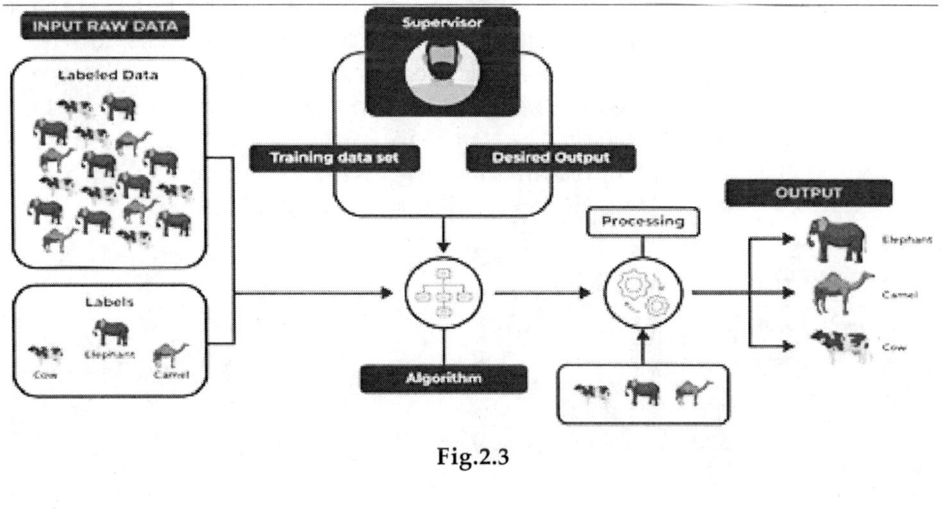

Fig.2.3

Example:

Let's say you have a fruit basket that you want to identify. The machine would first analyze the image to extract features such as its shape, color, and texture. Then, it would compare these features to the features of the fruits it has already learned about. If the new image's features are most similar to those of an apple, the machine would predict that the fruit is an apple.

For instance, suppose you are given a basket filled with different kinds of fruits. Now the first step is to train the machine with all the different fruits one by one like this:

- If the shape of the object is rounded and has a depression at the top, is red in color, then it will be labeled as –Apple.
- If the shape of the object is a long curving cylinder having Green-Yellow color, then it will be labeled as –Banana.

Now suppose after training the data, you have given a new separate fruit, say Banana from the basket, and asked to identify it. Since the machine has already learned the things from previous data and this time has to use it wisely. It will first classify the fruit with its shape and color and would confirm the fruit name as BANANA and put it in the Banana category. Thus the machine learns the things from training data(basket containing fruits) and then applies the knowledge to test data(new fruit).

Types of Supervised Learning: Supervised learning is classified into two categories of algorithms:

1. **Regression:** Regression is a type of supervised learning that is used to predict continuous values, such as house prices, stock prices, or customer churn. Regression algorithms learn a function that maps from the input features to the output value. Some common regression algorithms include Linear Regression, Polynomial Regression, Support Vector Machine Regression, Decision Tree Regression, and Random Forest Regression.
2. **Classification:** Classification is a type of supervised learning that is used to predict categorical values, such as whether a customer will churn or not, whether an email is spam or not, or whether a medical image shows a tumor or not. Classification algorithms learn a function that maps from the input features to a probability distribution over the output classes. Some common classification algorithms include Logistic Regression, Support Vector Machines, Decision Trees, Random Forests, and Naive Baye

Applications of Supervised Learning: Supervised learning can be used to solve a wide variety of problems, including:

1. **Spam Filtering:** Supervised learning algorithms can be trained to identify and classify spam emails based on their content, helping users avoid unwanted messages.

2. **Image Classification:** Supervised learning can automatically classify images into different categories, such as animals, objects, or scenes, facilitating tasks like image search, content moderation, and image-based product recommendations.
3. **Medical Diagnosis:** Supervised learning can assist in medical diagnosis by analyzing patient data, such as medical images, test results, and patient history, to identify patterns that suggest specific diseases or conditions.
4. **Fraud Detection:** Supervised learning models can analyze financial transactions and identify patterns that indicate fraudulent activity, helping financial institutions prevent fraud and protect their customers.
5. **Natural Language Processing (NLP):** Supervised learning plays a crucial role in NLP tasks, including sentiment analysis, machine translation, and text summarization, enabling machines to understand and process human language effectively.

Advantages of Supervised Learning

1. Supervised learning allows collecting data and produces data output from previous experiences.
2. Helps to optimize performance criteria with the help of experience.
3. Supervised machine learning helps to solve various types of real-world computation problems.
4. It performs classification and regression tasks.
5. It allows estimating or mapping the result to a new sample.
6. We have complete control over choosing the number of classes we want in the training data.

Disadvantages of Supervised Learning

1. Classifying big data can be challenging.
2. Training for supervised learning needs a lot of computation time. So, it requires a lot of time.
3. Supervised learning cannot handle all complex tasks in Machine Learning.
4. Computation time is vast for supervised learning.
5. It requires a labelled data set.
6. It requires a training process.

Unsupervised Learning

Unsupervised learning is a type of machine learning that learns from unlabeled data. This means that the data does not have any pre-existing labels or categories. The goal of unsupervised learning is to discover patterns and relationships in the data without any explicit guidance.

Unsupervised learning is the training of a machine using information that is neither classified nor labeled and allowing the algorithm to act on that information without guidance. Here the task of the machine is to group unsorted information according to similarities, patterns, and differences without any prior training of data.

Unlike supervised learning, no teacher is provided that means no training will be given to the machine. Therefore the machine is restricted to find the hidden structure in unlabeled data by itself.

You can use unsupervised learning to examine the animal data that has been gathered and distinguish between several groups according to the traits and actions of the animals. These groupings might correspond to various animal species, providing you to categorize the creatures without depending on labels that already exist. Some Key Points are as :

- Unsupervised learning allows the model to discover patterns and relationships in unlabeled data.
- Clustering algorithms group similar data points together based on their inherent characteristics.
- Feature extraction captures essential information from the data, enabling the model to make meaningful distinctions.
- Label association assigns categories to the clusters based on the extracted patterns and characteristics.

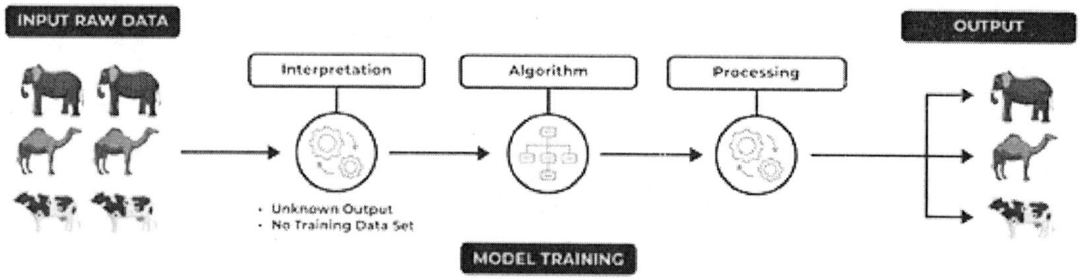

Fig.2.4

Example

Imagine you have a machine learning model trained on a large dataset of unlabeled images, containing both dogs and cats. The model has never seen an image of a dog or cat before, and it has no pre-existing labels or categories for these animals. Your task is to use unsupervised learning to identify the dogs and cats in a new, unseen image. For instance, suppose it is given an image having both dogs and cats which it has never seen.

Thus the machine has no idea about the features of dogs and cats so we can't categorize it as 'dogs and cats '. But it can categorize them according to their similarities, patterns, and differences, i.e., we can easily categorize the above picture into two parts. The first may contain all pics having dogs in them and the second part may contain all pics having cats in them. Here you didn't learn anything before, which means no training data or examples.

It allows the model to work on its own to discover patterns and information that was previously undetected. It mainly deals with unlabelled data.

Types of Unsupervised Learning: Unsupervised learning is classified into two categories of algorithms:

1. **Clustering:** Clustering is a type of unsupervised learning that is used to group similar data points together. Clustering algorithms work by iteratively moving data points closer to their cluster centers and further away from data points in other clusters. Clustering Types are Hierarchical clustering, K-means clustering, Principal Component Analysis, Singular Value Decomposition, Independent Component Analysis, Gaussian Mixture Models (GMMs) and Density-Based Spatial Clustering of Applications with Noise (DBSCAN).
2. **Association Rule Learning**: Association rule learning is a type of unsupervised learning that is used to identify patterns in a data. Association rule learning algorithms work by finding relationships between different items in a dataset. Some common association rule learning algorithms include Apriori Algorithm, Eclat Algorithm andFP-Growth Algorithm

Application of Unsupervised Learning: Non-supervised learning can be used to solve a wide variety of problems, including:

1. **Anomaly Detection:** Unsupervised learning can identify unusual patterns or deviations from normal behavior in data, enabling the detection of fraud, intrusion, or system failures.
2. **Scientific Discovery:** Unsupervised learning can uncover hidden relationships and patterns in scientific data, leading to new hypotheses and insights in various scientific fields.
3. **Recommendation Systems:** Unsupervised learning can identify patterns and similarities in user behavior and preferences to recommend products, movies, or music that align with their interests.
4. **Customer Segmentation:** Unsupervised learning can identify groups of customers with similar characteristics, allowing businesses to target marketing campaigns and improve customer service more effectively.
5. **Image Analysis:** Unsupervised learning can group images based on their content, facilitating tasks such as image classification, object detection, and image retrieval.

Advantages of Unsupervised Learning

1. It does not require training data to be labeled.
2. Dimensionality reduction can be easily accomplished using unsupervised learning.

3. Capable of finding previously unknown patterns in data.
4. Unsupervised learning can help you gain insights from unlabeled data that you might not have been able to get otherwise.
5. Unsupervised learning is good at finding patterns and relationships in data without being told what to look for. This can help you learn new things about your data.

Disadvantages of Unsupervised Learning

1. Difficult to measure accuracy or effectiveness due to lack of predefined answers during training.
2. The results often have lesser accuracy.
3. The user needs to spend time interpreting and label the classes which follow that classification.
4. Unsupervised learning can be sensitive to data quality, including missing values, outliers, and noisy data.
5. Without labeled data, it can be difficult to evaluate the performance of unsupervised learning models, making it challenging to assess their effectiveness.

Supervised vs. Unsupervised Learning

Table 2.5

S.No.	Aspect	Supervised Learning	Unsupervised Learning
1.	Definition	Learning from labeled data (input-output pairs).	Learning from unlabeled data (input only).
2.	Data Requirement	Requires a labeled dataset.	Works with unlabelled datasets.
3.	Goal	Predict outcomes or classify data points.	Discover patterns, group data, or reduce dimensionality.
4.	Applications	Spam detection, image classification, fraud detection.	Customer segmentation, anomaly detection, data compression.
5.	Evaluation Metrics	Accuracy, precision, recall, F1 score, RMSE.	Silhouette score, Davies-Bouldin index, visual inspection.
6.	Complexity	Generally requires more data preparation and labeling.	Can be more flexible but harder to evaluate.
7.	Examples of Algorithms	Linear Regression, Decision Trees, SVM, Neural Networks.	K-Means Clustering, Hierarchical Clustering, PCA.

Key Algorithms: Regression, Decision Trees, SVM, k-NN

Key algorithms in machine learning serve as foundational methods for solving various predictive and classification tasks. Key algorithms in machine learning are essential for tackling predictive and classification tasks. Regression models the relationship between input features and a continuous target variable, making it useful for applications like financial forecasting and real estate valuation. Decision Trees create a flowchart-like structure that splits data based on feature values, making them intuitive for classification tasks such as customer segmentation. Support Vector Machines (SVM) identify the optimal hyperplane to separate classes in high-dimensional space, excelling in areas like text classification and image recognition. k-Nearest Neighbors (k-NN) classifies data points by examining the majority class among their nearest neighbors, proving effective for recommendation systems and anomaly detection. Each algorithm has unique strengths and is chosen based on the specific needs of the problem, providing a robust toolkit for data analysis and predictive modeling.

Regression

Regression is used to predict continuous outcomes, modeling the relationship between input features and a target variable, commonly applied in financial forecasting and real estate valuation. It is a supervised machine learning technique, used to predict the value of the dependent variable for new, unseen data. It models the relationship between the input features and the target variable, allowing for the estimation or prediction of numerical values.

Regression analysis problem works with if output variable is a real or continuous value, such as "salary" or "weight". Many different models can be used, the simplest is the linear regression. It tries to fit data with the best hyper-plane which goes through the points.

Terminologies Related to the Regression Analysis in Machine Learning: Terminologies related to regression analysis:

1. **Response Variable:** The primary factor to predict or understand in regression, also known as the dependent variable or target variable.
2. **Predictor Variable:** Factors influencing the response variable, used to predict its values; also called independent variables.
3. **Outliers:** Observations with significantly low or high values compared to others, potentially impacting results and best avoided.
4. **Multicollinearity:** High correlation among independent variables, which can complicate the ranking of influential variables.
5. **Underfitting and Overfitting:** Overfitting occurs when an algorithm performs well on training but poorly on testing, while underfitting indicates poor performance on both datasets

Regression Algorithms: There are many different types of regression algorithms, but some of the most common include:

1. **Linear Regression:** Linear regression is one of the simplest and most widely used statistical models. This assumes that there is a linear relationship between

the independent and dependent variables. This means that the change in the dependent variable is proportional to the change in the independent variables.

2. **Polynomial Regression:** Polynomial regression is used to model nonlinear relationships between the dependent variable and the independent variables. It adds polynomial terms to the linear regression model to capture more complex relationships.
3. **Support Vector Regression (SVR):** Support vector regression (SVR) is a type of regression algorithm that is based on the support vector machine (SVM) algorithm. SVM is a type of algorithm that is used for classification tasks, but it can also be used for regression tasks. SVR works by finding a hyperplane that minimizes the sum of the squared residuals between the predicted and actual values.
4. **Decision Tree Regression:** Decision tree regression is a type of regression algorithm that builds a decision tree to predict the target value. A decision tree is a tree-like structure that consists of nodes and branches. Each node represents a decision, and each branch represents the outcome of that decision. The goal of decision tree regression is to build a tree that can accurately predict the target value for new data points.
5. **Random Forest Regression:** Random Forest regression is an ensemble method that combines multiple decision trees to predict the target value. Ensemble methods are a type of machine learning algorithm that combines multiple models to improve the performance of the overall model. Random forest regression works by building a large number of decision trees, each of which is trained on a different subset of the training data. The final prediction is made by averaging the predictions of all of the trees.

Characteristics of Regression: Here are the characteristics of the regression:

1. **Continuous Target Variable:** Regression deals with predicting continuous target variables that represent numerical values. Examples include predicting house prices, forecasting sales figures, or estimating patient recovery times.
2. **Error Measurement:** Regression models are evaluated based on their ability to minimize the error between the predicted and actual values of the target variable. Common error metrics include mean absolute error (MAE), mean squared error (MSE), and root mean squared error (RMSE).
3. **Model Complexity:** Regression models range from simple linear models to more complex nonlinear models. The choice of model complexity depends on the complexity of the relationship between the input features and the target variable.
4. **Overfitting and Underfitting:** Regression models are susceptible to overfitting and underfitting.
5. **Interpretability:** The interpretability of regression models varies depending

on the algorithm used. Simple linear models are highly interpretable, while more complex models may be more difficult to interpret.

Decision Trees

Decision trees are a popular and powerful tool used in various fields such as machine learning, data mining, and statistics. They provide a clear and intuitive way to make decisions based on data by modeling the relationships between different variables. A decision tree is a flowchart-like structure used to make decisions or predictions. It consists of nodes representing decisions or tests on attributes, branches representing the outcome of these decisions, and leaf nodes representing final outcomes or predictions. Each internal node corresponds to a test on an attribute, each branch corresponds to the result of the test, and each leaf node corresponds to a class label or a continuous value.

Structure of a Decision Tree

1. **Root Node:** Represents the entire dataset and the initial decision to be made.
2. **Internal Nodes:** Represent decisions or tests on attributes. Each internal node has one or more branches.
3. **Branches:** Represent the outcome of a decision or test, leading to another node.
4. **Leaf Nodes:** Represent the final decision or prediction. No further splits occur at these nodes.

Example: The tree can be explained by two entities, namely decision nodes and leaves. The leaves are the decisions or the final outcomes. And the decision nodes are where the data is split.

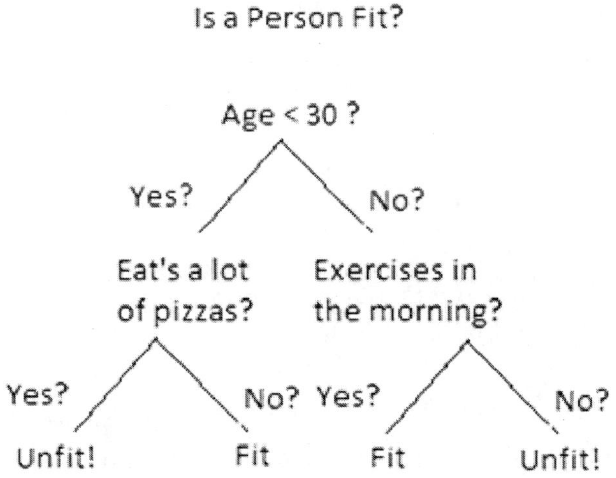

Fig.2.5

An example of a decision tree can be explained using above binary tree shown in fig.2.6. Let's say suppose we want to predict whether a person is fit given their information like age, eating habit, and physical activity, etc. The decision nodes here are questions like 'What's the age?', 'Does he exercise?', 'Does he eat a lot of pizzas'? And the leaves, which are outcomes like either 'fit', or 'unfit'. In this case this was a binary classification problem (a yes no type problem).

How Decision Trees Work?

The process of creating a decision tree involves:

1. **Selecting the Best Attribute:** Using a metric like Gini impurity, entropy, or information gain, the best attribute to split the data is selected.
2. **Splitting the Dataset:** The dataset is split into subsets based on the selected attribute.
3. **Repeating the Process:** The process is repeated recursively for each subset, creating a new internal node or leaf node until a stopping criterion is met (e.g., all instances in a node belong to the same class or a predefined depth is reached).

Why Decision Tree?

Decision trees are widely used in machine learning for a number of reasons:

1. Decision trees are so versatile in simulating intricate decision-making processes, because of their interpretability and versatility.
2. Their portrayal of complex choice scenarios that take into account a variety of causes and outcomes is made possible by their hierarchical structure.
3. They provide comprehensible insights into the decision logic, decision trees are especially helpful for tasks involving categorisation and regression.
4. They are proficient with both numerical and categorical data, and they can easily adapt to a variety of datasets thanks to their autonomous feature selection capability.
5. Decision trees also provide simple visualization, which helps to comprehend and elucidate the underlying decision processes in a model.

Advantages of Decision Trees

1. **Simplicity and Interpretability:** Decision trees are easy to understand and interpret. The visual representation closely mirrors human decision-making processes.
2. **Versatility:** Can be used for both classification and regression tasks.
3. **No Need for Feature Scaling:** Decision trees do not require normalization or scaling of the data.
4. **Handles Non-linear Relationships:** Capable of capturing non-linear relationships between features and target variables.

Disadvantages of Decision Trees

1. **Overfitting:** Decision trees can easily overfit the training data, especially if they are deep with many nodes.
2. **Instability:** Small variations in the data can result in a completely different tree being generated.
3. **Bias towards Features with More Levels:** Features with more levels can dominate the tree structure.
4. **Pruning:** To overcome **overfitting, pruning** techniques are used. Pruning reduces the size of the tree by removing nodes that provide little power in classifying instances. There are two main types of pruning as, pre-pruning (Early Stopping)tops the tree from growing once it meets certain criteria (e.g., maximum depth, minimum number of samples per leaf) whear as, post-pruning, this removes branches from a fully grown tree that do not provide significant power.

Applications of Decision Trees

1. **Business Decision Making:** Used in strategic planning and resource allocation.
2. **Healthcare:** Assists in diagnosing diseases and suggesting treatment plans.
3. **Finance:** Helps in credit scoring and risk assessment.
4. **Marketing:** Used to segment customers and predict customer behavior.

Support Vector Machine (SVM)

Support Vector Machine (SVM) is a powerful machine learning algorithm used for linear or non-linear classification, regression, and even outlier detection tasks. SVMs can be used for a variety of tasks, such as text classification, image classification, spam detection, handwriting identification, gene expression analysis, face detection, and anomaly detection. SVMs are adaptable and efficient in a variety of applications because they can manage high-dimensional data and nonlinear relationships. SVM algorithms are very effective as we try to find the maximum separating hyperplane between the different classes available in the target feature.

The main objective of the SVM algorithm is to find the optimal hyperplane in an N-dimensional space that can separate the data points in different classes in the feature space. The hyperplane tries that the margin between the closest points of different classes should be as maximum as possible. The dimension of the hyperplane depends upon the number of features. If the number of input features is two, then the hyperplane is just a line. If the number of input features is three, then the hyperplane becomes a 2-D plane. It becomes difficult to imagine when the number of features exceeds three.

Support Vector Machine Terminology

1. **Hyperplane:** Hyperplane is the decision boundary that is used to separate the data points of different classes in a feature space. In the case of linear classifications, it will be a linear equation i.e. $wx+b = 0$.

2. **Support Vectors:** Support vectors are the closest data points to the hyperplane, which makes a critical role in deciding the hyperplane and margin.
3. **Margin**: Margin is the distance between the support vector and hyperplane. The main objective of the support vector machine algorithm is to maximize the margin. The wider margin indicates better classification performance.
4. **Kernel:** Kernel is the mathematical function, which is used in SVM to map the original input data points into high-dimensional feature spaces, so, that the hyperplane can be easily found out even if the data points are not linearly separable in the original input space. Some of the common kernel functions are linear, polynomial, radial basis function(RBF), and sigmoid.
5. **Hard Margin:** The maximum-margin hyperplane or the hard margin hyperplane is a hyperplane that properly separates the data points of different categories without any misclassifications.
6. **Soft Margin:** When the data is not perfectly separable or contains outliers, SVM permits a soft margin technique. Each data point has a slack variable introduced by the soft-margin SVM formulation, which softens the strict margin requirement and permits certain misclassifications or violations. It discovers a compromise between increasing the margin and reducing violations.
7. **C:** Margin maximisation and misclassification fines are balanced by the regularisation parameter C in SVM. The penalty for going over the margin or misclassifying data items is decided by it. A stricter penalty is imposed with a greater value of C, which results in a smaller margin and perhaps fewer misclassifications.
8. **Hinge Loss:** A typical loss function in SVMs is hinge loss. It punishes incorrect classifications or margin violations. The objective function in SVM is frequently formed by combining it with the regularisation term.
9. **Dual Problem:** A dual Problem of the optimisation problem that requires locating the Lagrange multipliers related to the support vectors can be used to solve SVM. The dual formulation enables the use of kernel tricks and more effective computing.

Types of Support Vector Machine: Based on the nature of the decision boundary, Support Vector Machines (SVM) can be divided into two main parts:

1. **Linear SVM:** Linear SVMs use a linear decision boundary to separate the data points of different classes. When the data can be precisely linearly separated, linear SVMs are very suitable. This means that a single straight line (in 2D) or a hyperplane (in higher dimensions) can entirely divide the data points into their respective classes. A hyperplane that maximizes the margin between the classes is the decision boundary.
2. **Non-Linear SVM:** Non-Linear SVM can be used to classify data when it cannot

be separated into two classes by a straight line (in the case of 2D). By using kernel functions, nonlinear SVMs can handle nonlinearly separable data. The original input data is transformed by these kernel functions into a higher-dimensional feature space, where the data points can be linearly separated. A linear SVM is used to locate a nonlinear decision boundary in this modified space.

Example: SVM can be understood with the example that we have used in the KNN classifier. Suppose we see a strange cat that also has some features of dogs, so if we want a model that can accurately identify whether it is a cat or dog, so such a model can be created by using the SVM algorithm. We will first train our model with lots of images of cats and dogs so that it can learn about different features of cats and dogs, and then we test it with this strange creature. So as support vector creates a decision boundary between these two data (cat and dog) and choose extreme cases (support vectors), it will see the extreme case of cat and dog. On the basis of the support vectors, it will classify it as a cat, as shown in fig.2.6.

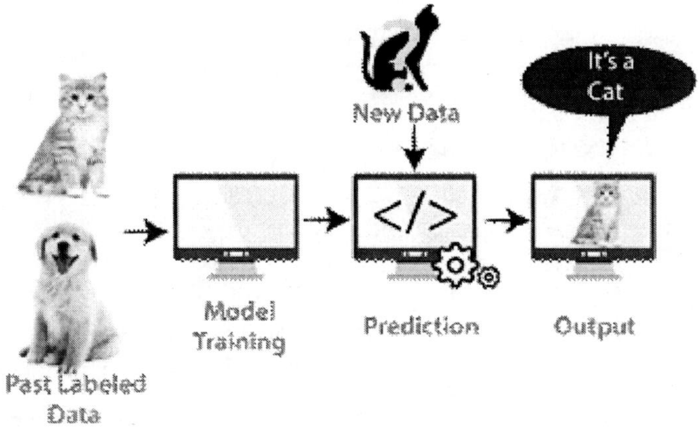

Fig.2.6

K-Nearest Neighbor (KNN)

The K-Nearest Neighbors (KNN) algorithm is a supervised machine learning method employed to tackle classification and regression problems. Evelyn Fix and Joseph Hodges developed this algorithm in 1951, which was subsequently expanded by Thomas Cover.

KNN is one of the most basic yet essential classification algorithms in machine learning. It belongs to the supervised learning domain and finds intense application in pattern recognition, data mining, and intrusion detection.

It is widely disposable in real-life scenarios since it is non-parametric, meaning it does not make any underlying assumptions about the distribution of data (as opposed to other algorithms such as GMM, which assume a Gaussian distribution of the given data). We are given some prior data (also called training data), which classifies coordinates into groups identified by an attribute.

As an example, consider the following table of data points containing two features:

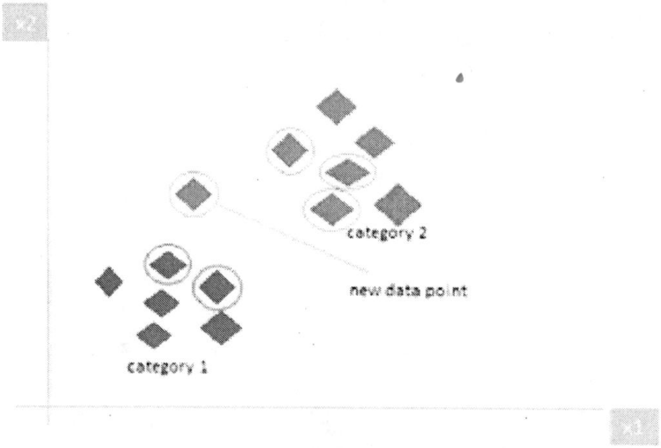

Fig.2.7 KNN Algorithm Working Visualization

Now, given another set of data points (also called testing data), allocate these points to a group by analyzing the training set. Note that the unclassified points are marked as 'White'.

Why do we need a KNN algorithm?

(K-NN) algorithm is a versatile and widely used machine learning algorithm that is primarily used for its simplicity and ease of implementation. It does not require any assumptions about the underlying data distribution. It can also handle both numerical and categorical data, making it a flexible choice for various types of datasets in classification and regression tasks. It is a non-parametric method that makes predictions based on the similarity of data points in a given dataset. K-NN is less sensitive to outliers compared to other algorithms.

The K-NN algorithm works by finding the K nearest neighbors to a given data point based on a distance metric, such as Euclidean distance. The class or value of the data point is then determined by the majority vote or average of the K neighbors. This approach allows the algorithm to adapt to different patterns and make predictions based on the local structure of the data.

Advantages of the KNN Algorithm

1. **Easy to implement:** This is easy to implement as the complexity of the algorithm is not that high.
2. **Adapts Easily:** As per the working of the KNN algorithm it stores all the data in memory storage and hence whenever a new example or data point is added then the algorithm adjusts itself as per that new example and has its contribution to the future predictions as well.
3. **Few Hyperparameters:** The only parameters which are required in the training

of a KNN algorithm are the value of k and the choice of the distance metric which we would like to choose from our evaluation metric.

Disadvantages of the KNN Algorithm

1. **Does not Scale:** As we have heard about this that the KNN algorithm is also considered a Lazy Algorithm. The main significance of this term is that this takes lots of computing power as well as data storage. This makes this algorithm both time-consuming and resource exhausting.
2. **Curse of Dimensionality:** There is a term known as the peaking phenomenon according to this the KNN algorithm is affected by the curse of dimensionality which implies the algorithm faces a hard time classifying the data points properly when the dimensionality is too high.
3. **Prone to Overfitting:** As the algorithm is affected due to the curse of dimensionality it is prone to the problem of overfitting as well. Hence generally feature selection as well as dimensionality reduction techniques are applied to deal with this problem.

Differences Between Key Algorithms: Regression, Decision Trees, SVM, K-NN

Table 2.6

S.No.	Aspect	Regression	Decision Trees	SVM	K-NN
1.	Model Structure	Linear or polynomial equation	Tree-like structure	Hyperplane in high-dimensional space	Instance-based
2.	Interpretability	Moderate (depends on complexity)	High (visual representation)	Low (complex decision boundary)	High (easy to understand)
3.	Handling non-linearity	Limited (requires transformations)	Handles non-linearity naturally	Handles non-linearity via kernels	Naturally handles non-linearity
4.	Overfitting Risk	Moderate (depends on regularization)	High without pruning	Low with appropriate tuning	High with small k values
5.	Overfitting Risk	Fast (depending on dataset size)	Moderate (varies with depth)	Slow (especially with large datasets)	Fast (but requires full dataset)
6.	Data Requirements	Requires labeled data	Requires labeled data	Requires labeled data	Requires labeled data
7.	Use Cases	Financial predictions, trend analysis	Customer segmentation, risk assessment	mage classification, text categorization	Recommendation systems, anomaly detection

Model Evaluation and Validation Techniques

Model evaluation and validation are essential components of the machine learning lifecycle. They ensure that models perform well not only on training data but also on unseen data. This article will explore various techniques for evaluating and validating machine learning models, covering key concepts, methodologies, metrics, and best practices.

Model Evaluation

Model evaluation is a critical phase in the machine learning lifecycle. It provides insights into how well a model performs on unseen data and helps ensure that the model generalizes well beyond the training dataset.

Model evaluation is the process that uses some metrics which help us to analyze the performance of the model. As we all know that model development is a multi-step process and a check should be kept on how well the model generalizes future predictions. Therefore evaluating a model plays a vital role so that we can judge the performance of our model. The evaluation also helps to analyze a model's key weaknesses. There are many metrics like Accuracy, Precision, Recall, F1 score, Area under Curve, Confusion Matrix, and Mean Square Error. Cross Validation is one technique that is followed during the training phase and it is a model evaluation technique as well.

Why is Evaluation necessary for a successful model?

Evaluation is necessary for ensuring that machine learning models are reliable, generalizable, and capable of making accurate predictions on new, unseen data, which is crucial for their successful deployment in real-world applications. Overfitting and underfitting are the two biggest causes of poor performance of machine learning algorithms.

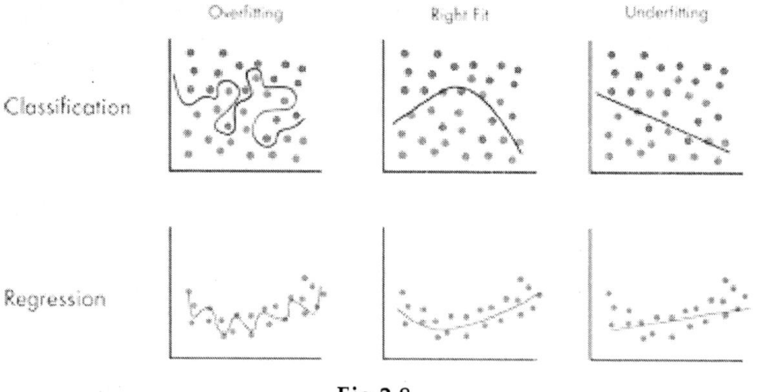

Fig.2.8

1. **Overfitting:** Occurs when the model is so closely aligned to the training data that it does not know how to respond to new data.
2. **Underfitting:** Occurs when the model cannot adequately capture the underlying structure of the data.
3. **Right Fit:** Occurs when both the training data error and the test data are minimal.

Error	Overfitting	Right Fit	Underfitting
Training	Low	Low	High
Test	High	Low	High

Model Evaluation Techniques: Model evaluation techniques are as follows:

1. **Data Splitting Techniques:** Data splitting is essential in machine learning to ensure that models can generalize well to unseen data. By dividing the dataset into different subsets, practitioners can evaluate model performance effectively. Here are the primary data splitting techniques:

   - **Train-Test Split:** This foundational method involves dividing the dataset into two parts: a training set to train the model and a test set to evaluate its performance. Typically, a common split ratio is 80/20 or 70/30.

     Pros: Simple and quick to implement.

     Cons: Can lead to unreliable estimates if the dataset is small or if the split is not representative.

   - **Stratified Sampling:** This technique ensures that each class is proportionally represented in both training and test sets, which is particularly important in imbalanced datasets.

     Pros: Maintains class distribution and provides more reliable evaluation metrics.

     Cons: Slightly more complex to implement than a standard split.

2. **Cross-Validation Techniques:** Cross-validation is a powerful technique for assessing how a model will generalize to an independent dataset. It helps to mitigate issues such as overfitting and provides a more reliable estimate of model performance. Here are the key cross-validation techniques:

   - **K-Fold Cross-Validation:** In K-Fold Cross-Validation, the dataset is divided into kkk subsets or folds. The model is trained on k"1k-1k"1 folds and validated on the remaining fold, repeating this process kkk times so that each fold serves as the validation set once.

     Example:

```
from sklearn.model_selection import KFold, cross_val_score

kf = KFold(n_splits=5, shuffle=True, random_state=42)
scores = cross_val_score(model, X, y, cv=kf)
```

     Pros: Provides a more robust estimate of model performance, reducing variance.

     Cons: Computationally intensive, especially with large datasets.

   - **Leave-One-Out Cross-Validation (LOOCV):** This is a special case of K-Fold Cross-Validation where kkk equals the number of data points. Each instance is used once as a validation set.

Example:

```
from sklearn.model_selection import LeaveOneOut

loo = LeaveOneOut()
for train_index, test_index in loo.split(X):
    X_train, X_test = X[train_index], X[test_index]
    y_train, y_test = y[train_index], y[test_index]
```

Pros: Uses almost all data for training, beneficial for small datasets.

Cons: Extremely computationally intensive, especially for large datasets.

3. **Performance Metrics:** Performance metrics are essential for evaluating how well a machine learning model performs on a given task. They provide quantitative assessments that guide model selection, tuning, and validation. The choice of metrics depends on whether the problem is a classification, regression, or clustering task. Here's an overview of key performance metrics for each category:

- **Accuracy:** The ratio of correctly predicted instances to the total instances. Useful for balanced datasets. Formula:

$$\text{Accuracy} = \frac{\text{True Positives} + \text{True Negatives}}{\text{Total Instances}}$$

- **Precision:** The ratio of true positive predictions to the total positive predictions made. Important in scenarios where false positives are costly. Formula:

$$\text{Precision} = \frac{\text{True Positives}}{\text{True Positives} + \text{False Positives}}$$

- **Recall (Sensitivity):** The ratio of true positive predictions to the total actual positives. Formula:

$$\text{Recall} = \frac{\text{True Positives}}{\text{True Positives} + \text{False Negatives}}$$

- **F1-Score:** The harmonic mean of precision and recall, balancing both metrics. Formula:

$$\text{F1-Score} = 2 \times \frac{\text{Precision} \times \text{Recall}}{\text{Precision} + \text{Recall}}$$

- **ROC-AUC (Receiver Operating Characteristic - Area Under Curve):**

Measures the area under the Receiver Operating Characteristic curve, reflecting the model's ability to discriminate between classes.

Regression Metrics

Mean Absolute Error (MAE): The average of absolute differences between predicted and actual values. Easy to interpret.

Mean Squared Error (MSE): The average of squared differences, emphasizing larger errors.

Root Mean Squared Error (RMSE): The square root of MSE, providing an error metric in the same units as the target variable.

4. **Visualization Techniques:** Visualization techniques play a crucial role in understanding model performance and data characteristics. They help convey complex information in an intuitive manner, making it easier to interpret results and identify areas for improvement. Here are some essential visualization techniques used in machine learning:
   - **Learning Curves:** Learning curves plot training and validation errors as a function of training set size. They help diagnose overfitting (high training accuracy, low validation accuracy) or underfitting (both low).
   - **Confusion Matrix:** This matrix summarizes true positives, false positives, true negatives, and false negatives, offering a detailed view of classification performance.
5. **Advanced Techniques:** Advanced visualization techniques can provide deeper insights into machine learning models and complex datasets. Here are some noteworthy methods:
   - **Ensemble Methods:** Techniques like bagging (e.g., Random Forest) and boosting (e.g., Gradient Boosting) combine multiple models to enhance accuracy and robustness.
   - **A/B Testing:** This method compares two models in a live environment to assess which performs better, helping ensure that changes lead to improved performance.

Best Practices for Advanced Techniques:

1. **Tailor Visualizations to Audience:** Consider the technical level and interests of your audience to choose the most effective visualization.
2. **Leverage Interactivity:** Interactive visualizations can facilitate exploration and deeper understanding of complex datasets.
3. **Incorporate Contextual Information:** Provide annotations and legends to clarify what viewers are seeing, especially in advanced or complex visualizations.

These advanced techniques can significantly enhance the understanding of machine learning models and their underlying data, leading to more informed decision-making and insights.

Model Validation

The process that helps us evaluate the performance of a trained model is called Model Validation. It helps us in validating the machine learning model performance on new or unseen data. It also helps us confirm that the model achieves its intended purpose.

Types of Model Validation

Model validation is the step conducted post Model Training, wherein the effectiveness of the trained model is assessed using a testing dataset. This dataset may or may not overlap with the data used for model training.

Model validation can be broadly categorized into two main approaches based on how the data is used for testing:

1. **In-Sample Validation:** This approach involves the use of data from the same dataset that was employed to develop the model.
   - **Holdout method:** The dataset is then divided into training set which is used to train the model and a hold out set which is used to test the performance of the model. This is a straightforward method, but it is prone to overfitting if the holdout sample is small.
2. **Out-of-Sample Validation:** This approach relies on entirely different data from the data used for training the model. This gives a more reliable prediction of how accurate the model will be in predicting new inputs.
   - **K-Fold Cross-validation:** The data is divided into k number of folds. The model is trained on k-1 folds and tested on the fold that is left. This is repeated k times, each time using a different fold for testing. This offers a more extensive analysis than the holdout method.
   - **Leave-One-Out Cross-validation (LOOCV):** This is a form of k-fold cross validation where k is equal to the number of instances. Only one piece of data is not used to train the model. This is repeated for each data point. Unfortunately, LOOCV is also time consuming when dealing with large datasets.
   - **Stratified K-Fold Cross-validation:** k-fold cross-validation in this type of cross-validation each fold has the same ratio of classes/categories as the overall dataset. This is useful especially where data in one class is very low compared to others.

Importance of Model Validation

Now that we've gained insight into Model Validation, it's evident how integral a component it is in the overall process of model development. Validating the outputs of a machine learning model holds paramount importance in ensuring its accuracy.

When a machine learning model undergoes training, a substantial volume of training data is utilized, and the primary objective of verifying model validation is to provide machine learning engineers with an opportunity to enhance both the quality and quantity of the data. Without proper checking and validation, relying on the predictions of the model is not justifiable. In critical domains such as healthcare and autonomous vehicles, errors in object detection can have severe consequences, leading to significant fatalities due to incorrect decisions made by the machine in real-world predictions. Therefore, validating the machine learning model during the training and development stages is crucial for ensuring accurate predictions. Additional benefits of Model Validation include the following.

- Enhance the model quality.
- Discovering more errors
- Prevents the model from overfitting and underfitting.

It is extremely important that data scientists assess machine learning models that are being trained for accuracy and stability. It is crucial since it must be made sure the model detects the majority of trends and patterns in the data without introducing excessive noise. It is now obvious that developing a machine learning model is not enough just to depend on its predictions; in order to guarantee the precision of the model's output and enable its use in practical applications, we also need to validate and assess the model's correctness.

Key Components of Model Validation

1. **Data Validation**
    - **Quality:** Dropping missing values, detecting outliers, and errors in the data. This prevents the model from learning from incorrect data or misinformation.
    - **Relevance:** Ensuring that the data is a true representation of the underlying problem that the model is designed to solve. Use of irrelevant information may end up leading to wrong conclusions.
    - **Bias:** Ensuring that the data has appropriate representation for the model to avoid reproducing biased or inaccurate results. Using methods such as analyzing data demographics and employing unbiased sampling can help.
2. **Conceptual Review**
    - **Logic:** Criticizing the logic of the model and examining whether it is useful for the problem under consideration. This includes finding out if the selected algorithms and techniques are suitable.
    - **Assumptions:** Understanding and critically evaluating the assumptions embedded in model building. Expectations that are not based on assumptions can result in inaccurate forecasts.
    - **Variables:** Relevance and informativeness of the selected variables about

the purpose of the model. Extraneous variables can also lead to poor model predictions.

3. **Testing**
   - **Train/Test Split:** Splitting the data into two – the training set to develop the model and the testing set to assess the model's prediction accuracy on new observations. This helps determine the capability of the model to make correct predictions with new data.
   - **Cross-validation:** The basic principle of cross-validation is that the data is divided into a user defined number of folds and each fold is considered as validation set while training on the remaining ones. This gives a better insight to model's performance than the train/test split approach.

Model Validation Techniques

Now that we know what model validation is, Let's discuss various methods or techniques using which a machine learning model can be evaluated. Let's discuss above listed methods for model validation:

1. **Train/Test Split:** Train/Test Split is a basic model validation technique where the dataset is divided into training and testing sets. The model is trained on the training set and then evaluated on the separate, unseen testing set. This helps assess the model's generalization performance on new, unseen data. Common split ratios include 70-30 or 80-20, where the larger portion is used for training.
2. **k-Fold Cross-Validation:** In k-Fold Cross-Validation, the dataset is divided into k subsets (folds). The model is trained and evaluated k times, each time using a different fold as the test set and the remaining as the training set. The results are averaged, providing a more robust evaluation and reducing the impact of dataset partitioning.
3. **Leave-One-Out Cross-Validation:** Leave-One-Out Cross-Validation (LOOCV) is an extreme case of k-Fold Cross-Validation where k equals the number of data points. The model is trained on all data points except one, and the process is repeated for each data point. It provides a comprehensive assessment but can be computationally expensive.
4. **Leave-One-Group-Out Cross-Validation:** This variation considers leaving out entire groups of related samples during each iteration. It is beneficial when the dataset has distinct groups, ensuring that the model is evaluated on diverse subsets.
5. **Nested Cross-Validation:** Nested Cross-Validation combines an outer loop for model evaluation with an inner loop for hyperparameter tuning. It helps assess how well the model generalizes to new data while optimizing hyperparameters.
6. **Time-Series Cross-Validation:** In Time-Series Cross-Validation, temporal

dependencies are considered. The dataset is split into training and testing sets in a way that respects the temporal order of the data, ensuring that the model is evaluated on future unseen observations.

7. **Wilcoxon Signed-Rank Test:** Wilcoxon Signed-Rank Test is a statistical method used to compare the performance of two models. It evaluates whether the differences in performance scores between models are significant, providing a robust way to compare models.

Differences Between Model Evaluation and Validation

Table 2.7

S.No.	Aspect	Model Evaluation	Model Validation
1.	Purpose	Assess the performance of a model	Ensure the model generalizes to unseen data
2.	Stage in Process	Occurs after model training	Can occur throughout the modeling process
3.	Data Used	Utilizes a distinct test dataset	Involves multiple subsets of training data
4.	Focus on Generalization	Primarily concerned with performance on a dataset	Emphasizes robustness and generalization
5.	Outcome Interpretation	Provides quantitative performance metrics	Offers insights into reliability and robustness
6.	Feedback Loop	Results guide future iterations	Creates a feedback loop for model adjustments

Introduction to Deep Learning and Neural Networks

Deep learning is a branch of machine learning that utilizes artificial neural networks to model complex patterns in data. These networks consist of layers of interconnected nodes, enabling tasks like image recognition, natural language processing, and speech recognition. Deep learning has significantly advanced AI capabilities across various fields.

Deep Learning

The definition of Deep learning is that it is the branch of machine learning that is based on artificial neural network architecture. An artificial neural network or ANN uses layers of interconnected nodes called neurons that work together to process and learn from the input data.

In a fully connected Deep neural network, there is an input layer and one or more hidden layers connected one after the other. Each neuron receives input from the previous layer neurons or the input layer. The output of one neuron becomes the input to other neurons in the next layer of the network, and this process continues until the final layer produces the output of the network. The layers of the neural network transform the input data through a series of nonlinear transformations, allowing the network to learn complex representations of the input data.

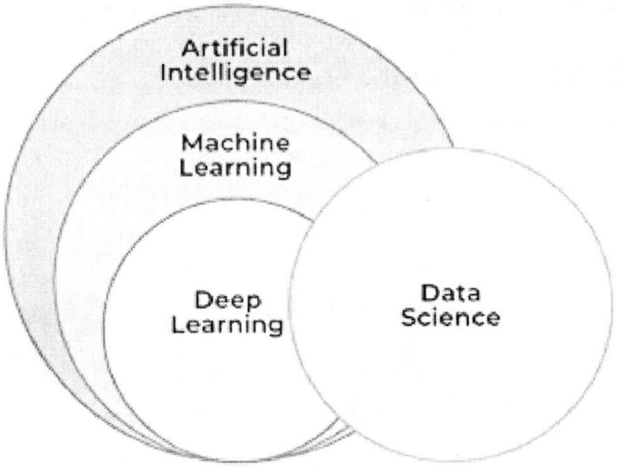

Fig.2.9 Scope of Deep Learning

Today Deep learning AI has become one of the most popular and visible areas of machine learning, due to its success in a variety of applications, such as computer vision, natural language processing, and Reinforcement learning.

Deep learning AI can be used for supervised, unsupervised as well as reinforcement machine learning, it uses a variety of ways to process these:

1. **Supervised Machine Learning:** Supervised machine learning is the machine learning technique in which the neural network learns to make predictions or classify data based on the labeled datasets. Here we input both input features along with the target variables. the neural network learns to make predictions based on the cost or error that comes from the difference between the predicted and the actual target, this process is known as backpropagation. Deep learning algorithms like Convolutional neural networks, Recurrent neural networks are used for many supervised tasks like image classifications and recognization, sentiment analysis, language translations, etc.
2. **Unsupervised Machine Learning:** Unsupervised machine learning is the machine learning technique in which the neural network learns to discover the patterns or to cluster the dataset based on unlabeled datasets. Here there are no target variables. while the machine has to self-determined the hidden patterns or relationships within the datasets. Deep learning algorithms like autoencoders and generative models are used for unsupervised tasks like clustering, dimensionality reduction, and anomaly detection.
3. **Reinforcement Machine Learning:** Reinforcement Machine Learning is the machine learning technique in which an agent learns to make decisions in an environment to maximize a reward signal. The agent interacts with the environment by taking action and observing the resulting rewards. Deep learning can be used to learn policies, or a set of actions, that maximizes the

cumulative reward over time. Deep reinforcement learning algorithms like Deep Q networks and Deep Deterministic Policy Gradient (DDPG) are used to reinforce tasks like robotics and game playing etc.

Artificial Neural Networks

Artificial neural networks are built on the principles of the structure and operation of human neurons. It is also known as neural networks or neural nets. An artificial neural network's input layer, which is the first layer, receives input from external sources and passes it on to the hidden layer, which is the second layer. Each neuron in the hidden layer gets information from the neurons in the previous layer, computes the weighted total, and then transfers it to the neurons in the next layer. These connections are weighted, which means that the impacts of the inputs from the preceding layer are more or less optimized by giving each input a distinct weight. These weights are then adjusted during the training process to enhance the performance of the model.

Simple Neural Network Architecture: Deep neural networks, or deep learning networks, have several hidden layers with millions of artificial neurons linked together. A number, called weight, represents the connections between one node and another. The weight is a positive number if one node excites another, or negative if one node suppresses the other. Nodes with higher weight values have more influence on the other nodes.

Theoretically, deep neural networks can map any input type to any output type. However, they also need much more training as compared to other machine learning methods. They need millions of examples of training data rather than perhaps the hundreds or thousands that a simpler network might need.

The architecture of netural network is shown in fig.2.10.

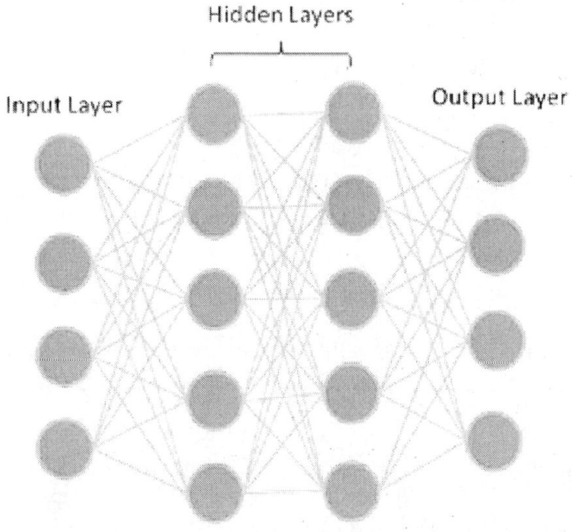

Fig.2.10

A basic neural network has interconnected artificial neurons in three layers:

1. **Input Layer:** Information from the outside world enters the artificial neural network from the input layer. Input nodes process the data, analyze or categorize it, and pass it on to the next layer.
2. **Hidden Layer:** Hidden layers take their input from the input layer or other hidden layers. Artificial neural networks can have a large number of hidden layers. Each hidden layer analyzes the output from the previous layer, processes it further, and passes it on to the next layer.
3. **Output Layer:** The output layer gives the final result of all the data processing by the artificial neural network. It can have single or multiple nodes. For instance, if we have a binary (yes/no) classification problem, the output layer will have one output node, which will give the result as 1 or 0. However, if we have a multi-class classification problem, the output layer might consist of more than one output node.

Application of Neural Network: The important applications of neural networks below.

1. **Computer Vision:** Computer vision is the ability of computers to extract information and insights from images and videos. With neural networks, computers can distinguish and recognize images similar to humans. Computer vision has several applications, such as the following:
   - Visual recognition in self-driving cars so they can recognize road signs and other road users
   - Content moderation to automatically remove unsafe or inappropriate content from image and video archives
   - Facial recognition to identify faces and recognize attributes like open eyes, glasses, and facial hair
   - Image labeling to identify brand logos, clothing, safety gear, and other image details
2. **Speech Recognition:** Neural networks can analyze human speech despite varying speech patterns, pitch, tone, language, and accent. Virtual assistants like Amazon Alexa and automatic transcription software use speech recognition to do tasks like these:
   - Assist call center agents and automatically classify calls
   - Convert clinical conversations into documentation in real time
   - Accurately subtitle videos and meeting recordings for wider content reach
3. **Natural Language Processing:** Natural language processing (NLP) is the ability to process natural, human-created text. Neural networks help computers gather insights and meaning from text data and documents. NLP has several use cases, including in these functions:

- Automated virtual agents and chatbots
- Automatic organization and classification of written data
- Business intelligence analysis of long-form documents like emails and forms
- Indexing of key phrases that indicate sentiment, like positive and negative comments on social media
- Document summarization and article generation for a given topic

4. **Recommendation Engines:** Neural networks can track user activity to develop personalized recommendations. They can also analyze all user behavior and discover new products or services that interest a specific user. For example, Curalate, a Philadelphia-based startup, helps brands convert social media posts into sales. Brands use Curalate's intelligent product tagging (IPT) service to automate the collection and curation of user-generated social content. IPT uses neural networks to automatically find and recommend products relevant to the user's social media activity. Consumers don't have to hunt through online catalogs to find a specific product from a social media image. Instead, they can use Curalate's auto product tagging to purchase the product with ease.

Differences Between Deep Learning and Neural Network

Table 2.8

S.No.	Aspect	Deep Learning	Neural Network
1.	Definition	A subset of machine learning that uses neural networks with multiple layers.	A type of model inspired by the human brain, consisting of interconnected neurons.
2.	Complexity	Typically involves complex architectures with many layers (deep networks).	Can refer to any neural network, including shallow networks with few layers.
3.	Data Requirement	Requires large datasets to effectively train deep models.	Can be effective with smaller datasets, especially in shallow architectures.
4.	Feature Learning	Automatically learns hierarchical features from raw data through multiple layers.	May require manual feature extraction for effective learning, especially in shallow networks.
5.	Computational Resources	Generally requires more computational power and resources (e.g., GPUs) due to complexity.	Typically less demanding, especially for simple or shallow networks.
6.	Applications	Used for advanced tasks like image and speech recognition, natural language processing.	Can be applied to simpler tasks, such as linear regression or basic pattern recognition.

4. Predictive Analytics

Predictive analytics refers to the use of statistical techniques, machine learning, and data mining to analyze historical data and make predictions about future events or outcomes. It leverages data, algorithms, and statistical models to identify patterns and trends that inform decision-making.

Predictive analytics is a powerful technique that utilizes statistical methods, machine learning, and data mining to analyze historical data and forecast future outcomes. By collecting and preparing large datasets from various sources, organizations can uncover patterns and trends that inform decision-making processes. The predictive modeling process typically involves regression analysis, classification, and time series forecasting, allowing businesses to make data-driven predictions about customer behavior, financial performance, and operational efficiency. Key applications of predictive analytics span multiple industries, including finance for credit scoring and fraud detection, healthcare for predicting patient outcomes, and retail for demand forecasting and personalized marketing strategies. This approach enables organizations to optimize resource allocation, enhance customer engagement, and gain a competitive advantage in their respective markets. However, challenges such as data quality, model complexity, and the need for ongoing monitoring must be addressed to ensure the reliability of predictions. By leveraging predictive analytics effectively, organizations can transform insights into actionable strategies, ultimately driving growth and improving overall performance in an increasingly data-driven world.

Key Components

1. **Data Collection:** Involves gathering historical data from various sources, including databases, sensors, transactions, and user interactions. This data serves as the foundation for analysis.
2. **Data Preparation:** The collected data is cleaned, transformed, and organized. This step includes handling missing values, normalizing data, and feature selection to ensure the data is suitable for analysis.
3. **Modeling:** Statistical and machine learning models are applied to the prepared data. Common techniques include:
   - **Regression Analysis:** For predicting continuous outcomes.
   - **Classification:** For predicting categorical outcomes.
   - **Time Series Analysis:** For forecasting future values based on historical trends.
4. **Validation:** Models are tested and validated using techniques like cross-validation to assess their accuracy and performance on unseen data. This step helps prevent overfitting and ensures reliability.
5. **Deployment:** Once validated, predictive models are deployed in real-world applications, integrating them into business processes or decision-making systems.
6. **Monitoring and Maintenance:** Ongoing monitoring is essential to ensure that

models remain accurate over time. This involves updating models with new data and recalibrating as necessary.

Time Series Analysis and Forecasting

A time series is a sequence of data points collected, recorded, or measured at successive, evenly-spaced time intervals.

Each data point represents observations or measurements taken over time, such as stock prices, temperature readings, or sales figures. Time series data is commonly represented graphically with time on the horizontal axis and the variable of interest on the vertical axis, allowing analysts to identify trends, patterns, and changes over time.

Time series data is often represented graphically as a line plot, with time depicted on the horizontal x-axis and the variable's values displayed on the vertical y-axis. This graphical representation facilitates the visualization of trends, patterns, and fluctuations in the variable over time, aiding in the analysis and interpretation of the data.

Components of Time Series Data: There are four main components of a time series:

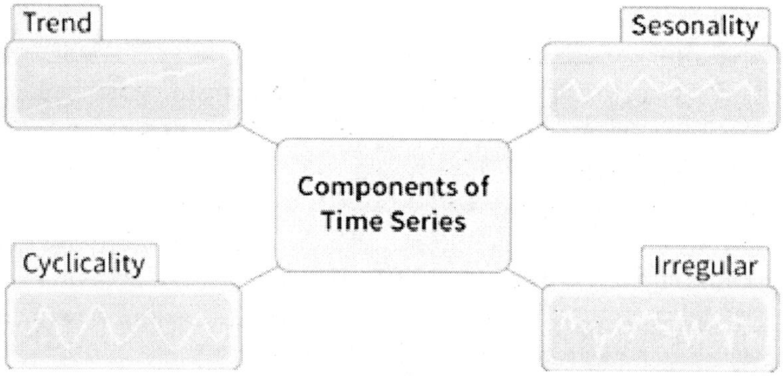

Fig.2.11

1. **Trend:** Trend represents the long-term movement or directionality of the data over time. It captures the overall tendency of the series to increase, decrease, or remain stable. Trends can be linear, indicating a consistent increase or decrease, or nonlinear, showing more complex patterns.
2. **Seasonality:** Seasonality refers to periodic fluctuations or patterns that occur at regular intervals within the time series. These cycles often repeat annually, quarterly, monthly, or weekly and are typically influenced by factors such as seasons, holidays, or business cycles.
3. **Cyclic variations:** Cyclical variations are longer-term fluctuations in the time series that do not have a fixed period like seasonality. These fluctuations represent economic or business cycles, which can extend over multiple years and are often associated with expansions and contractions in economic activity.

4. **Irregularity (or Noise):** Irregularity, also known as noise or randomness, refers to the unpredictable or random fluctuations in the data that cannot be attributed to the trend, seasonality, or cyclical variations. These fluctuations may result from random events, measurement errors, or other unforeseen factors. Irregularity makes it challenging to identify and model the underlying patterns in the time series data.

Importance of Time Series Analysis

1. **Predict Future Trends:** Time series analysis enables the prediction of future trends, allowing businesses to anticipate market demand, stock prices, and other key variables, facilitating proactive decision-making.
2. **Detect Patterns and Anomalies:** By examining sequential data points, time series analysis helps detect recurring patterns and anomalies, providing insights into underlying behaviors and potential outliers.
3. **Risk Mitigation:** By spotting potential risks, businesses can develop strategies to mitigate them, enhancing overall risk management.
4. **Strategic Planning**: Time series insights inform long-term strategic planning, guiding decision-making across finance, healthcare, and other sectors.
5. **Competitive Edge:** Time series analysis enables businesses to optimize resource allocation effectively, whether it's inventory, workforce, or financial assets. By staying ahead of market trends, responding to changes, and making data-driven decisions, businesses gain a competitive edge.

Time Series Visualization: Time series visualization is the graphical representation of data collected over successive time intervals. It encompasses various techniques such as line plots, seasonal subseries plots, autocorrelation plots, histograms, and interactive visualizations. These methods help analysts identify trends, patterns, and anomalies in time-dependent data for better understanding and decision-making. The different time series visualization graphs are as under:

1. **Line Plots:** Line plots display data points over time, allowing easy observation of trends, cycles, and fluctuations.
2. **Seasonal Plots:** These plots break down time series data into seasonal components, helping to visualize patterns within specific time periods.
3. **Histograms and Density Plots:** Shows the distribution of data values over time, providing insights into data characteristics such as skewness and kurtosis.
4. **Autocorrelation and Partial Autocorrelation Plots:** These plots visualize correlation between a time series and its lagged values, helping to identify seasonality and lagged relationships.
5. **Spectral Analysis:** Spectral analysis techniques, such as periodograms and spectrograms, visualize frequency components within time series data, useful for identifying periodicity and cyclical patterns.

6. **Decomposition Plots:** Decomposition plots break down a time series into its trend, seasonal, and residual components, aiding in understanding the underlying patterns.

These visualization techniques allow analysts to explore, interpret, and communicate insights from time series data effectively, supporting informed decision-making and forecasting.

Different Time Series Analysis & Decomposition Techniques

1. **Autocorrelation Analysis:** A statistical method to measure the correlation between a time series and a lagged version of itself at different time lags. It helps identify patterns and dependencies within the time series data.
2. **Partial Autocorrelation Functions (PACF):** PACF measures the correlation between a time series and its lagged values, controlling for intermediate lags, aiding in identifying direct relationships between variables.
3. **Trend Analysis:** The process of identifying and analyzing the long-term movement or directionality of a time series. Trends can be linear, exponential, or nonlinear and are crucial for understanding underlying patterns and making forecasts.
4. **Seasonality Analysis:** Seasonality refers to periodic fluctuations or patterns that occur in a time series at fixed intervals, such as daily, weekly, or yearly. Seasonality analysis involves identifying and quantifying these recurring patterns to understand their impact on the data.
5. **Decomposition:** Decomposition separates a time series into its constituent components, typically trend, seasonality, and residual (error). This technique helps isolate and analyze each component individually, making it easier to understand and model the underlying patterns.
6. **Spectrum Analysis:** Spectrum analysis involves examining the frequency domain representation of a time series to identify dominant frequencies or periodicities. It helps detect cyclic patterns and understand the underlying periodic behavior of the data.
7. **Seasonal and Trend Decomposition Using Loess:** STL decomposes a time series into three components: seasonal, trend, and residual. This decomposition enables modeling and forecasting each component separately, simplifying the forecasting process.
8. **Rolling Correlation:** Rolling correlation calculates the correlation coefficient between two time series over a rolling window of observations, capturing changes in the relationship between variables over time.
9. **Cross-correlation Analysis:** Cross-correlation analysis measures the similarity between two time series by computing their correlation at different time lags. It is used to identify relationships and dependencies between different variables or time series.

10. **Box-Jenkins Method:** Box-Jenkins Method is a systematic approach for analyzing and modeling time series data. It involves identifying the appropriate autoregressive integrated moving average (ARIMA) model parameters, estimating the model, diagnosing its adequacy through residual analysis, and selecting the best-fitting model.
11. **Granger Causality Analysis:** Granger causality analysis determines whether one time series can predict future values of another time series. It helps infer causal relationships between variables in time series data, providing insights into the direction of influence.

Time Series Forecasting

Time Series Forecasting is a statistical technique used to predict future values of a time series based on past observations. In simpler terms, it's like looking into the future of data points plotted over time. By analyzing patterns and trends in historical data, Time Series Forecasting helps make informed predictions about what may happen next, assisting in decision-making and planning for the future.

Different Time Series Forecasting Algorithms

1. **Autoregressive (AR) Model:** Autoregressive (AR) model is a type of time series model that predicts future values based on linear combinations of past values of the same time series. In an AR(p) model, the current value of the time series is modeled as a linear function of its previous p values, plus a random error term. The order of the autoregressive model (p) determines how many past values are used in the prediction.
2. **Autoregressive Integrated Moving Average (ARIMA):** ARIMA is a widely used statistical method for time series forecasting. It models the next value in a time series based on linear combination of its own past values and past forecast errors. The model parameters include the order of autoregression (p), differencing (d), and moving average (q).
3. **ARIMAX:** ARIMA model extended to include exogenous variables that can improve forecast accuracy.
4. **Seasonal Autoregressive Integrated Moving Average (SARIMA):** SARIMA extends ARIMA by incorporating seasonality into the model. It includes additional seasonal parameters (P, D, Q) to capture periodic fluctuations in the data.
5. **SARIMAX**: Extension of SARIMA that incorporates exogenous variables for seasonal time series forecasting.
6. **Vector Autoregression (VAR) Models:** VAR models extend autoregression to multivariate time series data by modeling each variable as a linear combination of its past values and the past values of other variables. They are suitable for analyzing and forecasting interdependencies among multiple time series.

7. **Theta Method:** A simple and intuitive forecasting technique based on extrapolation and trend fitting.
8. **Exponential Smoothing Methods:** Exponential smoothing methods, such as Simple Exponential Smoothing (SES) and Holt-Winters, forecast future values by exponentially decreasing weights for past observations. These methods are particularly useful for data with trend and seasonality.
9. **Gaussian Processes Regression:** Gaussian Processes Regression is a Bayesian non-parametric approach that models the distribution of functions over time. It provides uncertainty estimates along with point forecasts, making it useful for capturing uncertainty in time series forecasting.
10. **Generalized Additive Models (GAM):** A flexible modeling approach that combines additive components, allowing for nonlinear relationships and interactions.
11. **Random Forests:** Random Forests is a machine learning ensemble method that constructs multiple decision trees during training and outputs the average prediction of the individual trees. It can handle complex relationships and interactions in the data, making it effective for time series forecasting.
12. **Gradient Boosting Machines (GBM):** GBM is another ensemble learning technique that builds multiple decision trees sequentially, where each tree corrects the errors of the previous one. It excels in capturing nonlinear relationships and is robust against overfitting.
13. **State Space Models:** State space models represent a time series as a combination of unobserved (hidden) states and observed measurements. These models capture both the deterministic and stochastic components of the time series, making them suitable for forecasting and anomaly detection.
14. **Dynamic Linear Models (DLMs):** DLMs are Bayesian state-space models that represent time series data as a combination of latent state variables and observations. They are flexible models capable of incorporating various trends, seasonality, and other dynamic patterns in the data.
15. **Recurrent Neural Networks (RNNs) and Long Short-term Memory (LSTM) Networks:** RNNs and LSTMs are deep learning architectures designed to handle sequential data. They can capture complex temporal dependencies in time series data, making them powerful tools for forecasting tasks, especially when dealing with large-scale and high-dimensional data.
16. **Hidden Markov Model (HMM):** A Hidden Markov Model (HMM) is a statistical model used to describe sequences of observable events generated by underlying hidden states. In time series, HMMs infer hidden states from observed data, capturing dependencies and transitions between states. They are valuable for tasks like speech recognition, gesture analysis, and anomaly detection, providing a framework to model complex sequential data and extract meaningful patterns from it.

Regression Analysis: Linear, Logistic, and Polynomial

Regression analysis is a statistical method used to model the relationship between a dependent variable and one or more independent variables. The choice of regression type depends on the nature of the dependent variable and the relationship being analyzed. Three common types are:

1. **Linear Regression:** Linear regression models the relationship between a dependent variable and one or more independent variables using a linear equation.

   $$Y = a + bX + \epsilon,$$

   where,
   Y is the dependent variable,
   a is the y-intercept,
   b is the slope of the line,
   X is the independent variable,
   represents the error term.

   Use Cases: It is commonly used for predicting continuous outcomes, such as sales revenue based on advertising spend or house prices based on square footage.

   Assumptions: Assumes a linear relationship, homoscedasticity (constant variance of errors), and normally distributed errors.

2. **Logistic Regression:** Logistic regression is used when the dependent variable is binary (e.g., yes/no, 0/1). It models the probability that a given input belongs to a particular category. The model can be expressed as:

   $$p\colon \log\left(\frac{p}{1-p}\right) = a + bX$$

   Use Cases: Frequently applied in binary classification tasks, such as spam detection, credit scoring, and medical diagnosis (e.g., disease presence).

   Interpretation: The output is a probability between 0 and 1, often thresholded at 0.5 to determine class membership.

3. **Polynomial Regression:** Polynomial regression extends linear regression by fitting a polynomial equation to the data, allowing for non-linear relationships. The model can be expressed as:

   $$Y = a + b_1X + b_2X^2 + b_3X^3 + \ldots + b_nX^n + \epsilon$$

   Use Cases: Useful for modeling complex relationships where data points follow a curved pattern, such as growth trajectories or natural phenomena.

   Considerations: While it can model non-linear relationships effectively, using high-degree polynomials can lead to overfitting, where the model captures noise instead of the underlying trend.

Differences Between Regression Analysis:

Table 2.9

S.No.	Aspect	Linear Regression	Logistic Regression	Polynomial Regression
1.	Dependent Variable	Continuous variable	Binary variable (0/1, yes/no)	Continuous variable
2.	Use Case	Predicting values like sales or temperature	Classifying outcomes like spam detection or disease	Modeling non-linear relationships (e.g., growth patterns)
3.	Output	Direct prediction of the dependent variable	Probability of class membership	Prediction of the dependent variable based on polynomial terms
4.	Relationship Type	Assumes a linear relationship	Models the relationship in terms of odds	Can model complex, non-linear relationships
5.	Equation	$Y = a + bX + \epsilon$	$\log\left(\frac{p}{1-p}\right) = a + bX$	$Y = a + b_1X + b_2X^2 + b_3X^3 + ... + b_nX^n + \epsilon$

Predictive Modeling Techniques

Predictive modeling techniques use existing data to build (or train) a model that can predict outcomes for new data. Implementing such techniques enables businesses to optimize decision-making and generate new insights that lead to more effective and profitable actions.

Predictive Modelling Process

Once a set of current and historical data is ready for predictive analysis, the predictive modeling process can begin. To develop the predictive model, data science experts or analysts generate standard predictive algorithms and statistical models, train them using subsets of the data, and execute them against the entire data set. Let us understand how to build a predictive model using simple and easy-to-understand steps -

1. **Data Collection:** The process of data collection is acquiring the information needed for analysis, and it entails obtaining historical data from a reliable source to implement predictive analysis.
2. **Data Mining:** You cleanse your data sets through data mining or data cleaning. You delete incorrect data during the data cleansing process, and the data mining process entails removing identical and redundant data from your data collections.
3. **Exploratory Data Analysis (EDA):** Data exploration is essential for the predictive modeling process. You gather critical data and summarize it by recognizing patterns or trends. EDA is the final step in your data preparation phase.
4. **Predictive Model Development:** You will utilize various techniques to create predictive analytics models based on the patterns you've discovered.

Use Python, R, MATLAB, other programming languages, and standard statistical models to test your hypothesis.

5. **Model Evaluation:** Validation is a crucial phase in predictive analytics. You run a series of tests to see how effectively your model can predict outcomes. Given the sample data or input sets to evaluate the model's validity, you must assess the model's accuracy.
6. **Predictive Model Deployment:** Deployment allows you to test your model in a real-world scenario, which helps in practical decision making and makes it ready for implementation.
7. **Model Tracking:** Check the performance of your models constantly to ensure that you are receiving the best future outcomes possible. It involves comparing model predictions to actual data sets.

Types of Predictive Modelling

1. **Classification Model:** The classification model is one of the most popular predictive analytics models. These models perform categorical analysis on historical data. Various industries adopt classification models because they can retrain these models with current data and as a result, they obtain useful and detailed insights that help them build appropriate solutions. Classification models are customizable and are helpful across industries, including banking and retail.
2. **Clustering Model:** The clustering model gathers data and divides it into groups based on common characteristics. Hard clustering facilitates data classification, determining if each data point belongs to a cluster, and soft clustering allocates a probability to each data point. In some applications, such as marketing, the ability to partition data into distinct datasets depending on specific features is highly beneficial. A clustering model can help businesses plan marketing campaigns for certain groups of customers.
3. **Outliers Model:** Unlike the classification and forecast models, the outlier model deals with anomalous data items within a dataset. It works by detecting anomalous data, either on its own or with other categories and numbers. Outlier models are essential in industries like retail and finance, where detecting abnormalities can save businesses millions of dollars. Outlier models can quickly identify anomalies, so predictive analytics models are efficient in fraud detection.
4. **Forecast Model:** One of the most prominent predictive analytics models is the forecast model. It manages metric value predictions by calculating new data values based on historical data insights. Forecast models also generate numerical values in historical data if none are present. One of the most powerful features of forecast models is that they can manage multiple parameters at a time. As a result, they're one of the most popular predictive models in the market. Various industries can use a forecast model for different business

purposes. For example, a call center can use forecast analytics to predict how many supports calls they will receive in a day, or a retail store can forecast inventory for the upcoming holiday sales periods, etc.

5. **Time Series Model:** Time series predictive models analyze datasets where the input parameter is time sequences. The time series model develops a numerical value that predicts trends within a specific period by combining multiple data points (from the previous year's data). A Time Series model outperforms traditional ways of calculating a variable's progress because it may forecast for numerous regions or projects at once or focus on a single area or task, depending on the organization's needs. Time Series predictive models are helpful if organizations need to know how a specific variable changes over time. For example, if a small business owner wishes to track sales over the last four quarters, they will need to use a Time Series model. It can also look at external factors like seasons or periodical variations that could influence future trends.

Examples of Predictive Modelling

1. **Retail:** Predictive analytics helps retailers in multiple regions with inventory planning and dynamic pricing, evaluating the performance of promotional campaigns, and deciding which personalized retail offers are best for customers. By researching consumer behavior and acquiring a better understanding of its customers with the help of predictive models, Staples has achieved a 137 percent return on investment.
2. **Healthcare:** The healthcare industry employs predictive analytics and modeling to analyze and forecast future population healthcare needs by leveraging healthcare data. Predictive models in the healthcare industry help identify activities that increase patient satisfaction, resource usage, and budget control. Predictive modeling also enables the healthcare industry to improve financial management to optimize patient outcomes. The Centre for Addiction and Mental Health (CAMH), Canada's leading mental health teaching center, uses predictive modeling to streamline treatment for ALC patients and maximize bed space.
3. **Banking:** The banking industry benefits from predictive analytics by creating a credit risk-aware mindset, managing capital and liquidity, and satisfying regulatory obligations. Predictive analytics models provide more significant detection and protection and better control and compliance. Predictive models allow banks and other financial organizations to tailor each client interaction, reduce customer churn, earn customer trust, and generate remarkable customer experiences. OTP Bank Romania, part of the OTP Bank Group, implements predictive analytics to govern the quality of loan issuances, yield more precise business and risk forecasts, and meet profit goals for the bank's credit portfolios.

Applications of Predictive Analytics

Predictive analytics leverages historical data, statistical algorithms, and machine learning techniques to forecast future outcomes, enabling organizations to make informed decisions across various domains. Here are some key applications:

1. **Finance and Banking:** In the finance sector, predictive analytics plays a crucial role in assessing credit risk. Financial institutions use predictive models to evaluate the creditworthiness of applicants by analyzing historical data on repayment behavior, income levels, and other relevant factors. This helps in minimizing default rates and optimizing lending strategies. Additionally, predictive analytics is employed for fraud detection. By analyzing transaction patterns in real time, banks can identify anomalies that suggest fraudulent activity, allowing them to take immediate action to prevent losses.
2. **Healthcare:** Healthcare organizations leverage predictive analytics to improve patient outcomes and optimize resource allocation. For example, hospitals use predictive models to forecast patient readmissions, enabling them to develop targeted intervention strategies for at-risk patients. Predictive analytics also plays a key role in identifying disease outbreaks by analyzing data from various sources, including social media, healthcare reports, and environmental data. This proactive approach helps in timely responses to potential health crises.
3. **Retail and E-commerce:** In retail, predictive analytics is essential for sales forecasting. By analyzing historical sales data, seasonality, and market trends, retailers can accurately predict future sales and optimize inventory management. This not only helps in meeting customer demand but also reduces holding costs. Additionally, customer segmentation is enhanced through predictive analytics, allowing retailers to identify distinct customer groups based on purchasing behavior. This segmentation enables targeted marketing campaigns, improving customer engagement and conversion rates.
4. **Marketing:** Marketing departments utilize predictive analytics to evaluate the effectiveness of campaigns and optimize strategies. By analyzing past campaign performance, organizations can identify which tactics yield the best results, allowing for more efficient resource allocation. Predictive models also help in churn prediction, identifying customers likely to leave a service or unsubscribe. This information allows businesses to implement targeted retention strategies, such as personalized offers or improved customer service.
5. **Manufacturing:** In manufacturing, predictive analytics is used for predictive maintenance, a strategy that forecasts equipment failures before they occur. By analyzing data from machinery sensors and historical maintenance records, manufacturers can schedule maintenance activities proactively, reducing downtime and maintenance costs. Additionally, predictive analytics aids in quality control by identifying patterns that lead to defects, allowing manufacturers to adjust processes and improve product quality.

6. **Telecommunications:** Telecommunications companies use predictive analytics to optimize network performance and enhance customer satisfaction. By analyzing call data records and customer usage patterns, companies can improve service delivery and reduce dropped calls. Furthermore, predictive analytics helps identify customers at risk of switching providers, enabling companies to implement retention measures and improve customer loyalty.
7. **Transportation and Logistics:** In the transportation sector, predictive analytics is vital for route optimization. By forecasting traffic patterns and potential delays, companies can determine the most efficient routes for deliveries, reducing costs and improving customer satisfaction. Demand forecasting is another critical application, allowing companies to anticipate passenger or freight demand and adjust schedules and resources accordingly.
8. **Insurance:** Insurance companies use predictive analytics for risk assessment and premium pricing. By analyzing historical claims data and customer profiles, insurers can more accurately assess the risks associated with policyholders, leading to fairer premium rates. Additionally, predictive models help forecast potential claims, allowing for better financial planning and resource allocation.

5. Prescriptive Analytics

Prescriptive analytics is a type of data analytics that recommends actions based on data analysis and predictive modeling. It goes beyond simply forecasting future outcomes (as predictive analytics does) by providing actionable insights and specific recommendations to optimize decision-making. Prescriptive analytics is a branch of data analytics that focuses on providing actionable recommendations based on data analysis and predictive modeling. It goes beyond merely forecasting future outcomes by utilizing advanced algorithms and optimization techniques to suggest the best course of action for achieving specific goals. This approach involves scenario analysis, where various potential outcomes are evaluated to understand the implications of different decisions. Common applications include supply chain management, where it optimizes inventory and logistics; healthcare, where it recommends treatment plans based on patient data; and finance, where it aids in portfolio management and risk assessment. By analyzing historical and real-time data, prescriptive analytics empowers organizations to make informed, data-driven decisions that enhance efficiency and reduce costs. Its ability to simulate different scenarios allows businesses to anticipate challenges and adapt strategies proactively. Overall, prescriptive analytics serves as a vital tool for organizations looking to optimize their operations and improve decision-making in an increasingly complex and data-rich environment.

Key Features

1. **Action-oriented:** Prescriptive analytics focuses on providing recommendations for what actions to take to achieve desired outcomes, such as maximizing profit or minimizing risk.

2. **Optimization:** It utilizes mathematical and computational techniques, such as optimization algorithms, simulation models, and decision analysis, to determine the best course of action among various alternatives.
3. **Scenario Analysis:** Prescriptive analytics evaluates different scenarios and their potential outcomes, allowing organizations to understand the implications of various decisions.
4. **Real-Time Insights:** Many prescriptive analytics tools can analyze data in real-time, providing immediate recommendations based on current data.

Optimization Techniques

Optimization techniques are essential mathematical and computational methods used to identify the best solution from a set of feasible options. They play a crucial role in various fields, including operations research, finance, engineering, and machine learning, where maximizing or minimizing an objective function is desired. Some prominent optimization techniques and their applications:

1. **Linear Programming (LP):** Linear programming involves optimizing a linear objective function subject to linear constraints, which can be equalities or inequalities. The Simplex method is commonly used to solve LP problems. Applications of linear programming are abundant in resource allocation, such as maximizing profit or minimizing costs in manufacturing and transportation. For instance, a company may use LP to determine the optimal mix of products to manufacture while considering resource limitations.
2. **Integer Programming (IP):** Integer programming is a variation of linear programming where some or all decision variables must take integer values. This is particularly useful in scenarios where discrete items are involved, such as scheduling staff or assigning vehicles to routes. Mixed-integer programming (MIP) combines both integer and continuous variables, allowing for more complex modeling. For example, a delivery service can use IP to optimize vehicle assignments based on capacity and delivery time windows.
3. **Non-linear Programming (NLP):** Non-linear programming deals with optimization problems where the objective function or constraints are nonlinear. This type of programming is more complex than linear programming but is necessary for many real-world applications, such as portfolio optimization in finance or engineering design problems. NLP requires specialized algorithms, such as the Sequential Quadratic Programming (SQP) method, to find solutions effectively.
4. **Dynamic Programming (DP):** Dynamic programming is a method used to solve problems by breaking them down into simpler subproblems. It utilizes the principle of optimality, where the optimal solution to a problem can be constructed from optimal solutions to its subproblems. DP is particularly effective in problems involving decision making over time, such as inventory management and resource allocation in operations research.

5. **Genetic Algorithms (GA):** Genetic algorithms are heuristic search methods inspired by natural selection. They work by evolving a population of potential solutions over generations, applying operations like selection, crossover, and mutation. GAs is particularly useful for solving complex optimization problems where traditional methods may struggle, such as scheduling and vehicle routing problems. They are adaptable and can be applied to a wide range of scenarios.
6. **Simulated Annealing:** Simulated annealing is a probabilistic technique that aims to find an approximate solution to an optimization problem by mimicking the cooling process of metals. This method allows for worse solutions to be accepted at the beginning to escape local minima, gradually reducing the probability of accepting such solutions over time. Simulated annealing is useful for combinatorial optimization problems, such as the traveling salesman problem.
7. **Gradient Descent:** Gradient descent is an iterative optimization algorithm used to minimize a function by moving in the direction of the steepest descent of the function's gradient. It is widely employed in machine learning to optimize loss functions during model training. Variants like stochastic gradient descent (SGD) and mini-batch gradient descent are commonly used to improve convergence speed and reduce computational load.
8. **Convex Optimization:** Convex optimization deals with optimizing convex functions, where any local minimum is also a global minimum. This property simplifies the optimization process and ensures robust solutions. Convex optimization is widely used in various fields, including finance for risk management and machine learning for training algorithms.
9. **Constrained Optimization:** Constrained optimization involves optimizing an objective function while satisfying specific constraints. This approach is prevalent in resource allocation, project management, and logistics, where various limitations must be considered.

Conclusion

Optimization techniques are integral to solving complex decision-making problems across diverse industries. By selecting the appropriate method based on the problem's characteristics and requirements, organizations can enhance operational efficiency, reduce costs, and improve overall performance. As data and computational capabilities continue to evolve, the significance of optimization techniques in decision support systems will grow, enabling more effective and informed decision-making.

Decision Trees and Monte Carlo Simulations

Decision trees and Monte Carlo simulations are powerful analytical tools used for decision-making and risk assessment. Decision trees visually represent decisions, outcomes, and associated probabilities, making them easy to interpret for classification and regression tasks. In contrast, Monte Carlo simulations utilize randomness to model complex systems, generating a range of possible outcomes based on variable inputs and their probability distributions. This probabilistic approach helps quantify risks and uncertainties in various fields, including finance, project management, and engineering. Together, these methods enable organizations to make informed decisions and optimize strategies in uncertain environments.

Decision Trees

A decision tree is a powerful tool used in decision analysis, machine learning, and data mining. It visually represents decisions and their possible consequences, including chance event outcomes, resource costs, and utility.

Structure of a Decision Tree

1. **Root Node:** Represents the entire dataset and the initial decision to be made.
2. **Internal Nodes:** Represent decisions or tests on attributes. Each internal node has one or more branches.
3. **Branches:** Represent the outcome of a decision or test, leading to another node.
4. **Leaf Nodes:** Represent the final decision or prediction. No further splits occur at these nodes.

How Decision Trees Work?

The process of creating a decision tree involves:

1. **Selecting the Best Attribute:** Using a metric like Gini impurity, entropy, or information gain, the best attribute to split the data is selected.
2. **Splitting the Dataset:** The dataset is split into subsets based on the selected attribute.
3. **Repeating the Process:** The process is repeated recursively for each subset, creating a new internal node or leaf node until a stopping criterion is met (e.g., all instances in a node belong to the same class or a predefined depth is reached).

Advantages of Decision Trees

1. **Simplicity and Clarity:** Decision trees are easy to understand and interpret. They provide a clear and visual representation of the decision-making process, making it easier to communicate complex decisions.
2. **Versatility:** They can be used for both classification and regression tasks. In classification, they help in categorizing data into predefined classes, while in regression, they help in predicting continuous values.
3. **Non-parametric Nature:** Decision trees do not require any assumptions about the distribution of data, making them flexible and applicable to a wide range of problems.
4. **Handling of Non-linear Relationships:** They can capture non-linear

relationships between features and the target variable, which many linear models cannot.

Disadvantages of Decision Trees

1. **Overfitting:** Decision trees can easily overfit the training data, especially if they are not pruned. Overfitting occurs when the model learns the noise in the training data rather than the actual pattern.
2. **Instability:** Small changes in the data can result in a completely different tree structure, making them less robust.
3. **Bias:** Decision trees can be biased towards features with more levels. Techniques like random forests or boosting can help mitigate this issue.

Monte Carlo Simulations

Monte Carlo simulations are a statistical technique used to model and analyze complex systems that involve uncertainty and variability. Named after the famous Monte Carlo Casino in Monaco, this method utilizes random sampling to obtain numerical results. By simulating a wide range of scenarios, Monte Carlo simulations enable decision-makers to understand the probabilities of different outcomes, assess risks, and make informed decisions across various fields, including finance, engineering, and project management.

Steps of Monte Carlo simulation: The Monte Carlo simulation process typically involves the following steps:

1. **Define the Problem:** Clearly articulate the problem or decision to be analyzed, identifying the key variables and their relationships.
2. **Model the System:** Develop a mathematical model representing the system or process. This model should include all relevant variables and their interactions.
3. **Identify Probability Distributions:** For each uncertain variable, define a probability distribution that accurately reflects its potential values. Common distributions include normal, uniform, triangular, and log-normal distributions.
4. **Generate Random Samples:** Use random number generators to produce values for each variable based on its defined probability distribution. This step is crucial, as the quality of the simulation outcomes relies on the randomness and representativeness of these samples.
5. **Run Simulations:** Execute the model multiple times (often thousands or millions) using different sets of random inputs. Each iteration produces an outcome based on the random samples generated.
6. **Analyze Results:** After running the simulations, analyze the aggregated results to assess probabilities,

7. averages, variances, and other statistical metrics. This analysis provides insights into the likelihood of various outcomes.
8. **Make Decisions:** Utilize the insights gained from the simulations to inform decision-making, risk
9. management, and strategic planning.

Applications of Monte Carlo simulation

1. **Finance:** In finance, Monte Carlo simulations are widely used for risk assessment and investment analysis. They help quantify the uncertainty associated with asset prices, interest rates, and economic conditions. For example, a financial analyst may use Monte Carlo simulations to model the future value of an investment portfolio by simulating various market scenarios, accounting for the volatility of asset returns. This approach allows investors to understand potential risks and returns, enabling more informed investment decisions.
2. **Project Management:** Monte Carlo simulations are valuable tools for project managers when estimating project timelines and costs. By simulating different scenarios for task durations and resource allocations, project managers can identify the probability of meeting deadlines and budget constraints. This information helps in risk assessment, enabling proactive measures to mitigate potential delays and cost overruns. For instance, a project manager might simulate the completion dates of various project tasks, identifying the likelihood of completing the project on time.
3. **Engineering and Quality Control:** In engineering, Monte Carlo simulations are used for reliability analysis and quality control. By modeling potential failure scenarios and their associated probabilities, engineers can assess the reliability of systems and components. This approach is especially useful in industries such as aerospace and manufacturing, where safety and quality are critical. For example, an engineer might simulate the performance of a mechanical component under varying conditions to determine the likelihood of failure and inform design improvements.
4. **Environmental Science:** Monte Carlo simulations are employed in environmental modeling to assess the impact of uncertainties in environmental parameters. For instance, in risk assessment of hazardous materials, Monte Carlo simulations can estimate the potential exposure levels for different populations, considering uncertainties in factors like concentration levels, exposure duration, and population variability. This information aids in regulatory decision-making and environmental protection strategies.
5. **Healthcare:** In healthcare, Monte Carlo simulations are increasingly used to model disease spread, treatment outcomes, and resource allocation. For example, during the COVID-19 pandemic, public health officials used Monte Carlo simulations to forecast the spread of the virus under various intervention

scenarios. By modeling the effects of different public health measures, such as social distancing and vaccination rates, decision-makers could better understand potential outcomes and allocate resources accordingly.

Advantages of Monte Carlo Simulations

1. **Flexibility:** Monte Carlo simulations can be applied to a wide range of problems across various disciplines, making them highly versatile.
2. **Probabilistic Insight:** Unlike deterministic models that provide a single outcome, Monte Carlo simulations yield a distribution of possible outcomes, helping decision-makers understand the range of potential results and associated risks.
3. **Comprehensive Risk Assessment:** They facilitate the identification and quantification of risks, allowing organizations to make informed decisions based on a thorough understanding of uncertainties.
4. **Integration with Complex Models:** Monte Carlo simulations can be integrated with complex mathematical models, enabling the simulation of intricate systems with numerous interacting variables.

Limitations of Monte Carlo Simulations

1. **Computationally Intensive:** Running a large number of simulations can require significant computational resources and time, especially for complex models.
2. **Quality of Input Data:** The accuracy of the simulation outcomes relies heavily on the quality and validity of the input data and the assumptions made about probability distributions. Poorly defined distributions can lead to misleading results.
3. **Overfitting:** There is a risk of overfitting the model to historical data, which may not accurately represent future conditions. Decision-makers must be cautious when interpreting results.

Scenario Analysis and What-If Modeling

Scenario analysis and what-if modeling are powerful techniques used in decision-making and strategic planning. Both methods allow organizations to evaluate the potential impacts of different variables and assumptions, helping them prepare for uncertainty and make informed choices. While they share similarities, each approach has distinct characteristics and applications.

Scenario Analysis

Scenario analysis is a strategic planning tool used to visualize and evaluate potential future events and their impacts on a business or project. By developing multiple scenarios based on varying assumptions about key variables, organizations can assess risks and opportunities, enabling informed decision-making in uncertain environments. The primary goal of scenario analysis is to help organizations prepare for uncertainty. This method allows stakeholders to explore the implications of different external factors, such as economic shifts, regulatory changes, or technological advancements on their objectives. By anticipating various possible futures, businesses can develop strategies that are resilient and adaptable.

Key Components of Scenario Analysis

1. **Identify Key Drivers:** Determine the critical factors that can influence future outcomes. These drivers may include economic conditions, regulatory changes, technological advancements, market trends, and competitive dynamics.
2. **Define Scenarios:** Develop a range of plausible scenarios based on different assumptions about key drivers. Common scenarios include:
    - **Best-case scenario:** Optimistic outcomes with favourable conditions.
    - **Worst-case scenario:** Pessimistic outcomes with adverse conditions.
    - **Most-likely scenario:** A realistic assessment of future events based on current trends.
3. **Data Collection and Analysis:** Gather relevant quantitative and qualitative data to support the scenarios. This may include historical data, market research, expert opinions, and statistical models.
4. **Impact Assessment:** Analyze how each scenario affects key performance indicators (KPIs) and overall objectives. Assess the financial, operational, and strategic impacts of each scenario.
5. **Risk Identification:** Identify potential risks associated with each scenario. Consider factors such as market volatility, operational challenges, and external threats.
6. **Action Planning:** Develop strategic responses for each scenario. This includes creating contingency plans, resource allocations, and decision-making frameworks to navigate various potential futures.
7. **Monitoring and Review:** Establish a process for monitoring changes in key drivers and assumptions. Regularly review and update scenarios based on new information and evolving conditions.
8. **Communication and Collaboration:** Engage stakeholders throughout the scenario analysis process. Communicate findings and implications clearly to ensure alignment and facilitate informed decision-making.

Applications of Scenario Analysis

1. **Strategic Planning:** Organizations use scenario analysis to inform long-term strategic planning, enabling them to adapt to potential market changes or disruptions.

2. **Risk Management:** By exploring adverse scenarios, companies can identify potential risks and develop mitigation strategies, enhancing their overall risk management framework.

3. **Financial Forecasting:** Scenario analysis aids in financial modeling by providing insights into how different conditions might impact revenue, costs, and profitability.

4. **Project Management:** In project planning, scenario analysis helps assess the feasibility and risks of projects under various conditions, improving decision-making and resource allocation.

Example

Consider a company planning to launch a new product. The management team might develop three scenarios:

1. **Best-case Scenario:** Strong market demand, favorable regulatory conditions, and successful marketing efforts lead to high sales and profitability.

2. **Worst-case Scenario:** Economic downturn, increased competition, and regulatory hurdles result in low sales and financial losses.

3. **Most-likely Scenario:** Moderate demand, some competition, and manageable regulatory issues lead to steady sales growth but require ongoing adjustments.

By analyzing these scenarios, the company can devise strategies for product launch, marketing, and resource allocation that are robust across different potential futures.

Conclusion

Scenario analysis is a vital tool for organizations seeking to navigate uncertainty and complexity. By exploring various plausible futures and their implications, businesses can enhance their strategic planning, risk management, and overall decision-making processes. In a rapidly changing world, the ability to anticipate and adapt to different scenarios is crucial for achieving long-term success.

What-If Modeling

What-if modeling is a powerful analytical technique that allows organizations to explore the potential outcomes of varying specific inputs in a given model. This method provides valuable insights into how changes in one or more variables affect results, facilitating informed decision-making in various contexts, including finance, project management, and operational planning.

The primary goal of what-if modeling is to help decision-makers understand the impact of different scenarios on key outcomes. By manipulating variables within a model, organizations can assess the sensitivity of results to changes, identify critical factors influencing performance, and prepare for various possible futures. This capability is essential in today's fast-paced, uncertain business environment, where the ability to respond to changes can determine success or failure.

Key Components of What-If Modeling

1. **Base Model Definition:** Begin by creating a foundational model that accurately reflects the current state of operations, finances, or projects. This model should define all relevant variables and their interrelationships, along with clear assumptions about data sources and expected conditions.
2. **Identification of Key Variables:** Identify input variables that can be adjusted, such as sales volume, pricing, costs, and resource allocations. Determine the key performance indicators (KPIs) or outcomes that will be analyzed, like revenue or profit margins.
3. **Scenario Development:** Create scenarios by varying one or more input variables, including best-case, worst-case, and most-likely cases. Conduct sensitivity analysis to evaluate how sensitive outcomes are to changes in each variable, highlighting critical factors that influence results.
4. **Analysis and Simulation:** Run simulations with adjusted inputs to generate new outcomes. Utilize software tools for rapid calculations and visual tools like graphs and dashboards to present results clearly.
5. **Documentation and Interpretation:** Document the results of each scenario, noting key insights and their implications for decision-making. Analyze the outcomes to understand the relationships between input changes and resulting impacts.
6. **Communication:** Present findings to stakeholders, ensuring clarity in the implications of different scenarios. Encourage collaboration and feedback to refine scenarios.
7. **Review and Update:** Regularly review and update the model based on new data or changing conditions, implementing a monitoring process for key variables to maintain relevance and accuracy.

These components ensure effective use of what-if modeling for strategic planning and decision-making.

Applications of What-If Modeling

1. **Financial Planning and Analysis:** In finance, what-if modeling is extensively used for budgeting, forecasting, and investment analysis. Analysts can manipulate variables like revenue growth rates, expense assumptions, and capital costs to project various financial outcomes.

   Example: A company might use what-if modeling to evaluate the impact of a price increase on profitability. By adjusting the price and analyzing changes in sales volume and overall revenue, the finance team can determine if the price increase is feasible and beneficial.

2. **Project Management:** Project managers use what-if modeling to assess the potential impact of changes in project scope, timelines, or resource allocation. This approach helps identify critical paths, potential bottlenecks, and necessary adjustments to meet project objectives.

   Example: If a project encounter delays due to resource shortages, managers can model the effect of reallocating resources from less critical tasks. This helps determine if the project can still meet its deadline or if additional resources are required.

3. **Operations Management:** In operations, what-if modeling helps evaluate the effects of changes in production processes, supply chain dynamics, and inventory management. By simulating different operational scenarios, organizations can optimize efficiency and reduce costs.

   Example: A manufacturing company might model the impact of increasing production capacity on lead times and inventory levels. This analysis can guide decisions on whether to invest in additional machinery or adjust production schedules.

4. **Marketing and Sales:** Marketing teams use what-if modeling to explore the potential impacts of different marketing strategies, pricing models, and promotional campaigns on sales performance.

   Example: A marketing manager may evaluate the effect of increasing the advertising budget on sales growth. By adjusting the budget and analyzing projected sales outcomes, the team can make informed decisions about resource allocation.

5. **Human Resources and Workforce Planning:** HR departments utilize what-if modeling to assess the implications of changes in staffing levels, compensation structures, or training programs on overall productivity and employee satisfaction.

   Example: An HR team may model the impact of implementing a new training program on employee performance metrics. By adjusting training costs and expected performance improvements, the team can evaluate the program's potential ROI.

Conclusion

What-if modeling is a crucial tool for organizations seeking to navigate uncertainty and make informed decisions. By allowing decision-makers to explore the impacts of varying inputs, this method enhances strategic planning, risk assessment, and operational efficiency. In an ever-evolving business landscape, the ability to simulate different scenarios and analyze their potential outcomes equips organizations with the insights needed to adapt and thrive. Whether in finance, project management, marketing, or operations, what-if modeling serves as a valuable resource for optimizing strategies and achieving long-term success.

Differences Between Scenario Analysis and What-If Modelling

Table 2.10

S.No.	Feature	Scenario Analysis	What-if Modeling
1.	Focus	Explores multiple alternative futures.	Examines the impact of changing specific variables.
2.	Scope	Considers various assumptions and outcomes.	Primarily focuses on the sensitivity of outcomes.
3.	Complexity	Often involves more complex modeling and multiple scenarios.	Typically simpler, often focused on one change at a time.
4.	Output	Provides a range of potential outcomes and their probabilities.	Shows direct impacts of changes on outcomes
5.	Application	Used for long-term strategic planning and risk management.	Common in operational and tactical decision-making

Tools for Prescriptive Analytics: Gurobi, CPLEX

Gurobi

Gurobi is a leading optimization solver that excels in prescriptive analytics by offering powerful tools for linear programming (LP), mixed-integer programming (MIP), and quadratic programming (QP). Renowned for its speed and scalability, Gurobi allows users to solve complex optimization problems efficiently. It features user-friendly APIs in multiple programming languages, including Python, C++, and Java, making it accessible for various applications. Advanced capabilities like presolve techniques, cutting planes, and heuristics enhance model performance and solution quality. Gurobi's interactive environment facilitates quick testing and refinement of models. Additionally, it provides flexible deployment options, supporting both cloud and on-premise installations. These attributes make Gurobi an ideal choice for optimizing supply chains, financial portfolios, workforce scheduling, and production planning, enabling organizations to derive actionable insights and make informed decisions based on data-driven analysis.

Features of Gurobi's

1. **Advanced Optimization Solvers:** Gurobi excels in various optimization techniques, including:
   - **Linear Programming (LP)**: Users can model problems where the objective function and constraints are linear, making it suitable for a wide range of applications such as resource allocation and transportation.
   - **Mixed-Integer Programming (MIP)**: This feature allows for solving problems with both continuous and discrete variables, enabling complex decision-making scenarios, such as scheduling and facility location.
   - **Quadratic Programming (QP)**: Gurobi supports quadratic objectives, which are common in finance and portfolio optimization.

2. **High Performance and Scalability:** Gurobi is renowned for its speed and efficiency, which is critical for real-time decision-making in large-scale optimization problems. The solver leverages advanced algorithms and heuristics to quickly find optimal solutions, even for complex and high-dimensional problems. Its ability to handle large datasets and models makes it ideal for industries with extensive operational demands.
3. **User-Friendly APIs:** Gurobi provides intuitive APIs for various programming languages, including Python, C++, Java, and .NET. This flexibility allows users to integrate Gurobi seamlessly into their existing workflows and applications. The Python interface, in particular, is widely favored for its ease of use and integration with popular data science libraries.
4. **Interactive Environment:** Gurobi offers an interactive shell that allows users to quickly test and refine their models. This feature enables rapid prototyping and experimentation, which is invaluable during the model development phase.
5. **Cloud and On-Premise Options:** Gurobi provides flexibility in deployment, offering both cloud-based solutions and on-premise installations. This versatility allows organizations to choose the setup that best fits their infrastructure and operational requirements.
6. **Robust Support and Documentation:** Gurobi comes with extensive documentation, tutorials, and support resources to assist users in getting started and maximizing the solver's capabilities. The active user community also contributes to a rich ecosystem of shared knowledge and best practices.
7. **Real-world Applications:** Gurobi's features make it suitable for a wide range of applications, including supply chain optimization, financial portfolio management, workforce scheduling, production planning, and transportation logistics. Organizations across various sectors can leverage Gurobi to derive actionable insights and enhance decision-making processes.

Applications of Gurobi: Gurobi is applied across a wide range of domains, showcasing its versatility:

1. **Supply Chain Optimization:** Companies use Gurobi to minimize costs while managing complex logistics networks. This includes vehicle routing, inventory management, and production scheduling.
2. **Finance:** In the finance sector, Gurobi helps in portfolio optimization, risk management, and algorithmic trading by solving large-scale optimization problems that consider multiple constraints and objectives.
3. **Telecommunications:** Gurobi is employed in network design and optimization, helping companies optimize bandwidth allocation, minimize latency, and ensure quality of service.
4. **Manufacturing:** In manufacturing, Gurobi aids in optimizing production

schedules, resource allocation, and equipment utilization, contributing to improved efficiency and reduced operational costs.

Getting Started with Gurobi

To use Gurobi, users need to install the software and obtain a license. Gurobi offers various licensing options, including free academic licenses, which are available to students and educators.

Installation

1. **Download:** Users can download Gurobi from the official website. The installation package is available for different operating systems, including Windows, macOS, and Linux.
2. **License Setup:** After installation, users need to set up their license. The Gurobi license key is required to activate the software. For academic use, users can apply for a free license.
3. **Programming Environment:** Users typically write optimization models in their preferred programming language. The Gurobi Python interface is particularly user-friendly for those familiar with Python.

Basic Example in Python

A simple example to illustrate how to set up and solve a linear programming problem using Gurobi in Python:

```
from gurobipy import Model, GRB

# Create a new model
model = Model("example")

# Create variables
x = model.addVar(name="x", lb=0)  # x >= 0
y = model.addVar(name="y", lb=0)  # y >= 0

# Set objective
model.setObjective(3 * x + 4 * y, GRB.MAXIMIZE)

# Add constraints
model.addConstr(2 * x + y <= 8, "c0")
model.addConstr(x + 2 * y <= 8, "c1")

# Optimize model
model.optimize()

# Print the results
for v in model.getVars():
    print(f'{v.varName}: {v.x}')
print(f'Objective Value: {model.objVal}')
```

Conclusion

Gurobi is a powerful optimization solver that stands out for its performance, flexibility, and user-friendly features. Its wide-ranging applications across industries highlight its importance in solving complex decision-making problems. Whether for academic research or practical business applications, Gurobi equips users with the tools necessary to tackle optimization challenges effectively.

By continually improving its algorithms and expanding its capabilities, Gurobi remains at the forefront of optimization technology, making it an essential resource for anyone looking to harness the power of mathematical optimization.

CPLEX

IBM ILOG CPLEX Optimization Studio, commonly known as CPLEX, is a powerful optimization solver designed for solving linear programming (LP), mixed-integer programming (MIP), quadratic programming (QP), and other mathematical optimization problems. Since its inception in the late 1980s, CPLEX has evolved into a leading tool widely used in industries such as finance, logistics, telecommunications, and manufacturing.

Key Features of CPLEX

1. **High Performance:** CPLEX is renowned for its efficiency and speed. It employs advanced algorithms like the primal-dual simplex method, barrier method, and branch-and-cut techniques, allowing it to solve large-scale problems quickly.
2. **Support for Diverse Problem Types:** CPLEX can handle a variety of problem formulations, including LP, MIP, QP, and quadratic constrained programming (QCP). This flexibility makes it suitable for a wide array of applications.
3. **User-Friendly Interfaces:** CPLEX provides interfaces for several programming languages, including C, C++, Java, Python, and .NET. The Python API is particularly popular among data scientists for its simplicity and ease of integration with other data manipulation libraries.
4. **Modeling Capabilities:** The CPLEX Optimization Studio includes a powerful modeling language called OPL (Optimization Programming Language) that allows users to define complex models and constraints in a clear and concise manner.
5. **Concurrent Optimization:** CPLEX supports parallel processing, enabling it to utilize multi-threading to solve multiple instances of problems simultaneously. This feature is especially beneficial in environments where multiple scenarios need evaluation.
6. **Automatic Tuning:** CPLEX includes an automatic tuning feature that adjusts solver parameters based on the characteristics of the optimization problem, enhancing performance without manual intervention.

7. **Comprehensive Documentation and Support**: IBM provides extensive documentation, tutorials, and support resources, making it easier for users to learn and troubleshoot their optimization models.

Applications of CPLEX: CPLEX finds applications across a broad spectrum of fields, showcasing its versatility and effectiveness:

1. **Supply Chain Optimization:** Companies leverage CPLEX to minimize logistics costs, optimize inventory levels, and improve transportation routes, ensuring efficient supply chain operations.
2. **Finance and Investment:** In finance, CPLEX is used for portfolio optimization, risk assessment, and financial modeling, allowing firms to make data-driven investment decisions.
3. **Telecommunications:** CPLEX aids in optimizing network design, resource allocation, and bandwidth management, enhancing service quality and operational efficiency.
4. **Manufacturing:** CPLEX supports production planning, scheduling, and resource management, enabling manufacturers to maximize productivity and reduce operational costs.

Getting Started with CPLEX

To use CPLEX, users need to install the software and obtain a license. IBM offers various licensing options, including free academic licenses for students and educators.

Installation

1. **Download:** Users can download CPLEX from the IBM website. The installation package is available for different operating systems, including Windows, Linux, and macOS.
2. **License Setup:** After installation, users need to configure their license. Academic users can apply for a free license key through IBM's academic program.
3. **Development Environment:** Users can write optimization models using their preferred programming language or directly within the CPLEX Optimization Studio using OPL.

Basic Example in Python

Here's a simple example illustrating how to set up and solve a linear programming problem using the CPLEX Python API:

```
from cplex import Cplex

# Create a new CPLEX instance
model = Cplex()

# Set the problem type
model.set_problem_type(Cplex.problem_type.LP)

# Add variables
model.variables.add(names=["x", "y"], lb=[0.0, 0.0], ub=[Cplex.infinity, Cplex.infinity])

# Set the objective function
model.objective.set_sense(model.objective.sense.maximize)
model.objective.set_coefficients([3.0, 4.0])

# Add constraints
model.linear_constraints.add(
    names=["c1", "c2"],
    senses=["L", "L"],
    rhs=[8.0, 8.0],
    coefficients=[[0, 1], [2, 1], [1, 2]]
)

# Solve the model
model.solve()

# Print results
print("Solution status =", model.solution.get_status())
print("Objective value =", model.solution.get_objective_value())
for i in range(model.variables.get_num()):
    print(f"{model.variables.get_names()[i]} = {model.solution.get_values(i)}")
```

Performance Optimization: To get the best performance out of CPLEX, users can employ several strategies:

1. **Model Simplification**: Reducing the size of the model by eliminating redundant constraints and variables can significantly speed up the solution process.
2. **Parameter Tuning**: Manually adjusting CPLEX parameters can enhance performance for specific types of problems. The CPLEX documentation provides guidance on effective parameter settings.
3. **Utilizing the Callback Interface**: Advanced users can implement custom callbacks during the optimization process to gain insights into the solver's progress or to implement specific stopping criteria.

Conclusion

IBM ILOG CPLEX Optimization Studio is a powerful tool for solving complex optimization problems across various industries. With its high performance, versatility, and user-friendly interfaces, CPLEX enables businesses and researchers to make informed decisions based on data-driven optimization.

From supply chain management to financial modeling, CPLEX's applications are vast and varied, highlighting its importance in the optimization landscape. By continually improving its algorithms and expanding its features, CPLEX remains a leading choice for anyone looking to leverage the power of mathematical optimization in their decision-making processes. Whether for academic research or practical business applications, CPLEX equips users with the necessary tools to tackle optimization challenges effectively.

CASE STUDY OF CORE PRINCIPLES OF DATA ANALYTICS

Case Study 1: Retail Sales Optimization

Background

A national retail chain with over 200 stores across the country faced declining sales and increased competition from online retailers. The management sought to leverage data analytics to better understand customer behavior, optimize inventory, and improve marketing strategies. The core principles of data analytics—data collection, data cleaning, exploratory data analysis (EDA), and predictive modeling—were applied in this project.

Data Collection: The first step involved gathering data from various sources:

1. **Point of Sale (POS) Systems:** Sales data was collected from each store, including transaction details, product categories, and timestamps.
2. **Customer Loyalty Program:** Data from the loyalty program provided insights into customer demographics and purchase history.
3. **Online Presence:** Website traffic data, including page views and conversion rates, was also collected to analyze customer interactions online.

Data Cleaning: Once the data was collected, it underwent a rigorous cleaning process:

1. **Handling Missing Values:** Missing data points were identified and imputed based on the median values of corresponding attributes.
2. **Standardizing Formats:** Various date formats and product category names were standardized to ensure consistency across datasets.
3. **Removing Duplicates:** Duplicate entries in the sales records were eliminated to avoid skewed analysis.

Exploratory Data Analysis (EDA): With clean data, the team performed EDA to uncover insights:

1. **Sales Trends:** Time series analysis revealed seasonal sales trends, indicating peak sales during holidays and promotional events.
2. **Customer Segmentation:** Clustering techniques were applied to segment customers based on purchase behavior. This revealed that certain segments preferred specific product categories, allowing targeted marketing.
3. **Inventory Levels:** An analysis of inventory turnover rates highlighted slow-moving products that could be discounted to improve cash flow.

Predictive Modeling: The next step was to build predictive models to inform strategic decisions:

1. **Sales Forecasting:** A time series forecasting model was developed using historical sales data to predict future sales trends. This model incorporated external factors such as holidays and weather, which influenced buying patterns.
2. **Customer Lifetime Value (CLV):** A regression model was created to estimate the CLV for different customer segments, helping the marketing team allocate budgets effectively.

Implementation and Results: Based on insights derived from data analytics, the following strategies were implemented:

1. **Targeted Marketing Campaigns:** Personalized promotions were sent to different customer segments, leading to a 15% increase in response rates compared to previous campaigns.
2. **Inventory Optimization:** Adjustments were made to inventory levels based on the predictive model, reducing stockouts by 20% and minimizing excess inventory by 30%.
3. **Sales Growth:** Overall sales increased by 10% within six months of implementing these strategies.

Conclusion

This case study illustrates the core principles of data analytics in action. By leveraging data collection, cleaning, EDA, and predictive modeling, the retail chain was able to optimize its operations and significantly improve sales performance. The insights gained not only addressed immediate challenges but also established a data-driven culture within the organization for future decision-making.

Case Study 2: Healthcare Resource Allocation

Background

A regional healthcare provider faced challenges in managing patient flow and resource allocation. Increasing patient volumes and limited resources strained hospital operations, leading to longer wait times and decreased patient satisfaction. The healthcare provider decided to implement data analytics principles to optimize resource allocation and improve patient care.

Data Collection: The healthcare provider collected data from several sources:

Electronic Health Records (EHR): Patient demographics, visit histories, and treatment outcomes were aggregated from the EHR system.

Operational Data: Information on staffing levels, bed occupancy rates, and resource utilization was gathered from hospital management systems.

Patient Feedback: Surveys capturing patient satisfaction and feedback were included to understand service quality.

Data Cleaning: Data cleaning was crucial to ensure accurate analysis:

1. **Identifying Inconsistencies:** Patient records with missing demographic information were flagged, and efforts were made to obtain this data from primary care records.
2. **Standardizing Terminologies:** Medical terms and treatment codes were standardized to eliminate discrepancies across departments.

Exploratory Data Analysis (EDA): The cleaned data was subjected to EDA to extract actionable insights:

1. **Patient Flow Analysis:** The team conducted a flow analysis to understand peak admission times and patient demographics, revealing that certain departments were consistently over capacity.
2. **Resource Utilization:** An analysis of resource utilization showed that some departments had underutilized staff during peak hours, suggesting a mismatch between patient needs and available resources.

Predictive Modeling: With insights from EDA, predictive models were developed to guide resource allocation:

1. **Patient Admission Forecasting:** A predictive model using historical data identified patterns in-patient admissions. This model helped anticipate surges during flu season and other public health events.
2. **Staffing Optimization:** Regression analysis predicted the optimal number of staff needed for each department based on expected patient volume, leading to more efficient scheduling.

Implementation and Results: The healthcare provider implemented several strategies based on the analytics findings:

1. **Dynamic Staffing:** By aligning staffing levels with predicted patient volumes, the hospital reduced overtime costs by 25% and improved employee satisfaction.
2. **Resource Reallocation:** Resources were redistributed based on departmental needs, resulting in a 20% decrease in patient wait times.
3. **Improved Patient Satisfaction:** Following the changes, patient satisfaction scores increased by 30%, demonstrating the positive impact of data-driven decisions.

Conclusion

This case study exemplifies how core principles of data analytics can transform healthcare operations. Through effective data collection, cleaning, EDA, and predictive modeling, the healthcare provider optimized resource allocation, leading to enhanced patient care and operational efficiency. The success of this initiative underscores the importance of adopting a data-driven approach in the healthcare sector to meet growing demands and improve service delivery.

SUMMARY OF CORE PRINCIPLES OF DATA ANALYTICS

1. Statistical Foundations

Statistical foundations encompass key concepts like probability theory, hypothesis testing, confidence intervals, and the distinction between correlation and causation. Essential statistical tools, including R, SAS, and Python libraries, facilitate data analysis, enabling practitioners to make informed decisions based on empirical evidence and robust statistical methods.

Probability Theory and Distributions

Understanding probability is crucial for data analytics. It provides the mathematical foundation for making inferences from data. Common distributions include normal, binomial, and Poisson distributions, which help model different types of data and their behaviors.

Hypothesis Testing and Confidence Intervals

Hypothesis testing allows analysts to make decisions based on data. A hypothesis is tested to determine whether it can be rejected or not. Confidence intervals provide a range of values that likely contain the population parameter, offering a measure of uncertainty around estimates.

Correlation and Causation

Correlation measures the relationship between two variables, while causation implies that one variable influence another. Distinguishing between the two is essential to avoid misleading conclusions in data analysis.

Statistical Tools: R, SAS, Python Libraries

Tools like R and SAS are powerful for statistical analysis, providing a wide range of functions for conducting tests and visualizing data. Python libraries such as Pandas, NumPy, and SciPy are popular for data manipulation and statistical calculations.

2. Data Mining and Knowledge Discovery

Data mining and knowledge discovery involve extracting valuable patterns and insights from large datasets. Techniques include association rules, clustering, and classification, along with dimensionality reduction methods like PCA and LDA. These processes help organizations identify trends, segment customers, and enhance decision-making through actionable information derived from complex data.

Introduction to Data Mining Techniques

Data mining involves exploring large datasets to discover patterns and extract useful information. It encompasses various techniques and processes to analyze data and generate insights.

Association Rules, Clustering, and Classification

- **Association Rules:** These techniques identify relationships between variables, commonly used in market basket analysis to find items frequently purchased together.

- **Clustering:** This method groups similar data points together, helping identify natural groupings in data, such as customer segments.
- **Classification:** This involves predicting a categorical outcome based on input features, utilizing algorithms like decision trees and random forests.
- **Dimensionality Reduction: PCA, LDA:** Dimensionality reduction techniques, like PCA and LDA, simplify datasets by reducing features while preserving essential information, enhancing analysis and visualization.

Principal Component Analysis (PCA): Reduces the dimensionality of data while retaining its variance, making it easier to visualize and analyze.

Linear Discriminant Analysis (LDA): Focuses on finding a feature space that best separates different classes, enhancing classification tasks.

- **Case Studies in Data Mining:** Real-world examples, such as customer segmentation in retail or fraud detection in finance, illustrate how data mining techniques can yield actionable insights.

3. Machine Learning Fundamentals

Machine learning fundamentals cover supervised and unsupervised learning methods, including key algorithms like regression, decision trees, SVM, and k-NN. Model evaluation techniques, such as cross-validation and confusion matrices, assess performance. Additionally, deep learning utilizes neural networks to tackle complex patterns, significantly advancing fields like image and speech recognition.

Supervised vs. Unsupervised Learning: Supervised learning involves training models on labeled data, enabling predictions based on known outcomes, such as classification and regression tasks. In contrast, unsupervised learning analyzes unlabeled data to discover patterns or groupings, commonly used in clustering and association tasks, revealing hidden structures without predefined labels.

- **Supervised Learning:** The model is trained on labeled data, where input-output pairs are provided (e.g., predicting house prices based on features).
- **Unsupervised Learning:** The model works with unlabeled data to identify patterns or groupings without predefined outcomes (e.g., clustering customers).

Key Algorithms: Regression, Decision Trees, SVM, k-NN

Key algorithms in machine learning include regression for predicting continuous outcomes, decision trees for classification, support vector machines (SVM) for optimal separation of classes, and k-nearest neighbors (k-NN) for instance-based learning. These algorithms form the backbone of predictive modeling, enabling various applications across industries.

- **Regression:** Used for predicting continuous outcomes (e.g., linear regression).
- **Decision Trees:** A flowchart-like structure for decision-making, useful for classification tasks.

- **Support Vector Machines (SVM):** A powerful classifier that finds the optimal hyperplane to separate different classes.
- **k-Nearest Neighbors (k-NN):** A non-parametric method used for classification and regression based on the proximity of data points.

Model Evaluation and Validation Techniques

Techniques such as cross-validation, confusion matrices, and ROC curves are employed to assess model performance and generalizability.

Introduction to Deep Learning and Neural Networks

Deep learning utilizes neural networks with multiple layers to model complex patterns in large datasets. It has shown remarkable success in fields such as image and speech recognition.

4. Predictive Analytics

Predictive analytics utilizes statistical techniques and machine learning to forecast future outcomes based on historical data. Key methods include time series analysis, regression analysis, and predictive modeling. Applications span diverse fields, such as finance for risk assessment, marketing for customer behavior prediction, and operations for demand forecasting, enhancing decision-making processes.

Time Series Analysis and Forecasting

This technique focuses on analyzing data points collected or recorded at specific time intervals to identify trends and make future predictions (e.g., stock prices, sales forecasts).

Regression Analysis: Linear, Logistic, and Polynomial

Regression analysis is a statistical method used to model the relationship between dependent and independent variables. Key types include linear regression for predicting continuous outcomes, logistic regression for binary outcomes, and polynomial regression for non-linear relationships. It helps identify trends, assess impact, and make informed predictions across various fields.

- **Linear Regression:** Models the relationship between a dependent variable and one or more independent variables.
- **Logistic Regression:** Used for binary classification problems, predicting probabilities of outcomes.
- **Polynomial Regression:** Extends linear regression to model relationships between variables that are not linearly related.

Predictive Modeling Techniques

These encompass various statistical and machine learning methods used to predict outcomes, helping organizations make informed decisions based on data.

Applications of Predictive Analytics

Predictive analytics can be applied in diverse areas such as customer behavior forecasting, risk assessment in finance, and predictive maintenance in manufacturing.

5. Prescriptive Analytics

Prescriptive analytics provides recommendations for decision-making by analyzing data and applying optimization techniques. It includes methods like decision trees and Monte Carlo simulations to evaluate potential outcomes. Tools such as Gurobi and CPLEX assist in modeling complex scenarios, enabling organizations to optimize resources, mitigate risks, and enhance strategic planning.

Optimization Techniques

Prescriptive analytics employs optimization techniques to recommend actions based on data analysis. This includes linear programming, integer programming, and other mathematical optimization methods.

Decision Trees and Monte Carlo Simulations

Decision trees visually represent decisions and their potential outcomes, aiding in risk assessment and strategic planning. Monte Carlo simulations use random sampling to model uncertainty in complex systems, providing insights into possible future scenarios. Together, they enhance decision-making by evaluating risks and optimizing outcomes based on various inputs and probabilities.

- **Decision Trees:** Help visualize decisions and their potential consequences, useful in risk analysis.
- **Monte Carlo Simulations:** A computational algorithm that uses repeated random sampling to assess risk and uncertainty in predictive models.

Scenario Analysis and What-If Modeling

These techniques evaluate different scenarios to understand potential outcomes based on varying inputs, aiding in strategic decision-making.

Tools for Prescriptive Analytics: Gurobi, CPLEX

Gurobi and CPLEX are powerful optimization solvers that enable users to model complex decision problems, providing optimal solutions efficiently.

3

Tools and Technologies

"Tools and technologies" refer to the diverse range of instruments, software applications, systems, and methodologies utilized across various fields to enhance productivity, innovation, and efficiency. Tools can be physical, such as hammers and machinery in construction, or digital, like software development environments (IDEs), data analysis platforms, and design applications. Technologies, on the other hand, encompass the broader application of scientific knowledge for practical use, including web development technologies like HTML and CSS, information systems for data management, and cloud computing solutions that facilitate scalable infrastructure. The integration of tools and technologies plays a crucial role in transforming ideas into tangible outcomes, allowing businesses and individuals to streamline operations, improve collaboration, and drive progress in an increasingly digital world. By leveraging these resources, organizations can innovate, adapt to changing market demands, and optimize workflows, ultimately leading to better decision-making and enhanced competitiveness. As advancements continue to emerge, staying informed about the latest tools and technologies becomes essential for success in any industry, making them pivotal in shaping the future of work, education, and everyday life. Whether in software development, data science, or design, the effective use of tools and technologies empowers users to maximize their potential and achieve their goals, highlighting their indispensable role in modern society.

1. Data Analytics Tools Overview

Data analytics tools encompass a wide range of software and applications designed to facilitate data manipulation, analysis, and visualization. Commonly used tools include Excel for basic data handling and statistical analysis, offering user-friendly functionalities for data entry and graphing. For more advanced tasks, SQL (Structured Query Language) is essential for querying and managing relational databases. Programming languages like Python and R are popular for their extensive libraries and frameworks that support statistical analysis, machine learning, and data visualization. Python's libraries, such as Pandas and Matplotlib, enable users to manipulate and visualize data efficiently, while R excels in statistical modeling and advanced graphics. Data visualization tools, like Tableau and Power BI, allow users to create interactive dashboards and reports, making it easier to present insights visually. Additionally, cloud-based platforms such as Google Analytics provide tools for web data analysis, while Apache Hadoop and Spark are vital for handling large datasets in big data environments. Each of these tools plays a distinct role, with specific strengths tailored to various analytical tasks, from data cleaning to predictive modeling. The choice of tools often depends on the scale of the data, the complexity of the analysis, and the specific needs of the organization, emphasizing the importance of selecting the right tools to enhance data-driven decision-making.

Tools: R, Python, Excel, SQL

Instruments or software applications that help accomplish specific tasks or functions.

R Programming Language

R is a programming language and software environment specifically designed for statistical computing and data analysis. Developed in the early 1990s by statisticians Ross Ihaka and Robert Gentleman, R has become a vital tool in data science, statistics, and research across various fields. It offers an extensive suite of statistical techniques, including linear and nonlinear modeling, time-series analysis, and clustering. One of R's standout features is its robust data visualization capabilities, enabled by packages like ggplot2, which allow users to create intricate and informative graphics. The language is highly extensible, with thousands of packages available through the Comprehensive R Archive Network (CRAN), making it suitable for specialized analyses in areas such as finance, bioinformatics, and social sciences. R's syntax, while powerful, can present a learning curve for beginners, but its open-source nature and strong community support facilitate access to a wealth of resources and documentation. Additionally, R promotes reproducible research, enabling analysts to share their methodologies and results easily. Despite some limitations in handling large datasets compared to other languages, R remains a dominant choice for statisticians and data analysts who require advanced analytical tools and precise data representations, solidifying its position as an essential resource in today's data-driven world.

Features of R

1. **Statistical Modeling:** R is equipped with a vast array of statistical techniques, including linear and nonlinear modeling, time-series analysis, clustering, and more. This extensive library allows users to perform sophisticated analyses easily.

2. **Data Visualization:** One of R's standout features is its powerful data visualization capabilities. Libraries like **ggplot2** enable users to create complex and aesthetically pleasing graphics. This is vital for exploratory data analysis, allowing users to understand their data better.

3. **Extensibility:** R is highly extensible. Users can create their own packages, which can then be shared with the R community. This collaborative spirit fosters continuous improvement and expansion of R's capabilities.
4. **Comprehensive Package Ecosystem:** The Comprehensive R Archive Network (CRAN) hosts thousands of packages, allowing users to perform specialized analyses across various fields such as finance, bioinformatics, and social sciences.
5. **Data Handling:** R provides robust data manipulation functions, particularly through packages like **dplyr** and **tidyr**. These packages allow users to clean, transform, and reshape data efficiently.

Use Cases of R

1. **Academic Research:** R is extensively used in academic settings for statistical analysis and data visualization, enabling researchers to publish their findings with high-quality graphics and analyses.
2. **Data Science:** In the data science field, R is employed for predictive modeling, data cleaning, and visualization, making it a staple in many data-driven organizations.
3. **Finance:** Financial analysts use R for risk assessment, portfolio management, and quantitative analysis. R's statistical capabilities make it ideal for developing complex financial models.
4. **Healthcare and Bioinformatics:** R is commonly used in the healthcare industry for analyzing clinical trial data, genomics, and epidemiological studies, providing insights that drive medical research.

Advantages of R

1. **Free and Open Source:** R is available at no cost, making it accessible to a wide audience, including students and professionals in developing countries.
2. **Rich Community Support:** The R community is active and supportive, with numerous online forums, tutorials, and documentation available to help users troubleshoot issues and learn new techniques.
3. **Integration Capabilities:** R can integrate with other languages like Python and C++, as well as with databases such as SQL, enhancing its versatility.
4. **Reproducibility:** R promotes reproducible research, enabling users to document their analysis workflows and share them with others easily.

Disadvantages of R

1. **Steep Learning Curve:** While R is powerful, new users may find its syntax and functionalities challenging, especially if they lack programming experience.
2. **Performance with Large Datasets:** R can struggle with very large datasets, as

it loads data into memory, which may limit its ability to process massive datasets efficiently.

3. **Less Suitable for General Programming:** R is primarily focused on statistical analysis and may not be as effective for general-purpose programming compared to languages like Python.

Conclusion

R is a powerful tool for statistical analysis and data visualization, particularly suited for statisticians and data scientists. Its extensive libraries, strong community support, and focus on reproducibility make it an indispensable tool in various fields.

Python

Python is a versatile, high-level programming language known for its simplicity and readability, making it an ideal choice for both beginners and experienced developers. Created by Guido van Rossum and first released in 1991, Python supports multiple programming paradigms, including procedural, object-oriented, and functional programming. Its extensive standard library and a vibrant ecosystem of third-party packages enable developers to tackle a wide array of tasks, from web development and data analysis to artificial intelligence and scientific computing. Python's syntax emphasizes clarity and brevity, allowing developers to express concepts in fewer lines of code compared to many other languages. This ease of use has contributed to its widespread adoption across industries, with major companies like Google, Facebook, and Netflix utilizing it for various applications. The language is also popular in educational settings, as it provides a gentle introduction to programming concepts without the complexity of more rigid languages. Furthermore, Python's supportive community continually contributes to its growth, offering numerous resources, frameworks, and tools such as Django for web development and Pandas for data manipulation. With its ongoing evolution, including features like asynchronous programming and type hinting, Python remains a dynamic choice for modern software development, fostering innovation and collaboration in an increasingly digital world. Whether for scripting, automation, or building large-scale applications, Python's combination of power and simplicity makes it a staple in the toolkit of developers worldwide.

Features of Python

1. **Dynamic Typing:** Python is dynamically typed, meaning that you don't have to declare the type of a variable when you create it. This allows for greater flexibility in coding and enables rapid prototyping. However, this feature can also lead to runtime errors if types are not handled correctly, which is a trade-off that developers need to manage.

2. **Readability and Simplicity:** One of Python's most significant advantages is its clear and readable syntax. The use of indentation to define code blocks promotes a clean structure, making it easier to understand code at a glance.

This feature is particularly beneficial for beginners, as it reduces the cognitive load associated with understanding complex syntax.

3. **Extensive Standard Library:** Python comes with a rich standard library that provides modules and functions for various tasks, including file I/O, regular expressions, and web services. This extensive library reduces the need for external dependencies and allows developers to accomplish a wide range of tasks with minimal effort.
4. **Cross-Platform Compatibility:** Python is cross-platform, meaning that code written on one operating system can run on others with little to no modification. This feature is particularly advantageous in diverse computing environments, making Python a favourite for developers who need to deploy applications across different systems.
5. **Community and Ecosystem:** Python boasts a vibrant community that actively contributes to its growth. The Python Package Index (PyPI) hosts thousands of third-party libraries and frameworks that extend Python's capabilities. Popular libraries include NumPy for numerical computing, Pandas for data analysis, and Matplotlib for data visualization.

Use Cases of Python

1. **Web Development:** Python is widely used in web development, thanks to frameworks like Django and Flask. Django is a high-level framework that encourages rapid development and clean, pragmatic design. It comes with built-in features like authentication and an admin panel, allowing developers to focus on building applications rather than reinventing the wheel.

   Flask, on the other hand, is a micro-framework that is lightweight and modular, making it easier to customize. It is suitable for small to medium-sized applications and allows developers to choose components as needed.
2. **Data Science and Machine Learning:** Python has gained immense popularity in data science and machine learning. Libraries such as Pandas, NumPy, and SciPy provide powerful tools for data manipulation and numerical computations. For machine learning, libraries like Scikit-learn, TensorFlow, and PyTorch offer frameworks to build and train complex models efficiently.

   Python's simplicity allows data scientists to prototype quickly, facilitating experimentation and iteration, which are crucial in the data-driven world.
3. **Automation and Scripting:** Python is an excellent choice for automation and scripting tasks. Its straightforward syntax makes it easy to write scripts that can automate repetitive tasks, such as file manipulation, data entry, and web scraping. The language's compatibility with various operating systems enhances its utility in automating workflows.
4. **Game Development:** While not as prominent as other languages in game development, Python has frameworks like Pygame that allow developers to

create simple games. Its ease of use makes it suitable for educational purposes and for prototyping game concepts before moving to more complex languages like C++.

5. **Scientific Computing:** Python is widely used in scientific computing and research, especially in fields like physics, biology, and engineering. Libraries like SciPy and Matplotlib facilitate complex calculations and data visualization, enabling researchers to analyze data and present their findings effectively.
6. **Internet of Things (IoT):** With the rise of IoT devices, Python has emerged as a popular choice for programming microcontrollers and single-board computers like Raspberry Pi. Its simplicity and extensive library support make it suitable for developing applications that interact with sensors, motors, and other hardware components.

Python's Development Environment

Installation

Installing Python is straightforward. It is available for various operating systems, including Windows, macOS, and Linux. The official Python website provides downloadable installers, and many Linux distributions come with Python pre-installed. Additionally, tools like Anaconda simplify the installation of Python and its libraries, especially for data science applications.

Integrated Development Environments (IDEs): There are several IDEs and text editors available for Python development. Popular choices include:

1. **PyCharm:** A feature-rich IDE tailored for Python, offering code analysis, debugging tools, and version control integration.
2. **Visual Studio Code:** A lightweight and versatile code editor that supports Python through extensions, providing a customizable environment.
3. **Jupyter Notebook:** An interactive web application that allows users to create and share documents containing live code, equations, visualizations, and narrative text. It's particularly popular in data science and educational settings.

Best Practices in Python Programming

1. **Code Readability:** Maintaining readable code is crucial for collaboration and long-term maintenance. Using meaningful variable names, adhering to a consistent style guide (like PEP 8), and adding comments where necessary can enhance code clarity.
2. **Version Control:** Utilizing version control systems like Git is essential for tracking changes, collaborating with others, and maintaining code integrity. Platforms like GitHub and GitLab provide repositories where developers can host and share their projects.
3. **Testing:** Writing tests is an integral part of the development process. Frameworks like unittest and pytest help developers create and manage tests,

ensuring that code behaves as expected and reducing the likelihood of bugs.

4. **Documentation:** Good documentation is vital for any project. Python offers tools like Sphinx that can help generate documentation from docstrings in the code, making it easier for others (and your future self) to understand how to use the code.

The Future of Python

As technology continues to evolve, Python remains a relevant and powerful language. Its applications in emerging fields like artificial intelligence, machine learning, and big data ensure that it will remain in high demand. The Python community actively works on improving the language, with regular updates that enhance performance and introduce new features.

Additionally, the rise of educational resources and coding bootcamps focused on Python has increased accessibility, allowing more people to enter the programming field. This growing interest contributes to the continuous evolution of Python and its ecosystem.

Conclusion

Python's combination of simplicity, versatility, and a rich ecosystem makes it a leading choice for a wide range of applications. Whether you're a beginner looking to learn programming or an experienced developer working on complex projects, Python provides the tools and community support to succeed. Its applications span web development, data science, automation, and beyond, making it an invaluable language in the modern tech landscape. As Python continues to grow and adapt to new challenges, it will undoubtedly remain a cornerstone in the world of programming for years to come.

Excel

Microsoft Excel is a powerful spreadsheet application widely used for data organization, analysis, and visualization. Its user-friendly interface allows individuals and businesses to manage numerical data, perform calculations, and create charts with ease. Excel's capabilities include functions and formulas that facilitate complex computations, enabling users to manipulate data effectively. Features like pivot tables allow for dynamic data summarization, making it easier to extract insights from large datasets. Excel supports various data types, including text, numbers, and dates, and provides tools for data validation and conditional formatting to enhance data integrity and presentation. Users can automate repetitive tasks using macros, which are recorded sequences of actions that can be executed with a single command. Excel also supports collaboration through features like shared workbooks and real-time editing in Excel Online. Its extensive compatibility with other applications and formats, such as CSV and XML, makes it a versatile tool in both personal and professional settings. Whether for budgeting, project management, or statistical analysis, Excel is an essential tool for anyone needing to work with data efficiently and effectively.

Core Features of Excel

1. **Spreadsheet Basics:** Excel operates on a grid of rows and columns, creating cells where data can be entered. Each cell can hold text, numbers, or formulas, allowing for a versatile range of data manipulation. Users can format cells for better visibility and organization, utilizing options like font size, color, and borders.
2. **Formulas and Functions:** One of Excel's most powerful features is its ability to perform calculations using formulas and functions. Formulas are user-defined expressions that can involve arithmetic operations, while functions are pre-defined calculations. Excel includes a vast library of built-in functions for tasks such as:
   - **Mathematical calculations:** SUM, AVERAGE, MIN, MAX
   - **Text manipulation:** CONCATENATE, LEFT, RIGHT, TRIM
   - **Date and time functions:** TODAY, NOW, DATE, DATEDIF
   - **Logical operations:** IF, AND, OR, NOT
3. **Data Analysis Tools:** Excel offers several tools for data analysis that help users extract insights from datasets:
4. **Pivot Tables:** These allow users to summarize large amounts of data dynamically, enabling quick analysis and reporting.
5. **Data Filtering and Sorting:** Users can easily filter and sort data to find specific information, making it easier to manage large datasets.
6. **Conditional Formatting:** This feature enables users to apply formatting based on specific criteria, helping to visualize important trends and outliers in the data.
7. **Data Visualization:** Excel provides various chart types and graphical tools to visualize data effectively. Common chart types include:
8. **Column and Bar Charts:** Ideal for comparing different categories.
   - **Line Charts:** Useful for showing trends over time.
   - **Pie Charts:** Effective for displaying proportions within a whole.
   - **Scatter Plots:** Used for showing relationships between two variables.

   Users can customize charts by adjusting titles, labels, colors, and legends, making it easier to present data clearly.
9. **Automation with Macros:** Excel allows users to automate repetitive tasks through macros, which are recorded sequences of actions. Macros can be created using the built-in Macro Recorder or through Visual Basic for Applications (VBA), providing users with powerful customization options. This automation capability can save significant time and reduce the risk of errors in data processing.

10. **Collaboration and Sharing:** Excel supports collaboration features that enable multiple users to work on the same workbook simultaneously. Users can share workbooks via OneDrive or SharePoint, allowing real-time editing and updates. Comments and notes can also be added to cells, facilitating communication among team members.

11. **Importing and Exporting Data:** Excel can import data from various sources, including text files, databases, and web pages. Users can also export data in multiple formats, such as CSV, XML, and PDF. This flexibility makes Excel a versatile tool for data integration and reporting.

Applications of Excel

1. **Business and Finance:** Excel is widely used in business and finance for budgeting, forecasting, and financial analysis. Professionals leverage its calculation capabilities to create financial models, perform scenario analysis, and prepare financial statements. Excel's graphing tools help in presenting financial data visually, making it easier for stakeholders to understand.

2. **Project Management:** Excel serves as a valuable tool for project management. Users can create Gantt charts, timelines, and task lists to track project progress. Its built-in functions allow for resource allocation and budget management, facilitating efficient project planning and execution.

3. **Data Analysis and Reporting:** Data analysts frequently use Excel for data cleaning, transformation, and analysis. Its pivot tables and advanced functions make it easier to analyze trends and generate reports. Analysts can also use Excel to create dashboards that provide a visual overview of key performance indicators (KPIs).

4. **Education and Research:** In educational settings, Excel is often used for teaching mathematical concepts and data analysis techniques. Researchers utilize Excel for data collection, statistical analysis, and visualization of research findings. Its accessibility makes it a preferred choice for many academic projects.

Advanced Features of Excel

1. **Power Query:** Power Query is a powerful Excel add-in that allows users to connect, import, and transform data from various sources. It enables users to clean and reshape data easily, making it ideal for data preparation before analysis. Users can create automated data refresh processes, ensuring that reports are always up to date.

2. **Power Pivot:** Power Pivot is an advanced data modeling feature that enables users to create complex data models and perform powerful data analysis. It supports the use of Data Analysis Expressions (DAX) for creating calculated fields and measures, allowing for in-depth analysis across large datasets.

3. **What-If Analysis:** Excel's What-If Analysis tools, including Scenario Manager

and Goal Seek, allow users to forecast potential outcomes based on varying inputs. These tools are useful for financial modeling and decision-making, enabling users to explore different scenarios and their implications.

4. **Data Validation:** Data validation features in Excel help ensure the integrity of data entry by restricting input types and providing dropdown lists. This reduces errors and maintains data consistency, especially in large datasets.

Challenges and Limitations

1. **Scalability:** While Excel is powerful for many tasks, it may not handle extremely large datasets efficiently. Performance can degrade with large files, and users may encounter limitations in terms of the number of rows and columns available.
2. **Collaboration Issues:** Although Excel supports collaboration, simultaneous editing can lead to version control issues. Conflicts may arise when multiple users make changes at the same time, potentially resulting in data loss or inconsistencies.
3. **Data Security:** Excel files can be susceptible to unauthorized access, especially if sensitive data is not adequately protected. While Excel provides password protection and encryption options, users must be diligent in implementing these security measures.

Conclusion

Microsoft Excel is a versatile and powerful tool for data management, analysis, and visualization. Its extensive features, including formulas, pivot tables, and data visualization tools, make it indispensable for professionals in various fields. As organizations increasingly rely on data-driven decision-making, Excel remains a cornerstone in the toolkit of analysts, project managers, and business professionals alike. Despite its limitations, its flexibility and accessibility ensure that Excel will continue to be widely used for years to come.

Structured Query Language (SQL)

Structured Query Language (SQL) is a standard programming language used for managing and manipulating relational databases. SQL allows users to perform a variety of operations, including querying data, updating records, and managing database schemas. Its syntax is intuitive, making it accessible for both beginners and experienced developers. Common SQL commands include SELECT for retrieving data, INSERT for adding new records, UPDATE for modifying existing data, and DELETE for removing records. SQL is widely used in various database management systems (DBMS) like MySQL, PostgreSQL, Oracle, and Microsoft SQL Server. One of its strengths is the ability to join multiple tables, allowing for complex data retrieval and analysis. SQL also supports transactions, ensuring data integrity during operations. As organizations increasingly rely on data-driven decision-making, SQL has become an essential skill for data analysts, developers, and IT professionals. Its ability to handle large volumes of data efficiently makes SQL a cornerstone of modern database management and a critical tool for businesses seeking to leverage their data effectively.

Core Features of SQL

1. **Data Querying:** At the heart of SQL is its querying capability, which allows users to retrieve data from one or more tables. The basic SQL command for querying data is the SELECT statement, which can be customized with various clauses:
   - **WHERE Clause:** Filters records based on specified conditions.
   - **ORDER BY Clause:** Sorts the results based on one or more columns.
   - **GROUP BY Clause:** Groups records that have the same values in specified columns, often used with aggregate functions like COUNT, SUM, AVG, etc.
2. **Data Manipulation:** SQL provides commands for manipulating data within a database:
   - **INSERT:** Adds new records to a table.
   - **UPDATE:** Modifies existing records.
   - **DELETE:** Removes records from a table.

   These commands are fundamental for maintaining and updating database records.
3. **Data Definition:** SQL also includes commands for defining and managing database structures, known as Data Definition Language (DDL). Key DDL commands include:
   - **CREATE:** Creates a new table or database.
   - **ALTER:** Modifies an existing table structure.
   - **DROP:** Deletes a table or database.

   These commands help in structuring the database to fit the organization's data storage needs.
4. **Data Control:** SQL provides Data Control Language (DCL) commands to manage access to data within the database. These commands include:
   - **GRANT:** Gives specific privileges to users.
   - **REVOKE:** Removes previously granted privileges.

   These features are crucial for maintaining data security and integrity, ensuring that only authorized users can access sensitive information.

SQL Syntax and Structure

Basic Syntax

SQL syntax is relatively straightforward, allowing users to write queries in a natural language-like format. A typical SQL query might look like this:

```
SELECT first_name, last_name
FROM employees
WHERE department = 'Sales'
ORDER BY last_name;
```

This query retrieves the first and last names of employees in the Sales department, sorted by last name.

Joins: One of the strengths of SQL is its ability to join tables, allowing users to combine data from multiple sources. Common types of joins include:

1. **Inner Join:** Returns only the rows with matching values in both tables.
2. **Left Join:** Returns all rows from the left table and the matched rows from the right table, filling in NULLs for unmatched rows.
3. **Right Join:** Returns all rows from the right table and the matched rows from the left table.
4. **Full Outer Join:** Returns all rows when there is a match in either table.

Joins enable complex queries that aggregate data from different tables seamlessly.

Aggregate Functions: SQL provides various aggregate functions to perform calculations on sets of values:

1. **count():** Returns the number of rows that match a specified criterion.
2. **sum():** Returns the total sum of a numeric column.
3. **avg():** Returns the average value of a numeric column.
4. **min() and max():** Return the smallest and largest values in a set, respectively.

These functions are often used in conjunction with the GROUP BY clause for summarizing data.

Applications of SQL

1. **Data Management:** SQL is essential for managing databases, allowing users to store, retrieve, and manipulate large volumes of data. Its structured approach ensures that data remains organized and easily accessible.
2. **Business Intelligence and Analytics:** SQL is widely used in business intelligence (BI) applications to analyze data and generate insights. Analysts use SQL queries to extract relevant data for reporting and visualization, enabling informed decision-making.
3. **Web Development:** Many web applications rely on SQL databases to store user information, content, and application data. Frameworks like Django and Ruby on Rails integrate SQL, allowing developers to interact with databases easily.

4. **Data Warehousing:** In data warehousing, SQL is used to extract, transform, and load (ETL) data from various sources into a central repository. This process allows organizations to consolidate data for analysis and reporting.

5. **Data Science:** Data scientists often use SQL to access and analyze datasets stored in relational databases. SQL's querying capabilities allow for efficient data exploration and preprocessing before applying machine learning algorithms.

Advanced Features of SQL

1. **Stored Procedures:** Stored procedures are precompiled SQL statements that can be executed as a single unit. They enhance performance and maintainability by encapsulating complex logic within the database, allowing for reusable code.

2. **Triggers:** Triggers are special types of stored procedures that automatically execute in response to specific events on a table, such as INSERT, UPDATE, or DELETE operations. They are useful for maintaining data integrity and enforcing business rules.

3. **Views:** Views are virtual tables that present data from one or more tables in a specific format. They simplify complex queries by providing a stored representation of the data, enhancing security and access control by restricting direct access to the underlying tables.

4. **Indexing:** Indexing improves the speed of data retrieval operations on a database. By creating indexes on one or more columns, SQL databases can locate records more quickly, enhancing query performance. However, excessive indexing can slow down data modification operations.

Challenges and Limitations

1. **Complexity of Queries:** As the complexity of queries increases, the likelihood of errors also rises. Writing complex SQL statements can be challenging, requiring a deep understanding of the underlying database structure.

2. **Scalability Issues:** While SQL is effective for many applications, it may not scale well with extremely large datasets or high transaction volumes. In such cases, NoSQL databases may offer better performance and flexibility.

3. **Security Vulnerabilities:** SQL databases can be susceptible to security risks, such as SQL injection attacks. It is crucial for developers to implement proper input validation and security measures to protect sensitive data.

Conclusion

Structured Query Language (SQL) is a foundational tool for managing relational databases, providing users with powerful capabilities for data manipulation, querying, and management. Its wide range of applications, from business intelligence to web development and data science, underscores its significance in the modern data-driven landscape. As organizations continue to rely on data for decision-making, SQL remains an essential skill for professionals across various fields. Despite its challenges, the benefits of SQL in terms of data organization, analysis, and security make it a vital component of effective database management.

Comparison of Tools: R vs. Python, Excel, SQL

Table 3.1

S.No.	Features	R	Python	Excel	SQL
1.	Primary Use	Statistical analysis and visualization	General-purpose programming, data analysis	Spreadsheet management, data analysis	Data manipulation and querying
2.	Data Handling	Excellent for statistical data and complex analyses	Versatile; handles various data types and formats	Good for small to medium datasets	Optimized for large datasets in databases
3.	Libraries/Packages	Extensive libraries for stats (e.g., ggplot2, dplyr)	Rich ecosystem (e.g., Pandas, NumPy, Matplotlib)	Built-in functions and limited add-ins	No external libraries; standard SQL functions
4.	User Interface	Primarily code-based, RStudio is popular	Primarily code-based, many IDEs available (e.g., Jupyter, PyCharm)	GUI-based with drag-and-drop features	Code-based, typically executed in database management tools
5.	Learning Curve	Moderate; requires understanding of statistics	Moderate; accessible for beginners	Easy; user-friendly for basic tasks	Moderate; requires understanding of database concepts
6.	Visualization	Strong capabilities with libraries like ggplot2	Good visualization libraries (e.g., Matplotlib, Seaborn)	Basic charting tools; less flexible	Not primarily a visualization tool
7.	Statistical Analysis	Very strong; designed for statisticians	Good; libraries available, but not as specialized	Limited statistical tools	No statistical analysis features
8.	Automation	Scripting for analysis and reports	Scripting and automation with libraries	Macros for automation of tasks	Stored procedures and triggers for automation
9.	Best For	Academic research, statistical modeling	Data science, machine learning, general programming	Quick data tasks, budgeting, light analysis	Data retrieval, reporting, backend data management
10.	Cost	Free and open-source	Free and open-source	Requires a license; free alternatives exist (e.g., Google Sheets)	Free for many open-source databases; licensing may apply for commercial use

Data Visualization Tools: Tableau, Power BI, Qlik

Data visualization has become an essential component in the age of big data, enabling organizations to make informed decisions by presenting complex data in a visually appealing and understandable format. Among the myriads of tools available, Tableau, Power BI, and Qlik stand out as leaders in the data visualization space. Each of these tools offers unique features, capabilities, and advantages, catering to different business needs and user preferences. This article provides a comprehensive overview of these three powerful tools, comparing their functionalities, strengths, and potential use cases.

Tableau

Tableau is a leading data visualization tool designed to transform raw data into interactive and shareable dashboards, enabling users to analyze and interpret data easily. Founded in 2003, Tableau boasts a user-friendly, drag-and-drop interface that allows individuals to create complex visualizations without extensive technical knowledge. It connects seamlessly to various data sources, including spreadsheets, databases, and cloud services, supporting both live and extracted data. Tableau's powerful analytical capabilities include advanced calculations, trend analysis, and forecasting, making it ideal for in-depth business intelligence. Users can build interactive dashboards that facilitate data exploration through filtering, drill-downs, and dynamic visualizations. Additionally, Tableau's collaboration features allow teams to share insights securely via Tableau Server or Tableau Online. With its robust community and extensive resources, Tableau continues to be a go-to solution for organizations seeking to leverage data for informed decision-making and strategic planning.

Features of Tableau: Tableau offers a range of powerful features that make it a premier data visualization tool.

1. **User-friendly Interface:** With a drag-and-drop functionality, Tableau enables users to create complex visualizations easily, making it accessible for both beginners and experts.
2. **Data Connectivity:** It connects to numerous data sources, including spreadsheets, databases, and cloud services, allowing users to work with live data or static extracts.
3. **Advanced Analytics:** Tableau supports sophisticated analytical functions, such as trend lines, forecasts, and statistical summaries, facilitating in-depth data analysis.
4. **Interactive Dashboards:** Users can build dynamic dashboards that allow for filtering, drilling down, and navigating through visualizations, enhancing data exploration.
5. **Collaboration and Sharing:** Tableau Server and Tableau Online enable users to publish and share dashboards securely, fostering teamwork and real-time feedback.

6. **Mobile Accessibility:** Dashboards are optimized for mobile devices, allowing users to access and interact with data on the go.
7. **Extensive Visualization Options:** Tableau supports a variety of chart types bar, line, pie, scatter, maps, and more providing flexibility in how data is presented.
8. **Community and Resources:** A vibrant user community and extensive online resources provide support, tutorials, and shared best practices, enhancing user experience.

Use Cases for Tableau: Use cases of Tableau are follows:

1. **Business Intelligence:** Tableau is widely used for creating executive dashboards that provide insights into key performance indicators (KPIs) and business metrics.
2. **Sales and Marketing:** Teams use Tableau to analyze sales trends, customer segmentation, and campaign performance.
3. **Healthcare Analytics:** Tableau helps healthcare organizations visualize patient data, treatment outcomes, and operational efficiency.

Business Intelligence (BI)

Business Intelligence (BI) refers to the technologies, strategies, and practices that organizations use to collect, analyze, and present business data, enabling informed decision-making and strategic planning. BI encompasses a variety of tools and processes, including data mining, reporting, and performance management, aimed at transforming raw data into actionable insights. By utilizing data visualization techniques, dashboards, and reports, BI helps stakeholders understand complex datasets, track key performance indicators (KPIs), and identify trends and patterns. Key components of BI include data warehousing, which consolidates data from multiple sources for analysis; ETL (Extract, Transform, Load) processes that prepare data for analysis; and data analytics tools that provide insights through statistical and predictive modeling.

BI is essential for businesses in today's data-driven environment, as it enhances operational efficiency, improves customer satisfaction, and drives competitive advantage. Furthermore, BI solutions are increasingly adopting advanced technologies such as artificial intelligence and machine learning, which enable automated insights and deeper data exploration. As organizations continue to recognize the value of data, investing in robust BI systems has become crucial for achieving business objectives, fostering a data-driven culture, and ensuring long-term success in a rapidly changing marketplace.

Features of BI: Key features of Business Intelligence (BI):

1. **Data Integration:** Combines data from multiple sources, such as databases, spreadsheets, and cloud services, to provide a unified view for analysis.

2. **Data Warehousing:** Centralizes data storage, allowing for efficient querying and reporting, and ensuring data consistency across the organization.
3. **Data Visualization:** Offers tools to create interactive charts, graphs, and dashboards, making complex data easier to understand and interpret.
4. **Reporting and Dashboards:** Provides customizable reports and real-time dashboards that present key performance indicators (KPIs) and metrics at a glance.
5. **Ad Hoc Analysis:** Enables users to perform on-the-fly analysis without needing extensive technical skills, allowing for more agile decision-making.
6. **Predictive Analytics:** Uses statistical algorithms and machine learning techniques to forecast future trends and behaviors based on historical data.
7. **Data Mining:** Identifies patterns and relationships in large datasets, helping organizations uncover insights that inform strategic decisions.
8. **Collaboration Tools:** Facilitates sharing of insights and reports among team members, enhancing communication and decision-making processes.
9. **Mobile Accessibility:** Allows users to access BI tools and dashboards on mobile devices, ensuring data-driven decisions can be made anytime and anywhere.
10. **Security and Governance:** Ensures data protection through role-based access controls, auditing, and compliance measures, maintaining data integrity and security.

Use Cases for Power BI: Use cases of BI are follows:

1. **Financial Reporting:** Power BI is used to create financial dashboards that provide insights into revenue, expenses, and profitability.
2. **Retail Analytics:** Retailers leverage Power BI to analyze customer behavior, inventory levels, and sales performance.
3. **Project Management:** Power BI helps project managers visualize timelines, resource allocation, and project health.

Qlik

Qlik is a powerful data analytics platform renowned for its robust data visualization capabilities, particularly through its flagship product, Qlik Sense. Founded in 1993, Qlik is distinguished by its unique associative data model, which allows users to explore and analyze data in a non-linear fashion. This means that users can navigate freely through datasets, uncovering hidden relationships and insights without being confined to predefined queries. Qlik offers a user-friendly interface that empowers both technical and non-technical users to create interactive dashboards and reports with ease.

Key features of Qlik include extensive data connectivity, enabling integration with various data sources such as databases, spreadsheets, and cloud services. Its self-service analytics capabilities allow users to perform data preparation and analysis independently, promoting a culture of exploration and innovation. Qlik also provides advanced visualization options, with a wide variety of charts, graphs, and maps that enhance storytelling through data.

Collaboration is a key focus, with features that allow users to easily share insights and reports across teams. Additionally, Qlik incorporates artificial intelligence and augmented analytics, providing automated insights and natural language processing for intuitive data interaction. This combination of powerful features makes Qlik an ideal choice for organizations looking to leverage data for strategic decision-making and operational efficiency, fostering a data-driven culture across various industries.

Features of Qlik: Key features of Qlik are as follows:

1. **Associative Data Model:** Qlik's unique associative model allows users to explore data freely, uncovering insights and relationships without being restricted by predefined queries.
2. **Self-Service Analytics:** Users can create their own reports and dashboards without needing extensive technical skills, promoting a culture of data exploration.
3. **Data Connectivity:** Qlik connects to a wide range of data sources, including databases, cloud services, and spreadsheets, enabling comprehensive data integration.
4. **Advanced Visualization Options:** Offers a variety of charts, graphs, and maps, allowing users to present data in engaging and meaningful ways.
5. **Data Preparation:** Built-in tools facilitate data cleaning, transformation, and modeling, ensuring high-quality data for analysis.
6. **Collaborative Features:** Easy sharing of dashboards and insights enhances teamwork, allowing users to comment and discuss findings in real-time.
7. **Mobile Accessibility:** Qlik dashboards are mobile-responsive, providing access to insights anytime and anywhere.
8. **AI and Augmented Analytics:** Integrates AI-driven features, such as automated insights and natural language queries, making data interaction more intuitive.
9. **Security and Governance:** Ensures data protection with role-based access controls and compliance measures, maintaining data integrity.
10. **Scalability:** Suitable for organizations of all sizes, Qlik can handle large volumes of data and scale as business needs grow.

These features make Qlik a versatile and powerful tool for data-driven decision-making across various industries.

Use Cases of Qlik: Uses cases of Qlik are as follows:

1. **Business Intelligence:** Organizations use Qlik to create interactive dashboards and reports, enabling data-driven decision-making.
2. **Sales Analytics:** Sales teams analyze performance metrics, track sales pipelines, and identify trends to optimize sales strategies.
3. **Financial Reporting:** Finance departments leverage Qlik for budgeting, forecasting, and real-time financial analysis to improve financial planning.
4. **Supply Chain Management:** Businesses monitor inventory levels, supplier performance, and logistics to enhance supply chain efficiency.
5. **Customer Insights:** Marketers analyze customer behavior and preferences to tailor campaigns and improve customer satisfaction.

Conclusion

Qlik stands out as a robust and versatile data analytics platform that empowers organizations to harness their data effectively. By offering intuitive visualizations and powerful data integration capabilities, Qlik enables users to uncover insights, drive informed decision-making, and foster a data-driven culture. Its applications span diverse industries, from business intelligence and sales analytics to healthcare and education, making it a valuable tool for enhancing operational efficiency and strategic planning. As organizations continue to prioritize data analytics, Qlik remains a key player in transforming complex data into clear, actionable insights.

Differences Between Tableau, Power BI, Qlik

Table 3.2

S.No.	Aspect	Tableau	Power BI	Qlik
1.	Ease of Use	Intuitive, drag-and-drop interface; good for visual storytelling.	User-friendly with a familiar Microsoft interface.	Requires some technical skills, but intuitive once learned.
2.	Data Connectivity	Wide range of data connectors; excels in handling large datasets.	Strong integration with Microsoft products; numerous data sources.	Extensive connectivity options, particularly for real-time data.
3.	Visualization	Rich, customizable visualizations; great for detailed dashboards.	Good range of visualizations; strong in standard reports.	Strong in associative data exploration; effective visualizations.
4.	Deployment	On-premise and cloud options available.	Primarily cloud-based with desktop version.	On-premise, cloud, and hybrid deployment options.
5.	Collaboration	Good sharing options; requires Tableau Server for collaboration.	Excellent collaboration within Microsoft ecosystem.	Strong collaboration features with Qlik Sense.
6.	Pricing	Generally higher price point; varies by licensing.	More affordable; tiered pricing model.	Competitive pricing; flexible licensing options.

Cloud Platforms for Analytics: AWS, Azure, Google Cloud

Cloud platforms for analytics, including Amazon Web Services (AWS), Microsoft Azure, and Google Cloud Platform (GCP), provide organizations with the tools to manage and analyze large datasets without extensive on-premises infrastructure. AWS offers a comprehensive suite of services, such as Amazon Redshift for data warehousing and Amazon QuickSight for business intelligence, known for its scalability and extensive ecosystem. Microsoft Azure excels in integrating with existing Microsoft products, providing services like Azure Synapse Analytics and Azure Analysis Services, making it user-friendly for those familiar with Microsoft tools. Meanwhile, GCP is recognized for its BigQuery, a powerful serverless data warehouse that facilitates fast querying of large datasets, alongside Dataflow for data processing and Looker for business intelligence. GCP's strong focus on artificial intelligence and machine learning enhances its analytics capabilities. Each platform has distinct strengths: AWS is versatile with a wide service range, Azure offers seamless integration for Microsoft users, and GCP stands out for its performance and AI features. The choice among these platforms hinges on an organization's specific analytics needs, existing technology stack, and future goals, enabling businesses to effectively leverage their data for insights and decision-making.

Amazon Web Services (AWS)

Amazon Web Services (AWS) is a comprehensive cloud computing platform offering a wide range of services, including computing power, storage, databases, and analytics. Launched in 2006, AWS has become a leader in the cloud space, enabling organizations to scale their operations efficiently. Its core services, such as Amazon EC2 for scalable computing, Amazon S3 for storage, and Amazon RDS for managed databases, provide the flexibility and reliability needed for diverse workloads.

In the analytics domain, AWS provides powerful tools like Amazon Redshift for data warehousing, Amazon Athena for serverless querying of data in Amazon S3, and Amazon QuickSight for business intelligence. These services allow businesses to gain insights from their data quickly and at scale. AWS's extensive ecosystem also supports various third-party integrations, enhancing its capabilities further. With a pay-as-you-go pricing model and a global infrastructure, AWS is designed to meet the needs of startups, enterprises, and everything in between, making it a preferred choice for organizations looking to leverage cloud technology for innovation and growth. The challenges of AWS are as under:

1. **Complexity:** The breadth of services can be overwhelming, especially for new users. Proper management and configuration are required to optimize costs and performance.
2. **Cost Management:** While AWS offers flexibility, managing costs can be challenging without proper oversight, especially with pay-as-you-go pricing models.

AWS Fundamentals: In the Journey of AWS, understanding the key concepts such as Regions, Availability Zones, Global Network Infrastructure, etc is crucial. The fundamentals of AWS keep on maintaining the applications reliable and scalable with services globally with coming to a strategic deployment of resources for optimal performance and resilience. The following are the some of the main fundamentals of AWS:

1. **Regions:** AWS provide the services with respective division of regions. The regions are divided based on geographical areas/locations and will establish data centres. Based on need and traffic of users, the scale of data centres is depended to facilitate users with low-latencies of services.
2. **Availability Zones (AZ):** To prevent the Data centres for the Natural Calamities or any other disasters. The Datacentres are established as sub sections with isolated locations to enhance fault tolerance and disaster recovery management.
3. **Global Network Infrastructure:** AWS ensures the reliability and scalability of services through setting up its own AWS Network Infrastructure globally. It helps in better management of data transmissions for optimized performance and security reliance.

Top AWS Services: In the rapid revolution of Cloud Computing, AWS facilitates with wide variety of services respect to the fields and needs. The following are the top AWS services that are in wide usage:

1. **Amazon EC2 (Elastic Compute Cloud) :** It provides the Scalable computing power via cloud allowing the users to run applications and manage the workloads over their remotely.
2. **Amazon S3 (Simple Storage Service):** It offers scalable object Storage as a Service with high durability for storing and retrieving any amount of data.
3. **AWS Lambda:** It is a service in Serverless Architecture with Function as a Service facilitating serverless computing i.e., running the code on response to the events, the background environment management of servers is handled by AWS automatically. It helps the developers to completely focus on the logic of code build.
4. **Amazon RDS (Relational Database Service):** This is an AWS service that simplifies the management of database providing high available relational databases in the cloud.
5. **Amazon VPC (Virtual Private Cloud):** It enables the users to create isolated networks with option of public and private expose within the AWS cloud, providing safe and adaptable configurations of their resources.

AWS Cloud Computing Models: There are three cloud computing models available on AWS.

1. **Infrastructure as a Service (IaaS):** It is the basic building block of cloud IT. It generally provides access to data storage space, networking features, and

computer hardware (virtual or dedicated hardware). It is highly flexible and gives management controls over the IT resources to the developer. For example, VPC, EC2, EBS.

2. **Platform as a Service (PaaS):** This is a type of service where AWS manages the underlying infrastructure (usually operating system and hardware). This helps the developer to be more efficient as they do not have to worry about undifferentiated heavy lifting required for running the applications such as capacity planning, software maintenance, resource procurement, patching, etc., and focus more on deployment and management of the applications. For example, RDS, EMR, ElasticSearch.
3. **Software as a Service (SaaS):** It is a complete product that usually runs on a browser. It primarily refers to end-user applications. It is run and managed by the service provider. The end-user only has to worry about the application of the software suitable to its needs. For example, Saleforce.com, Web-based email, Office 365.

Microsoft Azure

Microsoft Azure is a comprehensive cloud computing platform that offers a wide range of services designed to help businesses build, deploy, and manage applications and services through Microsoft-managed data centers. Launched in 2010, Azure supports various programming languages, frameworks, and tools, making it versatile for developers and IT professionals. Key services include Azure Virtual Machines for scalable computing, Azure Blob Storage for unstructured data, and Azure SQL Database for managed relational database services. Azure also excels in analytics and business intelligence, featuring Azure Synapse Analytics for integrated data analytics, Power BI for data visualization, and Azure Machine Learning for building and deploying machine learning models. Its seamless integration with Microsoft products, such as Office 365 and Dynamics 365, enhances its appeal for organizations already invested in the Microsoft ecosystem. Furthermore, Azure provides strong hybrid cloud capabilities, allowing businesses to connect their on-premises infrastructure with the cloud, thereby ensuring flexibility and scalability. Security is a priority for Azure, with built-in features and compliance with numerous industry standards. With a pay-as-you-go pricing model and a vast global network of data centers, Microsoft Azure enables organizations to innovate rapidly while managing costs effectively, making it a preferred choice for enterprises looking to leverage cloud technology for digital transformation. The challenges of Microsoft Azure are as under:

1. **Learning Curve:** While user-friendly, some of Azure's advanced features may require a learning curve for users unfamiliar with cloud technologies.
2. **Service Limits:** Some services may have limitations in terms of scalability or features compared to competitors like AWS.

How does Microsoft Azure Work?

It is a private and public cloud platform that helps developers and IT professionals build deploy and manage applications. It uses the technology known as virtualization. Virtualization separates the tight coupling between the hardware and the operating system using an abstraction layer called a hypervisor. Hypervisor emulates all the functions of a computer in a virtual machine, it can run multiple virtual machines at the same time and each virtual machine can run any operating system, such as Windows or Linux.

Azure takes this virtualization technique and repeats it on a massive scale in the data center owned by Microsoft. Each data center has many racks filled with servers and each server includes a hypervisor to run multiple virtual machines. The network switch provides connectivity to all those servers.

Types of Azure Services: Microsoft Azure is a cloud computing platform which offers the following types of services:

1. **Infrastructure as a service (IaaS):** Infrastructure as a Service (IaaS) provides virtualized computing resources over the internet. In this model, cloud providers offer essential infrastructure components, such as virtual machines, storage, networks, and servers, allowing organizations to rent these resources instead of investing in physical hardware. Users can scale resources up or down based on demand, optimizing costs and enhancing flexibility. IaaS is particularly beneficial for businesses that require high-performance computing capabilities without the overhead of managing physical servers. Common use cases include hosting websites, storing large datasets, and running complex applications. Prominent IaaS providers include Amazon Web Services (AWS) EC2, Microsoft Azure Virtual Machines, and Google Cloud Compute Engine. IaaS enables businesses to focus on development and innovation, as they can leverage the underlying infrastructure managed by the provider, which also ensures security, backup, and disaster recovery services. This model supports various operating systems and software applications, offering businesses the freedom to customize their environments according to specific needs.

2. **Platform as a service (PaaS):** Platform as a Service (PaaS) offers a cloud-based environment for developers to build, deploy, and manage applications without the complexity of managing underlying infrastructure. PaaS provides a complete platform, including hardware, software, and tools necessary for application development. This model enables developers to focus on coding and application logic rather than dealing with server management, storage, or network configurations. PaaS solutions often include integrated development environments (IDEs), databases, middleware, and APIs, streamlining the development process and enhancing collaboration among teams. Popular PaaS providers include Google App Engine, Microsoft Azure App Service, and Heroku. PaaS is ideal for developing web applications, mobile apps, and microservices, offering scalability and flexibility as applications grow. Additionally, it allows for rapid prototyping and deployment, reducing time-to-market. By utilizing PaaS, organizations can accelerate innovation and

optimize resources, as they can easily integrate new technologies and services into their applications without extensive infrastructure management.

3. **Software as a service (SaaS):** Software as a Service (SaaS) delivers software applications over the internet on a subscription basis, eliminating the need for users to install and maintain software locally. In this model, applications are hosted in the cloud and accessed through web browsers, making them available from any device with internet connectivity. SaaS providers manage all aspects of the software, including updates, security, and infrastructure, allowing users to focus on utilizing the application rather than managing it. Common examples of SaaS include Microsoft 365, Google Workspace, Salesforce, and Dropbox. SaaS is particularly beneficial for businesses seeking cost-effective solutions, as it typically operates on a pay-as-you-go model, reducing upfront costs associated with software purchases and maintenance. Additionally, SaaS applications often include collaboration features and scalability, allowing organizations to easily add or remove users as needed. This flexibility supports remote work and enhances productivity, making SaaS an increasingly popular choice for businesses of all sizes across various industries.

Use Cases of Microsoft Azure: Following are the some of the use cases of Microsoft Azure:

1. **Deployment Of applications:** You can develop and deploy the application in the azure cloud by using the service called Azure App Service and Azure Functions after deploying the applications end users can access it.
2. **Identity and Access Management:** The application and data which is deployed and stored in the Microsoft Azure can be secured with the help of Identity and Access Management. It's commonly used for single sign-on, multi-factor authentication, and identity governance.
3. **Data Storage and Databases:** You can store the data in Microsoft azure in service like blob storage for unstructured data, table storage for NoSQL data, file storage, and Azure SQL Database for relational databases. The service can be scaled depending on the amount of data we are getting.
4. **DevOps and Continuous Integration/Continuous Deployment (CI/CD):** Azure DevOps will provide some tools like including version control, build automation, release management, and application monitoring.

Microsoft Azure Services: some of the services Microsoft Azure offers:

1. **Compute:** Includes Virtual Machines, Virtual Machine Scale Sets, Functions for serverless computing, Batch for containerized batch workloads, Service Fabric for microservices and container orchestration, and Cloud Services for building cloud-based apps and APIs.
2. **Networking:** With Azure, you can use a variety of networking tools, like the Virtual Network, which can connect to on-premise data centers; Load Balancer;

Application Gateway; VPN Gateway; Azure DNS for domain hosting, Content Delivery Network, Traffic Manager, ExpressRoute dedicated private network fibre connections; and Network Watcher monitoring and diagnostics

3. **Storage:** Includes Blob, Queue, File, and Disk Storage, as well as a Data Lake Store, Backup, and Site Recovery, among others.
4. **Web + Mobile:** Creating Web + Mobile applications is very easy as it includes several services for building and deploying applications.
5. **Containers:** Azure has a property that includes Container Service, which supports Kubernetes, DC/OS or Docker Swarm, and Container Registry, as well as tools for microservices.
6. **Databases:** Azure also included several SQL-based databases and related tools.
7. **Data + Analytics:** Azure has some big data tools like HDInsight for Hadoop Spark, R Server, HBase, and Storm clusters
8. **AI + Cognitive Services:** With Azure developing applications with artificial intelligence capabilities, like the Computer Vision API, Face API, Bing Web Search, Video Indexer, and Language Understanding Intelligent.
9. **Internet of Things:** Includes IoT Hub and IoT Edge services that can be combined with a variety of machine learning, analytics, and communications services.
10. **Security + Identity:** Includes Security Center, Azure Active Directory, Key Vault, and Multi-Factor Authentication Services.
11. **Developer Tools:** Includes cloud development services like Visual Studio Team Services, Azure DevTest Labs, HockeyApp mobile app deployment and monitoring, Xamarin cross-platform mobile development, and more.

Google Cloud

Google Cloud Platform (GCP) is a robust cloud computing service offered by Google, designed to provide a wide array of services for computing, storage, data analytics, and machine learning. Launched in 2008, GCP leverages Google's extensive infrastructure to deliver high-performance solutions that cater to businesses of all sizes. Key offerings include Google Compute Engine for scalable virtual machines, Google Cloud Storage for secure and scalable data storage, and BigQuery for powerful data analytics and real-time insights. GCP also excels in machine learning capabilities through services like TensorFlow and Google AI Platform, allowing organizations to build and deploy machine learning models easily. Its integration with popular tools such as Google Workspace enhances productivity by enabling seamless collaboration. GCP's serverless options, such as Google Cloud Functions, allow developers to execute code without managing servers, promoting agility and innovation. Security is a priority for GCP, which complies with various industry standards and offers robust security features to protect user data. With a pay-as-you-go pricing model and a commitment to sustainability, GCP provides organizations with flexible and cost-effective cloud solutions. By leveraging Google Cloud, businesses can harness advanced analytics and AI capabilities to drive innovation, streamline operations, and enhance their digital transformation journey. Strengths of Google Cloud Platform are as under:

1. **Performance and Scalability:** GCP is known for its exceptional performance and scalability. With its global network of data centers and the ability to scale resources on demand, organizations can easily accommodate varying workloads and traffic patterns. BigQuery, for instance, enables fast querying of large datasets, making it ideal for analytics.
2. **Integration with Google Services:** GCP seamlessly integrates with other Google services, such as Google Workspace and YouTube, enhancing productivity and collaboration. This integration provides a unified experience for users already familiar with Google products.
3. **Advanced Machine Learning Capabilities:** GCP's strong focus on machine learning and artificial intelligence sets it apart from competitors. With services like AutoML and TensorFlow, organizations can leverage advanced analytics and machine learning capabilities to drive innovation and improve decision-making.
4. **Strong Security Measures:** GCP implements a comprehensive security framework, including data encryption, IAM, and compliance with industry standards. These measures ensure that organizations can trust GCP with their sensitive data while adhering to regulatory requirements.

Architecture of Google Cloud Platform

1. **Global Infrastructure:** GCP operates on a robust global infrastructure designed to ensure high availability and low latency. The key components include:
   - **Regions:** GCP has multiple geographic regions worldwide, each comprising several data centers. Each region is independent, allowing for data redundancy and compliance with local regulations.
   - **Zones:** Within each region, GCP has multiple zones, which are isolated from each other to protect against failures. This design enables high availability and resilience for applications.
   - **Edge Network:** GCP benefits from Google's global private fiber-optic network, which enhances performance and reliability by optimizing data routes and minimizing latency.
2. **Core Services:** GCP provides a diverse set of core services categorized into several areas:
   - **Compute Services:** Google Compute Engine (GCE) offers virtual machines (VMs) with customizable configurations, while Google Kubernetes Engine (GKE) enables container orchestration for scalable applications. App Engine provides a fully managed platform for building applications without the need to manage the underlying infrastructure.

- **Storage Services:** Google Cloud Storage (GCS) provides scalable object storage for unstructured data. Google Persistent Disk offers block storage for VMs, and Google Cloud SQL supports managed relational databases.
- **Networking Services:** Google Virtual Private Cloud (VPC) allows users to create isolated networks. Google Cloud Load Balancing distributes traffic across multiple instances, and Cloud CDN accelerates content delivery through its extensive edge network.
- **Data Analytics:** BigQuery is GCP's serverless data warehouse designed for big data analytics. Google Cloud Dataflow enables stream and batch data processing, while Google Cloud Pub/Sub facilitates real-time messaging between applications.
- **Machine Learning and AI:** GCP offers TensorFlow, an open-source machine learning framework, and Google AI Platform for developing and deploying machine learning models. AutoML allows users with limited ML expertise to create custom models tailored to their data.

3. **Security and Compliance:** GCP prioritizes security and compliance, implementing robust measures to protect data. Features include:
   - **Identity and Access Management (IAM):** IAM allows organizations to control who can access resources and what actions they can perform, enabling fine-grained access control.
   - **Encryption:** Data is encrypted both at rest and in transit, ensuring that sensitive information is protected. GCP manages encryption keys, or users can manage their own keys through Cloud Key Management.
   - **Compliance Certifications:** GCP complies with various industry standards and regulations, including GDPR, HIPAA, and PCI DSS, making it suitable for industries with strict compliance requirements.

Key Services of Google Cloud

1. **Compute Services:** Google Cloud's compute services include Google Compute Engine for scalable virtual machines, Google Kubernetes Engine for container orchestration, and Google App Engine for fully managed application hosting. These services enable businesses to deploy, manage, and scale applications efficiently while optimizing performance and resource utilization in a flexible cloud environment.
   - **Google Compute Engine (GCE):** GCE provides scalable and flexible virtual machines that can run various workloads. Users can choose from predefined machine types or customize configurations to meet specific requirements. GCE also supports live migration of VMs, enhancing availability.
   - **Google Kubernetes Engine (GKE):** GKE simplifies the deployment, management, and scaling of containerized applications using Kubernetes.

It automates key tasks such as load balancing, scaling, and upgrades, allowing developers to focus on building applications.

- **Google App Engine:** App Engine is a fully managed platform for developing and hosting web applications. It automatically scales applications based on traffic and supports multiple programming languages, making it easy to build and deploy applications without managing infrastructure.

2. **Storage Services:** Google Cloud Storage provides scalable object storage for unstructured data, offering multiple classes for cost optimization. Google Persistent Disk delivers high-performance block storage for virtual machines, while Google Cloud SQL offers fully managed relational databases, simplifying maintenance and enhancing scalability for applications requiring structured data storage.
   - **Google Cloud Storage (GCS):** GCS offers a unified object storage solution for various data types, including images, videos, and backups. It provides multiple storage classes, allowing users to optimize costs based on data access patterns.
   - **Google Persistent Disk:** This service offers durable and high-performance block storage for VMs. It supports automatic backups and snapshots, ensuring data durability and recoverability.
   - **Google Cloud SQL:** Cloud SQL is a fully managed relational database service that supports popular databases like MySQL and PostgreSQL. It automates tasks such as patch management, backups, and replication, allowing users to focus on application development.
3. **Networking Services:** Google Cloud's networking services include Virtual Private Cloud (VPC) for isolated networks, enabling customizable IP address ranges and firewall rules. Cloud Load Balancing distributes incoming traffic for high availability, while Cloud CDN accelerates content delivery through its extensive edge network, reducing latency and enhancing user experience.
   - **Google Virtual Private Cloud (VPC):** VPC allows users to create isolated networks within GCP, providing control over IP address ranges, subnets, and firewall rules. It enables secure communication between resources while connecting to on-premises environments.
   - **Cloud Load Balancing:** This service distributes incoming traffic across multiple instances, improving application reliability and performance. It supports both HTTP(S) and TCP/UDP traffic, enabling seamless scaling.
   - **Cloud CDN:** Google Cloud CDN accelerates content delivery by caching content at edge locations around the world. This reduces latency and improves user experiences for applications requiring low-latency access to static and dynamic content.

4. **Data Analytics Services:** Google Cloud's data analytics services feature BigQuery, a serverless data warehouse enabling fast SQL queries on large datasets. Google Cloud Dataflow supports real-time and batch processing, allowing streamlined data workflows, while Google Cloud Pub/Sub facilitates real-time messaging and event-driven architectures, enhancing application responsiveness and scalability.
   - **BigQuery:** BigQuery is a serverless data warehouse that allows users to analyze large datasets using SQL queries. Its architecture supports high-speed queries and integrates with various data sources, enabling real-time analytics.
   - **Google Cloud Dataflow:** Dataflow is a fully managed service for stream and batch processing. It allows users to create data processing pipelines using Apache Beam, simplifying the management of data workflows.
   - **Google Cloud Pub/Sub:** This messaging service enables real-time messaging between applications, facilitating event-driven architectures and decoupled systems. It supports asynchronous communication and helps build scalable applications.
5. **Machine Learning and AI Services:** Google Cloud offers powerful machine learning services, including the AI Platform for developing and deploying models and AutoML for users with limited ML expertise to create custom models. TensorFlow provides a robust framework for building machine learning applications, facilitating advanced analytics and AI-driven insights across various industries.
   - **Google AI Platform:** This platform provides tools for developing and deploying machine learning models, from data preparation to training and serving. It integrates with TensorFlow, making it easy to build sophisticated models.
   - **AutoML:** AutoML enables users with limited machine learning expertise to create custom models tailored to their specific data. It provides a user-friendly interface for training models on various tasks, such as image classification and natural language processing.
   - **TensorFlow:** An open-source machine learning framework, TensorFlow is widely used for building and training machine learning models. GCP offers optimized environments for running TensorFlow workloads efficiently.

Use Cases of Google Cloud Platform: Uses cases of Google Cloud are as under:

1. **Data Analytics:** Organizations utilize GCP for big data analytics, leveraging BigQuery to analyze vast amounts of data quickly. Retail companies, for example, use BigQuery to gain insights into customer behavior and optimize inventory management.
2. **Application Development:** Developers use Google App Engine and GKE to

build and deploy applications without managing infrastructure. Startups can quickly launch products while focusing on coding and user experience, accelerating time-to-market.

3. **Machine Learning:** Companies in various industries employ GCP's machine learning services to create predictive models. For instance, financial institutions use GCP to develop fraud detection systems, leveraging TensorFlow for model training.
4. **Media and Entertainment:** Media companies utilize GCP to manage content delivery and streaming. With Cloud CDN and Compute Engine, they can efficiently serve media content to global audiences while maintaining performance.

Differences Between AWS, Microsoft Azure and Goggle Cloud

Table 3.3

S.No.	Aspect	AWS	Microsoft Azure	Goggle Cloud
1.	Launch Year	2006	2010	2008
2.	Market Share	Largest cloud service provider	Second largest	Third largest
3.	Core Services	Extensive range (compute, storage, databases)	Strong integration with Microsoft products	Focus on big data and machine learning
4.	Ease of Use	Complex, extensive options	User-friendly for Microsoft users	Simple interface, strong documentation
5.	Hybrid Cloud	AWS Outposts for hybrid setups	Strong hybrid capabilities with Azure Arc	Anthos for managing hybrid environments
6.	AI/ML Services	Amazon SageMaker	Azure Machine Learning	Google AI Platform and AutoML
7.	Pricing Model	Pay-as-you-go with Reserved Instances	Pay-as-you-go with various discounts	Pay-as-you-go with sustained use discounts
8.	Compliance & Security	Extensive compliance certifications	Strong compliance with enterprise features	Robust security features and compliance standards

2. Big Data Technologies

Big data technology is defined as software-utility. This technology is primarily designed to analyze, process and extract information from a large data set and a huge set of extremely complex structures. This is very difficult for traditional data processing software to deal with. Among the larger concepts of rage in technology, big data technologies are widely associated with many other technologies such as deep learning, machine learning, artificial intelligence (AI), and Internet of Things (IoT) that are massively augmented. In combination with these technologies, big data technologies are focused on analyzing and handling large amounts of real-time data and batch-related data.

Introduction to Big Data and Its Characteristics

Big Data technologies encompass a diverse set of tools and frameworks designed to manage, process, and analyze vast volumes of data generated at high speeds from various sources. Big Data deals with large data sets or deals with the deals with complexities handled by traditional data processing application software. It has three key concepts like volume, variety, and velocity. In volume, determining the size of data and in variety, data will be categorized means will determine the type of data like images, PDF, audio, video, etc. and in velocity, speed of data transfer or speed of processing and analyzing data will be considered. Big data works on large data sets, and it can be unstructured, semi-structured, and structured. It includes the following key parameters while considering big data like capturing data, search, data storage, sharing of data, transfer, data analysis, visualization, and querying, etc. In the case of analyzing, it will be used in A/B testing, machine learning, and natural language processing, etc. In the case of visualization, it will be used in charts, graphs, etc. In big data, the following technology will be used in Business intelligence, cloud computing, and databases, etc.

The Big Data ecosystem comprises a range of technologies and tools designed to handle various aspects of data management, processing, and analysis. Below are some of the key categories of Big Data technologies.

1. **Data Storage Technologies:** Data storage technologies include Hadoop Distributed File System (HDFS) for distributed file storage, and NoSQL databases like MongoDB and Cassandra for handling unstructured data. These solutions provide scalability and flexibility, allowing organizations to store large volumes of diverse data efficiently while ensuring accessibility and reliability.

   - **Hadoop Distributed File System (HDFS):** HDFS is the primary storage system for Hadoop, designed to store large files across multiple machines. It provides high-throughput access to application data and is highly fault-tolerant, ensuring data reliability.
   - **NoSQL Databases:** NoSQL databases are designed to handle unstructured and semi-structured data. They offer flexibility and scalability compared to traditional relational databases. Common NoSQL databases include:

     MongoDB: A document-oriented database that stores data in flexible, JSON-like documents.

     Cassandra: A distributed database that excels in handling high write and read volumes, designed for scalability and high availability.

     HBase: A column-family NoSQL database built on top of HDFS, suitable for real-time read/write access to large datasets.

2. **Data Processing Technologies:** Data processing technologies encompass frameworks like Apache Hadoop for batch processing and Apache Spark for

in-memory processing, enabling fast analytics. These tools allow organizations to process large datasets across distributed systems, facilitating efficient data manipulation and analysis, which is crucial for extracting insights from Big Data.

- **Apache Hadoop:** Apache Hadoop is an open-source framework that enables distributed storage and processing of large datasets across clusters of computers. Its key components include:

  Hadoop Common: The common utilities and libraries that support other Hadoop modules.

  Hadoop MapReduce: A programming model for processing large datasets in parallel.

  Hadoop YARN: A resource management layer that schedules and manages resources across the cluster.

- **Apache Spark:** Apache Spark is an open-source, distributed computing system that provides an alternative to Hadoop's MapReduce model. It offers in-memory processing, which significantly speeds up data processing tasks. Spark supports multiple programming languages, including Python, Java, and Scala, and includes libraries for machine learning (MLlib), graph processing (GraphX), and SQL querying (Spark SQL).

3. **Data Analytics Technologies:** Data analytics technologies include Apache Hive for SQL-like querying of large datasets and Apache Flink for real-time data processing. These tools enable organizations to analyze and derive insights from massive amounts of data, supporting informed decision-making and enhancing business intelligence capabilities through comprehensive analytics.

   - **Apache Hive:** Apache Hive is a data warehouse infrastructure built on top of Hadoop that enables SQL-like querying of large datasets. It allows users to write queries in HiveQL, which is then translated into MapReduce jobs for execution on Hadoop.
   - **Apache Pig:** Apache Pig is a high-level platform for creating programs that run on Hadoop. It provides a scripting language called Pig Latin, which simplifies data manipulation tasks by abstracting the complexity of MapReduce.
   - **Apache Flink:** Apache Flink is a stream processing framework that enables real-time data processing and analytics. It supports both batch and stream processing, providing low-latency data handling and
   - advanced event-time processing capabilities.

4. **Data Visualization Technologies:** Data visualization technologies, such as Tableau and Power BI, allow users to create interactive dashboards and visual reports from complex data. These tools transform raw data into intuitive visual

formats, making it easier for stakeholders to understand trends, patterns, and insights, thus facilitating better data-driven decisions.

- **Tableau:** Tableau is a powerful data visualization tool that allows users to create interactive and shareable dashboards. It connects to various data sources, enabling users to explore and analyze data visually without extensive coding.
- **Power BI:** Microsoft Power BI is a business analytics service that provides interactive visualizations and business intelligence capabilities. Users can create reports and dashboards from multiple data sources, facilitating data-driven decision-making.

Applications of Big Data Technologies: Key applications of Big Data Teachnologies are as under:

1. **Healthcare:** Big Data technologies are transforming the healthcare industry by enabling organizations to analyze patient data, monitor public health trends, and improve treatment outcomes. For instance, predictive analytics can identify potential health risks, allowing for proactive interventions.
2. **Retail:** Retailers leverage Big Data to analyze customer purchasing behavior, optimize inventory management, and enhance the shopping experience. Personalized marketing campaigns, informed by customer data analysis, can drive sales and improve customer loyalty.
3. **Finance:** In the finance sector, Big Data technologies are used for fraud detection, risk assessment, and algorithmic trading. By analyzing transaction patterns and market data, financial institutions can make more informed investment decisions and identify fraudulent activities more effectively.
4. **Transportation and Logistics:** Big Data plays a crucial role in optimizing transportation and logistics operations. Companies can analyze traffic patterns, weather data, and delivery routes to improve efficiency, reduce costs, and enhance customer satisfaction.
5. **Telecommunications:** Telecom companies use Big Data to monitor network performance, manage customer churn, and optimize service delivery. By analyzing call data records and customer interactions, providers can enhance service quality and customer retention.

Future Trends in Big Data Technologies

1. **Real-time Analytics:** The demand for real-time analytics is expected to grow as organizations seek to make timely decisions based on current data. Technologies like Apache Kafka and Apache Flink will play a significant role in enabling real-time data processing.
2. **Artificial Intelligence and Machine Learning Integration**: Integrating Big Data technologies with AI and machine learning will enhance predictive

analytics capabilities. Organizations will increasingly use advanced algorithms to derive insights from large datasets, improving decision-making processes.

3. **Edge Computing:** As IoT devices proliferate, edge computing will gain traction, allowing data processing to occur closer to the source. This approach reduces latency and bandwidth usage, enabling faster insights from real-time data streams.

4. **Enhanced Data Privacy Measures:** With growing concerns about data privacy, organizations will invest in technologies that ensure data protection and compliance with regulations. Techniques like differential privacy and encryption will become standard practices in Big Data analytics.

Conclusion

Big Data technologies are revolutionizing the way organizations manage, process, and analyze data. By leveraging these technologies, businesses can unlock valuable insights, enhance operational efficiency, and drive innovation. Despite the challenges associated with Big Data, the future holds immense potential for growth and advancement in this field. As organizations continue to adapt to the evolving data landscape, embracing Big Data technologies will be crucial for staying competitive and achieving success in the digital age.

Characteristics of Big Data Technologies

Big Data technology is reshaping industries by enabling organizations to process, analyze, and derive insights from vast and complex datasets. Understanding its characteristics is crucial for leveraging its potential effectively. This exploration delves into the defining features of Big Data technology, often encapsulated in the "Three Vs" and additional characteristics that provide a comprehensive view of its nature.

1. **Volume:** Volume refers to the sheer amount of data generated and collected by organizations. This data can range from terabytes to petabytes and even exabytes, far exceeding what traditional data processing tools can handle. Handling such vast quantities of data requires robust storage solutions. Technologies like Hadoop Distributed File System (HDFS) and cloud-based storage systems (e.g., Amazon S3, Google Cloud Storage) provide scalable options to store and retrieve large datasets efficiently. Organizations must also ensure that their infrastructure can handle increasing data loads over time.

   Example: Consider a social media platform like Facebook, which generates petabytes of data daily from user interactions, posts, and multimedia uploads. The ability to store and process this volume of data is essential for maintaining user engagement and delivering personalized experiences.

2. **Velocity:** Velocity refers to the speed at which data is generated, processed, and analyzed. In the modern digital landscape, data streams in real-time or near-real-time, necessitating immediate processing to extract actionable insights. Organizations must implement technologies capable of real-time data

processing, such as Apache Kafka for streaming data or Apache Flink for real-time analytics. The ability to process data quickly can significantly impact decision-making, particularly in industries where timing is crucial, such as finance, e-commerce, and healthcare.

Example: In the financial sector, stock market data is generated in milliseconds. Trading algorithms rely on real-time data analytics to execute trades based on current market conditions. Delays in processing this data can lead to substantial financial losses.

3. **Variety:** Variety highlights the diverse types of data organizations encounter, including structured, semi-structured, and unstructured data. This characteristic reflects the multifaceted nature of data in the digital age. Organizations need to adopt flexible data management and integration strategies to handle this variety. Traditional databases often struggle with unstructured data, leading to the rise of NoSQL databases like MongoDB and Cassandra, which can accommodate diverse data formats.

   Example: In a retail setting, data may come from various sources: structured data from sales transactions, semi-structured data from customer reviews, and unstructured data from social media interactions. Successfully integrating these data types can provide a holistic view of customer behavior and preferences.

4. **Veracity:** Veracity refers to the accuracy and reliability of the data. As organizations collect vast amounts of information, ensuring its quality becomes paramount. Inaccurate data can lead to misleading insights and poor decision-making. Organizations must implement robust data governance practices, including data validation, cleaning, and ongoing monitoring. This is critical to maintaining data integrity and ensuring that insights drawn from the data are trustworthy.

   Example: In marketing analytics, if a company uses outdated or incorrect customer data, it may misidentify target segments, leading to ineffective marketing campaigns. Ensuring data veracity is essential for achieving successful outcomes.

5. **Value:** Value refers to the actionable insights derived from analyzing Big Data. Ultimately, the goal of collecting and processing data is to extract value that drives business decisions and enhances operational efficiencies. Organizations must focus on building analytics capabilities that not only process data but also convert it into actionable insights. This may involve employing data scientists and analysts skilled in extracting value from complex datasets.

   Example: A telecommunications company might analyze call data records to identify patterns in customer behavior, leading to targeted marketing strategies that improve customer retention and enhance revenue.

6. **Variability:** Variability describes the changing nature of data and its meanings. Data can fluctuate in terms of structure, quality, and time, complicating analysis and processing. Organizations must be adaptable in their data handling practices. For example, seasonal trends may affect customer purchasing behavior, and data analytics models need to account for these variations to provide accurate predictions.

   Example: Retailers often experience variability in sales data based on seasonal trends, promotions, and market conditions. Understanding this variability allows companies to adjust inventory and marketing strategies accordingly.

7. **Complexity:** Complexity refers to the intricate relationships between various data sources, types, and formats. As data ecosystems grow, managing and integrating these diverse elements becomes increasingly challenging. Organizations need sophisticated data management and integration frameworks that can handle complex data relationships. This often involves the use of data lakes and advanced data integration tools that streamline data ingestion from multiple sources.

   Example: A healthcare organization may collect data from various sources, including electronic health records, wearable devices, and patient surveys. The complexity of integrating these diverse data sources is essential for gaining a comprehensive understanding of patient health.

8. **Scalability:** Scalability refers to the ability of a system to grow and manage increasing amounts of data effectively. As organizations collect more data over time, their infrastructure must be capable of scaling up to accommodate this growth. Cloud computing technologies, such as AWS, Azure, and Google Cloud, provide scalable solutions that allow organizations to adjust their storage and processing capacities as needed. This flexibility is crucial for managing fluctuating data loads.

   Example: An online streaming service like Netflix experiences fluctuating data loads due to varying user traffic. Their cloud-based architecture enables them to scale their infrastructure up or down to meet demand without sacrificing performance.

Conclusion

Understanding the characteristics of Big Data technology volume, velocity, variety, veracity, value, variability, complexity, and scalability is essential for organizations seeking to leverage data for competitive advantage. Each characteristic presents unique challenges and opportunities that require tailored strategies and technologies. By effectively managing these aspects, organizations can harness the full potential of Big Data, driving innovation and enhancing decision-making processes in an increasingly data-driven world. As Big Data technology continues to evolve, staying informed about these characteristics will be critical for success in the digital landscape.

Some Popular Big Data Technologies: Fig.3.2 shows big data technologies, each in detail are as follows:

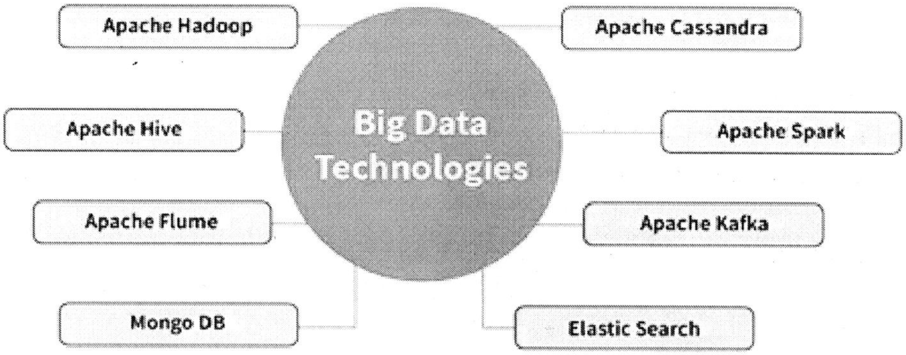

Fig.3.2

1. **Apache Cassandra:** It is one of the No-SQL databases which is highly scalable and has high availability. In this, we can replicate data across multiple data centers. Replication across multiple data centers is supported. In Cassandra, fault tolerance is one of the big factors in which failed nodes can be easily replaced without any downtime.
2. **Apache Hadoop:** Hadoop is one of the most widely used big data technology that is used to handle large-scale data, large file systems by using Hadoop file system which is called HDFS, and parallel processing like features using the MapReduce framework of Hadoop. Hadoop is a scalable system that helps to provide a scalable solution capable of handling large capacities and capabilities. For example: If you see real use cases like NextBio is using Hadoop MapReduce and HBase to process multi-terabyte data sets off the human genome.
3. **Apache Hive:** It is used for data summarization and ad hoc querying which means for querying and analyzing Big Data easily. It is built on top of Hadoop for providing data summarization, ad-hoc queries, and the analysis of large datasets using SQL-like language called HiveQL. It is not a relational database and not a language for real-time queries. It has many features like: designed for OLAP, SQL type language called HiveQL, fast, scalable, and extensible.
4. **Apache Flume:** It is a distributed and reliable system that is used to collect, aggregate, and move large amounts of log data from many data sources toward a centralized data store.
5. **Apache Spark:** The main objective of spark for speeding up the Hadoop computational computing software process, and it was introduced by Apache Software Foundation. Apache Spark can work independently because it has its own cluster management, and it is not an updated or modified version of Hadoop and if you delve deeper then you can say it is just one way to implement Spark with Hadoop. The Main idea to implement Spark with

Hadoop in two ways is for storage and processing. So, in two ways Spark uses Hadoop for storage purposes just because Spark has its own cluster management computation. In Spark, it includes interactive queries and stream processing, and in-memory cluster computing is one of the key features.

6. **Apache Kafka:** It is a distributed publish-subscribe messaging system and more specifically you can say it has a robust queue that allows you to handle a high volume of data, and you can pass the messages from one point to another as you can say from one sender to receiver. You can perform message computation in both offline and online modes, it is suitable for both. To prevent data loss Kafka messages are replicated within the cluster. For real-time streaming data analysis, it integrates Apache Storm and Spark and is built on top of the ZooKeeper synchronization service.
7. **MongoDB:** It is based on cross-platform and works on a concept like collection and document. It has document-oriented storage that means data will be stored in the form of JSON form. It can be an index on any attribute. It has features like high availability, replication, rich queries, support by MongoDB, Auto-Sharding, and Fast in-place updates.
8. **ElasticSearch:** It is a real-time distributed system, and open-source full-text search and analytics engine. It has features like scalability factor is high and scalable structured and unstructured data up to petabytes, it can be used as a replacement of MongoDB, RavenDB which is based on document-based storage. To improve the search performance, it uses denormalization. If you see the real use case then it is an enterprise search engine and big organizations using it, for example- Wikipedia, GitHub.

Hadoop Ecosystem: HDFS, MapReduce, Hive, Pig

The Hadoop ecosystem is a powerful framework designed to process and analyze large datasets across distributed computing environments. Developed by the Apache Software Foundation, Hadoop allows organizations to store and process vast amounts of data efficiently. The ecosystem comprises several components, each serving distinct functions that collectively enable effective data management and analytics. Key components of the Hadoop ecosystem include the Hadoop Distributed File System (HDFS), MapReduce, Hive, and Pig.

Hadoop Distributed File System (HDFS)

The Hadoop Distributed File System (HDFS) is a key component of the Hadoop ecosystem, designed to store and manage large datasets across a distributed computing environment. HDFS is built to handle massive volumes of data, providing high-throughput access and fault tolerance, which are essential for big data applications. Its architecture consists of two main components i.e., the NameNode and DataNodes. The NameNode acts as the master server, managing metadata and controlling access to files, while DataNodes store the actual data blocks. Data is split into large blocks, typically 128 MB or 256 MB, and replicated across multiple DataNodes to ensure reliability and availability even in the event of hardware failures. This replication strategy not only provides fault tolerance but also enhances data access speed by enabling parallel processing across the cluster. HDFS is designed for high throughput, making it suitable for batch processing workloads, and it optimizes data locality by moving computation closer to where the data resides, thus minimizing network congestion. Additionally, HDFS supports scalability, allowing organizations to add more nodes to accommodate growing data volumes seamlessly. Its capability to handle diverse data types, from structured to unstructured data, makes HDFS a versatile solution for modern data storage challenges, enabling organizations to leverage big data for insights and decision-making. The HDFS meaning and purpose is to achieve the following goals:

1. **Manage Large Datasets:** Organizing and storing datasets can be a hard talk to handle. HDFS is used to manage the applications that have to deal with huge datasets. To do this, HDFS should have hundreds of nodes per cluster.
2. **Detecting Faults:** HDFS should have technology in place to scan and detect faults quickly and effectively as it includes a large number of commodity hardware. Failure of components is a common issue.
3. **Hardware Efficiency:** When large datasets are involved, it can reduce the network traffic and increase the processing speed.

HDFS Architecture: As we see in fig.3.3, it focuses on NameNodes and DataNodes. The NameNode is the hardware that contains the GNU/Linux operating system and software. The Hadoop distributed file system acts as the master server and can manage the files, control a client's access to files, and overseas file operating processes such as renaming, opening, and closing files.

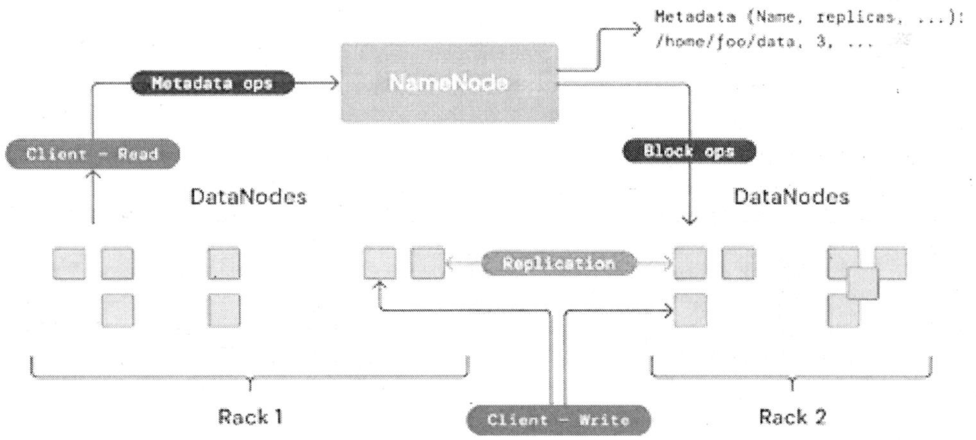

Fig.3.3

A DataNode is hardware having the GNU/Linux operating system and DataNode software. For every node in a HDFS cluster, you will locate a DataNode. These nodes help to control the data storage of their system as they can perform operations on the file systems if the client requests, and also create, replicate, and block files when the NameNode instructs. HDFS consists of two main components: the NameNode and DataNodes.

1. **NameNode:** This is the master server responsible for managing the file system namespace and regulating access to files by clients. It keeps metadata about files, such as their locations and replication status.
2. **DataNodes:** These are the worker nodes that store the actual data blocks. Each DataNode manages the storage attached to it and periodically sends heartbeat signals to the NameNode to confirm its status.

Key Features

1. **Scalability:** HDFS can scale horizontally by adding more nodes to the cluster, allowing organizations to accommodate growing data volumes easily.
2. **Fault Tolerance:** Data is automatically replicated across multiple nodes, typically three times, ensuring that data remains available even if one or more nodes fail.
3. **High Throughput:** HDFS is designed for high data transfer rates, making it suitable for large-scale data processing tasks.
4. **Data Locality:** By moving computation closer to the data, HDFS reduces network congestion and increases the speed of data processing.

MapReduce

MapReduce is a programming model and processing engine in the Hadoop ecosystem that enables the processing of large data sets across distributed clusters. It simplifies data processing tasks by dividing them into smaller, manageable units, allowing parallel execution on multiple nodes. The MapReduce model consists of two main functions: Map and Reduce. The Map function processes input data, generating intermediate key-value pairs, while the Reduce function aggregates these pairs to produce the final output. This design enhances efficiency and scalability, as tasks are distributed across various nodes, significantly speeding up data processing. One of the key advantages of MapReduce is its fault tolerance; if a node fails during processing, the framework automatically reallocates the tasks to other nodes, ensuring continuous operation. MapReduce is particularly well-suited for batch processing tasks, such as log analysis, data transformation, and large-scale machine learning applications. Developers can write MapReduce jobs in languages like Java, Python, or R, although the complexity of these jobs can be high compared to higher-level abstractions. As organizations increasingly rely on data-driven insights, MapReduce remains a cornerstone of big data processing, enabling scalable and efficient handling of vast data volumes across diverse industries.

MapReduce Architecture: The components of MapReduce architecture are as follows:

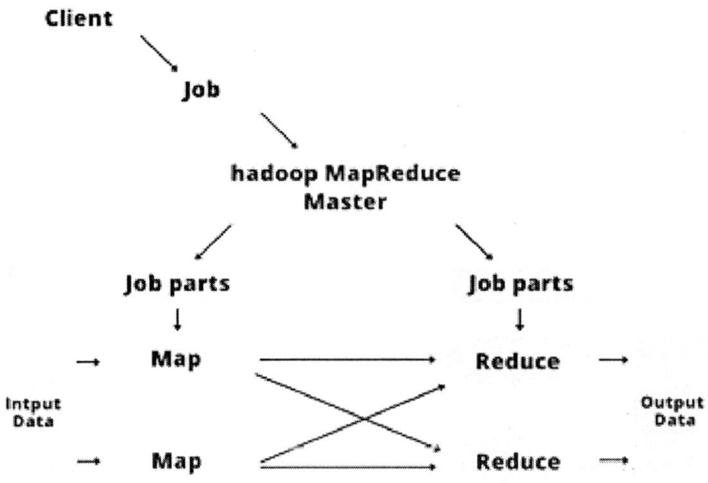

Fig.3.4

1. **Client:** The MapReduce client is the one who brings the Job to the MapReduce for processing. There can be multiple clients available that continuously send jobs for processing to the Hadoop MapReduce Manager.
2. **Job:** The MapReduce Job is the actual work that the client wanted to do which is comprised of so many smaller tasks that the client wants to process or execute.
3. **Hadoop MapReduce Master:** It divides the particular job into subsequent job-parts.
4. **Job-Parts:** The task or sub-jobs that are obtained after dividing the main job. The result of all the job-parts combined to produce the final output.
5. **Input Data:** The data set that is fed to the MapReduce for processing.
6. **Output Data:** The final result is obtained after the processing.

In MapReduce, we have a client. The client will submit the job of a particular size to the Hadoop MapReduce Master. Now, the MapReduce master will divide this job into further equivalent job-parts. These job-parts are then made available for the Map and Reduce Task. This Map and Reduce task will contain the program as per the requirement of the use-case that the particular company is solving. The developer writes their logic to fulfill the requirement that the industry requires. The input data which we are using is then fed to the Map Task and the Map will generate intermediate key-value pair as its output. The output of Map i.e. these key-value pairs are then fed to the Reducer and the final output is stored on the HDFS. There can be n number of Map and Reduce tasks made available for processing the data as per the requirement. The algorithm for Map and Reduce is made with a very optimized way such that the time complexity or space complexity is minimum.

MapReduce Model Function:

1. **The Map Function:** The Map function takes a set of input data and transforms it into a set of intermediate key-value pairs. This transformation occurs in parallel across multiple nodes in a distributed system, allowing for significant performance improvements. Key Characteristics of the Map Function:
   - **Input Splits:** The input data is divided into smaller chunks called splits. Each split is processed independently, which enables parallel execution.
   - **Key-Value Pairs:** The output of the Map function consists of key-value pairs. These pairs serve as input for the subsequent Reduce function.
   - **Data Locality:** To enhance performance, the framework attempts to run the Map function on the same node where the data resides, reducing the need for data transfer over the network.

   Example: Consider a scenario where a company wants to count the occurrences of words in a large text file. The Map function would read chunks of the file and emit a key-value pair for each word, with the word as the key and the number 1 as the value. For example, for the input "Hello World," the output would be:

   ```
   ("Hello", 1)
   ("World", 1)
   ```

2. **The Reduce Function:** The Reduce function takes the intermediate key-value pairs generated by the Map function and aggregates them to produce the final output. This function is also executed in parallel, allowing for efficient data processing. Key characteristics of the Reduce function:
   - **Aggregation**: The Reduce function processes the intermediate key-value pairs by grouping them based on their keys. It then applies an aggregation function to combine the values for each key.
   - **Final Output**: The output of the Reduce function is the final result of the MapReduce job, which can be written back to a file in HDFS or another storage system.

Example of the Reduce Function:

Continuing with the word count example, the Reduce function would receive the intermediate pairs from the Map function and sum the values for each unique word. For example:

```
("Hello", [1, 1]) => ("Hello", 2)
("World", [1]) => ("World", 1)
```

The final output would be:

```
("Hello", 2)
("World", 1)
```

Use Cases of MapReduce: MapReduce is widely used across various industries for different applications, including:

1. **Log Analysis:** Organizations can analyze server logs to monitor user behavior, identify trends, and troubleshoot issues.
2. **Data Transformation:** Businesses can transform large datasets from one format to another, facilitating data integration and preparation for analysis.
3. **Machine Learning:** MapReduce can be used to train machine learning models on large datasets by processing the data in parallel.
4. **Text Processing:** Applications like indexing web pages or performing natural language processing tasks leverage MapReduce for efficient text analysis.

Conclusion

MapReduce is a foundational technology in the big data landscape, enabling organizations to process and analyze vast datasets efficiently. Its distributed processing model, coupled with features like fault tolerance and scalability, makes it an ideal choice for handling large-scale data processing tasks. Despite its complexities and limitations, MapReduce continues to play a critical role in various applications across industries, from log analysis to machine learning. As organizations increasingly rely on data-driven insights, understanding MapReduce remains essential for leveraging the full potential of big data analytics. By mastering this powerful framework, businesses can unlock valuable insights, enhance decision-making, and drive innovation in an increasingly data-centric world.

Hive

Hive is a data warehousing solution built on top of the Hadoop ecosystem, designed to facilitate the querying and analysis of large datasets using a SQL-like language called HiveQL. It allows users to perform complex data queries without needing to write extensive MapReduce code, making it accessible for those familiar with traditional SQL databases. Hive operates on a schema-on-read model, meaning that data is structured at the time of querying rather than at the time of writing, providing flexibility in data management. Its architecture includes key components such as the Hive Metastore, which stores metadata about the data schema, and the execution engine that translates HiveQL queries into MapReduce jobs for execution. Hive supports partitioning and bucketing, which enhances query performance by organizing data in a way that minimizes the amount of data scanned during queries. This makes it particularly useful for data analysts and business intelligence professionals who need to extract insights quickly. Common use cases for Hive include data summarization, ad-hoc querying, and reporting on large datasets. As big data analytics becomes increasingly vital for businesses, Hive offers a user-friendly interface for leveraging the power of Hadoop without requiring in-depth programming knowledge.

Hive Architecture: Hive's architecture consists of several components that work together to facilitate data management and querying.

1. **Hive Metastore:** The Hive Metastore is a centralized repository that stores metadata about Hive tables, including their schema, location, and partitioning information. It acts as the interface between Hive and the data stored in HDFS, ensuring that queries can access the correct data.
2. **Driver:** The Hive Driver manages the execution of HiveQL queries. It compiles queries into a logical plan, optimizes execution paths, and interacts with the Metastore to retrieve metadata. The Driver then generates a series of MapReduce jobs (or other execution engines) to process the data.
3. **Execution Engine:** The execution engine is responsible for running the tasks generated by the Driver. Initially, Hive used MapReduce as its execution engine, but it has since expanded to support other engines, such as Apache Tez and Apache Spark, allowing for improved performance and faster query execution.
4. **User Interface:** Hive offers several user interfaces, including a command-line interface (CLI) and web-based interfaces. These interfaces allow users to submit queries, manage tables, and interact with the data stored in HDFS.

Challenges and Limitations: While Hive offers many advantages, it also has its challenges:

1. **Performance for Low-latency Queries:** Hive is optimized for batch processing rather than real-time analytics. Queries can exhibit latency, making it less suitable for applications requiring immediate results. Organizations with real-time needs may need to explore alternatives like Apache HBase or Apache Spark.
2. **Complexity of Optimizations:** Although Hive abstracts many complexities, achieving optimal performance can still require a deep understanding of data structures and query optimization techniques. Users may need to experiment with partitioning and bucketing strategies to maximize efficiency.
3. **Data Consistency:** As Hive relies on HDFS for storage, it inherits some limitations regarding data consistency. HDFS is optimized for write-once, read-many scenarios, which may lead to challenges in environments requiring frequent updates.

Conclusion

Apache Hive is a transformative tool for organizations seeking to harness the power of big data analytics. Its SQL-like interface, scalability, and integration with the Hadoop ecosystem make it accessible to a wide range of users, from data analysts to business intelligence professionals. By enabling efficient querying and management of large datasets, Hive empowers organizations to derive valuable insights that drive decision-making and innovation. As the big data landscape continues to evolve, Hive remains a cornerstone technology, continually adapting to meet the demands of modern data processing. Understanding Hive's features, architecture, and use cases is essential for any organization looking to leverage big data for competitive advantage in today's data-driven world.

Pig

Apache Pig is a high-level platform designed for creating programs that run on the Hadoop ecosystem, utilizing a scripting language known as Pig Latin. It provides a simpler and more intuitive way to process and analyze large datasets than writing complex MapReduce jobs. Pig Latin abstracts the complexities of the underlying MapReduce framework, allowing users to focus on data transformation and analysis through a straightforward syntax. Pig operates in two modes: Local mode, which runs on a single machine, and MapReduce mode, which executes on a Hadoop cluster, enabling it to handle large-scale data processing. One of Pig's notable features is its extensibility; users can define User Defined Functions (UDFs) to incorporate custom processing logic, making it adaptable to various data processing needs. The optimization opportunities inherent in Pig allow the execution engine to optimize scripts automatically, improving performance without user intervention. Common use cases for Pig include data cleansing, log analysis, and ETL (Extract, Transform, Load) operations. By simplifying the development process for big data analytics, Pig empowers data analysts and engineers to efficiently derive insights from complex datasets, contributing to data-driven decision-making in organizations across diverse industries.

Pig Architecture: Apache Pig has a well-defined architecture that consists of several components working together to facilitate data processing:

1. **Pig Latin:** Pig Latin is the scripting language used to write Pig scripts. It consists of a series of statements that describe the data transformation processes. The language provides built-in operators for common tasks such as filtering, grouping, and joining data.
2. **Pig Execution Engine:** The Pig execution engine is responsible for executing Pig Latin scripts. When a Pig script is run, the execution engine parses the script, translates it into a series of MapReduce jobs, and manages their execution across the Hadoop cluster. The execution engine can operate in two modes:
   - **Local Mode**: In this mode, Pig runs on a single machine, making it suitable for small datasets and quick development cycles.
   - **MapReduce Mode**: This mode enables Pig to execute on a Hadoop cluster, leveraging the distributed processing capabilities of MapReduce to handle larger datasets.

3. **Frontend Interfaces:** Pig offers several frontend interfaces, including a command-line interface (CLI) and a web-based interface. These interfaces allow users to submit Pig Latin scripts, manage data, and interact with the Hadoop ecosystem. The CLI is particularly popular among users who prefer a quick and interactive environment for testing and debugging scripts.
4. **User Defined Functions (UDFs):** Pig allows users to create custom UDFs to extend its functionality. These functions can be written in Java, Python, or other languages, enabling users to implement complex logic that may not be available in Pig's built-in functions. Once defined, UDFs can be reused across multiple Pig scripts, promoting code reuse and modularity.

Use Cases of Apache Pig: Apache Pig is widely used across various industries for different applications, including:

1. **Data Transformation and ETL:** Pig is particularly effective for ETL (Extract, Transform, Load) processes. Organizations use Pig to ingest data from various sources, apply transformations, and load it into data warehouses or analytical systems. Its ability to handle large datasets makes it a popular choice for data preparation tasks.
2. **Log Analysis:** Many organizations leverage Pig for analyzing log files generated by servers, applications, and user interactions. By processing and aggregating log data, businesses can gain insights into user behavior, system performance, and potential issues, enabling proactive management.
3. **Data Exploration:** Pig provides a flexible environment for data exploration, allowing data analysts to quickly run ad-hoc queries and test hypotheses. This capability is valuable in research and development environments, where insights need to be derived from large datasets rapidly.
4. **Machine Learning:** Pig can be used to preprocess data for machine learning applications. Data scientists often rely on Pig to clean and transform data, preparing it for analysis and model training. Its extensibility allows users to integrate custom algorithms directly into their Pig scripts.
5. **Social Media Analysis:** With the rise of social media, organizations are increasingly using Pig to analyze large volumes of social media data. By processing posts, comments, and interactions, businesses can gain insights into customer sentiment and engagement, informing marketing strategies.

Challenges and Limitations: While Apache Pig offers many advantages, it also has its challenges:

1. **Learning Curve:** Although Pig Latin is designed to be user-friendly, it may still present a learning curve for users unfamiliar with programming concepts. While data analysts with SQL experience may find it relatively easy to adopt, others may require training to fully leverage Pig's capabilities.
2. **Performance for Low-latency Queries:** Pig is primarily optimized for batch

processing, which may lead to latency issues for applications requiring real-time processing. Organizations with stringent real-time requirements might need to explore alternatives like Apache Spark.

3. **Debugging Complexity:** Debugging Pig scripts can be challenging, particularly in distributed environments. Errors may not be immediately apparent, requiring users to carefully review execution plans and logs to identify issues.

Conclusion

Apache Pig is a transformative tool for managing and processing large datasets within the Hadoop ecosystem. Its simplicity, extensibility, and ability to handle diverse data types make it an ideal choice for data engineers and analysts looking to work with big data efficiently. By providing a high-level abstraction over the complexities of MapReduce, Pig empowers organizations to derive valuable insights from their data. As the big data landscape continues to evolve, Apache Pig remains a relevant and powerful tool for data processing. Understanding its features, architecture, and use cases is essential for any organization aiming to harness the full potential of big data analytics. By leveraging Pig, businesses can enhance decision-making, drive innovation, and gain a competitive edge in an increasingly data-driven world.

Differences Between HDFS, MapReduce, Hive, Pig

Table 3.4

S.No.	Feature	HDFS	MapReduce	Hive	Pig
1.	Purpose	Data storage	Data processing	Data warehousing and querying	Data transformation and analysis
2.	Data Processing	None (focus on storage)	Distributed processing using Map and Reduce	Converts HiveQL to MapReduce jobs	Translates Pig Latin to MapReduce jobs
3.	User Interface	Command-line/ APIs	Java (or wrappers in other languages)	SQL-like (HiveQL)	Scripting language (Pig Latin)
4.	Complexity	Simple	Complex (requires programming)	Easier than MapReduce	More flexible but less intuitive
5.	Data Types	Schema-less	Schema-less (depends on input format)	Schema-based	Schema-aware but flexible
6.	Use Cases	Storing large datasets	Batch processing with custom logic	Analytics and reporting	Iterative processing and data flows

Real-time Data Processing with Spark and Kafka

In today's data-driven world, the ability to process and analyze data in real-time is paramount. Organizations are increasingly turning to big data technologies like

Apache Spark and Apache Kafka to meet their real-time processing needs. This comprehensive guide will explore how Spark and Kafka work together, their key features, use cases, and how to implement a real-time data processing pipeline.

Kafka

Apache Kafka is a distributed streaming platform designed for high-throughput, fault-tolerant data ingestion and real-time processing, originally developed by LinkedIn and now widely used in the big data ecosystem. Operating on a publish/subscribe model, Kafka allows producers to send messages to topics, which consumers can then read from. Its architecture includes brokers that store messages and manage client requests, with Zookeeper overseeing cluster state. Key features of Kafka include scalability, as it can handle thousands of messages per second and easily expand by adding more brokers; durability, with messages stored on disk and replicated for persistence; high throughput and low latency, making it suitable for real-time applications; and integrated stream processing capabilities via Kafka Streams, enabling the creation of real-time applications to process data streams. Common use cases include log aggregation, real-time analytics, event sourcing, and stream processing, while its compatibility with other big data tools like Apache Spark and Apache Flink enhances its utility in modern data architectures. Overall, Kafka serves as a cornerstone for organizations seeking efficient and timely handling of large volumes of data.

Key Features of Kafka: Apache Kafka is a powerful distributed streaming platform that has become essential for managing real-time data flows in modern applications. Here are the key features that make Kafka a popular choice for businesses seeking to handle large volumes of data efficiently:

1. **Publish/Subscribe Messaging Model:** Kafka employs a publish/subscribe architecture, allowing producers to send messages to topics while consumers subscribe to those topics to receive messages. This decouples data production from data consumption, enabling multiple applications to read the same stream of data independently.

2. **High Throughput and Low Latency:** Kafka is designed to handle high throughput, capable of processing millions of messages per second. Its architecture allows for low-latency message delivery, making it suitable for real-time applications that require quick data processing and immediate action.

3. **Scalability:** Kafka is highly scalable, allowing organizations to expand their data processing capabilities effortlessly. You can increase throughput by adding more partitions to a topic or by adding more brokers to the Kafka cluster. This horizontal scaling ensures that Kafka can meet growing data demands without a significant drop in performance.

4. **Durability and Reliability:** Messages in Kafka are stored on disk and can be replicated across multiple brokers, ensuring durability even in the event of

hardware failures. This replication feature allows for fault tolerance, ensuring that data is not lost and can be recovered if a broker goes down.

5. **Message Retention:** Kafka allows for configurable message retention policies. Messages can be retained for a specified period or until a certain size limit is reached. This flexibility enables applications to reprocess data or to recover from failures by reading historical messages.
6. **Stream Processing Capabilities:** With the introduction of Kafka Streams, developers can build real-time applications that process data streams directly within Kafka. Kafka Streams allows for complex event processing, enabling transformations, aggregations, and windowing operations on streaming data without requiring a separate processing framework.
7. **Exactly-once Semantics:** Kafka offers exactly-once processing semantics, which ensures that messages are neither lost nor duplicated during processing. This feature is crucial for applications that require strong consistency, such as financial transaction systems.
8. **Flexible Data Integration:** Kafka supports a variety of data formats and protocols, making it easy to integrate with existing systems. It has connectors for numerous data sources and sinks through the Kafka Connect framework, allowing seamless data ingestion from databases, cloud services, and other data systems.
9. **Strong Ecosystem and Community Support:** Kafka has a robust ecosystem that includes a variety of tools and libraries for stream processing, monitoring, and management. The active open-source community contributes to continuous improvements, ensuring that Kafka stays relevant and evolves to meet user needs.
10. **Security Features:** Kafka provides multiple security features, including authentication, authorization, and encryption. These security measures ensure that data is protected both in transit and at rest, making Kafka suitable for sensitive applications.
11. **Multi-tenancy:** Kafka supports multi-tenancy, allowing multiple applications and teams to use the same Kafka cluster without interference. This is achieved through isolation mechanisms and configurable access controls.

Use Cases: Apache Kafka is widely used across various industries due to its robust capabilities for handling real-time data streams. Here are some common use cases:

1. **Log Aggregation:** Kafka is ideal for collecting and aggregating logs from different services and applications, centralizing them for analysis and monitoring. This helps in troubleshooting and performance monitoring.
2. **Real-time Analytics:** Organizations use Kafka to process data in real-time for

insights and decision-making. For example, financial institutions can analyze transaction data immediately to detect fraud or anomalies.

3. **Event Sourcing:** Kafka allows systems to maintain a log of events that represent state changes, enabling easier recovery and auditing. This is particularly useful in applications where tracking state changes is crucial.
4. **Stream Processing:** With Kafka Streams, developers can build applications that process data on-the-fly, performing operations like filtering, aggregation, and joining streams for real-time insights.
5. **Data Integration:** Kafka serves as a backbone for connecting disparate data sources and sinks, enabling seamless data flow across systems. This is particularly useful for microservices architectures.
6. **IoT Data Ingestion:** Kafka can efficiently handle the large volumes of data generated by IoT devices, enabling real-time monitoring and analytics of sensor data.
7. **Messaging:** Kafka can also function as a message broker, facilitating communication between different microservices, ensuring messages are reliably delivered even under heavy loads.

These use cases highlight Kafka's versatility in managing real-time data and its significance in modern data architectures.

Conclusion

Overall, Kafka's combination of high throughput, scalability, durability, and flexibility makes it a powerful tool for building real-time data pipelines and applications. Its rich feature set, along with strong community support and a growing ecosystem, positions Kafka as a cornerstone in modern data architectures, enabling organizations to harness the power of their data effectively.

Spark

Apache Spark is an open-source distributed computing system designed for fast and efficient processing of large datasets. Known for its speed and ease of use, Spark leverages in-memory computing, which allows it to process data significantly faster than traditional disk-based systems like Hadoop MapReduce. It provides high-level APIs in languages such as Java, Scala, Python, and R, making it accessible to a wide range of developers. Spark supports various workloads, including batch processing, interactive queries, streaming data, machine learning, and graph processing, all within a unified framework. Its core abstraction, the Resilient Distributed Dataset (RDD), enables fault-tolerant distributed processing, allowing developers to perform complex transformations on large datasets effortlessly. Additionally, Spark integrates seamlessly with other big data tools and data sources, enhancing its versatility. With libraries like Spark SQL for structured data processing, MLlib for machine learning, and Spark

Streaming for real-time data processing, Spark has become a cornerstone of modern data analytics and big data solutions, empowering organizations to derive insights and make data-driven decisions quickly and efficiently.

Setting Up a Real-Time Data Processing Pipeline

Prerequisites: Before implementing a real-time data processing pipeline using Kafka and Spark, ensure you have the following:

1. A working installation of Apache Kafka.
2. A working installation of Apache Spark.
3. Java Development Kit (JDK) installed.
4. An IDE or code editor for development.

Step 1: Setting Up Kafka

1. **Download and Install Kafka:** Download the latest version of Kafka from the official website.
2. **Start Zookeeper:** Kafka requires Zookeeper to manage the brokers. Start Zookeeper using the following command:

```
bin/zookeeper-server-start.sh config/zookeeper.properties
```

3. **Start Kafka Broker:** Start a Kafka broker with the following command:

```
bin/kafka-server-start.sh config/server.properties
```

4. **Create a Kafka Topic:** Create a topic to which producers will publish data:

```
bin/kafka-topics.sh --create --topic my-topic --bootstrap-server localhost:9092
--partitions 1 --replication-factor 1
```

Step 2: Setting Up Spark Streaming

1. **Download and Install Spark:** Download the latest version of Spark from the official website.
2. **Add Kafka Dependency**: If you are using Maven, add the Kafka dependency to your pom.xml:

```
<dependency>
    <groupId>org.apache.spark</groupId>
    <artifactId>spark-streaming-kafka-0-10_2.12</artifactId>
    <version>3.0.0</version> <!-- Use the appropriate Spark version -->
</dependency>
```

3. **Create a Spark Streaming Application:** Below is a sample code snippet in Scala to create a Spark Streaming application that consumes data from Kafka:

```
import org.apache.spark.sql.SparkSession
import org.apache.spark.sql.streaming.Trigger

object KafkaSparkStreaming {
    def main(args: Array[String]): Unit = {
        val spark = SparkSession.builder
            .appName("KafkaSparkStreaming")
            .getOrCreate()

        import spark.implicits._

        // Define the Kafka source
        val kafkaStream = spark
            .readStream
            .format("kafka")
            .option("kafka.bootstrap.servers", "localhost:9092")
            .option("subscribe", "my-topic")
            .load()
```

```
        // Process the data (for example, select the value field)
        val processedStream = kafkaStream
            .selectExpr("CAST(value AS STRING) as message")

        // Output to console (for testing)
        val query = processedStream
            .writeStream
            .outputMode("append")
            .format("console")
            .trigger(Trigger.ProcessingTime("5 seconds"))
            .start()

        query.awaitTermination()
    }
}
```

4. **Run the Spark Streaming Application:** Package the application and run it using the Spark-submit command:

```
./bin/spark-submit --class KafkaSparkStreaming --master local[2] your-jar-file.jar
```

Step 3: Producing Data to Kafka

To see the real-time data processing in action, you can produce some sample data to the Kafka topic using the console producer:

```
bin/kafka-console-producer.sh --broker-list localhost:9092 --topic my-topic
```

Type messages into the console, and you should see them processed by your Spark Streaming application in real-time.

Use Cases of Spark: Here are several key use cases for Apache Spark:

1. **Real-time Data Processing:** Spark Streaming allows organizations to process

and analyze streaming data in real-time. For example, financial institutions can monitor transactions continuously to detect fraudulent activities or anomalies as they happen.

2. **Big Data Analytics:** Companies leverage Spark for large-scale data analytics, transforming and aggregating vast datasets to uncover insights into customer behavior, market trends, and operational efficiencies. Spark SQL enables complex queries on structured data, facilitating in-depth analysis.
3. **Machine Learning:** With MLlib, Spark supports scalable machine learning algorithms, enabling organizations to build, train, and deploy models on large datasets. This is beneficial in industries such as healthcare for predictive analytics, or retail for customer segmentation and recommendation systems.
4. **Data Integration and ETL:** Spark can act as a powerful ETL (Extract, Transform, Load) tool, allowing organizations to extract data from various sources, transform it for analysis, and load it into data warehouses or lakes. Its ability to handle diverse data formats enhances integration capabilities.
5. **Graph Processing:** Using GraphX, Spark allows for processing and analyzing large-scale graph data, useful in social network analysis, recommendation engines, and fraud detection in financial transactions.

These use cases highlight Spark's versatility and capability in handling a variety of data processing tasks across different industries.

Differences Between Kafka and Spark

Table 3.5

S.No.	Feature	Kafka	Spark
1.	Primary Function	A distributed messaging system for streaming data	A distributed computing framework for data processing
2.	Architecture	Publish/subscribe model with producers and consumers	Resilient Distributed Dataset (RDD) for processing data
3.	Data Processing	Focuses on real-time data ingestion and messaging	Supports batch processing, stream processing, and machine learning
4.	Message Retention	Stores messages for a configurable retention period	Processes data in-memory or on disk, with no inherent message retention
5.	Use Cases	Ideal for log aggregation, event sourcing, and real-time analytics	Best for ETL processes, big data analytics, and machine learning tasks
6.	State Management	Stateless by default, with additional frameworks for stateful processing	Stateful processing through RDDs and DataFrames, enabling complex transformations

NoSQL Databases: MongoDB, Cassandra, HBase

In the evolving landscape of data management, NoSQL databases have emerged as powerful alternatives to traditional relational databases. Designed to handle a wide variety of data types and structures, NoSQL databases cater to the needs of modern applications that require scalability, flexibility, and high performance. Among the prominent NoSQL databases, MongoDB, Apache Cassandra, and HBase stand out due to their unique features and use cases.

MongoDB

MongoDB is an open-source, document-oriented NoSQL database that provides a flexible and scalable solution for managing unstructured and semi-structured data. Launched in 2009 by 10gen, which later became MongoDB, Inc., it was designed to overcome the limitations of traditional relational databases by offering a more dynamic data model. It utilizes BSON (Binary JSON) to represent data, allowing for rich data structures that can include arrays and nested documents. This flexibility enables developers to work with dynamic schemas, making it easy to adapt to changing application requirements. MongoDB's architecture is built around collections, which group related documents, and databases, which house these collections. Key features include powerful querying capabilities, an aggregation framework for data processing, and support for geospatial indexing. Additionally, MongoDB offers high availability through replica sets, which provide data redundancy and failover capabilities. Its sharding mechanism allows for horizontal scaling, distributing data across multiple servers to handle large volumes of traffic and storage needs efficiently. MongoDB is widely used in various applications, including content management systems, real-time analytics, and e-commerce platforms, due to its ease of use and the ability to quickly evolve data models. With a strong community and a rich ecosystem of tools and libraries, MongoDB has become a cornerstone of modern data-driven applications.

Features of MongoDB: The core features of MangoDB are as follows:

1. **Document-Oriented Storage:** At the heart of MongoDB is its document-oriented storage model. Instead of storing data in rows and columns like traditional relational databases, MongoDB stores data in BSON (Binary JSON) documents. This allows for complex data structures, including nested documents and arrays. Each document can have a different schema, providing developers with the flexibility to evolve the data model as application requirements change.
2. **Collections and Databases:** In MongoDB, documents are grouped into collections, which are analogous to tables in relational databases. A collection can contain an unlimited number of documents, and since there is no fixed schema, developers can insert documents with varying fields. Each database can contain multiple collections, facilitating organized data management.
3. **High Scalability:** MongoDB is designed for horizontal scalability, allowing it to handle large volumes of data and high traffic loads efficiently. Through a process called sharding, MongoDB distributes data across multiple servers, known as shards. Each shard contains a subset of the data, allowing for increased capacity and load balancing as the application scales.

4. **High Availability:** MongoDB provides high availability through a feature called replica sets. A replica set is a group of MongoDB servers that maintain the same data set. One server is designated as the primary, while others serve as secondaries. If the primary server fails, one of the secondaries automatically takes over, ensuring minimal downtime and data loss.

5. **Rich Query Language:** MongoDB offers a powerful and flexible query language that allows developers to perform complex queries on documents. It supports various query types, including field queries, range queries, and even text searches. Additionally, MongoDB provides an aggregation framework, which enables data processing and transformation through a pipeline approach, allowing for filtering, grouping, and projecting data.

6. **Indexing:** MongoDB supports various indexing options to enhance query performance. Developers can create single-field or compound indexes on one or more fields of a document. Furthermore, MongoDB supports geospatial indexing, allowing for efficient querying of location-based data, making it suitable for applications that require geospatial capabilities.

7. **Built-in Aggregation Framework:** MongoDB's aggregation framework allows for advanced data processing and transformation directly within the database. It enables developers to perform operations such as filtering, grouping, and sorting, as well as performing calculations on data. The framework operates in a pipeline format, where each stage of the pipeline processes the data and passes it to the next stage.

8. **Flexible Data Model:** MongoDB's flexible schema enables developers to adjust the data structure as application requirements evolve. This adaptability is particularly beneficial for agile development, where requirements may change frequently. Developers can add or remove fields in documents without affecting other documents in the same collection.

9. **Strong Ecosystem and Community Support:** MongoDB boasts a strong ecosystem of tools, libraries, and community support. Various drivers are available for different programming languages, including Java, Python, Node.js, and Ruby. Additionally, MongoDB Atlas, the cloud-based version of MongoDB, offers managed database services with automatic scaling, backups, and monitoring, simplifying deployment and maintenance.

10. **Security Features:** MongoDB includes several security features, such as authentication, authorization, and encryption. Role-based access control allows administrators to define user roles and permissions, ensuring that only authorized users can access sensitive data. Furthermore, data can be encrypted both in transit and at rest, enhancing data security.

Use Cases of MongoDB: MongoDB is employed across various industries and applications due to its flexibility and scalability. Some common use cases include:

1. **Content Management Systems:** Many organizations utilize MongoDB for content management systems (CMS) because of its ability to store diverse content types. Its document-oriented model allows for the storage of articles, images, and metadata in a flexible manner, making it easier to manage and deliver content.
2. **Real-time Analytics:** With its high performance and aggregation capabilities, MongoDB is well-suited for real-time analytics applications. Organizations can analyze and visualize data in real time, enabling informed decision-making based on up-to-date information.
3. **E-Commerce Applications:** MongoDB is widely used in e-commerce platforms to manage product catalogs, user profiles, and shopping carts. Its flexible schema allows developers to handle varying product attributes and rapidly adapt to changing market conditions.
4. **Internet of Things (IoT):** As IoT devices generate massive amounts of data, MongoDB's scalability and flexibility make it an ideal choice for managing this data. It can store and process time-series data from sensors and devices, enabling real-time monitoring and analytics.
5. **Social Media Applications:** Social media platforms often require the ability to handle large volumes of user-generated content and interactions. MongoDB's document model allows for storing user profiles, posts, comments, and likes in a manner that supports fast retrieval and updates.
6. **Mobile Applications:** MongoDB is commonly used in mobile applications due to its ability to handle unstructured data and its flexibility in adapting to changing requirements. Developers can store user preferences, app settings, and content in a way that aligns with mobile app architectures.

Cassandra

Apache Cassandra is an open-source, highly scalable NoSQL database designed for handling large volumes of data across distributed systems without a single point of failure. Developed at Facebook, Cassandra employs a column-family data model that allows for flexible schema design, enabling efficient storage and retrieval of structured, semi-structured, and unstructured data. Its architecture is based on a peer-to-peer model, where each node in the cluster is equal, facilitating easy scalability by adding more nodes without downtime. Cassandra excels in write-heavy workloads, providing low-latency data access and high availability through its tunable consistency model, which allows users to balance consistency and availability based on application requirements. The database supports automatic data replication, ensuring durability and fault tolerance, while its built-in partitioning mechanism distributes data evenly across nodes. With CQL (Cassandra Query Language), developers can perform SQL-like queries, making it accessible to those familiar with traditional relational databases. Cassandra is ideal for use cases such as real-time analytics, IoT data management, and social media applications, where fast read and write operations are crucial for performance and scalability.

Architecture of Cassandra

1. **Peer-to-Peer Architecture:** Cassandra operates on a peer-to-peer architecture, meaning every node in the cluster is equal and plays a role in data storage and retrieval. This architecture eliminates bottlenecks, making it easier to scale horizontally by simply adding more nodes. Each node is responsible for a portion of the data and can serve both read and write requests, ensuring that no single node becomes a point of failure.
2. **Data Model:** Cassandra uses a flexible data model based on tables, rows, and columns, similar to a relational database but without a fixed schema. The primary elements include:
3. **Keyspace:** The outermost container in Cassandra, similar to a database in relational terms. It defines the replication strategy for the data contained within it.
4. **Table:** The structure within a keyspace, consisting of rows and columns. Each table can have a different set of columns, allowing for a dynamic schema.
5. **Row:** Each row is uniquely identified by a primary key, which can consist of one or more columns. This key determines how data is partitioned across the cluster.
6. **Column:** The individual data elements that are stored in a row. Columns can be added dynamically, making the data model highly flexible.
7. **Partitioning and Replication:** Cassandra employs a partitioning strategy to distribute data evenly across nodes, utilizing a consistent hashing algorithm. This ensures that no single node becomes a bottleneck. Each piece of data is replicated across multiple nodes based on the configured replication factor, which can be set per keyspace. This provides fault tolerance and high availability, as the system can continue to operate even if some nodes are down.
8. **Data Distribution:** Cassandra uses a ring-based architecture for data distribution. Each node is assigned a unique identifier, and data is distributed in a circular fashion. The distribution ensures that data is evenly spread across the cluster, allowing for efficient read and write operations.

Getting Started with Cassandra

Installation: To get started with Cassandra, you can install it on a local machine or a cloud server. The installation process typically involves:

1. **Downloading the Software:** Get the latest version of Cassandra from the official Apache website.
2. **Setting Up Dependencies:** Ensure that Java is installed, as Cassandra requires Java to run.

3. **Configuration:** Configure the cassandra.yaml file to set up the cluster, including node IP addresses and data directories.
4. **Starting the Service:** Launch the Cassandra server using the command line or service manager.

Basic Operations: Once installed, you can interact with Cassandra through the command-line interface (cqlsh) or using CQL. Basic operations include:

1. **Creating a Keyspace:**

```
CREATE KEYSPACE my_keyspace WITH REPLICATION = {'class': 'SimpleStrategy',
'replication_factor': 3};
```

2. **Creating a Table:**

```
CREATE TABLE users (user_id UUID PRIMARY KEY, name text, age int);
```

3. **Inserting Data:**

```
INSERT INTO users (user_id, name, age) VALUES (uuid(), 'Alice', 30);
```

4. **Querying Data:**

```
SELECT * FROM users WHERE user_id = <some-uuid>;
```

5. **Updating Data:**

```
UPDATE users SET age = 31 WHERE user_id = <some-uuid>;
```

6. **Deleting Data:**

```
DELETE FROM users WHERE user
```

Use Cases for Cassandra: Cassandra is widely used across various industries and applications due to its unique features and strengths. Some common use cases include:

1. **Internet of Things (IoT):** Cassandra is well-suited for IoT applications that require real-time data ingestion and analysis. Its ability to handle massive amounts of time-series data from sensors and devices makes it ideal for monitoring and analytics.
2. **Real-time Analytics:** Organizations use Cassandra for real-time analytics applications, where data is continuously ingested, processed, and analyzed. Its high write throughput and low-latency reads enable timely decision-making based on current data.
3. **Social Media and Messaging Applications:** Cassandra's ability to manage large volumes of user-generated content and interactions makes it a popular choice for social media platforms and messaging applications that require fast read and write operations.

4. **E-Commerce Platforms:** Cassandra is frequently employed in e-commerce solutions to manage product catalogs, user profiles, shopping carts, and order histories. Its flexible schema allows for rapid changes in product data and inventory.

HBase

Apache HBase is an open-source, distributed NoSQL database built on top of the Hadoop ecosystem, designed to provide real-time read and write access to large datasets. Modeled after Google's Bigtable, HBase uses a column-family data model, enabling efficient storage and retrieval of sparse data across massive tables. Its architecture consists of a master node that manages region servers, which handle the actual data storage and processing. HBase automatically partitions tables into regions, distributing them across the cluster for scalability and load balancing. It leverages HDFS (Hadoop Distributed File System) for fault-tolerant storage, ensuring data redundancy and reliability. HBase supports strong consistency, allowing immediate visibility of data after a write operation, which is crucial for applications requiring accurate real-time data access. It offers a Java-based API for operations and can handle large volumes of time-series data, making it ideal for use cases such as log processing, online transaction processing, and analytics on large datasets. With its integration into the Hadoop ecosystem, HBase can efficiently work alongside tools like Apache Spark and Apache Hive for big data processing and analytics.

Architecture of HBase

1. **HBase Components:** HBase consists of several key components that work together to manage large datasets efficiently:
   - **HMaster:** The master server that manages the HBase cluster. It coordinates region servers, handles load balancing, and performs administrative tasks such as schema changes and region assignments.
   - **Region Server:** The server that stores data and serves read and write requests. Each region server handles a subset of the data, divided into regions.
   - **Regions:** The basic unit of scalability in HBase, each region holds a portion of a table's data. Regions are dynamically split and distributed among region servers as data grows.
   - **HStore:** A storage mechanism within a region that holds data in the form of column families. Each HStore is responsible for reading and writing data to and from HDFS.
   - **HFile:** The underlying file format used to store data in HBase. HFiles are immutable and are written to HDFS, enabling efficient data retrieval and storage.
2. **Data Model:** HBase employs a flexible, schema-less data model based on tables, rows, and columns:

- **Tables:** Data is organized into tables, each identified by a unique name. Tables can have multiple column families.
- **Column Families:** Each table can contain one or more column families, which group related columns together. This allows for efficient storage and retrieval of data.
- **Rows:** Each row in a table is uniquely identified by a row key. Row keys are stored in sorted order, enabling fast retrieval.
- **Columns:** Columns can be added dynamically, allowing for a flexible schema that adapts to changing application requirements.

3. **Data Distribution:** HBase leverages HDFS (Hadoop Distributed File System) for data storage, enabling it to manage large volumes of data across a distributed cluster. The architecture supports horizontal scaling, allowing organizations to add more nodes to the cluster seamlessly.
4. **Write and Read Path**
   - **Write Path**: When data is written to HBase, it first goes into a write-ahead log (WAL) for durability. It is then stored in an in-memory structure called the MemStore. When the MemStore reaches a certain size, its contents are flushed to HDFS as HFiles.
   - **Read Path**: When a read request is made, HBase first checks the MemStore for data. If not found, it looks in the HFiles stored on HDFS. Bloom filters can be used to quickly determine whether a particular HFile may contain the requested data, optimizing read performance.

Getting Started with HBase

Installation: To get started with HBase, follow these steps:

1. **Install Hadoop:** HBase requires a Hadoop installation. Download and set up Hadoop on your cluster.
2. **Download HBase:** Obtain the latest version of HBase from the official Apache website.
3. **Configuration:** Configure the hbase-site.xml file to define settings such as Zookeeper connection, HDFS configuration, and other parameters.
4. **Start HBase:** Use the command line to start the HBase master and region servers.

Basic Operations: Once HBase is set up, you can interact with it using the HBase shell or Java API. Basic operations include:

1. **Creating a Table:**

```
create 'my_table', 'my_column_family'
```

2. **Inserting Data:**

```
put 'my_table', 'row1', 'my_column_family:my_column', 'value'
```

3. **Retrieving Data:**

```
get 'my_table', 'row1'
```

4. **Updating Data:**

```
put 'my_table', 'row1', 'my_column_family:my_column', 'new_value'
```

5. **Deleting Data:**

```
delete 'my_table', 'row1', 'my_column_family:my_column'
```

Monitoring and Management: HBase provides tools for monitoring and managing the cluster:

1. **HBase Web UI:** A web-based interface to monitor the status of the cluster, view table metrics, and manage region servers.
2. **HBase Shell:** The command-line interface for performing administrative tasks and querying data.
3. **Monitoring Tools:** Integration

Use Cases for HBase: HBase is employed across various industries and applications due to its unique features and strengths. Some common use cases include:

1. **Real-Time Analytics:** Organizations use HBase for real-time analytics applications that require immediate access to data. HBase's ability to handle high write and read throughput makes it ideal for analyzing live data streams.
2. **Internet of Things (IoT):** HBase is well-suited for IoT applications that generate massive amounts of time-series data. It can efficiently store and process data from sensors and devices in real time.
3. **Log and Event Data Management:** HBase is often used to manage log and event data generated by applications and services. Its ability to store large volumes of data and provide real-time access makes it suitable for monitoring and analysis.
4. **Content Management Systems:** Many organizations utilize HBase for content management systems that require scalable storage for diverse content types. Its flexible schema allows for rapid changes in content structure.
5. **Machine Learning:** HBase is used in machine learning applications to store training data and models. Its ability to handle large datasets and provide fast access to data makes it suitable for developing and deploying machine learning algorithms.

Differences Between MongoDB, Cassandra, HBase

Table 3.6

S.No.	Feature	MongoDB	Cassandra	HBase
1.	Data Model	Document-oriented, stores data in JSON-like BSON format, allowing nested structures.	Column-family store, organizes data into rows and columns, optimized for write-heavy workloads.	Column-family store similar to Cassandra, optimized for large datasets in a Hadoop ecosystem.
2.	Schema	Flexible schema, allows for dynamic changes to documents and fields.	Schema-less design with flexible column families; each row can have a different set of columns.	Requires a defined schema for tables, but supports adding columns dynamically.
3.	Query Language	Uses a rich query language (MongoDB Query Language) with support for ad-hoc queries and indexing.	CQL (Cassandra Query Language) provides SQL-like syntax but with limited capabilities for complex queries.	HBase Shell allows basic commands for CRUD operations; complex querying is not supported.
4.	Consistency Model	Strong consistency by default with options for eventual consistency; supports ACID transactions at the document level.	Tunable consistency levels, allowing users to balance between consistency and availability.	Strong consistency for read/write operations; ensures that the latest data is always read after a write.
5.	Scalability	Scales horizontally with sharding; easy to add new nodes.	Designed for horizontal scalability; handles large datasets across many nodes without a single point of failure.	Built on top of HDFS, providing scalability by adding region servers, but requires careful planning for performance.
6.	Use Cases	Ideal for content management, real-time analytics, and applications requiring flexible data models.	Best for applications needing high write throughput, such as IoT data and real-time analytics.	Suited for big data applications, real-time data processing, and time-series data management within the Hadoop ecosystem.

3. Business Intelligence and Reporting

Business Intelligence (BI) and reporting are essential for organizations aiming to leverage data for informed decision-making. BI encompasses a range of technologies and practices that collect, analyze, and present business data, enabling insights into operations, customer behavior, and market trends. Key components include data sources, integration, modeling, analysis, and visualization, which together facilitate effective reporting. Tools such as Tableau, Power BI, and Looker help transform complex datasets into understandable dashboards and reports. Organizations benefit from BI by improving operational efficiency, gaining competitive advantages, and fostering a data-driven culture. As trends evolve, the integration of AI, real-time analytics, and cloud solutions is enhancing BI capabilities, allowing businesses to respond quickly to changing environments. Ultimately, effective BI and reporting empower organizations to make strategic decisions based on accurate and timely data insights.

Business Intelligence (BI)

Business Intelligence (BI) refers to the technologies, processes, and practices that organizations use to collect, analyze, and present business data to drive informed decision-making. It encompasses a variety of tools and methodologies designed to transform raw data into actionable insights, enabling businesses to understand trends, improve operational efficiency, and enhance customer satisfaction. Key components of BI include data integration from multiple sources, data warehousing, and analytics, which can be both descriptive and predictive. By utilizing advanced visualization tools like Tableau and Power BI, users can create interactive dashboards and reports that simplify complex data sets. BI empowers organizations to make data-driven decisions, ensuring that strategies align with market dynamics and consumer behaviors. As businesses increasingly rely on data, the importance of BI has grown, leading to the adoption of self-service BI solutions that allow non-technical users to explore data independently. Additionally, the integration of artificial intelligence and machine learning is enhancing BI capabilities, enabling organizations to uncover deeper insights and automate reporting processes. Ultimately, BI not only helps in optimizing current operations but also plays a crucial role in strategic planning and long-term growth by providing a comprehensive view of performance metrics and market opportunities.

Key Components of Business Intelligence

1. **Data Sources:** BI systems gather data from various sources, including:
   - **Internal Databases:** Data from enterprise resource planning (ERP) systems, customer relationship management (CRM) systems, and transactional databases.
   - **External Data:** Information from social media, market research, and third-party data providers.
   - **Data Warehouses:** Central repositories that aggregate data from multiple sources, allowing for comprehensive analysis.
2. **Data Integration:** Data integration is a crucial aspect of BI, involving the consolidation of data from disparate sources into a unified format. Common methods include:
   - **ETL (Extract, Transform, Load):** The process of extracting data from source systems, transforming it into a suitable format, and loading it into a data warehouse.
   - **Data Lakes:** A storage solution that allows organizations to store large volumes of raw data in its native format until it is needed for analysis.

3. **Data Modeling:** Data modeling is the process of organizing data into structured formats that can be easily analyzed. Common models include:
   - **Star Schema:** A data modeling approach that organizes data into fact and dimension tables, optimizing query performance.
   - **Snowflake Schema:** An extension of the star schema that normalizes dimension tables into multiple related tables, allowing for more complex relationships.
4. **Data Analysis and Visualization:** BI tools provide various methods for analyzing and visualizing data, which include:
   - **Descriptive Analytics:** Summarizing historical data to identify trends and patterns.
   - **Predictive Analytics:** Using statistical models and machine learning techniques to forecast future outcomes based on historical data.
   - **Prescriptive Analytics:** Recommending actions based on data analysis to achieve desired outcomes.

   Data visualization is critical in presenting data effectively, utilizing charts, graphs, and dashboards to make complex information accessible.
5. **Reporting:** Reporting involves generating structured summaries of data to communicate insights effectively. Key aspects include:
   - **Automated Reporting:** Scheduled reports generated at regular intervals to keep stakeholders informed.
   - **Ad-Hoc Reporting:** Custom reports created on demand to address specific queries or analysis needs.

Business Intelligence Tools: Business Intelligence (BI) tools are essential for organizations looking to analyze data and derive actionable insights for informed decision-making. These tools encompass a variety of functionalities, including data visualization, reporting, and analytics. Key types of BI tools include:

1. **Data Visualization Tools:** Tools like Tableau and Power BI excel at transforming complex datasets into interactive, easy-to-understand visual representations, allowing users to explore trends and patterns intuitively.
2. **Dashboard Software:** Solutions such as Google Data Studio aggregate multiple data sources into a single interface, providing real-time monitoring of key performance indicators (KPIs) and business metrics.
3. **Reporting Tools:** Tools like SAP Crystal Reports generate structured reports, helping organizations summarize data for specific audiences and regulatory compliance.
4. **OLAP Tools:** Online Analytical Processing tools, such as Microsoft Analysis Services, enable users to perform multidimensional analysis, facilitating deeper insights into business data.

5. **Self-Service BI Tools:** Platforms like Looker empower non-technical users to explore data and create custom reports, reducing the dependency on IT teams.

Challenges in Business Intelligence

1. **Data Quality Issues:** Ensuring data quality is a significant challenge in BI. Inaccurate or inconsistent data can lead to misleading insights and poor decision-making.
2. **Integration Complexities:** Integrating data from multiple sources can be complex and time-consuming, requiring significant effort to ensure compatibility and consistency.
3. **Resistance to Change**: Cultural resistance within organizations can hinder the adoption of BI tools and practices, making it challenging to foster a data-driven culture.
4. **Skills Gap:** A shortage of skilled professionals in data analytics and BI tools can impede the effective implementation and utilization of BI initiatives.
5. **Data Security Concerns:** With the increasing volume of data being collected, ensuring data security and compliance with regulations is a growing challenge for organizations.

Future Trends in Business Intelligence

1. **AI and Machine Learning Integration:** The integration of artificial intelligence (AI) and machine learning (ML) with BI tools is enhancing data analysis capabilities. Organizations can leverage predictive analytics and automated insights, making BI more proactive and insightful.
2. **Real-time Analytics:** The demand for real-time analytics is increasing, allowing organizations to access and analyze data as it is generated. This capability is crucial for industries requiring immediate insights, such as finance and e-commerce.
3. **Cloud-based BI Solutions:** Cloud-based BI solutions are becoming more popular due to their scalability, cost-effectiveness, and accessibility. Organizations can access BI tools and data from anywhere, facilitating collaboration and remote work.
4. **Data Democratization:** Data democratization aims to make data accessible to all employees, regardless of their technical expertise. Self-service BI tools empower users to explore data and generate insights independently, fostering a culture of data-driven decision-making.
5. **Enhanced Data Visualization:** As the volume of data grows, the need for advanced data visualization techniques continues to rise. BI tools are incorporating more interactive and user-friendly visualizations to help users better understand complex data sets.

Conclusion

Business Intelligence is a vital component for organizations seeking to harness the power of data for strategic decision-making. By implementing effective BI practices, leveraging the right tools, and fostering a data-driven culture, organizations can gain valuable insights that drive growth and improve operational efficiency. As technology continues to evolve, staying informed about emerging trends in BI will be essential for maintaining a competitive advantage in an increasingly data-centric world. Through continuous investment in BI capabilities, organizations can not only respond to challenges but also proactively seize opportunities for innovation and success.

Reporting

Reporting in Business Intelligence (BI) refers to the systematic process of generating structured summaries of data to communicate insights effectively to stakeholders. This process encompasses various types of reports, including automated reports that are generated on a scheduled basis and ad-hoc reports created on demand to address specific analytical needs. Reporting tools, such as SAP Crystal Reports and Microsoft Power BI, allow users to visualize data through charts, graphs, and dashboards, making complex information more accessible and understandable. Effective reporting not only presents historical data but also incorporates real-time analytics, enabling organizations to monitor key performance indicators (KPIs) and assess business performance at a glance. Moreover, well-designed reports can highlight trends, identify anomalies, and provide actionable recommendations, thus facilitating informed decision-making. The integration of self-service reporting tools empowers business users to create and customize their reports without relying heavily on IT departments, promoting a culture of data-driven decision-making. As organizations increasingly focus on agility and responsiveness, reporting plays a crucial role in ensuring that relevant insights are communicated promptly, supporting strategic initiatives and operational improvements. Ultimately, robust reporting mechanisms are essential for aligning organizational goals with data-driven insights, fostering transparency, and enhancing overall business performance.

Importance of Reporting

1. **Informed Decision-making:** Reports provide essential information that guides strategic and operational decisions, reducing reliance on intuition alone.
2. **Performance Monitoring:** Regular reporting helps organizations track key performance indicators (KPIs), enabling proactive management of operations.
3. **Trend Identification:** By analyzing historical data, reports can reveal trends that inform future strategies and actions.
4. **Transparency:** Reporting fosters transparency within organizations by making data accessible to stakeholders, enhancing accountability and trust.

Types of Reporting

1. **Standard Reports:** Standard reports are pre-defined, regularly scheduled reports that provide consistent information over time. They often include:

- **Monthly Financial Reports**: Summarize financial performance against budgets and forecasts.
- **Sales Reports**: Track sales performance, identifying top-selling products and market trends.
- **Operational Reports**: Monitor daily operations, providing insights into productivity and efficiency.

2. **Ad-Hoc Reports:** Ad-hoc reports are created on demand to address specific business questions or analytical needs. Users can customize these reports based on their requirements, making them flexible and responsive to immediate concerns.
3. **Executive Dashboards:** Executive dashboards provide high-level summaries of key metrics and performance indicators. They offer real-time insights into critical areas such as sales, marketing, finance, and operations, allowing executives to monitor organizational performance at a glance.
4. **Operational Reports:** Operational reports focus on day-to-day operations and performance metrics. They provide detailed information about specific processes, helping managers identify inefficiencies and areas for improvement.
5. **Strategic Reports:** Strategic reports are designed to support long-term decision-making. They analyze data in relation to organizational goals and objectives, providing insights that guide strategic planning.

Reporting Process

1. **Data Collection:** The first step in the reporting process is data collection. This involves gathering data from various sources, including internal databases (e.g., ERP and CRM systems), external data providers, and data lakes.
2. **Data Integration:** Once data is collected, it must be integrated into a cohesive format. This can involve:
   - **ETL (Extract, Transform, Load):** Extracting data from different sources, transforming it to ensure consistency, and loading it into a data warehouse for analysis.
   - **Data Preparation:** Cleaning and preparing data to ensure accuracy and reliability, removing duplicates, and addressing inconsistencies.
3. **Data Analysis:** Data analysis involves examining the integrated data to uncover trends, patterns, and insights. This may include statistical analysis, data mining, and exploratory data analysis.
4. **Report Creation:** After analysis, reports are created using reporting tools. This includes selecting the appropriate format (e.g., tables, charts, graphs) and structuring the report to effectively communicate insights.
5. **Distribution:** Once reports are created, they must be distributed to the relevant

stakeholders. This can be done through various channels, including email, shared dashboards, or BI platforms.

6. **Feedback and Iteration:** After distribution, collecting feedback is crucial to improve future reporting efforts. Stakeholders may provide input on what information was useful, what could be improved, and what additional data might be needed.

Conclusion

Reporting in Business Intelligence is a vital process that enables organizations to convert data into actionable insights. By employing effective reporting practices, utilizing the right tools, and overcoming challenges, businesses can enhance decision-making, monitor performance, and foster a data-driven culture. As technology continues to evolve, staying informed about emerging trends in reporting will be essential for maintaining a competitive advantage in an increasingly data-centric landscape. Through continuous investment in reporting capabilities, organizations can not only respond to challenges but also proactively seize opportunities for innovation and success.

BI Frameworks

BI frameworks serve as blueprints for organizing BI initiatives. They outline the methodologies, processes, and technologies necessary to collect, analyze, and report data effectively. The goal of these frameworks is to ensure that BI aligns with organizational objectives and delivers valuable insights to decision-makers.

Key BI Frameworks: The key of BI Framework are as under:

1. **The BI Maturity Model:** The BI Maturity Model is a widely recognized framework that helps organizations assess their current BI capabilities and identify areas for improvement. It typically consists of several stages, each representing a level of sophistication in BI practices:
   - **Stage1: Descriptive Analytics:** Organizations at this stage focus on basic reporting and historical data analysis. They utilize tools to generate simple reports and dashboards that summarize past performance. The emphasis is on understanding "what happened."
   - **Stage 2: Diagnostic Analytics:** This stage allows organizations to analyze data to understand the reasons behind past performance. Techniques such as root cause analysis become prevalent, enabling teams to investigate anomalies and trends.
   - **Stage 3: Predictive Analytics:** Organizations in this stage leverage statistical models and machine learning algorithms to forecast future outcomes based on historical data. Predictive analytics helps organizations anticipate trends and prepare for upcoming challenges.

- **Stage 4: Prescriptive Analytics:** The final stage involves providing recommendations based on predictive models. Organizations can optimize decision-making by suggesting specific actions to achieve desired outcomes, often using advanced algorithms and simulations.

2. **The BI Lifecycle Framework:** The BI Lifecycle framework outlines the phases involved in implementing a BI solution, ensuring a systematic approach to BI initiatives. It typically includes the following stages:
   - **Planning:** Identifying objectives, scope, and resources for the BI initiative. This phase involves understanding stakeholder needs and determining the metrics that will drive analysis.
   - **Data Sourcing:** Gathering data from various internal and external sources, including operational databases, CRM systems, and third-party data providers. Data quality is critical at this stage.
   - **Data Integration:** Combining and preparing data for analysis through ETL (Extract, Transform, Load) processes. This stage ensures data consistency and reliability across sources.
   - **Data Storage:** Storing integrated data in data warehouses or lakes, optimizing it for query and analysis. Organizations often choose between traditional data warehouses and more flexible data lake solutions.
   - **Data Analysis:** Applying analytical methods to derive insights from stored data. This can include descriptive, diagnostic, predictive, and prescriptive analytics.
   - **Reporting and Visualization:** Presenting findings through dashboards, reports, and visualizations. Effective data visualization enhances the accessibility and comprehension of insights.
   - **Feedback and Iteration:** Collecting feedback from users to refine reports and analytical processes. Continuous improvement is vital for maintaining the relevance and effectiveness of BI initiatives.

Five Layers of BI Architecture: This framework outlines the components of a comprehensive BI system, divided into five layers:

1. **Data Source Layer:** This layer includes various data sources, such as operational databases, external data feeds, and APIs. The diversity of sources ensures a holistic view of organizational data.
2. **Data Integration Layer:** This layer encompasses ETL processes that prepare data for analysis. Data cleansing, transformation, and integration occur here to ensure consistency and quality.
3. **Data Storage Layer:** This includes data warehouses or data lakes where processed data is stored. The choice between a traditional data warehouse and a more flexible data lake depends on the organization's specific needs.
4. **Analytics Layer:** This layer consists of tools and techniques for data analysis, including OLAP (Online Analytical Processing) and data mining. Analytical capabilities enable organizations to uncover insights from their data.

5. **Presentation Layer:** The final layer includes interfaces for reporting and visualization, such as dashboards and BI applications. This layer is crucial for communicating insights to stakeholders effectively.

Benefits of BI Frameworks

1. **Structured Approach:** BI frameworks provide a systematic method for implementing BI initiatives, ensuring that all aspects of the process are covered.
2. **Alignment with Business Goals:** By focusing on organizational objectives, frameworks help ensure that BI initiatives deliver valuable insights that drive decision-making.
3. **Improved Data Quality:** Frameworks emphasize the importance of data quality and integration, leading to more accurate and reliable insights.
4. **Scalability:** Many BI frameworks are designed to grow with the organization, allowing for the addition of new data sources and analytical capabilities as needed.
5. **Enhanced Collaboration:** By involving stakeholders throughout the BI process, frameworks promote collaboration and ensure that the insights generated meet user needs.

Conclusion

Business Intelligence frameworks provide essential structures for organizations seeking to leverage data for improved decision-making and operational efficiency. By understanding key frameworks, organizations can implement BI initiatives that align with their goals and deliver actionable insights. Focusing on data quality, stakeholder involvement, and continuous improvement will enhance the effectiveness of BI efforts, enabling organizations to thrive in a data-driven landscape. As technology continues to evolve, staying informed about emerging trends in BI frameworks will be crucial for maintaining a competitive advantage and driving organizational success.

Dashboard Design and Best Practices

Dashboards are pivotal in Business Intelligence (BI) as they offer a visual representation of data, enabling organizations to monitor key metrics, analyze trends, and make informed decisions. Effective dashboard design enhances data comprehension, promotes user engagement, and facilitates swift decision-making.

A dashboard is a visual display of key information and metrics relevant to an organization's objectives, presented in a single interface. It aggregates data from various sources and presents it in a coherent manner, often using charts, graphs, and tables. Dashboards can serve different purposes, from high-level executive overviews to detailed operational insights, depending on the target audience. Types of Dashboards are as:

1. **Operational Dashboards**: Focus on real-time data and metrics to monitor day-to-day operations. These dashboards are often used by managers and operational teams.

2. **Strategic Dashboards**: Designed for executives and decision-makers, strategic dashboards provide high-level insights into overall business performance and long-term trends.
3. **Analytical Dashboards**: These dashboards enable users to explore data through in-depth analysis, often allowing for drill-down capabilities to investigate specific metrics or trends.

Key Principles of Dashboard Design: Effective dashboard design revolves around several core principles:

1. **Understand Your Audience:** Before designing a dashboard, it's crucial to understand who will use it. Different stakeholders have varying needs and preferences. Executives may require high-level insights, while operational staff might need detailed metrics. Engaging users during the design process can help tailor the dashboard to their requirements.
2. **Define Clear Objectives:** Establishing clear objectives for the dashboard is essential. Identify the key questions the dashboard aims to answer and the metrics that will support those objectives. This clarity will guide the selection of data and visualizations, ensuring that the dashboard remains focused and relevant.
3. **Prioritize Key Metrics:** Dashboards should highlight the most important metrics often referred to as Key Performance Indicators (KPIs). Prioritizing KPIs helps users quickly grasp performance and identify areas needing attention. Avoid cluttering the dashboard with excessive data; instead, focus on a few critical metrics that align with business goals.
4. **Use Visualizations Effectively:** The choice of visualizations plays a significant role in dashboard design. Different types of data require different visualization techniques:
   - **Bar and Column Charts**: Useful for comparing categories or showing changes over time.
   - **Line Charts**: Ideal for displaying trends over periods.
   - **Pie Charts**: Effective for illustrating proportions but should be used sparingly.
   - **Heat Maps**: Helpful for showing data density or variation across a geographic area.
   - **Tables**: Good for presenting detailed data but should be used in moderation to avoid overwhelming users.
5. **Ensure Clarity and Simplicity:** Dashboards should be easy to understand at a glance. Use clear labels, concise titles, and legends to guide users through the data. Avoid jargon or overly complex terminology that might confuse users. The design should be clean and uncluttered, with sufficient white space to enhance readability.

6. **Optimize for Interaction:** Incorporating interactive elements allows users to explore data more deeply. Features like drill-down capabilities, filtering options, and hover effects enable users to gain insights beyond what is immediately visible. Interactive dashboards encourage user engagement and enhance the overall analytical experience.
7. **Maintain Consistency:** Consistency in design elements such as colors, fonts, and layout—ensures that users can navigate the dashboard easily. Establishing a design system with predefined styles and formats promotes uniformity across different dashboards and reports.
8. **Focus on Performance:** The performance of a dashboard is critical. Users expect dashboards to load quickly and respond promptly to interactions. Optimize data queries and visualizations to minimize load times. Regularly monitor and assess dashboard performance, making necessary adjustments to improve speed and responsiveness.

Conclusion

Dashboard design is a critical aspect of Business Intelligence that can significantly impact an organization's ability to make informed decisions. By adhering to fundamental principles and best practices, organizations can create effective dashboards that enhance data visualization, facilitate user engagement, and drive strategic insights. Understanding the audience, defining clear objectives, prioritizing key metrics, and focusing on clarity and simplicity are essential steps in crafting impactful dashboards. As BI continues to evolve, staying abreast of emerging trends and technologies will further enhance the effectiveness of dashboard design, ensuring that organizations remain agile and informed in an increasingly data-driven world.

Self-service BI Tools

Self-Service BI refers to tools and processes that enable end-users to access and analyze data independently, without the need for specialized technical skills. Users can create reports, dashboards, and visualizations on their own, allowing them to explore data and derive insights in real time. This approach contrasts with traditional BI, where access to data and reporting was often limited to IT departments or data analysts. Key features of self-service BI tools are as:

1. **User-Friendly Interfaces:** Self-Service BI tools typically feature intuitive drag-and-drop interfaces that allow users to easily manipulate data and create visualizations without writing code.
2. **Data Connectivity:** These tools can connect to various data sources, including databases, cloud services, spreadsheets, and APIs, enabling users to access a wide range of data.
3. **Data Preparation:** Many self-services BI tools offer data preparation capabilities, such as cleaning, transforming, and aggregating data, making it easier for users to work with raw data.

4. **Interactive Visualizations:** Users can create interactive dashboards and visualizations that allow for dynamic exploration of data, helping them uncover insights quickly.
5. **Collaboration Features:** Self-Service BI tools often include features that facilitate sharing and collaboration among users, such as commenting, sharing dashboards, and exporting reports.
6. **Self-Help Resources:** Many tools come with built-in tutorials, documentation, and support forums to assist users in maximizing their use of the platform.

Popular Self-Service BI Tools: Several Self-Service BI tools are widely used in organizations today, each offering unique features and capabilities:

1. **Tableau:** Known for its powerful data visualization capabilities, Tableau allows users to create interactive dashboards and perform complex analyses with ease.
2. **Power BI:** Developed by Microsoft, Power BI integrates seamlessly with other Microsoft tools and offers a user-friendly interface for creating reports and dashboards.
3. **Qlik Sense:** Qlik Sense provides associative data modeling and intuitive visualizations, enabling users to explore data freely and uncover hidden insights.
4. **Looker:** Now part of Google Cloud, Looker focuses on data exploration and collaboration, allowing users to create customized data experiences.
5. **Domo:** Domo combines data integration, visualization, and collaboration in a single platform, making it suitable for organizations looking for an all-in-one solution.

Advanced Reporting Techniques

Advanced reporting refers to sophisticated methods and tools used to analyze and present data in a way that reveals deeper insights and supports strategic decision-making. It incorporates techniques such as data visualization, predictive analytics, real-time reporting, and interactive dashboards to enhance the clarity and effectiveness of reports.

Key Advanced Reporting Techniques

1. **Data Visualization:** Data visualization is the graphical representation of information and data. It uses visual elements like charts, graphs, and maps to convey complex data relationships and trends.
   - **Benefits:** Visualization simplifies data interpretation, highlights patterns, and makes it easier for stakeholders to grasp key insights quickly.
   - **Best Practices:** Use appropriate visualization types for the data (e.g., line charts for trends, bar charts for comparisons) and ensure clarity through labels and legends.

2. **Predictive Analytics:** Predictive analytics employs statistical techniques and machine learning algorithms to analyze historical data and make forecasts about future events.
   - **Benefits:** By anticipating future trends and behaviors, organizations can make proactive decisions and optimize strategies.
   - **Best Practices:** Use high-quality historical data for modeling, and validate models regularly to ensure accuracy in predictions.
3. **Interactive Dashboards:** Interactive dashboards allow users to manipulate data through filters, drill-downs, and what-if scenarios. This interactivity enhances user engagement and allows for tailored insights.
   - **Benefits:** Users can explore data on their terms, leading to deeper insights and more relevant findings.
   - **Best Practices:** Ensure intuitive navigation, provide contextual information, and allow users to save personalized views of the dashboard.
4. **Real-time Reporting: Real-time reporting** delivers data as it becomes available, enabling organizations to monitor key metrics continuously.
   - **Benefits:** Organizations can respond quickly to changing conditions, improving agility and decision-making.
   - **Best Practices:** Implement robust data integration processes to ensure data accuracy and consistency, and focus on the most critical KPIs for real-time monitoring.
5. **Drill-down and Drill-through Reporting:** Drill-down and drill-through reporting techniques enable users to explore data hierarchies. Drill-down allows users to click on data points to access more detailed views, while drill-through takes users to related reports or data sources.
   - **Benefits:** These techniques provide deeper insights into data, helping users understand the underlying factors affecting performance.
   - **Best Practices:** Clearly label interactive elements to guide users, and ensure that the underlying data is accessible and reliable.
6. **Data Blending:** Data blending combines data from different sources into a unified view, allowing for comprehensive analysis.
   - **Benefits:** This technique enables organizations to leverage data from multiple systems, uncovering insights that may not be visible when analyzing data in silos.
   - **Best Practices:** Use consistent data formats and ensure data quality across sources to avoid discrepancies in reporting.
7. **Storytelling with Data:** Data storytelling combines data visualization with narrative elements to convey insights more effectively. It involves presenting

data in a way that tells a story, engaging the audience emotionally and cognitively.

- **Benefits:** Storytelling helps communicate complex data insights in an accessible and compelling manner, enhancing understanding and retention.
- **Best Practices:** Use a clear structure (beginning, middle, end), incorporate visuals to support the narrative, and focus on key takeaways that drive action.

4. Text Analytics and Natural Language Processing (NLP)

Text analytics and Natural Language Processing (NLP) have emerged as critical fields within artificial intelligence, enabling computers to understand, interpret, and generate human language. As vast amounts of unstructured text data are generated daily ranging from social media posts and customer feedback to scientific articles organizations are increasingly leveraging these technologies to extract valuable insights, automate processes, and enhance customer experiences.

Text Analytics

Text analytics refers to the process of deriving meaningful insights from unstructured text data using various computational techniques. It involves converting text into structured data for analysis, enabling organizations to uncover patterns, sentiments, and trends. Text analytics encompasses several techniques, including:

1. **Text Mining:** The process of extracting information and patterns from text.
2. **Sentiment Analysis:** Assessing the emotional tone behind words to determine attitudes, opinions, and sentiments.
3. **Topic Modeling:** Identifying themes or topics within a corpus of text.
4. **Entity Recognition:** Identifying and classifying key entities in text, such as names, dates, and locations.

Importance of Text Analytics: Text analytics has become increasingly vital for organizations in the digital age, driven by the explosive growth of unstructured data generated from various sources like social media, emails, reviews, and documents. Here are several key reasons why text analytics is important:

1. **Data-driven Decision Making:** Text analytics enables organizations to convert unstructured text data into structured insights, supporting data-driven decision-making. By analyzing customer feedback, market trends, and social media sentiment, businesses can make informed strategic choices that align with customer needs and market demands.
2. **Enhanced Customer Understanding:** Through sentiment analysis and feedback mining, organizations can gain deeper insights into customer opinions, preferences, and behaviors. This understanding allows businesses to tailor their products, services, and marketing strategies to meet customer expectations effectively.

3. **Risk Management:** Text analytics can play a crucial role in identifying potential risks and compliance issues. By analyzing text data from reports, communications, and social media, organizations can detect early warning signs of fraud, misconduct, or regulatory violations.
4. **Operational Efficiency:** Automating the analysis of large volumes of text data can significantly reduce the time and effort required for manual analysis. This efficiency allows organizations to focus on strategic initiatives rather than data processing, improving overall productivity.
5. **Innovation and Product Development:** By analyzing customer feedback and industry trends, organizations can identify opportunities for innovation. Text analytics helps in understanding customer needs, leading to the development of products and services that address real-world problems.
6. **Social Media Monitoring:** Text analytics tools can monitor and analyze social media conversations in real time, providing insights into public sentiment about brands, products, and services. This capability allows organizations to respond quickly to customer feedback and manage their brand reputation effectively.

Natural Language Processing (NLP)

Natural language processing (NLP) is a subset of artificial intelligence that focuses on the interaction between computers and human language. It involves developing algorithms and models that enable computers to process, understand, and generate human language in a meaningful way. NLP combines computational linguistics with machine learning and data science to achieve its objectives. Key components of NLP are as:

1. **Tokenization:** Breaking down text into individual components, such as words or phrases, to facilitate analysis.
2. **Part-of-Speech Tagging:** Identifying the grammatical categories of words (e.g., noun, verb, adjective) to understand their roles in sentences.
3. **Named Entity Recognition (NER):** Detecting and classifying named entities (e.g., people, organizations, locations) within text.
4. **Sentiment Analysis:** Assessing the emotional tone of text to determine positive, negative, or neutral sentiments.
5. **Dependency Parsing:** Analyzing the grammatical structure of sentences to understand relationships between words.
6. **Word Embeddings:** Representing words as vectors in high-dimensional space, capturing their meanings and relationships.

Importance of NLP: Natural Language Processing (NLP) is a pivotal technology in today's data-driven world, enabling computers to understand, interpret, and generate human language. Its significance spans various sectors, driven by the increasing reliance on text and speech data. Here are some key reasons highlighting the importance of NLP:

1. **Enhanced Human-computer Interaction:** NLP facilitates more intuitive interactions between humans and machines. By enabling natural language queries and commands, NLP allows users to engage with technology in a way that feels more organic, improving user experience across applications like chatbots and virtual assistants.
2. **Data-driven Insights:** NLP allows organizations to extract valuable insights from vast amounts of unstructured text data, such as customer feedback, social media posts, and reports. This capability supports data-driven decision-making, helping businesses identify trends, sentiments, and opportunities.
3. **Improved Customer Support:** NLP powers intelligent customer service solutions, such as chatbots and virtual assistants, which can handle queries, provide support, and offer personalized recommendations. This leads to faster response times and improved customer satisfaction.
4. **Sentiment Analysis:** Businesses utilize NLP to perform sentiment analysis, allowing them to gauge public opinion and customer emotions regarding products, services, or brands. Understanding sentiments can inform marketing strategies and product development.
5. **Content Recommendation and Personalization:** NLP enables the analysis of user preferences and behaviors, facilitating personalized content recommendations. This personalization enhances user engagement and satisfaction across platforms like streaming services and e-commerce sites.
6. **Automation of Routine Tasks:** By automating text processing tasks, such as data entry, summarization, and categorization, NLP helps organizations save time and resources. This efficiency allows employees to focus on higher-value activities.

Techniques in Text Analytics and NLP

1. **Machine Learning Approaches:** Machine learning plays a pivotal role in NLP and text analytics. Various algorithms and techniques are employed to process text data, including:
   - **Supervised Learning:** Using labeled data to train models for tasks such as classification and sentiment analysis. Common algorithms include Support Vector Machines (SVM), Random Forests, and neural networks.
   - **Unsupervised Learning:** Analyzing text without labeled data to identify patterns and clusters. Techniques such as clustering and topic modeling (e.g., Latent Dirichlet Allocation) fall under this category.
   - **Deep Learning:** Leveraging neural networks to process and analyze large volumes of text data. Recurrent Neural Networks (RNNs), Long Short-Term

Memory networks (LSTMs), and Transformers are popular deep learning architectures in NLP.

2. **Rule-based Approaches:** In addition to machine learning, rule-based approaches utilize predefined linguistic rules to analyze text. These approaches often involve:
   - **Regular Expressions:** Patterns that can be used to match and manipulate text strings for tasks like data extraction and validation.
   - **Grammar Rules:** Employing linguistic rules to analyze sentence structure, allowing for the identification of relationships between words.
3. **Hybrid Approaches:** Many NLP applications combine machine learning and rule-based approaches to leverage the strengths of both methods. For example, a sentiment analysis model might use machine learning for classification while incorporating rule-based techniques for specific language patterns.

Applications of Text Analytics and NLP

1. **Sentiment Analysis:** Sentiment analysis is widely used to gauge public opinion and customer sentiments toward products, services, or brands. By analyzing social media posts, reviews, and customer feedback, organizations can gain insights into customer satisfaction and identify areas for improvement.
2. **Chatbots and Virtual Assistants:** NLP powers chatbots and virtual assistants, allowing them to understand user queries and provide relevant responses. These systems leverage NLP techniques to interpret language, enabling businesses to offer 24/7 customer support and streamline communication.
3. **Content Recommendation:** Text analytics can enhance content recommendation systems by analyzing user preferences and behavior. By understanding the context of user interactions, organizations can suggest relevant articles, products, or services.
4. **Information Retrieval:** NLP techniques improve information retrieval by enhancing search engines' ability to understand user queries and provide relevant results. Natural language search interfaces enable users to input questions in everyday language, improving the search experience.
5. **Document Summarization:** Text analytics enables the automatic summarization of large volumes of text, helping users quickly understand key points without reading the entire content. Techniques such as extractive and abstractive summarization are employed to achieve this.
6. **Fraud Detection and Compliance:** NLP can assist in identifying fraudulent activities by analyzing unstructured text data, such as emails or transaction records. By detecting anomalies and suspicious language patterns, organizations can enhance their fraud detection efforts.

Text Mining Techniques

Text mining involves extracting meaningful information and insights from unstructured text data. It leverages various techniques to analyze, interpret, and derive valuable insights from textual content. Here's an overview of the most commonly used text mining techniques:

1. **Tokenization:** Tokenization is the process of breaking down text into smaller units, known as tokens. These tokens can be words, phrases, or sentences, depending on the level of analysis required. Tokenization helps in simplifying the text for further processing.

   Use Case: Preparing text for analysis in sentiment analysis or natural language processing tasks.

2. **Text Preprocessing:** Before analysis, text data often requires cleaning and normalization. This process includes:
   - **Lowercasing:** Converting all text to lowercase to ensure uniformity.
   - **Removing Punctuation:** Eliminating punctuation marks to focus on the words.
   - **Stopword Removal:** Filtering out common words (e.g., "and," "the," "is") that do not contribute significant meaning.
   - **Stemming and Lemmatization:** Reducing words to their root form (e.g., "running" to "run") to treat different forms of a word as the same.

3. **Part-of-speech Tagging (POS):** Part-of-speech tagging involves assigning grammatical categories to each token in the text, such as noun, verb, adjective, etc. This technique helps in understanding the syntactic structure of sentences.

   Use Case: Enhancing information retrieval and improving the accuracy of text classification.

4. **Named Entity Recognition (NER):** NER identifies and classifies key entities in the text, such as names of people, organizations, locations, dates, and more. This technique is essential for extracting structured information from unstructured text.

   Use Case: Automating information extraction from news articles or social media posts.

5. **Sentiment Analysis:** Sentiment analysis determines the emotional tone behind a piece of text, categorizing it as positive, negative, or neutral. This technique helps organizations gauge public opinion and customer sentiment.

   Use Case: Analyzing customer reviews or social media mentions to assess brand reputation.

6. **Topic Modeling:** Topic modeling identifies underlying themes or topics in a collection of documents. Techniques like Latent Dirichlet Allocation (LDA)

and Non-negative Matrix Factorization (NMF) are commonly used for this purpose.

Use Case: Grouping news articles or research papers by common themes for easier navigation.

7. **Text Classification:** Text classification involves categorizing text into predefined classes or categories based on its content. Machine learning algorithms such as Support Vector Machines (SVM), Naive Bayes, and deep learning models are often employed for this task.

   Use Case: Spam detection in emails or categorizing support tickets based on their content.

8. **Clustering:** Clustering techniques group similar documents or text segments without predefined categories. Algorithms like K-means or hierarchical clustering can help identify patterns and relationships in text data.

   Use Case: Organizing customer feedback into clusters for better analysis and action.

9. **Text Summarization:** Text summarization techniques automatically condense lengthy documents into shorter versions, capturing the main ideas while retaining essential information. There are two types of summarizations:
   - **Extractive Summarization:** Selecting and extracting key sentences or phrases from the original text.
   - **Abstractive Summarization:** Generating a summary using new sentences that paraphrase the original content.

10. **Word Embeddings:** Word embeddings are a type of representation that captures the semantic meaning of words in a continuous vector space. Techniques like Word2Vec, GloVe, and FastText create word vectors that reflect the relationships between words.

    Use Case: Enhancing the performance of NLP tasks such as sentiment analysis and text classification.

Conclusion

Text mining techniques are essential for transforming unstructured text data into actionable insights. By leveraging these methods, organizations can enhance decision-making, improve customer experiences, and uncover valuable information hidden within large volumes of text. As the volume of text data continues to grow, mastering these techniques will be crucial for organizations looking to harness the power of information.

Sentiment Analysis and Topic Modeling

Sentiment analysis and topic modeling are two critical techniques in text mining and natural language processing (NLP) that enable organizations to extract meaningful insights from unstructured text data. While both techniques serve different purposes, they often complement each other in understanding customer opinions, market trends, and overall sentiment toward products, services, or events.

Sentiment Analysis

Sentiment analysis is a natural language processing technique that involves identifying and categorizing the emotional tone expressed in a piece of text, typically as positive, negative, or neutral. It enables organizations to gauge public sentiment, understand customer opinions, and monitor brand reputation by analyzing data from sources such as social media, product reviews, and surveys. The process begins with data collection, followed by text preprocessing to clean and prepare the data. Machine learning and deep learning models are then employed to classify sentiments based on extracted features. By providing insights into customer feelings and attitudes, sentiment analysis helps businesses enhance their products, improve customer service, and inform marketing strategies, ultimately driving better decision-making and fostering a deeper connection with their audience. As a vital tool for data-driven insights, sentiment analysis continues to evolve with advancements in natural language processing technologies.

Sentiment Analysis Works

1. **Data Collection:** Text data is collected from various sources such as social media, product reviews, surveys, and blogs.
2. **Text Preprocessing:** The text is cleaned and prepared for analysis. This includes tokenization, stopword removal, and normalization (lowercasing, stemming, etc.).
3. **Feature Extraction:** Key features are extracted from the text. This may involve using techniques like bag-of-words, term frequency-inverse document frequency (TF-IDF), or word embeddings.
4. **Modeling:** Various algorithms are employed to classify the sentiment. Common approaches include:
   - **Machine Learning Models:** Support Vector Machines (SVM), Naive Bayes, and Random Forests.
   - **Deep Learning Models:** Recurrent Neural Networks (RNNs), Long Short-Term Memory (LSTM) networks, and Transformers.
5. **Sentiment Classification:** The model predicts the sentiment class of the text based on the features extracted.

Applications of Sentiment Analysis: Sentiment analysis has a wide range of applications across various industries. Here are some key areas where it is effectively utilized:

1. **Customer Feedback and Reviews:** Businesses analyze customer reviews from platforms like Amazon, Yelp, and TripAdvisor to gauge overall satisfaction and identify areas for improvement. This helps in understanding consumer preferences and enhancing product offerings.

2. **Brand Monitoring:** Companies use sentiment analysis to track brand mentions on social media and news outlets. By assessing public sentiment, they can manage their reputation, respond to negative feedback, and engage with their audience more effectively.
3. **Market Research:** Organizations analyze public sentiment around products, services, or trends to inform marketing strategies. Understanding consumer attitudes can help in targeting campaigns more effectively and identifying emerging market opportunities.
4. **Political Analysis:** Sentiment analysis is widely used in political campaigns to gauge public opinion on candidates, policies, or events. By analyzing social media posts and news articles, political analysts can assess voter sentiment and adapt strategies accordingly.
5. **Financial Market Prediction:** Investors and analysts utilize sentiment analysis to predict stock market trends by analyzing news articles, earnings calls, and social media sentiment related to specific companies or industries. This helps in making informed investment decisions.

Topic Modeling

Topic modeling is a natural language processing technique used to discover hidden thematic structures in large collections of text. By identifying groups of words that frequently occur together, topic modeling reveals the underlying topics within a corpus of documents. Two popular algorithms for this purpose are Latent Dirichlet Allocation (LDA) and Non-negative Matrix Factorization (NMF). The process typically involves data collection, text preprocessing (such as tokenization and removing stopwords), and applying the chosen algorithm to extract topics. Each topic is represented by a set of keywords, allowing for better organization and understanding of content. Topic modeling has diverse applications, including document classification, content recommendation, and research analysis, helping organizations uncover trends and insights within their data. By leveraging this technique, businesses can improve information retrieval, enhance user experiences, and drive strategic decision-making based on the themes identified in textual data.

Topic Modeling Works: Topic modeling work in following points:

1. **Data Collection:** Similar to sentiment analysis, topic modeling begins with gathering a large set of text documents.
2. **Text Preprocessing:** Text is cleaned and pre-processed, which includes removing noise, tokenization, and filtering out stopwords.
3. **Model Selection:** Various algorithms can be used for topic modeling, including:
   - **Latent Dirichlet Allocation (LDA):** A generative probabilistic model that assumes each document is a mixture of topics, and each topic is characterized by a distribution of words.

- **Non-negative Matrix Factorization (NMF):** A matrix factorization technique that helps in identifying groups of related words.

4. **Model Training:** The selected model is trained on the pre-processed data to discover topics and the associated words.
5. **Interpretation:** The resulting topics are interpreted based on the words and documents associated with each topic.

Applications of Topic Modeling: Topic Modeling has a wide range of applications across various industries. Here are some key areas where it is effectively utilized:

1. **Document Classification:** Organizing large volumes of text into categories based on common topics.
2. **Content Recommendation:** Suggesting related articles or products based on topic similarity.
3. **Research Analysis:** Analyzing academic papers or articles to identify emerging trends and areas of interest.

Combining Sentiment Analysis and Topic Modeling: While sentiment analysis and topic modeling can be applied independently, combining them can yield powerful insights:

1. **Understanding Sentiment by Topic:** By applying both techniques, organizations can analyze sentiment within specific topics. For example, a company could assess customer sentiment regarding different product features by grouping feedback into topics using topic modeling.
2. **Contextual Sentiment Analysis:** Topic modeling can help identify the context in which sentiments are expressed, leading to more nuanced insights. For instance, knowing that sentiments about a product's price are negative can prompt further investigation into pricing strategies.

Conclusion

Sentiment analysis and topic modeling are invaluable tools in the realm of text analytics, offering complementary insights into customer opinions and thematic content within text data. By leveraging these techniques, organizations can enhance their understanding of customer sentiment, improve decision-making, and tailor their products and services to better meet market demands. As the volume of unstructured data continues to grow, mastering these techniques will be essential for deriving actionable insights and maintaining a competitive edge.

NLP Tools: NLTK, SpaCy, BERT

Natural Language Processing (NLP) tools are essential for analyzing and understanding human language through computational methods. Some of the most popular NLP tools are as:

Natural Language Toolkit (NLTK)

NLTK, or the Natural Language Toolkit, is a powerful and comprehensive library for Python that facilitates the development of natural language processing (NLP) applications. Designed for both education and research, NLTK provides a rich array of functionalities for text analysis, including tokenization, stemming, lemmatization, part-of-speech tagging, and named entity recognition. With access to over 50 corpora and lexical resources like WordNet, NLTK enables users to perform semantic analysis and understand linguistic relationships effectively. The library is particularly beneficial for preprocessing text data, making it an essential tool for tasks such as sentiment analysis and text classification. NLTK's user-friendly interface, extensive documentation, and numerous tutorials make it accessible to newcomers and experienced practitioners alike. It also integrates seamlessly with other Python libraries, such as NumPy and SciPy, enhancing its capabilities for data manipulation and analysis. Whether used for academic research, exploratory data analysis, or developing language models, NLTK serves as a foundational resource for anyone interested in the field of natural language processing. Its versatility and robust features empower users to extract insights from unstructured text, paving the way for innovative applications in linguistics and machine learning. As the field of NLP continues to evolve, NLTK remains a vital tool for researchers and developers seeking to harness the power of language data.

Key Features

1. **Extensive Libraries:** NLTK offers access to over 50 corpora and lexical resources, including WordNet, which helps with semantic analysis and understanding relationships between words.
2. **Text Processing Capabilities:** The toolkit supports various NLP tasks such as:
    - **Tokenization:** Splitting text into sentences or words.
    - **Stemming and Lemmatization:** Reducing words to their root forms.
    - **Part-of-speech Tagging:** Identifying the grammatical category of words.
    - **Named Entity Recognition:** Detecting and classifying named entities in text.
3. **Built-in Datasets:** NLTK provides various datasets for testing and training models, making it easier to prototype and validate NLP applications.
4. **Educational Focus:** The library is designed with education in mind, providing tutorials, documentation, and a supportive community to help newcomers learn NLP concepts.
5. **Integration with Other Libraries:** NLTK can be easily integrated with other Python libraries such as NumPy and SciPy for advanced data analysis.

Use Cases

1. **Text Preprocessing:** NLTK is commonly used for cleaning and preparing text data before analysis, making it ideal for machine learning pipelines.
2. **Building Language Models:** Researchers and developers use NLTK to create models for text classification, sentiment analysis, and other NLP applications.
3. **Academic Research:** NLTK serves as a valuable resource for students and researchers exploring linguistic concepts and conducting exploratory data analysis.
4. **Exploratory Text Analysis:** It enables users to perform tasks like topic modeling and semantic analysis, helping to uncover patterns in large text corpora.

Example: A simple example demonstrating basic NLTK functionalities, such as tokenization and part-of-speech tagging:

```
import nltk
from nltk.tokenize import word_tokenize, sent_tokenize
from nltk import pos_tag

# Sample text
text = "Natural language processing is an exciting field of study.

# Tokenization
sentences = sent_tokenize(text)
words = word_tokenize(text)

# Part-of-Speech Tagging
pos_tags = pos_tag(words)

print("Sentences:", sentences)
print("Words:", words)
print("Part-of-Speech Tags:", pos_tags)
```

Conclusion

NLTK is a powerful and versatile toolkit for anyone interested in natural language processing. Its extensive functionalities, rich resource libraries, and educational focus make it an excellent choice for both beginners and experienced practitioners. Whether you're working on text analysis, building language models, or conducting research, NLTK provides the tools you need to succeed in your NLP endeavors.

SpaCy

SpaCy is a modern, high-performance natural language processing (NLP) library designed for Python, optimized for real-world applications. Known for its speed and efficiency, SpaCy allows developers to process large volumes of text quickly and accurately. It offers a range of pre-trained models for multiple languages, facilitating tasks such as named entity recognition, part-of-speech tagging, and dependency parsing with minimal setup. The library features a user-friendly API that simplifies complex NLP tasks, making it accessible to both beginners and experienced developers. Additionally, SpaCy supports word vectors and contextual embeddings, enabling advanced semantic analysis and text representation. Its seamless integration with machine learning frameworks like TensorFlow and PyTorch further enhances its capabilities, allowing for the development of sophisticated models. Common use cases include building chatbots, content recommendation systems, and information extraction applications. By providing powerful tools for understanding and processing human language, SpaCy empowers organizations to leverage text data effectively, driving insights and enhancing user experiences across various domains. Its focus on performance and usability makes it a preferred choice for both academic research and industry projects in the field of natural language processing.

Key Features

1. **Industrial Strength:** SpaCy is optimized for performance, allowing for the processing of large volumes of text quickly. It leverages efficient algorithms and data structures to deliver fast results.

2. **Pre-trained Models:** The library provides a variety of pre-trained models for multiple languages, enabling users to perform tasks such as named entity recognition (NER), part-of-speech tagging, and dependency parsing with minimal setup.

3. **User-Friendly API:** SpaCy offers a clean and intuitive API that simplifies the implementation of complex NLP tasks, making it accessible for developers of all skill levels.

4. **Word Vectors and Embeddings:** SpaCy supports word vectors and contextual embeddings, allowing for advanced semantic understanding and text representation.

5. **Integration Capabilities:** It integrates seamlessly with other libraries, such as TensorFlow and PyTorch, facilitating the development of more sophisticated machine learning models.

Use Cases

1. **Chatbots and Virtual Assistants:** SpaCy is commonly used to build conversational agents that require understanding and processing user input.

2. **Content Recommendation Systems:** The library can analyze user behavior and preferences to suggest relevant articles or products.

3. **Information Extraction:** SpaCy's NER capabilities allow organizations to extract and categorize key information from unstructured text.

Example: A simple example demonstrating SpaCy's functionalities, such as tokenization and named entity recognition:

```
import spacy

# Load the English model
nlp = spacy.load("en_core_web_sm")

# Sample text
text = "Apple is looking at buying U.K. startup for $1 billion."

# Process the text
doc = nlp(text)

# Tokenization and named entity recognition
for token in doc:
    print(f"{token.text} ({token.pos_})")

for ent in doc.ents:
    print(f"{ent.text} ({ent.label_})")
```

Conclusion

SpaCy is a robust and efficient NLP library that empowers developers to build applications with advanced natural language understanding capabilities. Its speed, pre-trained models, and user-friendly interface make it a popular choice for both academic research and industry projects. Whether for developing chatbots, analyzing customer feedback, or extracting insights from text, SpaCy provides the tools necessary to harness the power of language data effectively.

Bidirectional Encoder Representations from Transformers (BERT)

Bidirectional Encoder Representations from Transformers (BERT) is a revolutionary natural language processing (NLP) model developed by Google that fundamentally changes how machines understand text. Unlike traditional models that process text in a single direction (either left-to-right or right-to-left), BERT uses a bidirectional approach, analyzing context from both sides of a word simultaneously. This enables it to capture nuanced meanings and relationships, significantly enhancing its understanding of language.

BERT is based on the transformer architecture, which employs attention mechanisms to focus on relevant words in a sentence, improving its ability to handle complex linguistic structures. The model is pre-trained on vast amounts of text data using unsupervised learning techniques, allowing it to grasp the intricacies of language. After pre-training, BERT can be fine-tuned for specific tasks such as sentiment analysis, question answering, and named entity recognition with minimal additional data.

Key Features

1. **Bidirectional Context:** BERT analyzes text in both directions simultaneously,

capturing nuanced meanings and relationships between words based on their surrounding context.

2. **Pre-training and Fine-tuning:** The model is initially pre-trained on vast amounts of text data using unsupervised learning and can then be fine-tuned on specific tasks, such as sentiment analysis or question answering, with relatively small datasets.
3. **Transformer Architecture:** BERT is based on the transformer architecture, which uses attention mechanisms to weigh the importance of different words in a sentence, enhancing its understanding of complex linguistic structures.
4. **State-of-the-art Performance:** BERT has achieved exceptional results on numerous NLP benchmarks, setting new standards in tasks like named entity recognition, sentiment analysis, and reading comprehension.

Use Cases

1. **Question Answering:** BERT is commonly used in systems that need to understand and retrieve answers from text based on user queries.
2. **Text Classification:** It improves the accuracy of categorizing text into predefined classes, such as spam detection or sentiment classification.
3. **Semantic Search:** BERT enhances search engines by improving their ability to understand user intent and deliver relevant results.

Example: A simple example using the Hugging Face Transformers library to implement BERT for text classification:

```
from transformers import BertTokenizer, BertForSequenceClassification
import torch

# Load pre-trained BERT model and tokenizer
tokenizer = BertTokenizer.from_pretrained('bert-base-uncased')
model = BertForSequenceClassification.from_pretrained('bert-base-uncased')

# Sample text
text = "BERT is transforming natural language processing."

# Tokenization
inputs = tokenizer(text, return_tensors='pt')

# Forward pass
outputs = model(**inputs)
logits = outputs.logits

print("Logits:", logits)
```

Conclusion

BERT has revolutionized the landscape of natural language processing, providing powerful capabilities for understanding context and meaning in text. Its bidirectional approach, combined with the transformer architecture, allows it to excel in various NLP tasks, making it a go-to choice for researchers and developers alike. By enabling machines to grasp the complexities of human language, BERT continues to drive advancements in AI applications across numerous fields.

Differences Between NLTK, SpaCy, BERT

Table 3.6

S.No.	Aspects	NLTK	SpaCy	BERT
1.	Type	Library for text processing and NLP	Library focused on production NLP	Pre-trained transformer model
2.	Architecture	Traditional NLP tools and algorithms	Based on modern NLP techniques	Transformer-based, bidirectional
3.	Performance	Slower for large datasets	Fast and efficient for real-time use	High accuracy, especially in contextual tasks
4.	Use Cases	Text preprocessing, linguistic research	Applications requiring fast processing	Contextual understanding, fine-tuning for tasks
5.	Ease of Use	More complex, requires additional setup	User-friendly API, easy to implement	Requires understanding of transformers

Applications in Social Media, Customer Feedback

Natural Language Processing (NLP) technologies are increasingly being utilized to analyze social media and customer feedback, providing valuable insights for businesses and organizations. Here are some key applications:

1. **Sentiment Analysis:** NLP techniques enable companies to assess public sentiment regarding their products, services, or brand. By analyzing social media posts, reviews, and comments, organizations can identify whether the sentiment is positive, negative, or neutral. This information helps businesses gauge customer satisfaction and address potential issues proactively.
2. **Brand Monitoring:** Businesses use NLP to monitor mentions of their brand across social media platforms. This involves tracking hashtags, keywords, and user-generated content to understand how the brand is perceived. Real-time monitoring allows for quick responses to customer inquiries or complaints, enhancing customer engagement and reputation management.
3. **Trend Analysis:** NLP tools can analyze large volumes of text data from social media to identify emerging trends and topics of interest. By understanding what consumers are discussing, brands can adapt their marketing strategies and product offerings to align with current interests, improving relevance and competitiveness.

4. **Customer Feedback Analysis:** Organizations leverage NLP to process and analyze customer feedback from surveys, reviews, and social media interactions. By extracting key themes and insights, businesses can identify common pain points, preferences, and suggestions for improvement, enabling data-driven decision-making.
5. **Chatbots and Virtual Assistants:** NLP powers chatbots and virtual assistants that engage with customers on social media and through customer service platforms. These tools can handle inquiries, provide support, and gather feedback in real-time, enhancing customer experience while reducing the workload on human agents.
6. **Crisis Management:** In the event of a PR crisis, NLP tools can quickly analyze social media conversations to assess the sentiment and volume of discussions. This allows companies to respond swiftly and effectively, managing their reputation and addressing customer concerns before they escalate.
7. **Personalization:** NLP helps analyze customer interactions to create personalized marketing strategies. By understanding customer preferences and behaviors through their feedback and social media activity, companies can tailor their communications, offers, and product recommendations, enhancing customer satisfaction and loyalty.

Conclusion

The application of NLP in social media and customer feedback analysis provides businesses with powerful tools to understand and engage with their audiences effectively. By harnessing the insights derived from sentiment analysis, trend monitoring, and customer feedback, organizations can make informed decisions, enhance customer experiences, and maintain a competitive edge in their industries.

5. Data Privacy and Security in Analytics

Data privacy and security are critical considerations in the realm of analytics, especially as organizations increasingly rely on data-driven decision-making. Protecting sensitive information while ensuring compliance with regulations is paramount. Here are key aspects of data privacy and security in analytics:

1. **Regulatory Compliance:** Organizations must adhere to various regulations regarding data privacy, such as the General Data Protection Regulation (GDPR) in Europe, the California Consumer Privacy Act (CCPA) in the U.S., and other regional laws. Compliance involves understanding data collection, processing, storage, and user consent requirements, ensuring that analytics practices align with legal frameworks.
2. **Data Encryption:** Encrypting data both at rest and in transit is essential for safeguarding sensitive information. Encryption converts data into a secure format that can only be accessed by authorized users, reducing the risk of data breaches. This practice is crucial for protecting personal identifiable information (PII) and other confidential data.

3. **Access Controls:** Implementing strict access controls ensures that only authorized personnel can access sensitive data. Role-based access control (RBAC) and least privilege principles help limit data exposure, minimizing the risk of unauthorized access and potential data leaks.
4. **Anonymization and De-identification:** To protect individual privacy, organizations can use techniques like data anonymization and de-identification. These methods remove or mask identifying information, allowing data to be analyzed without compromising user privacy. This is particularly important in analytics involving large datasets.
5. **Data Governance Frameworks:** Establishing a robust data governance framework helps organizations manage data privacy and security effectively. This includes defining data ownership, policies for data usage, and procedures for monitoring compliance. A strong governance framework fosters accountability and helps mitigate risks associated with data analytics.
6. **Risk Assessment and Management:** Regular risk assessments are essential to identify potential vulnerabilities in data analytics processes. Organizations should evaluate their data handling practices and implement risk management strategies to address identified threats. This proactive approach enhances overall data security.
7. **User Education and Training:** Educating employees about data privacy and security best practices is crucial for reducing risks. Regular training sessions can raise awareness about potential threats, such as phishing attacks, and promote a culture of data protection within the organization.

Conclusion

Data privacy and security in analytics are vital to maintaining trust and compliance in today's data-driven landscape. By implementing robust policies, technologies, and training programs, organizations can protect sensitive information while leveraging data analytics for strategic insights. Balancing innovation with responsibility is key to achieving sustainable and ethical data practices.

Understanding Data Privacy Laws: GDPR, CCPA

Data privacy laws have become increasingly important as organizations collect and process vast amounts of personal data. Two significant regulations in this landscape are the General Data Protection Regulation (GDPR) and the California Consumer Privacy Act (CCPA). Both aim to protect consumer rights and ensure responsible data handling, but they have distinct features and scopes.

General Data Protection Regulation (GDPR)

The General Data Protection Regulation (GDPR) is a comprehensive data protection law enacted by the European Union that came into effect on May 25, 2018. It aims to enhance individuals' control over their personal data and establish a unified framework for data privacy across EU member states. GDPR applies to any organization processing personal data of EU residents, regardless of the organization's location. Key principles include lawfulness, transparency, data minimization, accuracy, and security, ensuring that personal data is processed fairly and responsibly. Individuals are granted several rights, such as the right to access, rectify, erase, and transfer their data. Organizations must notify authorities of data breaches within 72 hours and face significant penalties for non-compliance, including fines up to €20 million or 4% of global revenue. Overall, GDPR sets a high standard for data privacy and has influenced global data protection regulations. Key principles are as under:

1. **Lawfulness, Fairness, and Transparency:** Organizations must process personal data lawfully, fairly, and transparently. Individuals should be informed about how their data is used.
2. **Purpose Limitation:** Data collection must be for specific, legitimate purposes, and data should not be processed in a manner incompatible with those purposes.
3. **Data Minimization:** Only the data necessary for the specified purposes should be collected and processed.
4. **Accuracy:** Organizations are required to ensure that personal data is accurate and kept up to date.
5. **Storage Limitation:** Personal data should be retained only as long as necessary for the purposes for which it was collected.
6. **Integrity and Confidentiality:** Organizations must implement appropriate security measures to protect personal data from unauthorized access, loss, or destruction.
7. **Accountability:** Data controllers must demonstrate compliance with GDPR principles and are responsible for their data processing activities.

Individual Rights Under GDPR: The GDPR grants individuals a set of rights regarding their personal data, empowering them to control how their information is handled. These rights include:

1. **Right to Access:** Individuals have the right to request access to their personal data held by organizations. They can obtain information about how their data is processed, the purposes of processing, and the retention periods.
2. **Right to Rectification:** Individuals can request corrections to inaccurate or incomplete personal data. Organizations must respond to such requests without undue delay.
3. **Right to Erasure:** Also known as the "right to be forgotten," individuals can request the deletion of their personal data under specific conditions, such as when the data is no longer necessary for the purposes for which it was collected.
4. **Right to Restrict Processing:** Individuals can request the restriction of processing their personal data in certain situations, such as when they contest the accuracy of the data or when they object to processing.

5. **Right to Data Portability:** Individuals can request their personal data in a structured, commonly used, and machine-readable format, allowing them to transfer their data to another data controller.
6. **Right to Object:** Individuals have the right to object to the processing of their personal data, particularly for direct marketing purposes. Organizations must stop processing data for such purposes upon receiving a valid objection.
7. **Rights Related to Automated Decision-making:** Individuals have the right not to be subjected to automated decision-making, including profiling, unless certain conditions are met, such as explicit consent or legal requirements.

Data Breach Notification: Under the GDPR, organizations are required to notify the relevant supervisory authority of a data breach within 72 hours of becoming aware of it. If the breach poses a high risk to individuals' rights and freedoms, affected individuals must also be informed without undue delay. This requirement emphasizes the importance of timely communication and transparency in the event of a data breach, enabling individuals to take necessary precautions.

Fines and Penalties: Non-compliance with GDPR can result in significant penalties. Organizations may face fines of up to €20 million or 4% of their global annual revenue, whichever is higher. Additionally, affected individuals can seek compensation for damages resulting from violations.

Conclusion

The GDPR represents a significant shift in data protection, emphasizing transparency, individual rights, and accountability. It sets a high standard for data privacy and security, influencing regulations worldwide. Organizations must ensure compliance to build trust with customers and avoid severe penalties, reinforcing the importance of responsible data management in today's digital landscape.

California Consumer Privacy Act (CCPA)

The California Consumer Privacy Act (CCPA) is a landmark piece of legislation aimed at enhancing privacy rights and consumer protection for residents of California. Enacted on June 28, 2018, and effective from January 1, 2020, the CCPA represents one of the most comprehensive privacy laws in the United States, addressing the growing concerns over data privacy in the digital age. The CCPA grants California residents greater control over their personal information and imposes specific obligations on businesses regarding data collection and processing practices.

The primary objectives of the CCPA are to empower consumers with more control over their personal data, increase transparency in data collection practices, and hold businesses accountable for protecting consumer privacy. By doing so, the CCPA aims to establish a consumer-centric framework for data privacy that promotes informed decision-making.

Key Features of CCPA: The key features of CCPA are as follows:

1. **Definition of Personal Information:** The CCPA broadly defines personal

information as any information that identifies, relates to, describes, or is capable of being associated with a particular individual or household. This includes names, addresses, email addresses, social security numbers, browsing history, and geolocation data, among other types of data.

2. **Consumer Rights:** The CCPA grants California residents several rights regarding their personal information:
   - **Right to Know:** Consumers can request information about the categories and specific pieces of personal data that businesses have collected about them, the purposes for which the data is used, and whether the data is sold or shared with third parties.
   - **Right to Delete:** Consumers have the right to request the deletion of their personal data held by businesses, subject to certain exceptions (e.g., when the data is necessary for completing a transaction).
   - **Right to Opt-out:** Consumers can opt out of the sale of their personal data to third parties. Businesses must provide a clear and accessible way for consumers to exercise this right.
   - **Right to Non-discrimination:** Businesses are prohibited from discriminating against consumers who exercise their rights under the CCPA. This means that consumers cannot be denied service or charged different prices for exercising their privacy rights.
3. **Business Obligations:** The CCPA imposes specific obligations on businesses that meet certain criteria:
   - **Notice Requirements:** Businesses must inform consumers at or before the point of data collection about the categories of personal information being collected and the purposes for which it will be used.
   - **Data Access and Deletion Requests:** Businesses must establish processes for handling consumer requests to access or delete their personal information and respond to these requests within a specified timeframe (generally within 45 days).
   - **Service Provider Contracts:** Businesses that share personal data with service providers must ensure that contracts are in place that specify the purpose of the data sharing and require service providers to comply with CCPA requirements.

Enforcement and Penalties: The enforcement of the CCPA is primarily the responsibility of the California Attorney General. Businesses that fail to comply with the CCPA can face civil penalties of up to $7,500 per violation. Additionally, consumers have the right to seek statutory damages in the event of a data breach, which can range from $100 to $750 per consumer per incident, or actual damages, whichever is greater.

Impact on Businesses: The CCPA has significant implications for businesses operating in California or collecting data from California residents:

1. **Compliance Costs:** Businesses must invest resources to ensure compliance with the CCPA, including legal consultations, technology upgrades, and employee training. Developing clear data privacy policies and procedures is essential.
2. **Increased Transparency:** The CCPA requires businesses to be more transparent about their data collection and processing practices, fostering trust among consumers. Clear privacy notices and accessible opt-out mechanisms are crucial for compliance.
3. **Consumer Trust:** By respecting consumer privacy rights and implementing robust data protection measures, businesses can build stronger relationships with customers. Demonstrating a commitment to data privacy can enhance brand loyalty and reputation.

Conclusion

The California Consumer Privacy Act represents a significant step toward enhancing consumer privacy rights and establishing a more transparent framework for data protection in the United States. By empowering consumers with greater control over their personal information, the CCPA sets a precedent for future privacy legislation at both state and national levels. As data privacy concerns continue to grow, organizations must prioritize compliance with the CCPA and adopt responsible data handling practices to build trust with consumers and safeguard their rights.

Data Anonymization and Masking Techniques

Data anonymization and masking are critical techniques used to protect sensitive information while still allowing for data analysis and processing. As organizations increasingly rely on data to drive decision-making, the need to safeguard personal and sensitive information has become paramount, particularly in light of regulations like the General Data Protection Regulation (GDPR) and the California Consumer Privacy Act (CCPA).

Data Anonymization

Data anonymization is the process of altering data in such a way that individuals cannot be identified. It involves removing or altering identifiable information from datasets, making it impossible to trace the data back to any individual. Types of anonymization techniques

1. **K-Anonymity:** K-anonymity ensures that each individual in a dataset cannot be distinguished from at least k"1k - 1k"1 other individuals. This is achieved by generalizing or suppressing certain attributes. For example, in a dataset with ages, instead of displaying specific ages, it might show age ranges (e.g., 20-30, 31-40).

2. **L-Diversity:** L-diversity enhances k-anonymity by ensuring that sensitive attributes within each group of k-anonymous records are diverse enough. This protects against attribute disclosure. For instance, if the dataset contains health information, it should ensure that each group includes various health conditions.
3. **T-Closeness:** T-closeness goes further by ensuring that the distribution of sensitive attributes in each group is similar to the distribution in the overall dataset. This reduces the risk of sensitive information being inferred.
4. **Differential Privacy:** Differential privacy introduces randomness into the dataset, providing a mathematical guarantee that the inclusion or exclusion of a single individual will not significantly affect the outcome of any analysis. This approach is often used in statistical data releases and machine learning.

Data Masking

Data masking is the process of obfuscating specific data within a database to protect it from unauthorized access while maintaining its usability for testing, analysis, or development purposes. Unlike anonymization, masked data can be reversed to retrieve the original information under controlled conditions. Types of masking techniques are as under:

1. **Static Data Masking:** In static data masking, a copy of the original data is created, and sensitive information is replaced with fictitious or scrambled data. This method is commonly used in non-production environments where realistic data is needed for testing.

   Example: Replacing customer names and addresses with dummy data while retaining the format.
2. **Dynamic Data Masking:** Dynamic data masking modifies the data in real-time based on the user's access rights. Users can see only the masked version of the data while the original data remains unchanged in the database.

   Example: A user may see "*****" in place of a social security number when accessing a database.
3. **Format-preserving Masking:** This technique replaces sensitive data with fictitious data that maintains the original data format. This is useful for applications where format consistency is necessary.

   Example: Replacing a credit card number with a valid-looking number that follows the same format (e.g., keeping the same length).
4. **Tokenization:** Tokenization involves substituting sensitive data with unique identification symbols (tokens) that retain essential information without compromising security. Tokens are stored in a separate database and can be mapped back to the original data.

   Example: Replacing credit card numbers with tokens that represent the original values.

Applications of Anonymization and Masking

1. **Compliance with Regulations:** Both anonymization and masking techniques help organizations comply with data protection regulations, ensuring that personal data is handled appropriately and reducing the risk of data breaches.
2. **Data Sharing and Collaboration:** Organizations often need to share data with third parties for analysis or research. Anonymizing or masking data allows for secure sharing without exposing sensitive information.
3. **Testing and Development:** In software development and testing environments, realistic data is often needed. Masking allows developers to work with data that resembles the production environment while protecting sensitive information.
4. **Research and Analytics:** Anonymized data can be used for research and analytics, enabling organizations to derive insights without compromising individual privacy.

Importance of Anonymization and Masking

1. **Enhancing Data Privacy:** Anonymization and masking are essential for protecting individuals' privacy rights, reducing the risk of identity theft and misuse of personal information.
2. **Building Trust:** By implementing robust data protection measures, organizations can build trust with customers and stakeholders, demonstrating a commitment to safeguarding their information.
3. **Reducing Compliance Risks:** Proper use of anonymization and masking techniques helps organizations mitigate the risk of non-compliance with data protection laws, which can result in severe penalties.
4. **Facilitating Data Utilization:** These techniques allow organizations to leverage data for analytics and decision-making while ensuring that sensitive information remains secure.

Conclusion

Data anonymization and masking are vital techniques in today's data-driven landscape, enabling organizations to protect sensitive information while still utilizing data for analysis and decision-making. By implementing these practices, organizations can enhance data privacy, build consumer trust, and comply with legal requirements. As data protection regulations continue to evolve, investing in effective anonymization and masking strategies will be essential for safeguarding personal information and ensuring responsible data handling.

Secure Data Storage and Access Control

In an era where data breaches and cyber threats are increasingly prevalent, ensuring the security of sensitive information is paramount. Secure data storage and effective access control are critical components of a comprehensive data protection strategy. Organizations must adopt robust practices to safeguard data integrity, confidentiality, and availability while providing authorized users with the necessary access to perform their tasks.

Methods of Secure Data Storage

1. **Encryption:** Encryption is one of the most effective ways to secure data at rest. It involves converting data into a coded format that can only be read by authorized users with the appropriate decryption key. Types of encryptions are:
   - **Symmetric Encryption**: The same key is used for both encryption and decryption. It is faster and suitable for large volumes of data but requires secure key management.
   - **Asymmetric Encryption**: Uses a pair of keys public and private. It is more secure but slower, often used for securing communications and transactions.
2. **Data Masking:** Data masking obscures specific data within a database to protect sensitive information. It allows organizations to use realistic data for development and testing without exposing the actual sensitive information.

   Example: Replacing actual customer names with fictitious names while maintaining the data structure.
3. **Access Control Mechanisms:** Effective access control is crucial for secure data storage. It involves implementing policies and technologies to regulate who can access data and under what circumstances. Types of access control are:
   - **Role-based Access Control (RBAC):** Access is granted based on the user's role within the organization. This ensures that users only have access to the information necessary for their job functions.
   - **Attribute-based Access Control (ABAC):** Access decisions are based on attributes (user attributes, resource attributes, environmental attributes). This allows for more granular control over who can access specific data.
4. **Data Segmentation:** Data segmentation involves dividing data into distinct sections based on sensitivity levels. This approach allows organizations to apply different security measures depending on the classification of the data.

   Example: Highly sensitive data, such as financial information, might be stored in a more secure environment compared to less sensitive operational data.
5. **Regular Backups:** Implementing regular data backups is essential for protecting against data loss due to breaches, corruption, or disasters. Secure backup solutions should also include encryption and access control measures to ensure the safety of backup data.

Importance of Access Control: Access control is the process of determining who can access specific data and what actions they can perform with that data. Proper access control is essential for several reasons:

1. **Preventing Unauthorized Access:** Access control helps restrict data access to authorized users only, reducing the risk of data breaches.
2. **Ensuring Compliance:** Many regulations require organizations to implement access controls to protect sensitive information. Non-compliance can lead to significant fines and reputational damage.
3. **Data Integrity:** Proper access controls ensure that only authorized individuals can modify or delete data, helping to maintain data integrity.
4. **Audit Trails:** Effective access control mechanisms allow organizations to maintain logs of who accessed what data and when. This is essential for audits and investigations.

Best Practices for Secure Data Storage and Access Control

1. **Implement Strong Encryption:** Use robust encryption methods for data at rest and in transit. Ensure that encryption keys are managed securely.
2. **Enforce Multi-Factor Authentication:** Require MFA for accessing sensitive data to add an extra layer of security.
3. **Regularly Review Access Controls:** Conduct periodic reviews of user access rights to ensure that only authorized individuals have access to sensitive data.
4. **Train Employees:** Provide training on data security best practices and the importance of protecting sensitive information.
5. **Establish Incident Response Plans:** Develop and maintain an incident response plan to address potential data breaches swiftly.
6. **Utilize Secure Backup Solutions:** Ensure that backup data is encrypted and stored securely, with access controls in place.

Conclusion

Secure data storage and access control are foundational elements of a robust data security strategy. By implementing effective storage solutions and access controls, organizations can protect sensitive information from unauthorized access and breaches, comply with regulatory requirements, and maintain the trust of customers and stakeholders. As cyber threats continue to evolve, prioritizing these practices will be essential for safeguarding data in an increasingly complex digital landscape.

Best Practices for Ensuring Data Security

In an increasingly digital world, ensuring data security is paramount for organizations of all sizes. With rising threats such as data breaches, ransomware, and cyberattacks, implementing best practices for data security is essential to protect sensitive information and maintain trust. Here are key strategies that organizations should adopt to enhance their data security posture.

1. **Conduct Regular Risk Assessments:** Regular risk assessments help organizations identify vulnerabilities in their data security frameworks.

Understanding potential threats allows for proactive measures to mitigate risks. Action steps are:

- **Identify Assets:** Catalog all data assets, including databases and applications.
- **Evaluate Threats:** Assess threats such as cyberattacks, insider threats, and environmental risks.
- **Prioritize Risks:** Create a risk matrix to prioritize vulnerabilities based on their potential impact.

2. **Implement Strong Access Control:** Access controls are critical for ensuring that only authorized personnel can access sensitive data, reducing the risk of unauthorized access. Action steps are:
   - **Role-based Access Control (RBAC):** Grant access based on user roles to limit data exposure.
   - **Multi-factor Authentication (MFA):** Require additional verification steps to enhance security.
   - **Regular Reviews:** Conduct periodic audits of access rights to ensure compliance.
3. **Encrypt Sensitive Data:** Encryption protects data by transforming it into a format that can only be accessed with a decryption key, safeguarding it against unauthorized access. Action steps are:
   - **Data at Rest:** Use strong encryption algorithms (e.g., AES) for stored data.
   - **Data in Transit:** Implement SSL/TLS for secure data transmission over networks.
4. **Keep Software and Systems Updated:** Outdated software is a common target for cybercriminals. Regular updates patch vulnerabilities and enhance security. Action steps are:
   - **Automatic Updates:** Enable automatic updates for critical software and systems.
   - **Patch Management:** Establish a schedule for manually checking and applying security patches.
5. **Regularly Backup Data:** Regular backups are essential for data recovery in case of breaches, corruption, or disasters. A robust backup strategy ensures business continuity. Action steps are:
   - **Backup Frequency:** Schedule daily or weekly backups, depending on data volatility.
   - **Offsite Storage:** Store backups securely in offsite locations or cloud solutions.

6. **Educate Employees on Data Security:** Employees are often the weakest link in data security. Educating them on best practices helps prevent human errors that can lead to breaches. Action steps are:
   - **Training Programs:** Conduct regular training on topics such as phishing and password management.
   - **Create a Security Culture:** Encourage employees to report suspicious activity and participate in security discussions.
7. **Monitor and Audit Data Access:** Continuous monitoring of data access helps identify unauthorized attempts and potential breaches early on. Action steps are:
   - **Access Logs:** Implement logging mechanisms to track who accesses sensitive data and when.
   - **Regular Audits:** Conduct audits of access logs to identify anomalies and take corrective actions.
8. **Implement Data Loss Prevention (DLP) Solutions:** DLP solutions help prevent data breaches by monitoring and controlling the transfer of sensitive information. Action steps are:
   - **Deploy DLP Tools:** Utilize software that monitors data use, including email and file sharing.
   - **Define Policies:** Establish data handling policies that dictate how sensitive data can be used and shared.
9. **Develop an Incident Response Plan**: An incident response plan outlines how to respond to security breaches, minimizing damage and recovery time. Action steps are:
   - **Assign Roles:** Define roles and responsibilities for incident response team members.
   - **Create Procedures:** Develop clear procedures for identifying, containing, and recovering from incidents.
   - **Conduct Drills:** Regularly test the plan through drills to ensure team readiness.
10. **Secure Physical Access to Data Centers:** Physical security is as important as cybersecurity. Unauthorized physical access can lead to data breaches. Action steps are:
    - **Access Controls:** Implement key card systems, biometric scanners, and visitor logs.
    - **Surveillance:** Use video monitoring and security personnel to safeguard facilities.

Conclusion

Implementing these best practices for data security is essential for protecting sensitive information in today's digital landscape. By conducting regular risk assessments, establishing strong access controls, encrypting data, and fostering a culture of security awareness, organizations can significantly enhance their security posture. As threats continue to evolve, staying vigilant and adapting these practices will be key to ensuring the safety and integrity of data.

CASE STUDIES OF TOOLS AND TECHNOLOGIES

Case Study 1: Using Tableau for Data Visualization in a Retail Chain

Overview

A leading retail chain, with over 500 stores across the country, faced challenges in analyzing and visualizing sales data. Despite having access to vast amounts of data from various sources, the company struggled to generate actionable insights due to the complexity and volume of the data. To address this, the organization decided to implement Tableau, a powerful data visualization tool, to improve its analytics capabilities.

Implementation

Step 1: Data Integration

The first step was to integrate data from multiple sources, including point-of-sale systems, inventory databases, and customer relationship management (CRM) systems. Tableau's ability to connect to various data sources, such as SQL databases, Excel files, and cloud services, made this process seamless.

Step 2: Building Dashboards

Once the data was integrated, the analytics team created interactive dashboards that displayed key performance indicators (KPIs) such as sales trends, inventory levels, and customer demographics. Tableau's drag-and-drop interface allowed team members with varying levels of technical expertise to create visualizations easily.

Step 3: Training and Adoption

To ensure effective use of Tableau, the company conducted training sessions for employees across departments. This training focused on how to navigate dashboards, interpret data visualizations, and use the insights for decision-making.

Results

1. **Enhanced Decision-making:** The retail chain experienced a 30% improvement in decision-making speed due to the accessibility of real-time data visualizations. Managers could quickly identify trends and make informed decisions regarding inventory management and promotional strategies.
2. **Sales Growth:** By analyzing customer buying patterns through the dashboards, the company optimized its product placements and promotional campaigns, resulting in a 15% increase in sales over six months.

3. **Operational Efficiency:** The insights gained from Tableau allowed for better inventory management, reducing excess stock by 20%. This not only minimized storage costs but also improved cash flow.

Conclusion

The implementation of Tableau transformed the retail chain's data analysis capabilities, enabling it to leverage data for strategic decision-making effectively. By integrating diverse data sources and creating user-friendly dashboards, the company was able to enhance its operational efficiency, increase sales, and improve overall performance.

Case Study 2: Implementing Salesforce for Customer Relationship Management in a Financial Services Firm

Overview

A mid-sized financial services firm providing investment and insurance solutions was facing challenges in managing customer relationships and tracking sales leads. The company relied on outdated manual processes and disparate systems, leading to inefficiencies and missed opportunities. To improve its customer relationship management (CRM) capabilities, the firm decided to implement Salesforce, a leading cloud-based CRM platform.

Implementation

Step 1: Needs Assessment

The first step involved conducting a needs assessment to identify the specific requirements of different departments, including sales, marketing, and customer support. This assessment helped tailor Salesforce to the organization's needs.

Step 2: Customization and Integration

Salesforce was customized to fit the firm's workflow, including features like lead tracking, opportunity management, and customer service automation. The team integrated Salesforce with existing tools, such as email systems and financial planning software, to streamline operations.

Step 3: User Training and Onboarding

To facilitate a smooth transition, the company organized comprehensive training sessions for employees. The training covered Salesforce functionalities, best practices for lead management, and customer interaction techniques.

Results

1. **Improved Customer Engagement:** The firm saw a 40% increase in customer engagement due to improved tracking of customer interactions and preferences. Salesforce allowed for personalized communication, enhancing customer satisfaction.

2. **Increased Sales Efficiency:** Sales teams reported a 25% increase in lead

conversion rates as a result of better tracking and follow-up processes. Salesforce provided insights into lead behavior, enabling more targeted sales strategies.

3. **Data-Driven Decision-making:** With Salesforce's reporting tools, management could access real-time analytics to evaluate sales performance and marketing effectiveness. This data-driven approach led to a
4. more proactive business strategy.

Conclusion

By implementing Salesforce, the financial services firm transformed its customer relationship management processes. The platform provided a unified view of customer interactions, improved sales efficiency, and enhanced customer engagement. This case study highlights the importance of leveraging CRM tools to optimize business operations and drive growth.

Final Thoughts

These case studies demonstrate how the effective use of advanced tools and technologies can lead to significant improvements in operational efficiency, customer engagement, and overall business performance. Whether through data visualization with Tableau in a retail environment or customer relationship management with Salesforce in the financial sector, organizations that embrace innovative technologies are better positioned to thrive in a competitive landscape. By investing in the right tools and ensuring proper implementation, companies can unlock the full potential of their data and resources, ultimately driving long-term success.

SUMMARY OF TOOLS AND TECHNOLOGIES

1. Data Analytics Tools Overview

Data analytics tools encompass a variety of technologies for analyzing and visualizing data. Key tools include R and Python for statistical analysis, Excel for basic tasks, and SQL for database queries. Visualization platforms like Tableau and Power BI, along with cloud services like AWS and Azure, enhance data accessibility and insights.

Comparison of Tools: R vs. Python, Excel, SQL

The landscape of data analytics tools is rich and varied, catering to different user needs and expertise. R is primarily favored for statistical analysis and visualization, making it popular among statisticians and data scientists. Its vast repository of packages, such as ggplot2 and dplyr, enhances its functionality for data manipulation and graphical representation. In contrast, Python has emerged as a versatile tool that supports a wide range of applications, including machine learning, web development, and data analytics. Libraries such as Pandas, NumPy, and Matplotlib empower users to handle data processing and visualization effectively.

Excel remains a staple for data analysis, particularly in business environments, due to its user-friendly interface and powerful functions. It is suitable for small to medium datasets and basic analysis tasks but can struggle with larger data volumes. SQL (Structured Query Language) is essential for managing and querying relational databases, allowing users to manipulate and extract data efficiently. Each tool has its strengths, and the choice depends on the specific requirements of the analysis task, data size, and user expertise.

Data Visualization Tools: Tableau, Power BI, Qlik

Data visualization tools are crucial for translating complex data into understandable insights. Tableau is renowned for its intuitive drag-and-drop interface, allowing users to create interactive and shareable dashboards. It supports a variety of data sources and enables real-time data visualization, making it a favourite among analysts and business intelligence professionals. Power BI, developed by Microsoft, integrates seamlessly with other Microsoft products and provides robust analytics capabilities. Its ease of use and strong data connectivity options make it an attractive choice for organizations already using Microsoft services.

Qlik, known for its associative data model, allows users to explore data intuitively, revealing insights that might be missed with traditional query-based tools. It emphasizes self-service analytics, enabling users to generate reports and dashboards without extensive IT involvement. Overall, these visualization tools enhance data interpretation, facilitating better decision-making across organizations.

Cloud Platforms for Analytics: AWS, Azure, Google Cloud

Cloud platforms have revolutionized data analytics by providing scalable resources and infrastructure. Amazon Web Services (AWS) offers a comprehensive suite of tools, including Amazon Redshift for data warehousing, Amazon S3 for storage, and AWS Glue for data integration. Its flexibility and extensive service offerings make it a preferred choice for many businesses.

Microsoft Azure is another powerful cloud platform, integrating seamlessly with other Microsoft services. Azure offers services like Azure Synapse Analytics for big data analytics and Azure Machine Learning for predictive modeling. Its hybrid cloud capabilities also allow businesses to balance between on-premises and cloud environments.

Google Cloud provides tools such as BigQuery, a serverless data warehouse that enables fast SQL queries and analytics on large datasets. Its focus on machine learning and AI tools enhances its appeal to organizations looking to leverage advanced analytics. All three platforms enable businesses to process and analyze data at scale while ensuring flexibility and cost-effectiveness.

2. Big Data Technologies

Big Data technologies encompass tools and frameworks for managing and analyzing vast datasets characterized by volume, velocity, and variety. Key components include the Hadoop ecosystem (HDFS, MapReduce, Hive, Pig), real-time processing with Spark and Kafka, and NoSQL databases like MongoDB, Cassandra, and HBase, enabling efficient data handling and insights.

Introduction to Big Data and Its Characteristics

Big Data refers to the vast volumes of structured and unstructured data generated at high velocity and variety. It is characterized by the "Three Vs": volume (the sheer amount of data), velocity (the speed at which data is generated and processed), and variety (the different types of data, including text, images, and videos). The ability to analyze Big Data is crucial for organizations seeking to gain insights, enhance customer experiences, and improve operational efficiency.

Hadoop Ecosystem: HDFS, MapReduce, Hive, Pig

The Hadoop ecosystem is a foundational framework for managing and processing Big Data. Hadoop Distributed File System (HDFS) is designed to store vast amounts of data across multiple machines, providing high throughput access and fault tolerance. **MapReduce** is the processing engine that allows for the distributed processing of data stored in HDFS, breaking down tasks into smaller, manageable parts.

Hive is a data warehousing solution built on top of Hadoop, enabling users to query and manage large datasets using a SQL-like language called HiveQL. It simplifies the process of data analysis for users familiar with traditional databases. Pig is a high-level platform for creating programs that run on Hadoop, allowing users to write complex data transformations using a scripting language known as Pig Latin. Together, these components form a robust ecosystem for handling Big Data efficiently.

Real-time Data Processing with Spark and Kafka

Apache Spark is an open-source data processing engine designed for speed and ease of use. It provides in-memory processing capabilities, allowing for faster data analysis compared to traditional disk-based systems. Spark supports various data processing tasks, including batch processing, stream processing, and machine learning. When combined with **Apache Kafka**, a distributed streaming platform, organizations can handle real-time data feeds effectively. Kafka serves as a messaging system that enables the continuous flow of data between applications, making it ideal for scenarios requiring real-time analytics.

NoSQL Databases: MongoDB, Cassandra, HBase

NoSQL databases are designed to handle unstructured data and provide scalability, flexibility, and high availability. MongoDB is a document-oriented database that stores data in flexible, JSON-like documents, allowing for easy data retrieval and indexing. It is particularly well-suited for applications requiring rapid development and iteration.

Cassandra is a wide-column store known for its ability to handle large amounts of data across many servers without a single point of failure. It excels in scenarios requiring high write and read throughput, making it ideal for real-time analytics applications. HBase, built on top of Hadoop, provides a scalable, distributed database that supports random, real-time access to large datasets. Each of these NoSQL databases addresses specific needs in handling Big Data and provides organizations with the tools to manage and analyze diverse data types.

3. Business Intelligence and Reporting

Business Intelligence (BI) and reporting involve analyzing data to drive informed decision-making. Key elements include BI frameworks, effective dashboard design, self-service BI tools, and advanced reporting techniques. These practices enable organizations to visualize insights, monitor performance, and respond quickly to changing business conditions, fostering a data-driven culture.

BI Concepts and Frameworks

Business Intelligence (BI) encompasses the strategies and technologies used by organizations to analyze business data and gain actionable insights. Key concepts include data warehousing, data mining, and analytics. BI frameworks provide structured approaches for gathering, analyzing, and presenting data, enabling businesses to make informed decisions based on real-time insights.

Dashboard Design and Best Practices

Effective dashboard design is crucial for conveying insights clearly and concisely. Best practices include keeping layouts simple and intuitive, using appropriate visualizations (such as graphs and charts), and ensuring that key metrics are prominently displayed. Dashboards should be interactive, allowing users to drill down into data for deeper analysis while maintaining a focus on high-level insights.

Self-Service BI Tools

Self-service BI tools empower users to create reports and dashboards without relying on IT departments. These tools provide intuitive interfaces that enable business users to access and analyze data independently. The adoption of self-service BI enhances agility, allowing organizations to respond quickly to changing business needs and fosters a data-driven culture across departments.

Advanced Reporting Techniques

Advanced reporting techniques involve the use of predictive analytics, data modeling, and data visualization to uncover trends and patterns. Organizations leverage these techniques to create reports that not only summarize historical data but also forecast future outcomes. This proactive approach enables businesses to make strategic decisions based on predictive insights, driving growth and efficiency.

4. Text Analytics and Natural Language Processing (NLP)

Text Analytics and Natural Language Processing (NLP) focus on extracting insights from unstructured text data. Techniques include sentiment analysis, topic modeling, and text mining. Tools like NLTK, SpaCy, and BERT enhance text understanding, enabling applications in customer feedback analysis and social media monitoring to drive informed business decisions.

Text Mining Techniques

Text analytics involves extracting meaningful insights from unstructured text data. Common techniques include text mining, which involves discovering patterns and trends from textual data, and natural language processing (NLP), which enables machines to understand and interpret human language. These techniques allow organizations to analyze customer feedback, social media interactions, and other textual sources to gain valuable insights.

Sentiment Analysis and Topic Modeling

Sentiment analysis is a specialized form of text analytics that determines the sentiment expressed in a piece of text, categorizing it as positive, negative, or neutral. This technique is widely used in monitoring brand perception and customer satisfaction. Topic modeling involves identifying themes or topics within large volumes of text, helping organizations understand the main subjects being discussed and enabling targeted responses.

NLP Tools: NLTK, SpaCy, BERT

Several NLP tools have emerged to facilitate text analysis. NLTK (Natural Language Toolkit) is a comprehensive library for text processing in Python, providing tools for tasks like tokenization and stemming. SpaCy is another popular NLP library known for its efficiency and ease of use, particularly in production settings. BERT (Bidirectional Encoder Representations from Transformers), developed by Google, is a powerful model for understanding the context of words in text, significantly improving the performance of various NLP tasks, including sentiment analysis and question answering.

Applications in Social Media and Customer Feedback

NLP and text analytics have numerous applications in analyzing social media interactions and customer feedback. Organizations leverage these technologies to gain insights into customer sentiment, identify trends, and inform marketing strategies. By understanding public perception and addressing customer concerns promptly, businesses can enhance their reputation and improve customer experiences.

5. Data Privacy and Security in Analytics

Data privacy and security in analytics involve protecting sensitive information through compliance with laws like GDPR and CCPA, employing techniques such as data anonymization and masking, and implementing secure storage and access control measures. These practices ensure user privacy while enabling organizations to leverage data for informed decision-making.

Understanding Data Privacy Laws: GDPR, CCPA

Data privacy laws such as the General Data Protection Regulation (GDPR) and the California Consumer Privacy Act (CCPA) set stringent requirements for data handling and user privacy. GDPR emphasizes user consent and data protection rights, while CCPA grants consumers greater control over their personal information.

Organizations must understand these regulations to ensure compliance and avoid legal repercussions.

Data Anonymization and Masking Techniques

Data anonymization involves removing personally identifiable information (PII) from datasets to protect user privacy. Techniques such as data masking replace sensitive data with fictional values, allowing organizations to use real data for testing and development without exposing personal information. These techniques are essential for maintaining compliance with data privacy laws while leveraging data for analytics.

Secure Data Storage and Access Control

Secure data storage and access control involve encrypting sensitive data, implementing strict access policies, using strong authentication, conducting regular backups, monitoring access, and training employees.

Best Practices for Ensuring Data Security

Best practices for ensuring data security include encrypting data, implementing access controls, using multi-factor authentication, conducting regular backups, monitoring logs, and training employees on security awareness.

4

Applications and Case Studies

Data analytics has become a cornerstone across various industries, driving significant advancements and efficiencies through diverse applications and case studies. In healthcare, for instance, predictive analytics is revolutionizing patient care by analyzing historical health data to forecast disease outbreaks and patient readmission rates. A notable case is Mount Sinai Health System, which implemented predictive models to identify high-risk patients, allowing for targeted interventions that reduced readmission rates by over 20%. Similarly, in retail, companies like Amazon leverage data analytics to enhance customer experiences through personalized recommendations based on browsing and purchasing history. Their recommendation engine, which accounts for a significant portion of their revenue, demonstrates the power of data-driven insights in shaping consumer behavior and increasing sales.

In finance, data analytics is used for fraud detection and risk management. PayPal employs machine learning algorithms to analyze transaction patterns in real-time, flagging suspicious activities and minimizing losses from fraudulent transactions. This approach has proven highly effective, significantly reducing fraud rates and enhancing customer trust. In the manufacturing sector, companies like General Electric utilize data analytics for predictive maintenance, analyzing machine performance data to predict failures before they occur, thus minimizing downtime and maintenance costs. This proactive strategy has led to substantial cost savings and improved operational efficiency. Furthermore, in the field of marketing, businesses are employing analytics to measure campaign effectiveness and customer engagement. Coca-Cola, for instance, uses data analytics to track customer preferences and optimize marketing strategies, resulting in increased brand loyalty and sales growth. These applications illustrate the transformative potential of data analytics, showcasing its ability to drive innovation, improve decision-making, and create competitive advantages across a wide range of sectors. As organizations continue to recognize the value of data, the scope and impact of analytics are expected to expand further, leading to more informed and strategic business practices.

1. Marketing Analytics

Marketing analytics involves the systematic collection, measurement, and analysis of data to evaluate the effectiveness of marketing strategies and campaigns. By leveraging various analytical tools and techniques, businesses can gain deep insights into customer behavior, preferences, and trends. This data-driven approach allows marketers to understand which strategies resonate with their target audience, identify high-performing channels, and allocate resources more effectively. Techniques such as A/B testing, customer segmentation, and conversion tracking enable organizations to refine their messaging and optimize campaigns in real time. For instance, by analyzing engagement metrics from email marketing campaigns, businesses can determine the ideal send times, subject lines, and content types that lead to higher open and conversion rates. Ultimately, marketing analytics transforms raw data into actionable insights, driving more informed decision-making and enhancing overall marketing effectiveness.

Moreover, the advent of advanced technologies, including machine learning and artificial intelligence, is reshaping the landscape of marketing analytics. These technologies enable predictive analytics, where businesses can forecast future customer behavior based on historical data. For example, Netflix employs sophisticated algorithms to recommend content based on users' viewing histories, significantly enhancing user engagement and retention. Additionally, social media platforms provide rich datasets that marketers can analyze to gauge brand sentiment, monitor competitor activities, and identify emerging trends. By integrating data from multiple sources, such as CRM systems, web analytics, and social media, organizations can develop a holistic view of their marketing efforts. This comprehensive perspective empowers marketers to tailor campaigns to specific audience segments, measure return on investment (ROI) more accurately, and adjust strategies dynamically. As data continues to proliferate, the importance of marketing analytics will only grow, enabling businesses to stay competitive in an increasingly complex and fast-paced marketplace.

Key Components of Marketing Analytics: Marketing analytics encompasses various processes and methodologies that help organizations assess their marketing performance and optimize strategies. Understanding the key components of marketing analytics is essential for leveraging data effectively to drive business outcomes. Here are the primary components:

1. **Data Collection:** The foundation of effective marketing analytics is robust data collection. Organizations gather data from a multitude of sources, including:
   - **Web Analytics:** Tools like Google Analytics provide insights into website traffic, user behavior, and conversion rates.
   - **Social Media Metrics:** Platforms such as Facebook, Twitter, and Instagram offer analytics that track engagement, reach, and audience demographics.
   - **Customer Relationship Management (CRM) Systems:** CRMs store

valuable customer data, including purchase history, preferences, and interactions, which can inform marketing strategies.

- **Email Marketing Tools:** Services like Mailchimp and Constant Contact collect data on open rates, click-through rates, and subscriber engagement.

By aggregating data from these various sources, marketers can gain a comprehensive view of their audience and campaign performance.

2. **Data Processing and Cleaning:** Raw data is often messy and may contain errors, duplicates, or inconsistencies. Data processing involves cleaning and preparing the data for analysis. This step includes:
   - **Removing Duplicates:** Ensuring that each entry in the dataset is unique.
   - **Correcting Errors:** Identifying and fixing inaccuracies in the data, such as incorrect dates or values.
   - **Standardizing Formats:** Ensuring consistency in data formats, such as date formats or categorical variables.

   Effective data cleaning is crucial for obtaining reliable insights, as inaccuracies can skew analysis results.

3. **Descriptive Analytics:** Descriptive analytics focuses on summarizing historical data to understand what has happened. This component employs various techniques, such as:
   - **Data Visualization:** Tools like Tableau and Power BI help present data through graphs and charts, making it easier to identify trends and patterns.
   - **Summary Statistics:** Metrics such as mean, median, and standard deviation provide a quick overview of data characteristics.
   - **Reporting:** Regular reports summarizing key performance indicators (KPIs) help stakeholders understand marketing performance at a glance.

   Descriptive analytics sets the stage for deeper analysis and helps marketers evaluate past campaign effectiveness.

4. **Predictive Analytics:** Predictive analytics utilizes statistical models and machine learning techniques to forecast future outcomes based on historical data. This component is essential for:
   - **Customer Segmentation:** Identifying distinct customer groups based on behavior and preferences, allowing for targeted marketing.
   - **Sales Forecasting:** Predicting future sales trends based on past performance and market conditions.
   - **Churn Prediction:** Identifying customers at risk of leaving and developing strategies to retain them.

   By anticipating future behaviors, marketers can proactively tailor their strategies for better outcomes.

5. **Prescriptive Analytics:** Prescriptive analytics goes a step further by recommending specific actions based on data insights. This component helps marketers understand not just what is likely to happen, but what they should do about it. Techniques include:
   - **Optimization Models:** These models suggest the best course of action, such as budget allocation across marketing channels.
   - **Scenario Analysis:** Evaluating different scenarios to determine potential outcomes of various marketing strategies.

   Prescriptive analytics empowers marketers to make informed decisions that maximize their impact.
6. **Performance Measurement and KPIs:** A critical aspect of marketing analytics is measuring performance through key performance indicators (KPIs). KPIs vary depending on the goals of a campaign but may include:
   - **Conversion Rate:** The percentage of users who complete a desired action.
   - **Customer Acquisition Cost (CAC):** The total cost of acquiring a new customer.
   - **Customer Lifetime Value (CLV):** The total revenue a customer is expected to generate over their lifetime.

   Regularly tracking these metrics helps marketers assess their effectiveness and make data-driven adjustments.

Importance of Marketing Analytics: Marketing analytics has become a vital component of modern business strategy, enabling organizations to harness the power of data to drive effective marketing initiatives. The importance of marketing analytics can be understood through several key aspects:

1. **Data-driven Decision-making:** At its core, marketing analytics transforms raw data into actionable insights. Instead of relying on gut feelings or assumptions, organizations can make informed decisions based on empirical evidence. This data-driven approach minimizes risks and increases the likelihood of success by allowing marketers to evaluate the effectiveness of their strategies with tangible metrics.
2. **Evaluating Campaign Effectiveness:** One of the primary benefits of marketing analytics is the ability to assess campaign performance. By analyzing key performance indicators (KPIs) such as conversion rates, click-through rates, and customer engagement metrics, marketers can identify which channels and tactics yield the best results. This evaluation is crucial for understanding what resonates with the target audience and for refining future marketing efforts.
3. **Optimizing Resource Allocation:** Effective resource allocation is essential for maximizing return on investment (ROI). Marketing analytics enables organizations to determine which campaigns and channels are most effective,

allowing them to allocate their budgets accordingly. By focusing on high-performing strategies and cutting back on less effective ones, businesses can enhance their overall marketing efficiency.

4. **Understanding Customer Behavior:** Marketing analytics provides a deep understanding of customer preferences and behaviors. By analyzing data from various sources, such as website interactions, social media engagement, and purchase histories, organizations can segment their audience more effectively. This segmentation allows for personalized marketing efforts that resonate with specific customer groups, leading to increased engagement and higher conversion rates.

5. **Enhancing Personalization:** In today's market, personalization is key to successful marketing. With insights gained from marketing analytics, organizations can create tailored marketing messages and offers that speak directly to individual customers' needs and preferences. This targeted approach not only enhances customer satisfaction but also fosters loyalty, as consumers are more likely to engage with brands that understand and cater to their specific desires.

6. **Predictive Analytics for Future Planning:** Predictive analytics is a powerful tool within the marketing analytics framework. It utilizes historical data and statistical algorithms to forecast future trends and customer behaviors. By anticipating what customers are likely to want or need, organizations can adapt their strategies proactively, positioning themselves to meet market demands before they arise.

Types of Digital Marketing Analytics: Digital marketing analytics encompasses a range of techniques and tools designed to measure, analyze, and optimize online marketing performance. Understanding the different types of digital marketing analytics is crucial for businesses looking to enhance their strategies and drive better results. Some primary types of digital marketing analytics:

1. **Web Analytics:** Web analytics is the foundation of digital marketing analytics. It involves tracking and analyzing website traffic and user behavior to understand how visitors interact with a site. Key metrics include page views, session duration, bounce rates, and conversion rates. Tools like Google Analytics provide valuable insights, allowing marketers to identify which pages perform best, where users drop off, and how to optimize the user experience. This information is essential for improving site navigation and content effectiveness.

2. **Social Media Analytics:** Social media analytics focuses on measuring engagement and performance across various social media platforms. Key metrics include likes, shares, comments, follower growth, and engagement rates. By analyzing these metrics, businesses can gauge the effectiveness of their social media campaigns, understand audience demographics, and

identify trends in user interaction. Tools like Hootsuite and Sprout Social provide comprehensive dashboards for tracking social media performance and refining strategies accordingly.

3. **Email Marketing Analytics:** Email marketing analytics evaluates the performance of email campaigns. Important metrics include open rates, click-through rates (CTR), conversion rates, and unsubscribe rates. Analyzing these metrics helps marketers understand what types of content resonate with their audience, optimize send times, and improve targeting. A/B testing can also be employed to refine subject lines and content based on recipient engagement.
4. **SEO Analytics:** SEO analytics focuses on measuring the effectiveness of search engine optimization efforts. Key metrics include organic traffic, keyword rankings, backlinks, and click-through rates from search engine results pages (SERPs). Tools like Google Search Console and SEMrush allow marketers to analyze their website's performance in search engines and identify opportunities for improvement. This type of analytics is essential for ensuring visibility and driving organic traffic.
5. **PPC (Pay-Per-Click) Analytics:** PPC analytics measures the performance of paid advertising campaigns, such as Google Ads and social media ads. Key metrics include cost per click (CPC), click-through rates, conversion rates, and return on ad spend (ROAS). This analysis helps marketers understand which ads and keywords are most effective, allowing for better budget allocation and strategy refinement. Insights gained from PPC analytics are critical for maximizing the efficiency of paid advertising.
6. **Conversion Rate Optimization (CRO) Analytics:** CRO analytics focuses on understanding and improving the percentage of website visitors who complete desired actions, such as making a purchase or signing up for a newsletter. Techniques like A/B testing, heatmaps, and user flow analysis are commonly used to identify barriers to conversion. This type of analytics helps businesses optimize landing pages and calls to action, ultimately increasing conversion rates.
7. **Attribution Analytics:** Attribution analytics assigns credit to various marketing channels and touchpoints that contribute to conversions. By understanding the customer journey, marketers can determine which channels are most effective in driving sales or leads. This type of analysis helps optimize marketing strategies based on data-driven insights about where to invest resources for maximum impact.
8. **Content Marketing Analytics:** Content marketing analytics tracks the performance of content across multiple platforms. Metrics include page views, time on page, social shares, and engagement rates. Analyzing this data helps businesses understand what types of content resonate with their audience, allowing for the development of more targeted and effective content strategies.

Customer Segmentation and Targeting

Customer segmentation and targeting are fundamental components of effective marketing strategy. They involve dividing a broad market into smaller, more manageable groups of consumers with similar characteristics, preferences, or behaviors, and then targeting these segments with tailored marketing messages. This approach allows businesses to optimize their marketing efforts, improve customer satisfaction, and ultimately drive sales. In this comprehensive exploration, we will delve into the significance, methods, benefits, challenges, and best practices associated with customer segmentation and targeting.

Importance of Customer Segmentation: The importance of customer segmentation are as follows:

1. **Enhanced Understanding of Customers:** Segmentation helps businesses gain deeper insights into their customer base. By understanding the unique needs and preferences of different segments, companies can craft messages and offerings that resonate more effectively.
2. **Improved Marketing Efficiency:** Targeting specific segments allows for more focused marketing efforts. Instead of employing a one-size-fits-all approach, businesses can allocate resources efficiently, reducing wastage and maximizing ROI.
3. **Increased Customer Satisfaction:** Tailored marketing messages and products that address the specific needs of a segment lead to higher customer satisfaction. When customers feel understood and valued, they are more likely to remain loyal to a brand.
4. **Competitive Advantage:** Organizations that effectively segment and target their markets can differentiate themselves from competitors. By catering to niche segments, businesses can establish a stronger market presence and brand loyalty.
5. **Better Product Development:** Understanding customer segments can inform product development and innovation. Companies can create offerings that directly meet the needs of specific groups, leading to higher adoption rates and success.

Methods of Customer Segmentation: Customer segmentation can be approached in various ways, often categorized into the following methods:

1. **Demographic Segmentation:** This method divides the market based on demographic factors such as age, gender, income, education, and family size. For example, a luxury brand may target high-income individuals, while a budget brand may focus on lower-income consumers.
2. **Geographic Segmentation:** Geographic segmentation considers the location of customers. It can be as broad as continents or countries or as specific as neighbourhoods. Local preferences and cultural factors often influence buying

behavior, making this method essential for businesses operating in multiple regions.

3. **Psychographic Segmentation:** This approach groups customers based on their lifestyles, values, interests, and personalities. Psychographic segmentation delves into the motivations behind purchasing decisions, allowing for more personalized marketing. For instance, an outdoor gear company may target adventurous, eco-conscious consumers.
4. **Behavioral Segmentation:** Behavioral segmentation focuses on customers' interactions with a brand. It considers factors such as purchase history, usage frequency, brand loyalty, and responses to marketing campaigns. Businesses can identify segments like frequent buyers, occasional users, and brand switchers to tailor their strategies.

Targeting Strategies

Targeting strategies are approaches businesses use to engage specific customer segments identified through segmentation. Common strategies include mass marketing, which addresses the entire market with a single message, and differentiated marketing, where distinct marketing mixes are tailored for each segment. Concentrated marketing focuses on a single segment, allowing for deeper specialization, while micromarketing targets individuals with highly personalized messages. Finally, hybrid marketing combines elements of multiple strategies to maximize outreach and impact. By selecting the right targeting strategy, businesses can optimize their marketing efforts, enhance customer engagement, and improve overall conversion rates.

Once segmentation is complete, the next step is targeting. Businesses can choose from several strategies:

1. **Mass Marketing:** This approach targets the entire market with a single message. It's less common today due to the rise of personalized marketing but can still be effective for products with universal appeal, such as basic necessities.
2. **Differentiated Marketing:** In this strategy, businesses develop different marketing mixes for each segment. For example, a cosmetics brand might create distinct product lines for teenagers, working professionals, and seniors, each with tailored messaging and positioning.
3. **Concentrated Marketing:** Concentrated marketing focuses on a single market segment. This approach allows businesses to become experts in that niche and build strong brand loyalty. A small artisan bakery, for instance, may target health-conscious consumers with gluten-free products.
4. **Micromarketing:** Micromarketing takes targeting to the individual level, using personalized marketing strategies tailored to individual customers. This approach is often facilitated by advanced data analytics and AI technologies, allowing brands to deliver highly relevant content and offers.

5. **Hybrid Marketing:** This strategy combines elements of multiple targeting approaches. For instance, a brand may use differentiated marketing for various segments while also employing micromarketing tactics to personalize outreach within those segments.

Benefits of Customer Segmentation and Targeting: The benefits of customer segmentation and targeting are as under:

1. **Higher Conversion Rates:** Tailored messaging that resonates with specific segments tends to yield higher conversion rates, as customers are more likely to respond to offers that align with their interests and needs.
2. **Cost Efficiency:** By focusing resources on the most promising segments, businesses can reduce overall marketing costs. Targeted campaigns typically require less budget than broad-reaching campaigns.
3. **Improved Customer Retention:** Personalized marketing fosters stronger relationships with customers, leading to increased loyalty and retention. Satisfied customers are more likely to return and recommend the brand to others.
4. **Strategic Resource Allocation:** Segmentation enables businesses to allocate marketing resources effectively, focusing on segments that offer the highest potential for profitability.
5. **Market Insights:** Continuous segmentation and targeting efforts generate valuable insights into customer preferences and market trends, allowing businesses to adapt quickly to changing consumer behavior.

Conclusion

Customer segmentation and targeting are essential strategies that enable businesses to connect more effectively with their audience. By understanding the unique needs and preferences of different market segments, organizations can craft tailored marketing messages that resonate, ultimately driving higher engagement and sales. While challenges exist, leveraging data analytics, embracing best practices, and continually optimizing strategies can lead to significant competitive advantages. In today's dynamic market environment, businesses that excel in segmentation and targeting will foster stronger relationships with their customers and achieve sustainable growth.

Campaign Effectiveness Analysis

Campaign effectiveness analysis is a crucial aspect of marketing that assesses the performance of marketing campaigns. It involves measuring various metrics to determine how well a campaign meets its objectives, whether those are increasing brand awareness, generating leads, or driving sales. By evaluating the effectiveness of campaigns, businesses can refine their strategies, allocate resources more efficiently, and ultimately achieve better results. This comprehensive exploration will cover the importance of campaign effectiveness analysis, methodologies for conducting the analysis, key metrics to consider, tools and technologies available, challenges faced, and best practices for optimizing marketing campaigns.

Importance of Campaign Effectiveness Analysis: Importance of Campaign effectiveness analysis are as under:

1. **Informed Decision-making:** Understanding the effectiveness of a marketing campaign enables businesses to make data-driven decisions. Insights gained from analysis help marketers determine what worked, what didn't, and why, allowing them to optimize future campaigns based on empirical evidence rather than assumptions.
2. **Resource Allocation:** Campaign analysis provides clarity on which marketing strategies yield the best results. This enables organizations to allocate resources such as time, budget, and personnel more effectively, directing investment towards high-performing campaigns and reducing spending on less effective ones.
3. **Continuous Improvement:** By consistently analyzing campaign performance, businesses can foster a culture of continuous improvement. Marketers can test new ideas, learn from failures, and adapt strategies in real time, ensuring campaigns evolve in response to market dynamics and customer feedback.
4. **Enhanced Customer Understanding:** Campaign effectiveness analysis offers insights into customer behavior, preferences, and engagement. By understanding how different segments respond to various marketing tactics, businesses can tailor their messaging and approach, ultimately improving customer satisfaction and loyalty.
5. **Justification of Marketing Spend:** In an era where marketing budgets are scrutinized, being able to demonstrate the return on investment (ROI) of marketing campaigns is vital. Effective analysis provides the data needed to justify marketing expenditures to stakeholders and secure future funding.

Key Metrics for Campaign Effectiveness Analysis: Analyzing the effectiveness of marketing campaigns requires a clear understanding of key metrics that gauge performance across various dimensions. These metrics provide insights into how well a campaign meets its objectives, whether those are related to brand awareness, lead generation, or sales conversion. Here are some of the most crucial metrics to consider:

1. **Conversion Rate:** The conversion rate is a fundamental metric that measures the percentage of users who complete a desired action, such as making a purchase, signing up for a newsletter, or downloading a resource. It's calculated by dividing the number of conversions by the total number of visitors and multiplying by 100. A high conversion rate indicates that the campaign is effective in persuading users to take action.
2. **Click-Through Rate (CTR):** CTR measures the percentage of people who click on a specific link or call-to-action (CTA) within a campaign. It is calculated by dividing the number of clicks by the total impressions (or views) and

multiplying by 100. A high CTR suggests that the campaign's messaging and targeting are resonating well with the audience, while a low CTR may indicate a need for refinement.

3. **Return on Investment (ROI):** ROI evaluates the profitability of a campaign by comparing the revenue generated to the costs incurred. It is calculated as:

   A positive ROI signifies that the campaign has generated more revenue than it cost, making it a key metric for justifying marketing expenditures.

4. **Customer Acquisition Cost (CAC):** CAC measures the cost associated with acquiring a new customer through a specific campaign. This metric is calculated by dividing the total costs of the campaign by the number of new customers acquired. Understanding CAC helps businesses evaluate the efficiency of their marketing efforts and ensure that the cost of acquiring customers aligns with their long-term value.

5. **Customer Lifetime Value (CLV):** CLV estimates the total revenue a customer is expected to generate throughout their relationship with a business. By comparing CLV to CAC, marketers can assess the long-term viability of their customer acquisition strategies. A high CLV relative to CAC indicates that a campaign is not only acquiring customers effectively but also attracting valuable long-term clients.

6. **Engagement Metrics:** Engagement metrics, such as likes, shares, comments, and time spent on content, provide insights into how audiences interact with a campaign. Higher engagement levels typically correlate with more successful campaigns, as they indicate that the content resonates with the audience. Social media analytics tools can help track these metrics effectively.

7. **Lead Generation:** For campaigns focused on generating leads, tracking the quantity and quality of leads produced is essential. Metrics such as lead conversion rates (the percentage of leads that become paying customers) provide insights into the effectiveness of the campaign in attracting and nurturing prospects.

8. **Brand Awareness Metrics:** Brand awareness can be assessed through surveys, social media reach, and website traffic. Metrics such as impressions, reach, and changes in brand sentiment before and after a campaign help gauge its impact on overall brand visibility and recognition.

9. **Sales Revenue:** For campaigns with direct sales objectives, tracking the total revenue generated during and after the campaign is critical. This metric provides a clear indication of the financial impact and success of the campaign.

10. **Retention Rate:** Retention rate measures the percentage of customers who continue to engage with a brand over a specific period. A high retention rate indicates successful customer engagement and satisfaction, often resulting from effective marketing campaigns.

Best Practices for Optimizing Campaign Effectiveness: To ensure marketing campaigns achieve their objectives and maximize return on investment, it's essential to implement best practices that enhance effectiveness. Here are some key strategies:

1. **Set Clear Goals and Objectives:** Establish specific, measurable, achievable, relevant, and time-bound (SMART) goals before launching a campaign. Clear objectives guide the strategy, making it easier to measure success and adjust tactics as needed.
2. **Identify Key Performance Indicators (KPIs):** Select relevant KPIs that align with your campaign goals. Metrics such as conversion rates, click-through rates, customer acquisition cost, and return on investment provide insight into performance, enabling effective tracking and optimization.
3. **Leverage Data Analytics Tools:** Utilize analytics platforms like Google Analytics, CRM systems, and social media analytics to collect and analyze data. These tools provide valuable insights into user behavior, campaign performance, and audience demographics, informing decisions.
4. **Conduct A/B Testing:** Implement A/B testing to compare different versions of your campaign materials—such as headlines, images, or calls to action. This allows you to identify what resonates best with your audience and optimize accordingly.
5. **Segment Your Audience:** Divide your audience into distinct segments based on demographics, behavior, or preferences. Tailor messaging and offers to each segment to increase relevance and engagement, ultimately improving conversion rates.
6. **Monitor and Adjust in Real-time:** Continuously monitor campaign performance and be prepared to make adjustments as needed. Real-time data allows for quick pivots, ensuring that campaigns remain aligned with audience responses and market conditions.
7. **Focus on Customer Experience:** Ensure that the customer journey is smooth and engaging. Optimize landing pages for clarity and speed, simplify forms, and ensure a seamless transition from marketing materials to the final action.
8. **Utilize Multi-channel Strategies:** Reach your audience through multiple channels social media, email, content marketing, and paid ads. A multi-channel approach enhances visibility and increases the chances of engagement, as different audiences respond to various platforms.

Conclusion

Campaign effectiveness analysis is a vital aspect of modern marketing that enables businesses to measure the success of their campaigns, optimize their strategies, and drive better outcomes. By employing robust methodologies, leveraging key metrics, utilizing advanced tools, and overcoming challenges, marketers can create a culture of continuous improvement. This ongoing evaluation not only enhances marketing performance but also fosters deeper customer understanding and loyalty, ultimately leading to greater business success.

Customer Lifetime Value (CLV) Prediction

Customer Lifetime Value (CLV) prediction is a crucial metric that estimates the total revenue a business can expect from a customer throughout their relationship. By calculating CLV, companies can strategically allocate resources, optimize marketing efforts, and tailor customer engagement initiatives to maximize profitability. Various methodologies exist for predicting CLV, including historical calculations based on actual revenue, predictive models utilizing statistical techniques and machine learning, and simplified formulas that estimate value based on average purchase behavior. Data quality plays a significant role in the accuracy of these predictions; thus, businesses must focus on integrating and cleansing data from multiple sources, including transaction history, customer demographics, and behavioral insights. While CLV prediction offers numerous benefits, such as improved customer segmentation and retention strategies, challenges like data limitations and changing consumer behavior can complicate the process. To effectively predict CLV, organizations should adopt best practices like continuous model refinement, advanced analytics, and customer-centric approaches that prioritize customer experience. By understanding and accurately predicting CLV, businesses can foster long-term relationships, enhance customer satisfaction, and drive sustainable growth.

Importance of Customer Lifetime Value Prediction

1. **Strategic Resource Allocation:** Predicting CLV allows businesses to allocate resources more effectively. By understanding which customers are likely to bring in the most revenue over time, organizations can tailor their marketing strategies and budget allocations accordingly. This ensures that investment is directed toward high-value customers, maximizing ROI.
2. **Enhanced Customer Segmentation:** CLV prediction aids in customer segmentation, enabling businesses to categorize customers based on their predicted lifetime value. This segmentation allows for personalized marketing approaches, ensuring that high-value customers receive targeted communications and offers that encourage loyalty and retention.
3. **Improved Customer Acquisition Strategies:** Knowing the predicted CLV of different customer segments helps businesses develop more efficient acquisition strategies. By understanding how much they can afford to spend to acquire a customer based on their expected lifetime value, organizations can optimize their marketing budgets and improve customer acquisition costs (CAC).
4. **Retention Efforts:** Predicting CLV can inform retention strategies by identifying customers at risk of churn. Businesses can implement targeted retention campaigns aimed at high-value customers who are showing signs of disengagement, thereby improving overall customer retention rates and lifetime value.

5. **Long-term Planning:** A reliable CLV prediction model supports long-term strategic planning. It enables organizations to forecast revenue, plan product development, and optimize customer experience initiatives based on anticipated customer behavior and value.

Methodologies for Calculating Customer Lifetime Value: There are several methodologies for calculating CLV, each with its advantages and disadvantages. The choice of methodology depends on the nature of the business, available data, and the desired level of complexity in the analysis.

1. **Historical CLV Calculation:** The historical CLV calculation is based on the actual revenue generated by a customer during their relationship with the business. The formula is straightforward:

$$\text{CLV} = \sum \text{Revenue}_t - \text{Cost}_t$$

   where, t is the time period (months, years) over which the customer has been active. This method is simple but may not accurately predict future value, especially for newer customers with limited purchase history.

2. **Predictive CLV Models:** Predictive models use historical data to estimate the future behavior of customers. These models often employ statistical techniques and machine learning algorithms to analyze customer interactions and predict future purchases. Common approaches include:

   - **Regression Analysis:** Linear regression can model the relationship between customer characteristics and their purchasing behavior, enabling predictions based on historical trends.
   - **Cohort Analysis:** By grouping customers based on shared characteristics or behaviors, businesses can analyze the purchasing patterns of each cohort over time and predict future value.
   - **Machine Learning Models:** Advanced machine learning techniques such as decision trees, random forests, or neural networks can uncover complex relationships in customer data, improving prediction accuracy.

3. **Discounted Cash Flow (DCF) Model:** The DCF model takes into account the time value of money, providing a more nuanced understanding of CLV. The formula is:

$$\text{CLV} = \sum \left(\frac{\text{Revenue}_t}{(1+r)^t} \right) - \text{Cost}$$

   where, r is the discount rate. This method is particularly useful for businesses with long customer relationships, as it accounts for the diminishing value of future revenue.

4. Simplified CLV Calculation: For businesses seeking a quick estimation, a simplified CLV formula can be used:

$$\text{CLV} = \text{Average Purchase Value} \times \text{Average Purchase Frequency} \times \text{Average Customer Lifespan}$$

While this method provides a useful ballpark figure, it may lack the granularity needed for strategic decision-making.

Role of Data in CLV Prediction: Data plays a pivotal role in accurately predicting Customer Lifetime Value (CLV), serving as the foundation for insights and strategies that drive business success. Here's a breakdown of the various aspects in which data influences CLV prediction:

1. **Data Sources:** Effective CLV prediction relies on diverse data sources, including:
   - **Transactional Data:** Information on customer purchases, such as frequency, amount, and product details, helps establish historical revenue patterns.
   - **Demographic Data:** Attributes like age, gender, location, and income level enable businesses to segment customers and tailor marketing strategies.
   - **Behavioral Data:** Tracking customer interactions across channels such as website visits, social media engagement, and email responses provides insights into preferences and engagement levels.
   - **Feedback and Surveys:** Customer feedback, reviews, and survey responses help assess satisfaction and loyalty, informing retention strategies.
2. **Data Quality:** High-quality, accurate data is essential for reliable CLV predictions. Organizations must focus on:
   - **Data Cleansing:** Regularly updating and correcting errors in datasets to ensure completeness and accuracy.
   - **Integration:** Combining data from various sources into a unified view of the customer journey, facilitating more comprehensive analysis.
3. **Analytics Techniques:** Data analytics techniques, including statistical modeling and machine learning, enable organizations to derive insights from complex datasets:
   - **Predictive Modeling:** Statistical methods and machine learning algorithms analyze historical data to predict future customer behavior and potential revenue.
   - **Cohort Analysis:** Grouping customers based on shared characteristics allows businesses to observe and predict purchasing trends within specific segments.
4. **Real-time Data Usage:** Utilizing real-time data enhances the ability to adapt CLV predictions dynamically. By continuously monitoring customer behavior and interactions, businesses can refine their predictions and strategies, responding promptly to changing market conditions.
5. **Attribution and Tracking:** Data enables effective attribution of customer interactions across multiple touchpoints, helping to understand which

marketing efforts contribute to customer acquisition and retention. This insight informs future marketing strategies and resource allocation.

Role of Data in Customer Lifetime Value (CLV) Prediction: Data plays a pivotal role in accurately predicting Customer Lifetime Value (CLV), serving as the foundation for insights and strategies that drive business success. Here's a breakdown of the various aspects in which data influences CLV prediction:

1. **Data Sources:** Effective CLV prediction relies on diverse data sources, including:
    - **Transactional Data:** Information on customer purchases, such as frequency, amount, and product details, helps establish historical revenue patterns.
    - **Demographic Data**: Attributes like age, gender, location, and income level enable businesses to segment customers and tailor marketing strategies.
    - **Behavioral Data:** Tracking customer interactions across channels such as website visits, social media engagement, and email responses provides insights into preferences and engagement levels.
    - **Feedback and Surveys:** Customer feedback, reviews, and survey responses help assess satisfaction and loyalty, informing retention strategies.
2. **Data Quality:** High-quality, accurate data is essential for reliable CLV predictions. Organizations must focus on:
    - **Data Cleansing:** Regularly updating and correcting errors in datasets to ensure completeness and accuracy.
    - **Integration:** Combining data from various sources into a unified view of the customer journey, facilitating more comprehensive analysis.
3. **Analytics Techniques:** Data analytics techniques, including statistical modeling and machine learning, enable organizations to derive insights from complex datasets:
    - **Predictive Modeling:** Statistical methods and machine learning algorithms analyze historical data to predict future customer behavior and potential revenue.
    - **Cohort Analysis:** Grouping customers based on shared characteristics allows businesses to observe and predict purchasing trends within specific segments.
4. **Real-time Data Usage:** Utilizing real-time data enhances the ability to adapt CLV predictions dynamically. By continuously monitoring customer behavior and interactions, businesses can refine their predictions and strategies, responding promptly to changing market conditions.
5. **Attribution and Tracking:** Data enables effective attribution of customer interactions across multiple touchpoints, helping to understand which

marketing efforts contribute to customer acquisition and retention. This insight informs future marketing strategies and resource allocation.

Case Studies: Real-world Applications

In today's data-driven landscape, marketing analytics has become an essential tool for businesses seeking to understand consumer behavior, optimize campaigns, and improve ROI. This document explores several case studies that illustrate the successful application of marketing analytics across various industries, showcasing how companies leverage data to drive strategic decision-making and achieve measurable results.

1. Netflix: Personalization Through Data

Background: Netflix, a leading streaming service, has transformed the entertainment industry by utilizing advanced marketing analytics to personalize user experiences. With over 230 million subscribers, the company relies heavily on data to inform its content offerings and marketing strategies.

Implementation: Netflix employs several analytics-driven strategies:

- **User Behavior Analysis:** Netflix tracks viewing habits, such as watch time, genre preferences, and user ratings. This data helps the platform recommend content tailored to individual users, enhancing engagement and retention.
- **A/B Testing:** The company continuously tests various marketing materials, such as thumbnails and trailers, to determine which versions yield higher click-through rates. By analyzing user interactions, Netflix optimizes its marketing approach in real-time.
- **Content Development:** Data analytics informs decisions about original content creation. For instance, the success of shows like "Stranger Things" was partly due to data indicating strong interest in 1980s nostalgia and supernatural themes.

Results: Netflix's personalized recommendations have led to significant increases in user engagement, with 80% of content watched stemming from these suggestions. This strategy has contributed to a retention rate of over 93% for new subscribers, highlighting the effectiveness of data-driven personalization.

2. Amazon: Predictive Analytics for Customer Insights

Background: Amazon, the global e-commerce giant, uses marketing analytics to enhance customer experience and drive sales. The company's sophisticated algorithms analyze customer data to predict purchasing behavior and optimize inventory management.

Implementation: Amazon employs several analytics-driven strategies:

Recommendation Engine: Amazon's recommendation system uses collaborative filtering and machine learning to suggest products based on browsing history, past purchases, and similar user profiles. This personalized shopping experience increases the likelihood of impulse buys.

Dynamic Pricing: By analyzing market trends, competitor pricing, and customer demand, Amazon adjusts prices in real-time. This strategy maximizes sales while maintaining competitive advantage.

Customer Segmentation: Amazon uses analytics to segment its customer base into distinct groups based on purchasing behavior, preferences, and demographics. This segmentation allows for targeted marketing campaigns and personalized promotions.

Results: Amazon's recommendation engine drives approximately 35% of its total sales. Additionally, the company's dynamic pricing strategy has led to increased market share and improved profit margins, underscoring the power of predictive analytics in e-commerce.

3. Coca-Cola: Social Media Analytics for Brand Engagement

Background: Coca-Cola, one of the world's most recognizable brands, has successfully leveraged marketing analytics to enhance its social media presence and engage with consumers effectively.

Implementation: Coca-Cola employs various analytical strategies, including:

- **Sentiment Analysis:** The company utilizes social media analytics tools to monitor brand mentions, customer sentiments, and trending topics. This real-time feedback allows Coca-Cola to respond promptly to consumer needs and adjust marketing strategies accordingly.
- **Content Optimization:** By analyzing engagement metrics (likes, shares, comments), Coca-Cola tailors its social media content to resonate with target audiences. The brand uses this data to refine its messaging and improve overall engagement rates.
- **Campaign Performance Tracking:** Coca-Cola measures the impact of marketing campaigns across social media platforms. By evaluating key performance indicators (KPIs), the company can optimize future campaigns based on what resonates most with consumers.

Results: Coca-Cola's social media analytics have led to increased engagement and brand loyalty. Campaigns like "Share a Coke" generated over 500,000 photos shared on social media, significantly boosting brand visibility and consumer interaction. The company's ability to adapt to consumer feedback has solidified its position as a leader in brand engagement.

4. Spotify: Data-driven Marketing and Personalization

Background: Spotify, a leading music streaming service, harnesses marketing analytics to provide personalized music recommendations and enhance user engagement. With over 500 million users, the platform prioritizes data-driven decision-making.

Implementation: Spotify's marketing analytics strategies include:

- **User Data Analysis:** By analyzing listening habits, user preferences, and playlist creations, Spotify creates tailored playlists such as "Discover Weekly" and "Release Radar." These features enhance user satisfaction and retention.
- **Targeted Advertising:** Spotify uses demographic and behavioral data to deliver personalized ads to users. By ensuring that advertisements are relevant, the platform increases the likelihood of user engagement with sponsored content.
- **Real-time Insights:** Spotify analyzes data in real-time to identify emerging trends and popular tracks, enabling timely marketing campaigns that capitalize on current listener interests.

Results: Spotify's personalized playlists have significantly increased user engagement, with over 40 million playlists created by users and billions of streams generated. The targeted advertising approach has also improved ad performance metrics, leading to higher conversion rates and advertiser satisfaction.

5. Target: Predictive Analytics for Customer Engagement

Background: Target, a major retail corporation, employs marketing analytics to understand consumer behavior and enhance customer engagement. The company uses predictive analytics to anticipate customer needs and optimize its marketing strategies.

Implementation: Key strategies include:

- **Predictive Modeling:** Target analyzes purchasing patterns and demographic data to predict future buying behaviors. This approach allows the company to tailor marketing efforts and product offerings to specific customer segments.
- **Customized Promotions:** By leveraging predictive analytics, Target creates personalized promotions and coupons for individual shoppers based on their shopping history, increasing the likelihood of purchase.
- **Location-based Analytics:** Target utilizes location data to optimize inventory management and marketing efforts for specific stores. This ensures that local customers find relevant products and promotions in-store.

Results: Target's predictive analytics have led to increased sales and enhanced customer loyalty. For instance, the company reported a 5% increase in sales attributed to its customized promotions. By understanding and anticipating consumer needs, Target has successfully differentiated itself in a competitive retail landscape.

Conclusion

The case studies presented illustrate the transformative impact of marketing analytics across various industries. Companies like Netflix, Amazon, Coca-Cola, Spotify, and Target have successfully harnessed data to enhance customer experiences, drive sales, and improve brand engagement. As the business landscape continues to evolve, the strategic application of marketing analytics will remain a vital component for organizations seeking to thrive in a competitive environment. By leveraging data-driven insights, businesses can make informed decisions, optimize their marketing strategies, and ultimately achieve sustainable growth.

2. Financial Analytics

Financial analytics is the process of using data analysis techniques to assess and interpret financial data, enabling organizations to make informed decisions regarding their financial health and strategy. This discipline encompasses a variety of activities, including budgeting, forecasting, performance measurement, and risk management. By employing descriptive, predictive, and prescriptive analytics, businesses can gain insights into past performance, forecast future trends, and optimize financial strategies. For instance, descriptive analytics might analyze historical revenue and expense data to identify trends, while predictive analytics could forecast future cash flows based on various scenarios. Additionally, financial analytics helps in assessing investment opportunities, managing risks, and ensuring compliance with regulations. Organizations leverage financial analytics to enhance their decision-making processes, improve operational efficiency, and achieve strategic goals. The rise of advanced technologies, such as machine learning and artificial intelligence, has further empowered financial analytics, allowing for real-time insights and deeper analysis of complex financial datasets. Ultimately, effective financial analytics provides a competitive advantage by enabling organizations to adapt to market changes, optimize resource allocation, and enhance overall financial performance. As businesses increasingly rely on data-driven insights, financial analytics has become essential for navigating the complexities of today's financial landscape.

What does a Financial Analyst do?

A financial analyst analyzes financial data to help businesses or individuals make decisions. They examine financial statements, market trends, and economic conditions to assess the company's performance, estimate future earnings or cash flow, provide investment recommendations, and manage financial risks.

Financial analysts work in various segments and across almost all industries. Most businesses employ some sort of financial analyst, but other types of companies such as investment banks, mutual funds, hedge funds, insurance companies, and other financial institutions may employ a great deal more of them.

A financial analyst's primary role is to analyze financial data and trends to support the decision-making processes. The specific responsibilities of a financial analyst can vary depending on their role and where they work but generally include:

1. **Analyzing Financial Statements:** Reviewing the balance sheet, income statement, and cash flow statement to assess a company's financial health.
2. **Forecasting and Predictive Analysis:** Developing financial models to predict future trends, revenue, expenses, and cash flows, based on historical data and market conditions.

3. **Building Visualizations and Dashboards:** Creating visual representations of financial data, such as graphs and charts, to make complex data more accessible and actionable.
4. **Regression and Statistical Analysis:** Applying regression models (linear, logistic, etc.) to uncover relationships between variables, assess risk factors, or optimize financial strategies.
5. **Investment Analysis:** Evaluating investment opportunities by analyzing market trends, economic conditions, and financial performance of potential investments.
6. **Risk Assessment:** Identifying financial risks by data-driven models like regression analysis and machine learning to predict and quantify risks, and recommending strategies to mitigate them.
7. **Market Research:** Researching industry trends, market conditions, and competitor performance using financial data such as revenue, profit margins, and economic indicators to make informed strategic planning and decisions.

Financial Analytics Important: In a data-driven business environment, the ability to analyze and interpret financial data is more crucial than ever. Financial analytics affects all parts of a business and is key in helping companies predict and plan for the future. By using advanced analytical techniques, businesses can better understand their financial health, anticipate challenges, and uncover growth opportunities. In the following sections, we will explore nine important reasons why financial analytics is indispensable for organizations.

1. **Informed Decision-making:** Financial analysts and financial analytics make it possible to get accurate and actionable insights from data so you can make better decisions about how to expand or improve your business. Here are two examples of ways financial analysts contribute to this:
   - **Scenario Planning:** Financial analytics perform scenario planning, where different strategies are tested under various market conditions. This can help you understand potential outcomes and prepare for unexpected events.
   - **Data-driven Strategies:** Financial analytics can lead to more effective strategies for pricing, budgeting, investment, and resource allocation. This reduces guesswork and enhances the likelihood of achieving desired financial outcomes.
2. **Performance Measurement and Benchmarking:** Financial analytics is essential for measuring and benchmarking a company's performance against industry standards or competitors. This process helps identify areas where the company excels or needs improvement. Here are two ways financial analysts help support this:
   - **Key Performance Indicators (KPIs):** Financial analysts will collect, set, and use KPIs to monitor specific aspects of performance such as revenue growth,

profit margins, return on investment (ROI), and operating costs. These metrics help provide company leaders with a clear picture of how well the company is performing in relation to its goals.

- **Performance Benchmarks:** By comparing performance data with industry benchmarks, financial analysts help determine competitiveness. This can highlight operational inefficiencies, lack of pricing competitiveness, or reveal other opportunities to capitalize on market trends.

3. **Risk Management:** One of the critical roles of financial analytics is identifying, assessing, and managing financial risks. This includes credit risk, market risk, liquidity risk, and operational risk.
   - **Credit Risk Analysis:** Financial analytics can assess the creditworthiness of customers or counterparties by analyzing their financial statements, payment histories, and market conditions. This helps in making lending decisions and setting credit limits.
   - **Market Risk Management:** By analyzing market trends and volatility, an analyst can better understand potential risks associated with changes in interest rates, foreign exchange rates, and commodity prices. This allows you to hedge against adverse movements and protect your financial positions.
   - **Predictive Analytics for Risk:** Advanced predictive models can forecast potential risks and their impact on financial performance. For example, predictive analytics can be used to anticipate defaults in loan portfolios or identify patterns that indicate fraudulent activity.
4. **Strategic Planning and Forecasting:** Financial analytics provides a foundation for strategic planning and forecasting by offering insights into past performance and future trends. This can help your company set realistic goals, allocate resources efficiently, and plan for long-term growth.
   - **Budgeting and Forecasting:** Financial analytics can help you create and monitor budgets and forecasts that guide operational and financial planning. These forecasts consider various factors such as market conditions, economic indicators, and historical performance, ensuring more accurate and reliable financial planning.
   - **Long-Term Strategy Development:** With the help of financial analytics, you can develop long-term strategies that align with your financial goals. This involves assessing potential investments, mergers, and acquisitions, or exploring new markets based on financial feasibility and projected returns.
5. **Enhancing Operational Efficiency:** Financial analytics can uncover inefficiencies in business processes and identify cost-saving opportunities. By analyzing financial data, you can streamline operations, reduce waste, and improve productivity.

- **Cost Management:** Through detailed analysis of cost structures, financial analytics helps you to identify areas where costs can be reduced without affecting quality or performance. This might include negotiating better terms with suppliers, optimizing inventory levels, or reducing overhead expenses.
- **Process Optimization:** Financial analytics can reveal inefficiencies in workflows or supply chains that, when addressed, can lead to significant savings and improved profitability. For example, analyzing production costs and timelines can help identify bottlenecks and improve manufacturing efficiency.
- **Revenue Generation and Margins:** Financial analysts have a role in setting and modeling pricing options, which can help move companies towards goals or earn more margin on sales.

6. **Facilitating Capital Allocation:** Effective capital allocation is crucial for maximizing shareholder value. Financial analytics assists in determining how capital should be allocated across different projects or business units to achieve the highest returns.
   - **Investment Analysis:** By evaluating potential investment opportunities using techniques like discounted cash flow (DCF) analysis, internal rate of return (IRR), and net present value (NPV), financial analysts can help you select the projects that offer the best potential for growth and profitability.
   - **Capital Budgeting:** Financial analytics support you in the capital budgeting process by providing a clear picture of the expected costs and benefits of various investment options. This ensures that capital is allocated to projects that are aligned with the company's strategic objectives and have the potential to generate significant returns.
7. **Supporting Mergers and Acquisitions (M&A):** In M&A transactions, financial analytics is vital for evaluating the financial health and value of potential target companies. This involves due diligence processes to assess financial statements, understand revenue drivers, and identify any hidden liabilities.
   - **Valuation Analysis:** Financial analytics is used to determine the fair value of a company or its assets. This includes analyzing financial statements, cash flows, and market conditions to arrive at an accurate valuation, which is crucial for negotiating the terms of an acquisition or merger.
   - **Post-Merger Integration:** After a merger or acquisition, financial analytics helps in integrating the financial systems of the merged entities, aligning financial reporting, and ensuring that the combined company meets its financial goals.
8. **Improving Investor Relations:** Financial analytics also plays a key role in maintaining healthy investor relations by providing transparent and accurate financial information.

- **Financial Reporting:** Regular financial reporting backed by robust analytics helps in building trust with investors by providing a clear and accurate picture of the company's financial health and performance.
- **Earnings Guidance:** You can use financial analytics to provide earnings guidance to investors, helping them set realistic expectations and avoid surprises. This improves investor confidence and can positively impact stock prices.

9. **Enhancing Regulatory Compliance:** Financial analytics helps companies comply with various financial regulations and standards by ensuring accurate and timely reporting.
   - **Compliance Monitoring:** Financial analytics can be used to monitor compliance with regulatory requirements such as the Sarbanes-Oxley Act (SOX) in the U.S., International Financial Reporting Standards (IFRS), or local tax laws.
   - **Audit Readiness:** By maintaining accurate and detailed financial records, financial analytics ensures that you are always prepared for audits, reducing the risk of non-compliance penalties.

Financial Analytics Use Cases: Financial analytics can be applied in many ways across different industries. That makes it difficult to pin down globally relevant use cases. However, you can use KNIME to automate tasks in any finance department. Some several use cases of financial analytics across different sectors:

1. **Budgeting and Forecasting in Corporations:** Companies use financial analytics to create accurate budgets and forecasts by analyzing historical financial data and market trends. For instance, a manufacturing company may analyze production costs, sales forecasts, and seasonal trends to prepare its annual budget. By employing variance analysis, the company can compare actual results to its budget, helping identify areas for cost control and strategic adjustments.
2. **Risk Management in Banking:** Banks leverage financial analytics to assess credit risk and enhance their lending processes. By analyzing historical data on borrowers, transaction behaviors, and macroeconomic indicators, banks can develop predictive models to evaluate the likelihood of default. This helps them make informed lending decisions and adjust interest rates accordingly, minimizing potential losses.
3. **Investment Portfolio Management:** Investment firms use financial analytics to optimize asset allocation in portfolios. By analyzing market trends, historical performance, and economic indicators, firms can develop quantitative models that inform their investment strategies. For example, a hedge fund might employ machine learning algorithms to predict stock movements, helping portfolio managers adjust their positions for maximum returns.

4. **Sales Performance Analysis in Retail:** Retail companies utilize financial analytics to evaluate sales performance across different channels and regions. By analyzing point-of-sale data, customer behavior, and promotional effectiveness, retailers can identify high-performing products and areas needing improvement. This analysis informs inventory management, pricing strategies, and targeted marketing campaigns.
5. **Expense Management in Non-Profits:** Non-profit organizations apply financial analytics to track and manage expenses effectively. By analyzing funding sources, program costs, and operational expenses, these organizations can assess their financial sustainability. This data-driven approach helps non-profits allocate resources more efficiently and justify their spending to stakeholders.
6. **Cost-benefit Analysis for New Projects:** Companies often use financial analytics to conduct cost-benefit analyses when considering new projects or investments. By projecting costs, revenues, and potential risks, organizations can evaluate the viability of projects before committing resources. For example, a tech company might analyze the expected return on investment for developing a new software product against the associated development costs.
7. **Regulatory Compliance in Finance:** Financial institutions employ analytics to ensure compliance with regulatory requirements. By analyzing transaction data and monitoring financial activities, banks can detect anomalies that may indicate fraudulent activities or compliance breaches. This proactive approach minimizes regulatory risks and enhances transparency.

Financial Analysis Challenges: Financial analysis is a critical function for organizations, enabling informed decision-making and strategic planning. However, it is not without its challenges. Here are some of the key obstacles that professionals face:

1. **Data Quality and Integrity:** Ensuring high data quality and integrity is crucial for effective financial analysis. Inaccurate, outdated, or incomplete data can lead to flawed insights and poor decision-making. Organizations must invest in robust data management practices to maintain reliable data sources and enhance analytical accuracy.
   - **Inaccurate Data:** Poor data quality can lead to flawed analysis and misinformed decisions. Inaccuracies may arise from manual entry errors, outdated systems, or incomplete data.
   - **Data Silos:** Organizations often have data stored in various systems, making it difficult to obtain a comprehensive view. This fragmentation can hinder effective analysis.
2. **Complex Regulatory Environment:** Navigating a complex regulatory environment poses significant challenges for financial analysts. Compliance with various local and international regulations requires constant vigilance

and adaptation. Failure to adhere to these regulations can result in severe penalties, affecting an organization's financial standing and reputation.

- **Compliance Requirements:** Financial analysts must navigate a maze of regulations and compliance standards, which can vary by industry and region. Keeping up with these changes can be resource-intensive.
- **Reporting Standards:** Adhering to different reporting frameworks (e.g., GAAP, IFRS) can complicate financial analysis, especially for multinational companies.

3. **Rapid Market Changes:** The financial landscape is constantly evolving due to factors like economic shifts, technological advancements, and changing consumer behavior. These rapid market changes can complicate financial analysis, making it difficult for organizations to adapt their strategies and forecasts in real-time, potentially impacting profitability.
   - **Economic Volatility:** Fluctuations in the economy, such as recessions or rapid growth, can significantly impact financial performance, complicating forecasting and analysis.
   - **Changing Consumer Behavior:** Shifts in consumer preferences or unexpected trends can affect revenue projections and require analysts to adapt quickly.
4. **Integration of Advanced Technologies:** Integrating advanced technologies, such as AI and machine learning, into existing financial analysis processes can be challenging. Organizations may struggle with costs, technical expertise, and employee resistance. Ineffective integration can lead to underutilization of these powerful tools, limiting their potential benefits.
   - **Adoption Barriers:** While tools like AI and machine learning can enhance analysis, integrating these technologies into existing processes poses challenges, including costs, training, and resistance to change.
   - **Complexity of Tools:** Advanced analytical tools can be complex and may require specialized skills that current staff may lack, leading to underutilization.
5. **Limited Resources and Budget Constraints:** Organizations frequently face constraints on financial analysis resources, impacting their ability to conduct thorough analyses. Limited budgets can restrict access to advanced tools, hiring of skilled personnel, and necessary training. These constraints can lead to rushed analyses and compromised decision-making quality.
   - **Resource Allocation:** Financial analysis often competes with other functions for limited resources, making it difficult to allocate sufficient budget and personnel for effective analysis.
   - **Time Constraints:** Analysts are often under pressure to deliver insights quickly, which can lead to rushed analyses and overlooked details.

6. **Skills Gap:** The rapid evolution of financial analytics tools has created a skills gap in many organizations. Professionals often lack the necessary training to effectively utilize advanced analytics techniques. This shortage of skilled analysts hampers the ability to derive meaningful insights from complex data, limiting strategic decision-making.
   - **Training Needs:** The fast-paced evolution of financial analytics tools necessitates ongoing training and upskilling, which can be challenging to implement effectively.
   - **Shortage of Talent:** There is a growing demand for skilled analysts who can interpret complex data, leading to a talent shortage in many organizations.
7. **Forecasting Challenges:** Forecasting involves predicting future financial performance, which is inherently uncertain. Unforeseen events, such as economic downturns or market disruptions, can derail projections. Additionally, reliance on historical data may not accurately reflect future conditions, leading to potential inaccuracies in budgeting and strategic planning.
   - **Uncertainty:** Predicting future financial performance involves uncertainty, and unexpected events (like natural disasters or political changes) can disrupt forecasts.
   - **Model Limitations:** Financial models are often based on historical data, which may not accurately reflect future conditions, leading to potential errors in forecasting.

Future of Financial Analytics: The landscape of financial analytics is rapidly evolving, driven by technological advancements, changing market dynamics, and the increasing need for data-driven decision-making. Here are key trends and predictions shaping the future of financial analytics:

1. **Automation and AI:** The future of financial analytics is increasingly tied to automation and artificial intelligence. Advanced algorithms can process large datasets faster and with greater accuracy, providing real-time insights that enhance decision-making.
2. **Predictive and Prescriptive Analytics:** As technology continues to evolve, predictive and prescriptive analytics will become more sophisticated. Organizations will be able to forecast outcomes with greater precision and receive actionable recommendations based on real-time data.
3. **Increased Focus on ESG Metrics:** Environmental, Social, and Governance (ESG) factors are becoming critical in financial analytics. Companies are increasingly analyzing these metrics to assess risk and align with sustainable business practices, influencing investment decisions.

Conclusion

Financial analytics is a vital component of modern business strategy, providing organizations with the insights needed to navigate complex financial landscapes. By leveraging data-driven techniques, businesses can enhance decision-making, optimize performance, and mitigate risks. As technology advances, the capabilities of financial analytics will continue to grow, enabling organizations to adapt to changing market conditions and achieve sustainable success. The integration of AI, predictive models, and ESG metrics will shape the future of financial analytics, ensuring its relevance in an increasingly data-centric world.

Portfolio Optimization and Asset Valuation

Portfolio optimization and asset valuation are key components of investment strategy. Portfolio optimization focuses on selecting the ideal mix of assets to maximize returns while minimizing risk, often employing techniques like mean-variance optimization and the efficient frontier. This process involves diversifying investments across various asset classes to achieve a balanced risk-return profile. Asset valuation, on the other hand, determines the worth of an asset through methods such as discounted cash flow (DCF) analysis, comparative analysis, and asset-based valuation. Accurate valuation is essential for making informed investment decisions, assessing market opportunities, and guiding mergers and acquisitions.

Integrating both concepts allows investors to identify undervalued assets and strategically allocate resources, ensuring their portfolios align with financial goals and risk tolerance. Together, portfolio optimization and asset valuation enhance the decision-making process, leading to improved investment outcomes in an ever-changing financial landscape.

Portfolio optimization

Portfolio optimization is the process of selecting the best combination of assets to maximize expected returns while minimizing risk. It involves constructing a portfolio that aligns with an investor's financial goals and risk tolerance. The foundational principle is the risk-return trade-off higher potential returns typically come with higher risk.

Key methodologies include mean-variance optimization, developed by Harry Markowitz, which uses historical return data to identify the most efficient portfolios those that offer the highest expected return for a given level of risk. Investors plot these portfolios on the efficient frontier, a curve representing optimal asset allocations. Diversification is a critical aspect of portfolio optimization, as it reduces the impact of any single asset's poor performance. By spreading investments across different asset classes such as stocks, bonds, and real estate investors can mitigate risk.

Additionally, advanced techniques like Capital Asset Pricing Model (CAPM) and multi-factor models assess expected returns based on systematic risk factors. With the advent of technology, algorithms and machine learning are increasingly utilized for dynamic optimization, allowing for real-time adjustments to portfolios based on changing market conditions. Overall, effective portfolio optimization is essential for achieving sustainable investment success.

Key Concepts in Portfolio Optimization: Some of the key concepts in portfolio optimization:

1. **Risk and Return:** Risk is the potential for loss or variability in returns. Investors must understand their risk tolerance, which varies based on individual circumstances whereas the return is the profit or loss generated by an investment over time. Higher returns typically come with higher risk.
2. **Diversification**: Spreading investments across various assets to reduce overall risk. By holding a mix of asset classes, sectors, and geographies, investors can mitigate the impact of poor performance in any single investment.
3. **Efficient Frontier:** A graphical representation of optimal portfolios that offer the highest expected return for a given level of risk. Portfolios on the frontier are considered efficient, while those below are suboptimal.
4. **Mean-variance Optimization (MVO):** A mathematical framework developed by Harry Markowitz that seeks to identify the best asset allocation by analyzing expected returns, variances, and covariances of asset returns.
5. **Capital Asset Pricing Model (CAPM):** A model that describes the relationship between expected return and systematic risk. It helps investors evaluate whether an asset is fairly valued based on its risk relative to the market.
6. **Multi-factor Models:** These extend CAPM by considering multiple risk factors (e.g., size, value, momentum) that may influence asset returns, providing a more comprehensive analysis of risk.
7. **Optimization Algorithms:** Techniques such as genetic algorithms, simulated annealing, and Monte Carlo simulations that are used to dynamically adjust portfolios based on changing market conditions.
8. **Asset Allocation:** The strategic decision of distributing investments among different asset classes (e.g., stocks, bonds, real estate) to balance risk and return according to the investor's goals.
9. **Rebalancing:** The process of periodically adjusting the weights of assets in a portfolio to maintain the desired level of risk and return as market conditions change.
10. **Performance Measurement:** Evaluating how well a portfolio has performed against benchmarks and risk-adjusted metrics, such as Sharpe ratio, to assess investment success.

Methodologies for Portfolio Optimization: Some of the key methodologies for portfolio optimization are as under:

1. **Mean-Variance Optimization:** Mean-variance optimization (MVO) is a mathematical framework used to construct an optimal portfolio based on

expected returns, variances, and covariances of asset returns. The process involves the following steps:

- **Estimate Expected Returns**: Investors forecast the expected returns for each asset based on historical performance, economic indicators, and market analysis.
- **Calculate Risk**: The risk associated with each asset is quantified using standard deviation, while the relationship between asset returns is assessed using covariance.
- **Construct the Efficient Frontier**: By plotting the risk-return combinations of various portfolios, the efficient frontier is created, showing the optimal portfolios.
- **Select the Optimal Portfolio**: Based on an investor's risk tolerance, the optimal portfolio is identified along the efficient frontier.

2. **Capital Asset Pricing Model (CAPM):** The Capital Asset Pricing Model (CAPM) is a widely used financial model that establishes a relationship between expected return and systematic risk (beta). CAPM helps investors determine whether an asset is fairly valued, taking into account its risk relative to the market. The formula is as follows:

$$\text{Expected Return} = R_f + \beta \times (R_m - R_f)$$

Where:

- R_f = Risk-free rate
- β = Measure of asset risk
- R_m = Expected market return

CAPM assists in identifying which assets to include in a portfolio based on their risk-adjusted returns.

3. **Multi-factor Models:** Multi-factor models extend CAPM by considering multiple risk factors that may affect asset returns. Common factors include market risk, size risk, value risk, and momentum. These models provide a more comprehensive framework for understanding the risks associated with different investments and can improve portfolio performance.

4. **Optimization Algorithms:** With advancements in technology, various algorithms and techniques are now employed for complex portfolio optimization. Methods such as genetic algorithms, simulated annealing, and Monte Carlo simulations allow for dynamic adjustments to portfolios based on market conditions. These tools enable investors to explore a vast number of potential asset combinations, identifying optimal allocations more effectively than traditional methods.

Practical Application of Portfolio Optimization

1. **Establishing Investment Goals:** The first step in portfolio optimization is defining clear investment objectives. Investors should consider their financial goals, risk tolerance, investment horizon, and liquidity needs. This foundational understanding will guide the optimization process.
2. **Asset Selection**: Investors must conduct thorough research to identify suitable assets for inclusion in their portfolio. This involves analyzing potential investments, considering factors such as historical performance, volatility, and correlations with other assets.
3. **Asset Allocation:** Once suitable assets are identified, the next step is to determine the allocation of funds across the selected assets. This allocation should align with the investor's risk tolerance and investment goals, as well as capitalize on the benefits of diversification.
4. **Continuous Monitoring and Rebalancing:** The financial markets are dynamic, and portfolio optimization is not a one-time task. Regular monitoring of portfolio performance is essential, and rebalancing may be necessary to maintain the desired asset allocation. Rebalancing involves adjusting the weights of assets in response to market changes, ensuring the portfolio remains aligned with the investor's goals.

Future of Portfolio Optimization: # Future of Portfolio Optimization: The landscape of portfolio optimization is evolving rapidly, influenced by technological advancements, changing market dynamics, and evolving investor preferences. Here are key trends and predictions that are shaping the future of portfolio optimization:

1. **Integration of Artificial Intelligence and Machine Learning**
   - **Advanced Analytics:** AI and machine learning algorithms will increasingly be employed to analyze vast datasets and identify patterns that traditional methods may miss. These technologies can enhance predictive modeling, helping investors make more informed decisions.
   - **Automated Insights:** AI can provide real-time insights and recommendations, allowing for dynamic adjustments to portfolios based on market changes.
2. **Real-time Data Utilization**
   - **Instantaneous Analysis:** The ability to access real-time data will revolutionize portfolio optimization, enabling investors to make timely decisions that respond to market fluctuations.
   - **Enhanced Responsiveness:** Real-time analytics will facilitate quicker portfolio rebalancing and risk assessment, improving overall performance.
3. **Focus on Environmental, Social, and Governance (ESG) Factors**

- **Sustainable Investing:** As awareness of ESG issues grows, investors will increasingly integrate these factors into their optimization strategies. This trend will influence asset selection and allocation, reflecting a broader commitment to sustainable practices.
- **Performance Metrics:** New methodologies will emerge to quantify the impact of ESG factors on financial performance, allowing investors to optimize portfolios while aligning with their values.

4. **Personalization and Goal-Based Investing**
   - **Customized Strategies:** Advances in data analytics will enable more personalized investment strategies tailored to individual investor goals, risk tolerance, and preferences.
   - **Dynamic Goal Alignment:** Portfolio optimization will increasingly focus on aligning investments with specific financial objectives, allowing for more targeted asset allocation.
5. **Increased Use of Multi-factor Models**
   - **Diverse Risk Assessment:** Multi-factor models will gain traction, allowing investors to evaluate asset performance based on multiple risk factors, leading to more robust portfolio construction.
   - **Enhanced Diversification:** By considering a wider range of influences, investors can achieve better diversification and risk management.
6. **Automation and Robo-Advisors**
   - **Rob-advisory Services:** The rise of robo-advisors will democratize portfolio optimization, making advanced investment strategies accessible to a broader audience. Automated platforms will provide personalized portfolio management with minimal human intervention.
   - **Cost Efficiency:** Automation will reduce costs associated with portfolio management, enabling more investors to access optimization tools.
7. **Advanced Risk Management Techniques**
   - **Scenario Analysis and Stress Testing:** Enhanced tools for scenario analysis will help investors assess portfolio resilience under various market conditions, informing better risk management practices.
   - **Real-time Risk Assessment:** Continuous monitoring of risk metrics will allow for timely interventions, improving portfolio stability during volatile market periods.
8. **Blockchain and Decentralized Finance (DeFi)**
   - **Transparent Transactions:** Blockchain technology can provide greater transparency and security in asset transactions, enhancing trust in portfolio management processes.
   - **Innovative Investment Opportunities:** The emergence of DeFi will

introduce new asset classes and investment opportunities, requiring updated optimization strategies to account for these innovations.

9. **Collaboration Between Human and Machine**
   - **Hybrid Models:** The future of portfolio optimization will likely involve collaboration between human intuition and machine intelligence. Human analysts will guide strategic decisions while algorithms handle complex data analysis.
   - **Enhanced Decision-making:** This synergy will enable more nuanced and informed investment strategies.

10. **Continuous Learning and Adaptation**
    - **Agile Strategies:** As markets evolve, portfolio optimization strategies will need to be agile and adaptable. Continuous learning algorithms will improve over time, refining investment approaches based on historical performance and new data.
    - **Feedback Loops:** Incorporating feedback mechanisms will allow for ongoing optimization and better alignment with changing market conditions.

Asset Valuation

Asset valuation is the process of determining the worth of an asset or investment, a critical aspect of financial decision-making. Accurate valuation enables investors to assess potential returns, make informed buying or selling choices, and evaluate associated risks. Common methods include Discounted Cash Flow (DCF) analysis, which estimates the present value of an asset based on expected future cash flows, discounted by an appropriate rate. Comparative analysis, or relative valuation, involves assessing an asset against similar assets using metrics like price-to-earnings (P/E) and price-to-book (P/B) ratios. Asset-based valuation focuses on the underlying assets and liabilities of tangible items, making it particularly useful for real estate and companies with significant physical assets. Additionally, option pricing models, such as the Black-Scholes model, are employed to value financial derivatives by calculating fair values based on the movements of underlying asset prices. Mastering these valuation techniques is essential for investors and financial professionals, as they provide the framework for developing investment strategies and conducting thorough financial analysis, ultimately influencing investment success.

Importance of Asset Valuation: Importance of asset valuation are as follows:

1. **Informed Investment Decisions:** One of the primary reasons asset valuations is important is that it enables investors to make informed decisions. By accurately assessing an asset's worth, investors can identify opportunities for buying undervalued assets or selling overvalued ones. This informed decision-making is crucial for optimizing returns and managing investment risk effectively. A well-valued asset can enhance portfolio performance, while poor

valuation may lead to significant financial losses.

2. **Financial Reporting Compliance:** For corporations, accurate asset valuation is essential for compliance with accounting standards and regulations. Companies must regularly assess their assets to ensure that their financial statements reflect true economic value. This transparency is not only vital for compliance but also helps build trust among stakeholders, including investors, analysts, and regulatory bodies. Accurate financial reporting is critical for maintaining credibility in the market, which can impact a company's ability to raise capital and secure financing.
3. **Mergers and Acquisitions (M&A):** In the realm of mergers and acquisitions, precise asset valuation becomes even more critical. M&A transactions often hinge on the valuation of the involved entities. Accurate valuations help negotiators establish fair prices and assess potential synergies that could arise from the merger or acquisition. Misevaluation can lead to overpayment, underpayment, or even failed deals, making it essential for companies to invest in robust valuation processes during M&A activities.
4. **Risk Assessment:** Asset valuation is also integral to risk assessment. Understanding an asset's intrinsic value allows investors and companies to evaluate the risks associated with that asset more effectively. For instance, if the market value of an asset is significantly lower than its intrinsic value, it may indicate a potential buying opportunity. Conversely, if the market value is high without justification, it could signal a riskier investment. Effective risk management strategies are built on solid valuation principles.
5. **Capital Budgeting:** In capital budgeting, accurate asset valuation assists companies in assessing the feasibility of projects and investments. Valuation techniques provide insights into potential returns and associated risks, guiding organizations in their capital allocation decisions. By understanding the true value of assets, businesses can prioritize projects that align with their strategic goals, ensuring that resources are allocated efficiently.

Key Valuation Methods: The key valuation methods are as follows:

1. **Discounted Cash Flow (DCF) Analysis:** The Discounted Cash Flow (DCF) method is one of the most widely used approaches for valuing assets. It estimates the present value of an asset based on its expected future cash flows, discounted back to their present value using a required rate of return.

   Steps Involved

   - **Estimate Future Cash Flows:** Forecast the asset's future cash flows over a specified period, typically 5 to 10 years. This includes revenue projections, operating costs, and capital expenditures.
   - **Determine the Discount Rate:** Establish an appropriate discount rate, often based on the Weighted Average Cost of Capital (WACC) or required rate

of return for investors.

- **Calculate Present Value:** Discount the estimated future cash flows back to their present value using the formula:

$$PV = \sum \frac{CF_t}{(1+r)^t}$$

where, CF_t is the cash flow in year t and r is the discount rate.

- **Terminal Value:** Estimate the terminal value at the end of the projection period to account for cash flows beyond that timeframe, often using the Gordon Growth Model or exit multiple approach.
- **Sum of Cash Flows:** Add the present value of future cash flows and the terminal value to arrive at the total asset value.

Advantages: DCF analysis provides a detailed understanding of an asset's intrinsic value based on fundamental financial data. It is flexible and can be tailored to various types of assets.

Limitations: DCF relies heavily on projections and assumptions, which can introduce significant uncertainty. Small changes in assumptions can lead to vastly different valuations.

2. **Comparative Analysis (Relative Valuation):** Comparative analysis, also known as relative valuation, involves assessing an asset's value by comparing it to similar assets or companies. This method uses valuation multiples derived from comparable entities to estimate the target asset's value.

Steps Involved

- **Identify Comparable:** Select a group of similar companies or assets that operate in the same industry and have comparable characteristics.
- **Calculate Multiples:** Calculate the relevant valuation multiples for the comparable assets.
- **Apply Multiples:** Apply the average or median multiples to the target asset's financial metrics (e.g., earnings, book value) to derive an estimated value.

Advantages: Comparative analysis is straightforward, quick, and relies on market data, making it useful for investors seeking a relative perspective on asset values.

Limitations: It may overlook unique characteristics of the asset being valued and can be influenced by market sentiment, leading to potential inaccuracies.

3. **Asset-Based Valuation:** Asset-based valuation focuses on determining the value of an asset based on its underlying assets and liabilities. This approach is particularly useful for tangible assets like real estate and companies with significant physical assets.

Steps Involved

- **Identify Assets and Liabilities:** List all tangible and intangible assets, as well as liabilities associated with the asset or company.
- **Valuation of Assets:** Assign values to each asset based on market prices, replacement costs, or appraisals.
- **Net Asset Value Calculation:** Subtract total liabilities from total assets to arrive at the net asset value (NAV):

$$NAV = \text{Total Assets} - \text{Total Liabilities}$$

Advantages: This method provides a clear picture of an asset's intrinsic value based on its balance sheet. It is straightforward and easy to understand.

Limitations: Asset-based valuation may not fully capture the value of intangible assets (e.g., brand equity) and can underestimate the value of a business with strong earnings potential.

4. **Option Pricing Models:** Option pricing models, such as the Black-Scholes model and the binomial model, are used to value financial derivatives, specifically options. These models estimate the fair value of options based on underlying asset price movements and other variables.

Key Components

- **Underlying Asset Price:** Current price of the asset on which the option is based.
- **Strike Price:** The price at which the option can be exercised.
- **Time to Expiration:** The remaining time until the option expires.
- **Volatility:** The expected volatility of the underlying asset's price.
- **Risk-free Rate:** The theoretical return on a risk-free investment, typically based on government bonds.

Advantages: Option pricing models provide a rigorous framework for valuing complex financial instruments and help investors assess risk in derivatives trading.

Limitations: These models rely on assumptions that may not always hold true, such as constant volatility and efficient markets, potentially leading to inaccuracies.

Emerging Trends in Asset Valuation

1. **Technological Advancements:** Technological advancements have revolutionized asset valuation through big data analytics, artificial intelligence, and machine learning. These innovations enhance predictive modeling, automate valuation processes, and provide real-time insights, enabling more accurate assessments. As a result, investors and financial professionals can make informed decisions faster and more effectively than ever before.

- **Data Analytics:** The rise of big data and advanced analytics tools allows for more accurate forecasts and valuations. Investors can analyze vast datasets to identify trends and correlations that inform asset valuations.
- **Artificial Intelligence:** AI and machine learning algorithms are being used to enhance valuation models, improve predictive analytics, and automate the valuation process.

2. **Integration of ESG Factors:** The integration of Environmental, Social, and Governance (ESG) factors into asset valuation is increasingly important as investors seek sustainable returns. By assessing ESG metrics, investors can evaluate long-term risks and opportunities, aligning investments with ethical standards while potentially enhancing financial performance and resilience in changing market dynamics.
   - **Sustainability Metrics**: As Environmental, Social, and Governance (ESG) factors gain importance, asset valuations are increasingly incorporating these metrics. Investors are recognizing that sustainable practices can influence long-term financial performance and risk.
   - **Impact Investing**: The growing demand for socially responsible investments has prompted the development of valuation frameworks that assess both financial returns and social impact.
3. **Globalization and Market Dynamics:** Globalization and shifting market dynamics have transformed asset valuation practices. Investors must consider international factors, such as regulatory differences and economic conditions, that affect asset worth. This complexity requires a nuanced understanding of global trends, enabling more informed investment decisions and effective risk management in diverse markets.
   - **Cross-Border Valuation**: As investment opportunities become more global, understanding international market dynamics and valuation standards becomes crucial. Differences in regulations, market practices, and economic conditions can impact asset values significantly.
   - **Market Volatility**: In an era of rapid market changes and increased volatility, real-time valuation methods and scenario analysis will become essential for effective asset valuation.

Conclusion

Asset valuation is a vital process that influences investment decisions, financial reporting, and corporate strategy. Understanding various valuation methods such as DCF analysis, comparative analysis, asset-based valuation, and option pricing models equips investors and financial professionals with the tools needed to assess asset worth accurately. As technology advances and market dynamics evolve, asset valuation will continue to adapt, incorporating new methodologies and considerations, such as ESG factors and big data analytics. A thorough grasp of these trends and techniques will empower stakeholders to make informed decisions in an increasingly complex financial landscape.

Differences Between Portfolio Optimization and Asset Valuation

Table 4.1

S.No.	Aspects	Portfolio Optimization	Asset Valuation
1.	Definition	The process of selecting the best mix of assets to maximize returns for a given level of risk.	The process of determining the worth of an individual asset or investment.
2.	Objective	To create an optimal investment portfolio based on risk-return trade-offs.	To assess the intrinsic value of an asset for informed decision-making.
3.	Focus	Emphasizes the relationship between multiple assets in a portfolio.	Concentrates on the value of a single asset or entity.
4.	Methods	Mean-Variance Optimization, Black-Litterman Model, Risk Parity.	DCF Analysis, Comparative Analysis, Asset-Based Valuation, Option Pricing Models.
5.	Outcome	An optimal asset allocation that maximizes returns or minimizes risk.	A monetary value assigned to an asset based on valuation techniques.
6.	Time Horizon	Often considers short-term and long-term investment strategies.	Typically focuses on the current value, though projections can extend into the future.
7.	Risk Assessment	Evaluates the overall risk of a portfolio through diversification and correlation of assets.	Assesses risk related to a specific asset, considering factors like market volatility and performance.
8.	Application	Used by portfolio managers, individual investors, and financial advisors for investment strategies.	Used by investors, financial analysts, and accountants for investment decisions, financial reporting, and M&A activities.

Fraud Detection Techniques

Fraud detection is a process that detects and prevents fraudsters from obtaining money or property through false means. It is a set of activities undertaken to detect and block the attempt of fraudsters from obtaining money or property fraudulently. Fraud detection is prevalent across banking, insurance, medical, government, and public sectors, as well as in law enforcement agencies.

Traditional Fraud Detection Techniques

Fraud detection techniques include manual audits, data analysis, rule-based systems, machine learning, behavioral analytics, and real-time monitoring. These methods identify anomalies, assess risks, and adapt to evolving fraud tactics, ensuring organizations can effectively safeguard against financial loss and maintain operational integrity. Fraud detection techniques are:

1. **Manual Audits:** Manual audits involve systematically reviewing financial records and transactions to identify discrepancies or anomalies. This process

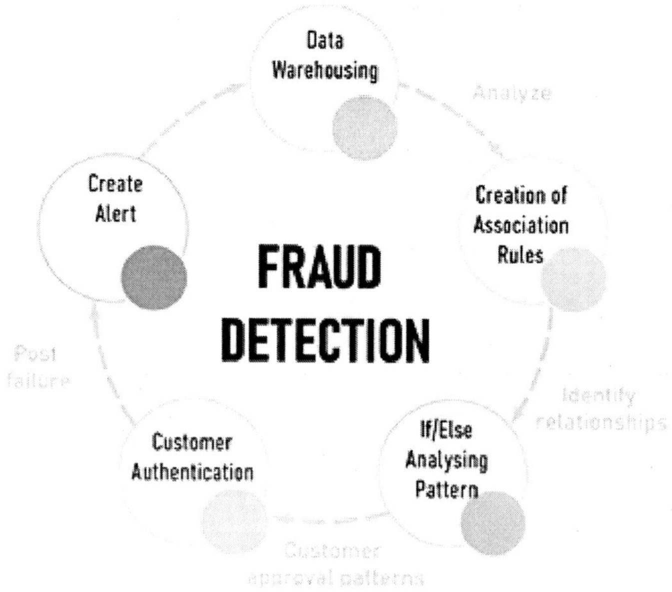

Fig.4.1

can uncover issues such as improper accounting practices or fraudulent activities. Manual audits play a crucial role in fraud detection and prevention within organizations. This traditional method involves a systematic examination of financial records, transactions, and operational processes to identify discrepancies, irregularities, or potentially fraudulent activities. Despite the rise of automated solutions and advanced technologies, manual audits remain an essential component of an organization's overall fraud detection strategy.

Purpose of Manual Audits: The primary goal of manual audits is to ensure the accuracy and integrity of financial reporting. By reviewing transactions and accounting practices, auditors can detect errors or manipulations that could indicate fraudulent behavior. Manual audits also help organizations comply with regulatory requirements, enhancing transparency and accountability.

Audit Process: The manual audit process typically involves several key steps:

- **Planning:** Auditors define the scope and objectives of the audit. This includes identifying the areas to focus on, such as specific departments, financial statements, or transaction types. Planning also involves assessing risks and determining the resources needed for the audit.
- **Data Collection:** Relevant documents and records are gathered, including financial statements, transaction logs, invoices, and receipts. Auditors may

also conduct interviews with employees to gain insights into operational processes and controls.

- **Analysis:** The collected data is meticulously analyzed. Auditors compare actual transactions against expected patterns, rules, and benchmarks. This analysis can involve reviewing financial ratios, conducting trend analyses, and employing techniques like Benford's Law to identify anomalies in numerical data.
- **Reporting:** Findings from the audit are documented in a comprehensive report. This report outlines identified discrepancies, potential fraud indicators, and recommendations for corrective actions. The audit report is then presented to management or relevant stakeholders.

Practices for Effective Manual Audits: To maximize the effectiveness of manual audits, organizations should consider the following best practices:

- **Regular Audits:** Conduct audits on a regular basis to ensure continuous oversight and timely identification of issues.
- **Training and Development:** Invest in ongoing training for auditors to keep them updated on the latest fraud schemes, regulatory changes, and audit techniques.
- **Cross-functional Teams:** Involve professionals from different departments to provide diverse perspectives and insights during the audit process.
- **Follow-up Actions:** Ensure that recommendations from audit reports are implemented promptly to address identified issues and strengthen internal controls.

2. **Data Analysis Techniques:** Data analysis involves examining and interpreting financial data to uncover patterns indicative of fraud. Data analysis techniques are essential tools in the fight against fraud, allowing organizations to identify anomalies, patterns, and trends that may indicate fraudulent activity. By systematically analyzing financial data, organizations can enhance their fraud detection capabilities and respond proactively to potential threats.

   - **Trend Analysis:** Trend analysis involves examining data over a specified time period to identify patterns or shifts that could suggest fraudulent behavior. By comparing historical data to current figures, auditors can detect unusual spikes or drops in activity. Process:

     Collect historical data related to transactions, revenue, or expenditures.

     Use statistical methods to identify trends and compare current figures against historical norms.

     Highlight any significant deviations for further investigation.

   - **Ratio Analysis:** Ratio analysis involves calculating and comparing financial ratios to assess the health of an organization and detect inconsistencies. Ratios can reveal discrepancies between related financial metrics.

Process: Identify key financial ratios, such as profit margins, return on assets, and liquidity ratios.

Compare these ratios over time or against industry benchmarks.

Investigate any unusual fluctuations or inconsistencies.

- **Benford's Law:** Benford's Law states that in many naturally occurring datasets, the distribution of the leading digits is not uniform. For example, the number '1' appears as the leading digit more frequently than '9'. This principle can help detect anomalies in numerical data. Process:

  Analyze the leading digits of numerical datasets (e.g., transaction amounts).

  Compare the observed distribution of leading digits against the expected distribution as per Benford's Law.

  Identify significant deviations that may indicate manipulation.

- **Anomaly Detection:** Anomaly detection involves identifying data points that deviate significantly from the norm. This technique can uncover unexpected transactions that warrant further investigation. Process:

  Use statistical methods or machine learning algorithms to establish baseline behaviors.

  Flag data points that fall outside predefined thresholds.

  Investigate flagged anomalies to determine if they are fraudulent.

- **Data Visualization:** Data visualization techniques, such as graphs and dashboards, help present complex data in a more digestible format. Visual representations can make it easier to spot trends, patterns, and outliers. Process:

  Gather and process data into visual formats, such as charts or heat maps.

  Use visualization tools to highlight areas of concern.

  Share visual insights with stakeholders for decision-making.

3. **Rule-based Systems:** Rule-based systems apply predefined rules to transactions to flag potentially fraudulent activities. For example, transactions above a certain dollar amount or from unusual locations may trigger alerts. Rule-based systems are a fundamental approach in fraud detection, employing predefined rules and criteria to identify potentially fraudulent transactions or activities. These systems leverage structured guidelines to flag anomalies, making them a crucial part of many organizations' fraud prevention strategies.

Rule-based Systems Working:

- **Rule Definition:** The first step in creating a rule-based system involves defining a set of rules based on historical data, industry best practices, and known fraud patterns. These rules can cover various aspects, such as transaction amounts, frequency of transactions, geographic locations, and customer behaviors.

- **Rule Application:** Once the rules are established, they are applied to incoming transactions or activities. The system evaluates each transaction against the defined rules to determine if it meets any criteria for further investigation. For example, a rule might flag any transaction over a specific amount or multiple transactions from the same account within a short period.
- **Alert Generation:** When a transaction meets one or more predefined criteria, the system generates an alert for further review. These alerts are prioritized based on the severity of the rule violated, allowing fraud analysts to focus on the most suspicious activities first.

Practices for Implementing Rule-Based Systems: To maximize the effectiveness of rule-based systems, organizations should consider the following best practices:

- **Regularly Review and Update Rules:** Periodic assessment of rules is crucial to ensure they remain relevant and effective against evolving fraud tactics.
- **Integrate with Other Techniques:** Combining rule-based systems with other detection methods, such as data analysis and machine learning, can enhance overall fraud detection capabilities.
- **Balance between Sensitivity and Specificity:** Striking the right balance in rule thresholds can help minimize false positives while ensuring legitimate fraud cases are identified.
- **Training and Support:** Provide ongoing training for fraud analysts to effectively interpret alerts and investigate flagged transactions.

Financial Modeling Case Studies

Financial modeling is a crucial skill for professionals in finance, investment, and corporate strategy. It allows for the analysis of financial performance, forecasting future earnings, and supporting strategic decision-making. In this article, we will explore several case studies that illustrate the application of financial modeling across different industries and scenarios.

Case Study 1: Valuation of a Technology Startup

Background: A venture capital firm is considering investing in a tech startup focused on developing a new software solution for small businesses. The firm needs to determine the potential value of the startup and the expected return on investment.

Financial Model Structure:

1. **Revenue Projections:**
   - Estimate user growth based on market research and industry trends.
   - Model revenue streams: subscription fees, tiered pricing based on features, and upselling additional services.

Differences Between Manual Audits, Data Analysis, Rule-based Systems

Table 4.2

S.No.	Aspect	Manual Audits	Data Analysis	Rule-based Systems
1.	Definition	Systematic review of financial records and transactions.	Examination of data to identify patterns and anomalies.	Application of predefined rules to identify suspicious transactions.
2.	Process	Planning, data collection, analysis, reporting.	Data gathering, statistical analysis, pattern recognition.	Rule definition, application, alert generation.
3.	Human Involvement	High; relies on auditors' judgment and expertise.	Varies; can be automated or manual but often requires interpretation.	Low; primarily automated with predefined criteria.
4.	Flexibility	Flexible; can adapt to unique circumstances during audits.	Moderately flexible; adaptable based on data context.	Rigid; rules must be manually updated to adapt to new fraud tactics.
5.	Speed	Time-consuming; often takes weeks to complete.	Can be quick, especially with automated tools.	Fast; real-time processing of transactions.
6.	False Positives	Generally low; focuses on specific instances.	Variable; depends on the analysis method and thresholds used.	Often high; many legitimate transactions may be flagged as suspicious.
7.	Scope	Limited; may not cover all transactions, especially in large volumes.	Broad; can analyze large datasets for patterns Limited; may not cover all transactions, especially in large volumes. various dimensions.	Focused on specific criteria, potentially missing complex fraud patterns.
8.	Cost	Can be expensive due to labour-intensive processes.	Varies; can be cost-effective if automated but may require specialized tools.	Generally lower upfront costs compared to advanced analytics but requires ongoing rule maintenance.
9.	Outcome	In-depth insights into fraud and compliance issues.	Identification of trends, anomalies, and data relationships.	Immediate alerts for further investigation of flagged transactions.

2. **Cost Structure:**
   - Analyze fixed costs (e.g., salaries, office space) and variable costs (e.g., customer acquisition, hosting services).
   - Include research and development expenses to maintain competitive advantage.
3. **Cash Flow Analysis:**
   - Project cash inflows from sales and cash outflows for expenses.
   - Calculate free cash flow (FCF) to determine the amount available for distribution to investors.
4. **Valuation Methods:**

- Use Discounted Cash Flow (DCF) analysis to calculate the present value of future cash flows.
- Compare results with market comps to validate assumptions.

Outcome: The financial model indicated a robust growth potential, showing a 30% annual growth rate in revenue over five years. The DCF analysis yielded a valuation of $10 million, providing the venture capital firm with a basis for negotiation. The firm decided to invest, believing the potential returns justified the risk.

Case Study 2: Mergers and Acquisitions in the Healthcare Sector

Background: large pharmaceutical company is evaluating the acquisition of a smaller biotech firm with promising drug candidates. The goal is to assess the financial impact of the acquisition on the parent company's earnings.

Financial Model Structure

1. **Pro Forma Financial Statements:**
   - Develop pro forma income statements, balance sheets, and cash flow statements for the combined entity.
   - Incorporate projected revenues from the biotech firm's drugs after approval.
2. **Synergy Assessment:**
   - Identify potential cost synergies, such as reduced overhead and shared R&D expenses.
   - Estimate revenue synergies from cross-selling opportunities in existing markets.
3. **Impact on Valuation:**
   - Analyze how the acquisition will affect the overall valuation of the parent company.
   - Adjust financial metrics to reflect the additional revenue and costs associated with the acquisition.
4. **Sensitivity Analysis:** Perform sensitivity analyses to understand how changes in key assumptions (e.g., drug approval timelines, market penetration rates) affect the valuation.

Outcome: The analysis revealed significant synergies, estimating a combined EBITDA increase of $50 million within three years. The acquisition would create a stronger product pipeline and enhance the parent company's market position. Based on these findings, the board approved the acquisition, leading to successful integration and enhanced shareholder value.

Case Study 3: Real Estate Investment Analysis

Background: A real estate investment firm is considering purchasing a commercial property to generate rental income and potential appreciation. The firm needs to build a financial model to evaluate the investment's viability.

Financial Model Structure

1. **Revenue Projections:**
   - Forecast rental income based on current lease agreements and market rates.
   - Include potential rental increases and additional revenue from ancillary services (e.g., parking, advertising).
2. **Expense Estimates:**
   - Model operating expenses, including property management, maintenance, property taxes, and insurance.
   - Consider capital expenditures for renovations or improvements.
3. **Cash Flow Analysis:**
   - Calculate net operating income (NOI) by subtracting operating expenses from rental income.
   - Determine cash flow available for debt service and investor returns.
4. **Exit Strategy:**
   - Project the property's resale value based on expected appreciation rates and market conditions.
   - Use DCF analysis to evaluate the investment's overall return over a holding period.

Outcome: The financial model showed a projected IRR (Internal Rate of Return) of 12% over a five-year holding period, primarily driven by stable rental income and property appreciation. The firm decided to proceed with the acquisition, leading to successful cash flow generation and eventual profitable sale.

Case Study 4: Corporate Financial Planning for a Manufacturing Firm

Background: A manufacturing company is looking to optimize its production capacity and assess the financial implications of expanding its facilities. The leadership team needs a financial model to guide its decision-making.

Financial Model Structure

1. **Capacity Analysis:**
   - Evaluate current production capacity and forecast future demand based on market trends.
   - Identify required investment for new equipment and facilities.
2. **Cost Analysis:**
   - Analyze fixed costs (e.g., facility costs, salaries) and variable costs (e.g., raw materials, labor).
   - Project potential economies of scale with increased production.

3. **Profitability Assessment:**
   - Model the impact of increased production on overall profitability.
   - Calculate contribution margins and break-even analysis for various production levels.
4. **Scenario Analysis:** Develop multiple scenarios (e.g., best case, worst case, most likely) to assess risks and uncertainties associated with the expansion.

Outcome: The financial model indicated that expanding production could yield significant profit increases, with a projected ROI (Return on Investment) of 15%. By using scenario analysis, the company prepared for various market conditions, ultimately deciding to proceed with the expansion, which resulted in increased market share and profitability.

Case Study 5: Financial Forecasting for a Retail Chain

Background: A national retail chain aims to improve its financial forecasting to better manage inventory, staffing, and promotional strategies. The management team needs a robust financial model to guide these decisions.

Financial Model Structure

1. **Sales Forecasting:**
   - Analyze historical sales data, incorporating seasonality and economic indicators.
   - Use regression analysis to identify relationships between sales and external factors (e.g., consumer confidence).
2. **Cost of Goods Sold (COGS):**
   - Project COGS based on sales forecasts and historical margins.
   - Include factors such as supplier pricing and inventory turnover rates.
3. **Operating Expenses:**
   - Estimate fixed and variable operating expenses, such as rent, utilities, and salaries.
   - Consider the impact of promotions and marketing on expenses.
4. **Cash Flow Projections:**
   - Create cash flow forecasts based on revenue and expense projections.
   - Assess working capital requirements to ensure liquidity.

Outcome: The financial forecasting model enabled the retail chain to optimize inventory levels, resulting in a 20% reduction in holding costs. Improved forecasting accuracy also led to better staffing decisions and targeted marketing campaigns, ultimately increasing overall sales by 10%.

Conclusion

These case studies illustrate the diverse applications of financial modeling across various industries. From valuing startups and assessing acquisitions to analyzing real estate investments and optimizing corporate financial strategies, financial modeling is a critical tool for informed decision-making. By leveraging structured financial models, organizations can navigate complexities, enhance performance, and drive sustainable growth. As businesses continue to evolve, mastering financial modeling techniques will remain essential for professionals aiming to contribute effectively to their organizations' success.

3. Healthcare Analytics

Healthcare analytics involves the systematic analysis of health data to enhance patient outcomes, streamline operations, and improve decision-making. With the growing volume of data generated from electronic health records (EHRs), wearable devices, and health information exchanges, healthcare organizations can leverage analytics to identify trends, assess risks, and optimize resource allocation. Descriptive, predictive, and prescriptive analytics play key roles in transforming raw data into actionable insights, enabling providers to deliver personalized care and effectively manage population health.

Despite its significant benefits, healthcare analytics faces challenges such as data quality, privacy concerns, and interoperability issues. Ensuring accurate and secure data integration across various platforms is crucial for effective analysis. Additionally, the healthcare sector often grapples with a shortage of skilled professionals who can interpret data and apply analytics in clinical settings. As the industry continues to embrace advanced technologies like artificial intelligence and machine learning, the future of healthcare analytics promises to enhance real-time decision-making and foster patient-centric care, ultimately leading to improved health outcomes and operational efficiencies.

Importance of Healthcare Analytics: Healthcare analytics plays a crucial role in modern healthcare systems, fundamentally transforming the way providers deliver care and manage operations. By leveraging data derived from various sources, including electronic health records (EHRs), medical devices, and patient surveys, healthcare analytics empowers organizations to enhance patient outcomes, streamline operations, and optimize resource allocation. The importance of healthcare analytics can be understood through several key dimensions.

1. **Improving Patient Outcomes:** One of the primary benefits of healthcare analytics is its ability to improve patient outcomes. By analyzing historical data, healthcare providers can identify trends, recognize potential health risks, and tailor interventions accordingly. For instance, predictive analytics can assess the likelihood of hospital readmissions, enabling providers to implement targeted discharge planning and follow-up care. This proactive approach not

only enhances the quality of care delivered to patients but also reduces the financial burden on healthcare systems.

2. **Population Health Management:** Healthcare analytics is essential for effective population health management. It allows organizations to segment patient populations based on various factors, such as demographics, chronic conditions, and social determinants of health. By identifying at-risk groups, healthcare providers can implement preventive measures, promote wellness initiatives, and allocate resources more effectively. This data-driven approach leads to better health outcomes for communities and helps mitigate healthcare disparities.

3. **Operational Efficiency:** Operational efficiency is another critical aspect where healthcare analytics shines. By analyzing data related to patient flow, staffing, and resource utilization, organizations can identify inefficiencies and areas for improvement. For example, operational analytics can reveal patterns in-patient admissions and discharge processes, helping hospitals optimize staffing schedules and reduce wait times. Streamlining operations not only enhances patient satisfaction but also contributes to cost savings and better resource management.

4. **Financial Performance:** Financial analytics is vital for ensuring the economic viability of healthcare organizations. By analyzing billing patterns, reimbursement rates, and financial performance metrics, healthcare providers can identify opportunities for revenue optimization. For instance, analytics can help detect billing discrepancies, reduce claim denials, and improve the overall revenue cycle. This financial insight is crucial for sustainability, especially in an environment characterized by increasing costs and changing reimbursement models.

5. **Enhancing Clinical Decision-making:** Healthcare analytics also supports clinical decision-making by providing healthcare professionals with evidence-based insights. Real-time data analytics can assist clinicians in diagnosing conditions, recommending treatments, and monitoring patient responses to therapies. By integrating clinical guidelines and best practices into analytics tools, providers can ensure that decisions are informed by the most current and relevant information, ultimately leading to improved patient safety and care quality.

6. **Addressing Challenges:** Despite its many advantages, healthcare analytics does face challenges. Issues related to data quality, privacy concerns, and interoperability between different health IT systems can hinder the effective use of analytics. Ensuring that data is accurate, secure, and easily accessible is critical for maximizing the benefits of healthcare analytics. Furthermore, there is a growing need for skilled professionals who can interpret complex data and derive actionable insights.

Types of Healthcare Analytics: Healthcare analytics encompasses various methodologies and approaches to analyze health data for improving patient care, operational efficiency, and financial performance. Understanding the different types of healthcare analytics is crucial for organizations looking to leverage data effectively. The main categories include descriptive, predictive, prescriptive, and diagnostic analytics.

1. **Descriptive Analytics:** Descriptive analytics focuses on summarizing historical data to understand past events and trends. It answers questions such as "What happened?" by using techniques like data aggregation, visualization, and reporting. In healthcare, descriptive analytics can provide insights into patient demographics, treatment outcomes, and resource utilization. For example, hospitals might use descriptive analytics to assess the number of patients treated for specific conditions over a given period, which can inform staffing and resource allocation. Healthcare organizations often utilize dashboards and reports generated from descriptive analytics to track key performance indicators (KPIs) such as patient satisfaction scores, readmission rates, and operational metrics. By offering a clear view of historical performance, descriptive analytics helps organizations identify areas needing improvement and supports compliance with regulatory requirements.
2. **Predictive Analytics:** Predictive analytics builds on descriptive insights to forecast future events and outcomes. It utilizes statistical algorithms and machine learning techniques to analyze historical data and identify patterns that can indicate future trends. For example, predictive analytics can be employed to determine the likelihood of a patient being readmitted to the hospital based on factors such as age, medical history, and treatment compliance. Healthcare providers can use predictive models to stratify patient populations, allowing for more targeted interventions. For instance, by identifying high-risk patients, providers can implement proactive care plans, thus reducing the chances of complications or readmissions. This type of analytics not only enhances patient care but also contributes to more efficient use of resources.
3. **Prescriptive Analytics:** Prescriptive analytics goes a step further by recommending specific actions based on predictive insights. It answers questions like "What should we do?" by providing actionable recommendations derived from data analysis. This type of analytics often uses advanced algorithms and optimization techniques to identify the best course of action among multiple alternatives. In healthcare, prescriptive analytics can help in various scenarios, such as treatment planning, resource allocation, and operational management. For instance, a hospital might use prescriptive analytics to determine the optimal staffing levels needed during peak hours based on projected patient inflow. This capability helps organizations make data-driven decisions that improve both patient outcomes and operational efficiency.

4. **Diagnostic Analytics:** Diagnostic analytics focuses on understanding the reasons behind past events. It answers the question "Why did it happen?" by exploring relationships within the data. This type of analytics is crucial for investigating adverse events, treatment failures, or unexpected outcomes. For example, if a spike in hospital-acquired infections occurs, diagnostic analytics can help identify contributing factors such as specific procedures, staff practices, or patient demographics. Healthcare organizations can use diagnostic analytics to conduct root cause analyses, ultimately leading to improved practices and policies aimed at enhancing patient safety and care quality. By understanding the underlying causes of issues, providers can implement corrective actions that mitigate risks and improve overall performance.

Application of Healthcare Analytics: Healthcare analytics has become a transformative force within the industry, offering a wide array of applications that enhance patient care, streamline operations, and improve financial outcomes. By harnessing data from diverse sources, healthcare organizations can gain valuable insights that inform decision-making and drive strategic initiatives. Here are several key applications of healthcare analytics:

1. **Clinical Decision Support:** One of the most critical applications of healthcare analytics is in clinical decision support systems (CDSS). These systems leverage data analytics to provide healthcare providers with evidence-based recommendations at the point of care. For instance, predictive models can identify patients at risk for conditions like sepsis or readmissions, enabling timely interventions. By integrating clinical guidelines and patient data, CDSS enhances diagnostic accuracy and treatment effectiveness, ultimately improving patient outcomes.

2. **Population Health Management:** Healthcare analytics is essential for effective population health management, allowing organizations to analyze health trends across different demographics. By segmenting populations based on factors such as age, chronic conditions, and social determinants of health, providers can identify at-risk groups and implement targeted prevention and intervention strategies. For example, analytics can reveal high rates of diabetes in a specific community, prompting initiatives focused on education, screening, and lifestyle modifications to mitigate risk.

3. **Operational Efficiency:** Analytics plays a crucial role in optimizing healthcare operations. By analyzing data related to patient flow, staffing levels, and resource utilization, organizations can identify inefficiencies and improve workflows. For instance, operational analytics can help hospitals forecast patient admissions based on historical data, allowing for better staffing and resource allocation. This not only enhances patient experience by reducing wait times but also leads to cost savings through improved operational efficiency.

4. **Financial Management:** In the realm of financial management, healthcare analytics aids organizations in optimizing revenue cycles and controlling costs. By analyzing billing patterns, payer reimbursements, and operational expenses, providers can identify areas for improvement. For example, analytics can help detect billing discrepancies or reduce claim denials by pinpointing common issues in the billing process. This proactive approach ensures timely revenue collection and contributes to the financial stability of healthcare organizations.
5. **Quality Improvement Initiatives:** Healthcare analytics is instrumental in driving quality improvement initiatives. By tracking key performance indicators (KPIs) such as patient satisfaction, treatment outcomes, and adherence to clinical guidelines, organizations can assess the effectiveness of care delivery. For example, analytics can help evaluate the impact of new protocols on infection rates or medication errors, guiding continuous quality improvement efforts. This data-driven approach ensures that care standards are consistently met and enhanced over time.
6. **Research and Development:** In the realm of medical research, healthcare analytics facilitates clinical trials and research studies. By analyzing patient populations, trial data, and outcomes, researchers can identify trends and evaluate the efficacy of new treatments or interventions. Analytics also supports the recruitment of appropriate participants for trials by leveraging demographic and clinical data, ultimately speeding up the research process and bringing new therapies to market more efficiently.
7. **Telemedicine and Remote Monitoring:** The rise of telemedicine and remote patient monitoring has underscored the importance of healthcare analytics. By collecting and analyzing data from wearable devices and telehealth platforms, providers can monitor patient health in real time. Analytics can identify patterns in vital signs or symptom reports, allowing for timely interventions and improved management of chronic conditions.

Future Trends in Healthcare Analytics: The future of healthcare analytics is poised for significant transformation, driven by advancements in technology, evolving healthcare needs, and a growing emphasis on patient-centered care. Here are several key trends expected to shape the landscape of healthcare analytics in the coming years:

1. **Artificial Intelligence and Machine Learning:** The integration of artificial intelligence (AI) and machine learning (ML) into healthcare analytics is set to revolutionize data interpretation and decision-making processes. These technologies can analyze vast amounts of data rapidly, uncovering patterns and insights that may not be apparent through traditional analytical methods. For example, AI algorithms can enhance predictive analytics by accurately forecasting patient outcomes, enabling proactive interventions. Machine learning models will continuously improve over time as they learn from new data, refining predictions and recommendations.

2. **Real-time Analytics:** As healthcare systems increasingly prioritize timely decision-making, the demand for real-time analytics will grow. Real-time data processing allows healthcare providers to access up-to-date information about patient conditions, resource availability, and operational metrics. This capability enhances clinical decision-making and improves response times in critical situations, such as emergency care. For example, real-time analytics can help emergency departments manage patient flow more effectively, reducing wait times and optimizing resource allocation.
3. **Interoperability and Data Integration:** The future of healthcare analytics will see a strong emphasis on interoperability, enabling seamless data sharing between disparate health information systems. Effective data integration will provide a more comprehensive view of patient health, allowing for more accurate analytics. This trend is critical for facilitating care coordination among different providers and improving population health management. As standards for data exchange evolve, healthcare organizations will be better equipped to harness insights from diverse data sources, including EHRs, claims data, and wearable devices.
4. **Patient-centric Analytics:** The shift towards patient-centered care is driving the development of analytics focused on individual patient experiences and preferences. This trend emphasizes the importance of involving patients in their care processes and utilizing their feedback to improve services. Patient-centric analytics can analyze data from surveys, wearable health devices, and patient portals to tailor care plans to meet individual needs. This approach fosters greater patient engagement and satisfaction while enhancing clinical outcomes.
5. **Data Privacy and Security Enhancements:** As healthcare analytics relies heavily on sensitive patient data, ensuring data privacy and security will be paramount. Future trends will involve implementing advanced encryption, anonymization techniques, and robust cybersecurity measures to protect patient information. Regulatory frameworks will also evolve, requiring organizations to comply with stringent data protection standards. As patients become more aware of their data privacy rights, healthcare providers will need to prioritize transparent data practices to build trust.
6. **Predictive and Prescriptive Analytics Expansion:** While predictive analytics is already prevalent, its future applications will expand significantly. By combining predictive insights with prescriptive analytics, healthcare organizations will be able to not only forecast outcomes but also receive actionable recommendations for interventions. This combination will enhance clinical decision-making, optimize treatment plans, and improve resource management, ultimately leading to better patient outcomes and more efficient care delivery.

7. **Telehealth and Remote Monitoring Integration:** The rise of telehealth has underscored the importance of integrating healthcare analytics with remote monitoring technologies. As patients increasingly engage in remote care, analytics will play a crucial role in tracking health data collected from wearable devices and telehealth platforms. This integration will facilitate real-time monitoring, enabling providers to respond promptly to changes in patient health and adjust care plans accordingly.

Differences Between Marketing Analytics, Financial Analytics and Healthcare Analytics

Table 4.3

S.No.	Aspect	Marketing Analytics	Financial Analytics	Healthcare Analytics
1.	Purpose	To measure and optimize marketing performance and customer engagement.	To measure and optimize marketing performance and customer engagement.	To improve patient outcomes, operational efficiency, and resource allocation.
2.	Data Sources	Customer data, social Data Sources, website analytics, sales data, surveys.	Financial statements, transaction data, budgeting information, market data.	Electronic health records (EHRs), patient surveys, clinical data, operational metrics.
3.	Key Metrics	Customer acquisition cost, return on investment (ROI), conversion rates, customer lifetime value (CLV).	Profit margins, revenue growth, return on equity (ROE), cash flow, expenses.	Patient outcomes (e.g., readmission rates), treatment effectiveness, resource utilization, patient satisfaction scores.
4.	Analytical Techniques	Descriptive analytics, predictive modeling, segmentation analysis, A/B testing.	Variance analysis, trend analysis, forecasting, budgeting models.	Predictive analytics, diagnostic analytics, real-time monitoring, quality improvement metrics.
5.	Stakeholders	Marketing teams, sales departments, product managers, executives.	Finance departments, investment analysts, executives, auditors.	Healthcare providers, hospital administrators, public health officials, researchers.
6.	Timeframe	Short to medium-term (campaigns, quarterly performance).	Short to long-term (monthly, quarterly, annual reporting and forecasting).	Ongoing (real-time monitoring, continuous quality improvement).
7.	Outcome Focus	Brand awareness, customer engagement, sales growth.	Financial stability, profitability, investment decisions.	Improved patient care, operational efficiency, cost savings.
8.	Challenges	Data integration, measuring ROI, evolving customer behaviors.	Data accuracy, regulatory compliance, market volatility.	Data privacy, interoperability, quality of care measurements.

Conclusion

Healthcare analytics is revolutionizing the way care is delivered, providing valuable insights that drive improvements in patient outcomes and operational efficiencies. Despite the challenges it faces, the potential benefits far outweigh the obstacles. As technology continues to evolve, the integration of advanced analytics into healthcare practices will lead to a more data-driven, patient-centered approach, ultimately transforming the landscape of healthcare delivery. The ongoing commitment to harnessing the power of analytics will be crucial in meeting the future demands of the healthcare industry.

Supply Chain and Operations Analytics

Supply chain and operations analytics involve the systematic use of data to enhance decision-making, optimize processes, and improve overall efficiency within an organization. By leveraging historical and real-time data, businesses can gain valuable insights into demand forecasting, inventory management, supplier performance, and logistics operations. These analytics enable companies to identify inefficiencies, reduce costs, and respond proactively to market changes, ultimately enhancing customer satisfaction. The applications of supply chain analytics are diverse, including demand forecasting, inventory optimization, logistics management, and production planning. With the integration of advanced technologies such as artificial intelligence (AI) and the Internet of Things (IoT), organizations can achieve real-time visibility and predictive capabilities, further refining their operations. However, challenges such as data quality, integration, and cybersecurity risks must be addressed to fully harness the power of analytics. As organizations increasingly focus on sustainability and collaboration, supply chain analytics will play a crucial role in navigating complexities and driving long-term success in today's dynamic business environment.

Importance of Supply Chain and Operations Analytics: Supply chain and operations analytics play a pivotal role in enhancing the effectiveness and efficiency of organizations across various industries. As businesses face increasing complexity in their supply chains due to globalization, technological advancements, and evolving consumer demands, the need for robust analytics becomes paramount. Here are several key reasons highlighting the importance of supply chain and operations analytics.

1. **Enhanced Decision-making:** At the core of supply chain analytics is the ability to provide data-driven insights that inform strategic and operational decisions. By analyzing historical data, real-time metrics, and market trends, organizations can better understand their supply chain dynamics. This capability allows decision-makers to identify potential issues before they escalate, enabling proactive measures to optimize operations. For instance, predictive analytics can forecast demand fluctuations, allowing businesses to adjust inventory levels accordingly.
2. **Cost Reduction:** Effective supply chain and operations analytics significantly

contribute to cost reduction. By identifying inefficiencies and waste throughout the supply chain, organizations can streamline processes and optimize resource utilization. For example, analytics can highlight bottlenecks in production or logistics, enabling timely interventions that lower operational costs. Through techniques such as inventory optimization and demand forecasting, businesses can minimize carrying costs and reduce stockouts, leading to improved profitability.

3. **Improved Customer Satisfaction:** In today's competitive landscape, customer satisfaction is paramount. Supply chain analytics helps organizations enhance service levels by ensuring timely delivery and product availability. By accurately forecasting demand and managing inventory, companies can align their operations with customer needs. Analytics enables businesses to understand customer preferences and behavior, leading to personalized offerings and improved responsiveness. This, in turn, fosters loyalty and long-term relationships with customers.

4. **Risk Management:** Supply chains are inherently vulnerable to various risks, including supply disruptions, natural disasters, and geopolitical uncertainties. Analytics provides organizations with the tools to assess and mitigate these risks effectively. By analyzing data related to supplier performance, demand variability, and market trends, businesses can develop contingency plans to address potential disruptions. This proactive risk management approach enhances operational resilience and helps maintain continuity in challenging circumstances.

5. **Sustainability and Compliance:** With a growing emphasis on sustainability, organizations are increasingly seeking to minimize their environmental impact. Supply chain analytics can assist in monitoring practices related to sourcing, transportation, and waste management, ensuring compliance with environmental regulations. By analyzing data on emissions and resource consumption, companies can identify areas for improvement and implement more sustainable practices. This not only enhances their corporate social responsibility (CSR) efforts but also appeals to environmentally conscious consumers.

6. **Enhanced Collaboration:** In today's interconnected world, collaboration among supply chain partners is vital for optimizing operations. Supply chain analytics facilitates data sharing and collaboration, enabling organizations to work together more effectively. By providing a comprehensive view of the supply chain, analytics fosters transparency and trust among stakeholders. Enhanced collaboration leads to improved visibility and responsiveness, ultimately driving better overall performance.

7. **Continuous Improvement:** The application of analytics in supply chain and operations fosters a culture of continuous improvement. By regularly analyzing performance metrics and operational data, organizations can identify trends

and areas for enhancement. Techniques such as Six Sigma and Lean management can be reinforced through data-driven insights, allowing businesses to implement strategies that promote efficiency, quality, and agility.

Types of Supply Chain and Operations Analytics: Supply chain and operations analytics encompass a range of techniques and methodologies that help organizations improve decision-making, enhance efficiency, and optimize performance. These analytics can be categorized into several types, each serving distinct purposes and providing unique insights. Here are the main types of supply chain and operations analytics:

1. **Descriptive Analytics:** Descriptive analytics focuses on summarizing historical data to provide insights into past performance. This type involves the collection and analysis of data from various sources, such as sales figures, inventory levels, and order fulfilment rates. Organizations use descriptive analytics to generate reports and dashboards that track key performance indicators (KPIs), identify trends, and assess the effectiveness of supply chain operations. By understanding what has happened, businesses can gain insights into operational strengths and weaknesses.
2. **Predictive Analytics:** Predictive analytics uses statistical techniques and machine learning algorithms to forecast future events based on historical data. This type of analytics is particularly valuable in supply chain management for demand forecasting, inventory management, and risk assessment. By analyzing patterns in past sales data, market trends, and external factors, organizations can make informed predictions about future demand. This foresight allows businesses to optimize inventory levels, reduce stockouts, and plan production schedules more effectively.
3. **Prescriptive Analytics:** Prescriptive analytics goes beyond predicting future outcomes by recommending specific actions to achieve desired results. This type of analytics utilizes optimization algorithms and simulation techniques to analyze various scenarios and suggest the best course of action. For example, prescriptive analytics can help organizations determine the optimal inventory levels, identify the most cost-effective suppliers, or design efficient logistics routes. By evaluating multiple options and their potential impacts, businesses can make data-driven decisions that align with their strategic goals.
4. **Diagnostic Analytics:** Diagnostic analytics focuses on understanding the reasons behind past events and performance. This type of analysis investigates historical data to identify root causes of issues, such as supply chain disruptions, quality problems, or operational inefficiencies. By employing techniques like correlation analysis and data mining, organizations can uncover patterns and relationships within the data. Diagnostic analytics provides actionable insights that enable businesses to implement corrective measures and prevent similar issues in the future.

5. **Real-time Analytics:** Real-time analytics involves the continuous monitoring and analysis of data as it is generated. This type of analytics is particularly valuable for managing supply chain operations, where timely information is crucial for decision-making. Real-time analytics allows organizations to track key metrics, such as inventory levels, order status, and transportation performance, in real-time. By leveraging IoT devices and advanced data processing technologies, businesses can respond swiftly to changes in demand, address supply chain disruptions, and optimize resource allocation.
6. **Network Analytics:** Network analytics focuses on analyzing the entire supply chain network, including suppliers, manufacturers, distributors, and retailers. This type of analytics examines relationships, dependencies, and flows of goods and information across the network. By visualizing and analyzing these connections, organizations can identify vulnerabilities, optimize logistics routes, and assess the impact of potential changes to the network structure. Network analytics is essential for understanding the complexity of supply chains and making informed decisions regarding resource allocation and collaboration.

Challenges in Supply Chain and Operations Analytics: Supply chain and operations analytics offer valuable insights for enhancing efficiency and decision-making, but organizations face several challenges in effectively leveraging these tools.

1. **Data Quality and Integration:** One of the primary challenges is ensuring the quality and consistency of data across various sources. Inconsistent, incomplete, or inaccurate data can lead to misleading insights. Additionally, integrating data from multiple systems, such as suppliers, distributors, and internal platforms, poses significant difficulties, making it challenging to achieve a unified view of the supply chain.
2. **Resistance to Change:** Implementing analytics initiatives often meets resistance from employees accustomed to traditional processes. Change management is crucial to foster a culture that embraces data-driven decision-making. Without proper training and communication, employees may be hesitant to adopt new analytics tools and methodologies.
3. **Complexity of Supply Chains:** Modern supply chains are intricate, involving numerous stakeholders and multiple tiers of suppliers. Analyzing data within this complexity can be overwhelming. Organizations need robust frameworks and technologies to manage and analyze vast amounts of data effectively.
4. **Cybersecurity Risks:** As organizations increasingly rely on digital tools and analytics, they become more vulnerable to cybersecurity threats. Protecting sensitive data and ensuring compliance with regulations is paramount, requiring strong cybersecurity measures to safeguard analytics systems.

Demand Forecasting and Inventory Management

Demand forecasting and inventory management are critical components of supply chain management, significantly influencing a company's operational efficiency and profitability. Accurate demand forecasting helps businesses anticipate customer needs, while effective inventory management ensures that products are available when needed, without incurring excessive carrying costs.

Demand Forecasting

Demand forecasting is the process of predicting future customer demand for a product or service. It plays a crucial role in various sectors, including retail, manufacturing, and supply chain management, by helping businesses optimize inventory levels, reduce costs, and enhance customer satisfaction.

Accurate demand forecasts rely on a combination of quantitative and qualitative methods. Quantitative techniques include statistical models and historical sales data analysis, such as time series analysis and regression models. These methods can identify patterns and trends over time, allowing businesses to make informed predictions based on past performance. Qualitative methods, on the other hand, involve expert opinions, market research, and consumer surveys. These approaches can capture nuances that quantitative data may miss, especially in dynamic markets where consumer preferences change rapidly. Effective demand forecasting also requires consideration of external factors, such as economic conditions, seasonal trends, and competitive actions. By incorporating these elements, businesses can create more robust forecasts.

Types of Demand Forecasting: Demand forecasting can be categorized into various types based on methodology, time frame, and purpose. The types of demand forecasting are as follows:

1. **Quantitative Forecasting:** Quantitative forecasting relies on numerical data and statistical methods to predict future demand. It primarily encompasses two approaches: time series analysis and causal models. Time series analysis examines historical data to identify patterns, trends, and seasonal variations, often using techniques like moving averages or exponential smoothing. This approach is effective for stable products with consistent sales patterns. Causal models, on the other hand, analyze relationships between demand and external factors, such as price changes, marketing efforts, or economic indicators. By understanding how these variables influence demand, businesses can create more accurate forecasts. While quantitative methods provide data-driven insights, they may fall short in rapidly changing markets where qualitative factors play a significant role. Combining quantitative forecasting with qualitative insights often leads to better overall predictions.
2. **Qualitative Forecasting:** Qualitative forecasting relies on subjective judgment and insights rather than numerical data. It is particularly useful in scenarios where historical data is limited or unavailable, such as new product launches or entering new markets. Key methods include expert judgment, where industry professionals share their knowledge and predictions, and market

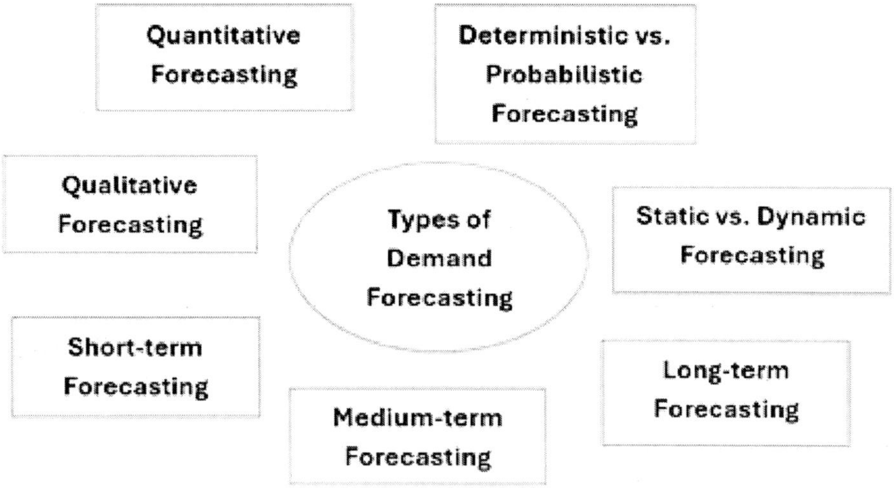

Fig.4.2

research techniques like surveys and focus groups that capture consumer preferences and behaviors. These methods help businesses understand market dynamics and customer sentiments, allowing for more nuanced forecasts. While qualitative forecasting offers valuable insights, it can be influenced by biases and may lack the objectivity of quantitative methods. Therefore, many organizations integrate qualitative and quantitative approaches to enhance forecasting accuracy and ensure a well-rounded understanding of potential demand.

3. **Short-term Forecasting:** Short-term forecasting focuses on predicting demand for a limited time frame, typically ranging from a few days to a few months. This type of forecasting is essential for day-to-day operational decisions, such as inventory management, staffing, and production scheduling. Businesses rely on short-term forecasts to avoid stockouts or excess inventory, which can significantly impact cash flow and customer satisfaction. Techniques commonly used include moving averages and recent sales trends, which provide quick insights based on the most relevant data. Short-term forecasts often adjust rapidly in response to market fluctuations, seasonal trends, or promotional activities. However, while these forecasts can be accurate in the short run, they may be less reliable for long-term planning, emphasizing the need for a balanced approach that incorporates both short- and long-term forecasts.

4. **Medium-term Forecasting:** Medium-term forecasting spans several months to a couple of years and is crucial for budgeting, resource allocation, and strategic planning. This type of forecasting allows businesses to anticipate market trends and adjust their operations accordingly. Techniques employed often include a blend of statistical methods, such as regression analysis, and

qualitative inputs from market research. Medium-term forecasts help companies make informed decisions about production capacity, marketing strategies, and investment opportunities. They are particularly useful for industries with seasonal variations or cyclical demand patterns, enabling businesses to prepare for fluctuations without significant overcapacity. However, medium-term forecasts must be continually refined as market conditions evolve, making it important for organizations to maintain flexibility and adapt their strategies based on updated information.

5. **Long-term Forecasting:** Long-term forecasting involves predicting demand over an extended period, typically several years. It is essential for strategic planning, capital investments, and major business decisions. Long-term forecasts consider various factors, including economic trends, demographic shifts, and technological advancements, to anticipate changes in consumer behavior and market conditions. Techniques like trend analysis and scenario planning are often employed to visualize potential future states and prepare organizations for different outcomes. While long-term forecasts provide a broad view of the market landscape, they inherently carry more uncertainty due to the extended time frame. Factors such as changes in consumer preferences, regulatory shifts, or unexpected economic events can significantly impact accuracy. As a result, companies often use long-term forecasts as a guiding framework rather than definitive predictions, allowing for adaptability in a dynamic business environment.

6. **Static vs. Dynamic Forecasting:** Static and dynamic forecasting represent two contrasting approaches to demand prediction. Static forecasting assumes that historical patterns and relationships remain unchanged over the forecasting period. This method provides a straightforward, fixed estimate based on historical data, making it easy to implement and interpret. However, its simplicity can be a drawback in rapidly changing markets, as it fails to account for new trends or shifts in consumer behavior. Dynamic forecasting, conversely, is more adaptable, adjusting predictions based on real-time data and evolving market conditions. It incorporates feedback loops and continuous updates, allowing businesses to respond quickly to changes, such as seasonality, market disruptions, or competitive actions. While dynamic forecasting offers enhanced accuracy, it requires more sophisticated data analysis tools and ongoing data collection efforts. Organizations often choose between these methods based on their specific needs, resources, and the volatility of the market in which they operate.

7. **Deterministic vs. Probabilistic Forecasting:** Deterministic and probabilistic forecasting are two distinct approaches to predicting future demand. Deterministic forecasting provides a single, fixed outcome based on set inputs and assumptions, often using historical data and established models. This method is straightforward, making it easy for organizations to plan based on

specific predictions. However, it does not account for uncertainty or variability in demand, which can be a significant limitation in volatile markets. In contrast, probabilistic forecasting offers a range of potential outcomes, each with associated probabilities. This approach acknowledges the inherent uncertainty in demand prediction and provides businesses with a more comprehensive view of possible scenarios. Probabilistic methods, such as Monte Carlo simulations, help organizations prepare for various market conditions and make informed decisions based on risk assessment. While more complex, probabilistic forecasting can enhance resilience and adaptability in planning, particularly in uncertain environments. Organizations often blend these approaches to strike a balance between clarity and adaptability.

Steps of Demand Forecasting: Demand forecasting is a systematic process that helps businesses predict future customer demand for products or services. A well-structured forecasting process can enhance inventory management, optimize production, and improve customer satisfaction. Below are the key steps involved in demand forecasting:

1. **Define the Objective:** The first step in demand forecasting is to clearly define the objective of the forecast. This involves identifying what the organization aims to achieve with the forecast. Objectives can vary significantly, including:
   - **Inventory Management:** Ensuring sufficient stock levels to meet anticipated demand without overstocking.
   - **Production Planning:** Aligning production schedules with expected demand to optimize resources.
   - **Financial Planning:** Assisting in budgeting and financial forecasting based on expected sales.
   - **Market Analysis:** Understanding market trends to identify opportunities for growth.

   Clear objectives help guide the entire forecasting process, influencing the selection of methods and the scope of the analysis.
2. **Collect Historical Data:** Historical data is foundational for demand forecasting. This step involves gathering relevant data that can provide insights into past demand patterns. Key data sources include:
   - **Sales Data:** Historical sales records over specific periods (daily, weekly, monthly).
   - **Market Research:** Data from surveys and studies that provide insights into consumer preferences and market trends.
   - **Economic Indicators:** Data related to broader economic conditions that can influence demand, such as GDP growth, unemployment rates, and consumer confidence indexes.

- **Competitor Analysis:** Information about competitors' performance and market share can help contextualize demand predictions.

  Data collection should focus on ensuring accuracy and completeness. Data integrity is crucial, as any discrepancies can lead to misleading forecasts.

3. **Analyze Historical Data:** Once historical data is collected, the next step is to analyze it to identify trends, seasonality, and patterns. This analysis can be performed using various techniques:

   - **Trend Analysis:** Identifying long-term movements in the data, such as increasing or decreasing sales over time.
   - **Seasonal Analysis:** Examining variations in demand that occur at specific times of the year, such as holiday sales peaks.
   - **Cyclical Patterns:** Identifying demand fluctuations that occur in cycles, often influenced by economic factors.

   Statistical tools such as graphs, charts, and software applications (like Excel or specialized forecasting software) can aid in visualizing and analyzing the data.

4. **Select the Forecasting Method:** Based on the objectives and historical data analysis, the next step is to select an appropriate forecasting method. The choice of method depends on the type of data available, the time frame of the forecast, and the complexity of the demand patterns. Common forecasting methods include:

   - **Quantitative Methods:** Quantitative methods in demand forecasting utilize numerical data and statistical techniques to predict future demand. Key approaches include time series analysis, which identifies patterns from historical data, and causal models, which analyze relationships between demand and external factors. These methods provide data-driven insights for more accurate forecasts.

     Time Series Analysis: Uses historical data to forecast future demand by identifying patterns.

     Causal Models: Examines relationships between demand and other factors, such as advertising spend or economic conditions.

   - **Qualitative Methods:** Qualitative methods in demand forecasting rely on subjective insights rather than numerical data. Key approaches include expert judgment, where industry specialists provide forecasts based on experience, and market research, which gathers consumer opinions through surveys and focus groups. These methods help capture nuances in consumer behavior and market trends.

     Expert Judgment: Involves consulting industry experts for insights and predictions.

Market Research: Utilizing consumer surveys and focus groups to gather insights about future demand.

Selecting the right method is critical, as different methods yield varying levels of accuracy and are suited to different forecasting scenarios.

5. **Develop the Forecast:** With the method selected, the next step is to develop the forecast itself. This involves applying the chosen forecasting method to the historical data. Key considerations during this step include:
   - **Model Calibration:** Adjusting the model parameters to fit historical data accurately.
   - **Running Simulations:** In cases of complex models, running simulations to validate the results and ensure robustness.
   - **Incorporating External Factors:** Including any relevant external variables that could impact demand, such as economic trends, marketing campaigns, or changes in consumer behavior.

   It's essential to document assumptions made during this process, as they can significantly influence the outcome of the forecast.
6. Validate the Forecast: After developing the forecast, it is critical to validate its accuracy. This involves comparing the forecasted values with actual sales data from the same period. Validation techniques may include:
   - **Mean Absolute Error (MAE):** Measures the average magnitude of errors in a set of forecasts, without considering **their direction.**
   - **Mean Squared Error (MSE):** Squares the errors before averaging, giving more weight to larger errors.
   - **Tracking Signals:** Monitoring the forecast over time to determine if it consistently overestimates or underestimates actual demand.

   Validation helps to assess the reliability of the forecasting model and can guide necessary adjustments for future forecasts.
7. **Refine the Forecast:** Based on the validation results, the forecasting process may require refinement. This step involves:
   - **Adjusting Parameters:** Modifying the model parameters based on validation feedback to improve accuracy.
   - **Incorporating New Data:** Updating the model with new sales data or market insights to reflect recent trends.
   - **Continuous Improvement:** Establishing a feedback loop to continually refine forecasting methods and models over time.

   Refinement is crucial for maintaining forecasting accuracy, especially in dynamic markets where conditions frequently change.

8. **Communicate the Forecast:** Once the forecast is refined and validated, it is essential to communicate the results to relevant stakeholders. Effective communication involves:
   - **Presenting Results:** Using clear and visually engaging formats (charts, graphs) to present the forecast data.
   - **Explaining Assumptions:** Clearly outlining the assumptions and methodology used in the forecasting process to build trust and understanding.
   - **Engaging Stakeholders:** Involving key stakeholders in discussions about the forecast to gather their insights and foster collaboration.

   Transparent communication ensures that all relevant parties understand the forecast and can make informed decisions based on it.
9. **Monitor and Adjust:** The final step in the demand forecasting process is continuous monitoring and adjustment. Demand forecasting is not a one-time activity; it requires ongoing attention. Key actions during this phase include:
   - **Tracking Performance:** Regularly comparing actual demand against forecasts to identify discrepancies.
   - **Responding to Changes:** Being proactive in adjusting forecasts based on new market data, economic shifts, or unexpected events (e.g., supply chain disruptions).
   - **Reviewing Processes:** Periodically reviewing the forecasting process itself to identify areas for improvement, whether in data collection, analysis methods, or communication strategies.

   By establishing a culture of continuous monitoring and adjustment, organizations can enhance their forecasting capabilities and responsiveness to market dynamics.

Importance of Demand Forecasting: Demand forecasting is essential for businesses across various sectors due to its significant impact on operations, financial planning, and strategic decision-making. Here are key points highlighting its importance:

1. **Inventory Management:** Accurate demand forecasting helps businesses maintain optimal inventory levels, reducing the risk of stockouts or overstock situations. This ensures that products are available when customers need them, improving customer satisfaction and reducing holding costs.
2. **Production Planning:** Forecasting allows companies to align production schedules with anticipated demand, optimizing resource utilization and minimizing waste. This is particularly crucial in manufacturing, where inefficient production can lead to increased costs and missed opportunities.
3. **Cost Efficiency:** By predicting demand accurately, organizations can reduce

excess inventory and associated carrying costs. This leads to more efficient use of resources and better cash flow management.

4. **Financial Planning:** Demand forecasts are critical for budgeting and financial forecasting. They help organizations project revenues, manage expenses, and allocate resources effectively, ensuring financial stability and growth.
5. **Market Understanding:** Forecasting provides insights into market trends and consumer behavior, enabling businesses to adapt their strategies to changing conditions. This helps in identifying new opportunities and potential risks.
6. **Improved Customer Service:** By anticipating customer demand, businesses can enhance service levels, ensuring timely deliveries and availability of products. This fosters customer loyalty and enhances brand reputation.
7. **Strategic Decision-making:** Accurate forecasts support long-term strategic planning, guiding decisions related to new product development, market expansion, and resource allocation. This ensures that organizations remain competitive in their industries.
8. **Supply Chain Optimization:** Effective demand forecasting improves collaboration with suppliers and partners by enabling better planning and communication, leading to a more efficient supply chain.
9. **Risk Management:** Forecasting helps identify potential fluctuations in demand, allowing businesses to develop contingency plans and mitigate risks associated with unexpected changes in the market.

Inventory Management

Inventory management is a critical function for businesses that handle physical goods, encompassing the planning, controlling, and overseeing of inventory levels to meet customer demand while minimizing costs. Effective inventory management ensures that the right products are available at the right time, ultimately leading to improved customer satisfaction and operational efficiency.

Inventory management is the systematic process of overseeing and controlling a company's inventory levels to ensure the right products are available at the right time, minimizing costs and maximizing efficiency. It involves tracking raw materials, work-in-progress, and finished goods, utilizing various techniques such as Just-In-Time (JIT), Economic Order Quantity (EOQ), and ABC analysis. Effective inventory management helps businesses avoid stockouts and overstock situations, directly impacting customer satisfaction and operational efficiency.

Key components of successful inventory management include accurate demand forecasting, regular audits, and the use of advanced inventory management software that provides real-time tracking and reporting. Challenges such as demand variability, supply chain disruptions, and maintaining inventory accuracy can complicate the process. However, adopting best practices such as fostering strong supplier relationships, implementing automation, and leveraging data analytics can significantly enhance inventory performance. Ultimately, effective inventory management is essential for optimizing cash flow, reducing costs, and ensuring businesses can respond swiftly to changing market conditions, thereby maintaining a competitive edge.

Methods of Inventory Management: Effective inventory management is essential for ensuring that businesses maintain the right amount of stock to meet customer demand while minimizing costs. Here are some key methods used in inventory management:

1. **Just-In-Time (JIT):** JIT inventory management minimizes inventory levels by ordering goods only as needed for production or sales. This method reduces holding costs and waste but requires precise coordination with suppliers to avoid stockouts.
2. **Economic Order Quantity (EOQ):** EOQ is a formula used to determine the optimal order quantity that minimizes total inventory costs, including ordering and holding costs. It helps businesses balance the costs of ordering too frequently against carrying excess inventory.
3. **ABC Analysis:** This technique categorizes inventory into three groups based on value and importance:
   - **A Items:** High-value items with low sales frequency (10-20% of items, 70-80% of value).
   - **B Items:** Moderate value and frequency.
   - **C Items:** Low-value items with high sales frequency (50-70% of items, 10-20% of value).

   This prioritization allows businesses to focus their management efforts on the most critical items.
4. **Safety Stock:** Safety stock acts as a buffer against uncertainties in demand or supply chain disruptions. It helps prevent stockouts while balancing carrying costs.
5. **Demand Forecasting:** Accurate demand forecasting involves using historical data and market trends to predict future demand. Techniques can be quantitative (statistical models) or qualitative (expert opinions), enabling better inventory planning.
6. **Inventory Management Software:** Modern software solutions automate inventory tracking, provide real-time data, and enable better decision-making through analytics. These systems help streamline processes and improve accuracy.

Importance of Inventory Management: Inventory management plays a crucial role in the overall success of a business. Here are key reasons highlighting its importance:

1. **Meeting Customer Demand:** Effective inventory management ensures that products are available when customers want them, enhancing customer satisfaction and loyalty.
2. **Cost Control:** By optimizing inventory levels, businesses can reduce holding costs, such as warehousing and insurance, while avoiding expenses related to stockouts or excess inventory.
3. **Improved Cash Flow:** Efficient inventory management enables better cash flow by reducing capital tied up in inventory, allowing businesses to invest in other areas.
4. **Enhanced Operational Efficiency:** Streamlined inventory processes improve overall operational efficiency, reducing lead times and enabling quicker responses to market changes.
5. **Risk Mitigation:** Proper inventory management helps mitigate risks associated with demand fluctuations and supply chain disruptions, allowing businesses to adapt quickly to changing conditions.
6. **Data-driven Decision Making:** Inventory management systems provide valuable data and insights that support informed decision-making, from procurement to sales strategies.
7. **Competitive Advantage:** Companies that effectively manage their inventory can better respond to market demands, stay ahead of competitors, and achieve greater market share.

Process Optimization and Simulation

Process optimization and simulation are essential methodologies employed by organizations to enhance operational efficiency, reduce costs, and improve overall performance. These approaches allow businesses to analyze existing processes, identify bottlenecks, and implement data-driven improvements.

Process Optimization

Process optimization refers to the systematic effort to improve a process's efficiency and effectiveness. The primary goals include maximizing productivity, minimizing costs, improving quality, and enhancing customer satisfaction. Process optimization is the systematic approach to improving an organization's workflows, efficiency, and effectiveness. By identifying bottlenecks, reducing waste, and enhancing resource allocation, businesses can significantly lower costs while improving quality and customer satisfaction. Key methodologies such as Lean Manufacturing, Six Sigma, and the Theory of Constraints provide structured frameworks for analyzing and refining processes.

The optimization process typically begins with defining clear objectives, followed by thorough analysis of existing workflows through data collection and process mapping. Once inefficiencies are identified, organizations can develop targeted strategies for improvement, implementing changes that may include technology upgrades, streamlined operations, or enhanced employee training. Continuous monitoring of key performance indicators (KPIs) ensures that these improvements are sustained over time. Ultimately, effective process optimization not only boosts productivity and profitability but also fosters a culture of continuous improvement, allowing organizations to adapt swiftly to changing market demands and remain competitive in their respective industries. Common techniques for process optimization include:

1. **Lean Manufacturing:** Focuses on eliminating waste and improving value through streamlined workflows.
2. **Six Sigma:** A data-driven approach aimed at reducing defects and variability in processes.
3. **Theory of Constraints (TOC):** Identifies the limiting factor (bottleneck) in a process and systematically improves it to enhance throughput.
4. **Kaizen:** Emphasizes continuous, incremental improvements through employee involvement and feedback.

Simulation

Simulation involves creating a digital model of a real-world process to analyze its behavior under various conditions. This technique enables organizations to test changes and assess their impact without disrupting actual operations. Simulation is a powerful technique used to model and analyze the behavior of real-world systems through a virtual environment. By creating digital representations of processes, organizations can test various scenarios and observe potential outcomes without disrupting actual operations. This capability is crucial for decision-making, risk assessment, and process optimization across various fields, including manufacturing, logistics, finance, and healthcare.

There are several types of simulation, including Discrete Event Simulation (DES), which models systems as a sequence of discrete events over time, and Monte Carlo Simulation, which uses random sampling to analyze risk and uncertainty. By running simulations, businesses can evaluate the impact of changes, optimize resource allocation, and identify potential bottlenecks before implementing real-world modifications. The insights gained from simulation not only enhance operational efficiency but also improve strategic planning by providing data-driven evidence for decision-making. Ultimately, simulation enables organizations to innovate and adapt in a rapidly changing environment while minimizing risks associated with change.

Types of Simulation: Key types of simulation include:

1. **Discrete Event Simulation (DES):** Models the operation of a system as a sequence of events over time, useful in manufacturing and logistics.
2. **Monte Carlo Simulation:** Uses random sampling to assess risk and uncertainty in processes, commonly applied in finance and project management.

3. **System Dynamics:** Focuses on the behavior of complex systems over time, considering feedback loops and time delays.

Relationship Between Optimization and Simulation

Optimization and simulation often complement each other. Simulation provides insights into current performance, helping identify areas for improvement. Once potential optimizations are identified, simulation can be used to validate these changes, ensuring they will lead to the desired outcomes.

Steps in Process Optimization and Simulation

1. **Define Objectives:** Clearly outline the goals for optimization and simulation.
2. **Data Collection:** Gather relevant data about current processes, including performance metrics and resource utilization.
3. **Process Mapping:** Create detailed maps of existing processes to visualize workflows and identify inefficiencies.
4. **Simulation Modeling:** Develop simulation models based on collected data, choosing the appropriate type of simulation.
5. **Analysis:** Run simulations to evaluate different scenarios and their potential impacts on performance.
6. **Optimization:** Identify and implement changes based on simulation results, targeting improvements in efficiency or quality.
7. **Validation:** Re-run simulations to ensure that proposed changes yield the expected benefits.
8. **Continuous Improvement:** Establish a cycle of regular review and adaptation of processes to maintain efficiency.

Conclusion

Process optimization and simulation are integral to achieving operational excellence. By leveraging these techniques, organizations can make informed decisions that lead to substantial improvements in efficiency, quality, and cost-effectiveness, positioning themselves for long-term success in a competitive landscape.

Transportation and Logistics Analytics

Transportation and logistics analytics involve the systematic collection and analysis of data related to the movement of goods and services. This field leverages advanced analytics techniques, including predictive modeling, optimization algorithms, and machine learning, to enhance supply chain efficiency and decision-making. By analyzing data such as shipment times, costs, inventory levels, and customer demand patterns, organizations can identify inefficiencies, forecast future needs, and optimize routes to minimize delays and transportation costs. For instance, route optimization tools can suggest the most efficient paths for delivery vehicles, while demand forecasting helps companies adjust inventory levels to meet customer needs without overstocking. Additionally, real-time tracking and performance metrics provide insights into operational performance, enabling proactive management of potential disruptions. The integration of transportation and logistics analytics ultimately leads to improved service levels, reduced operational costs, and enhanced customer satisfaction, making it a critical component in today's competitive marketplace. By harnessing the power of data, organizations can make informed strategic decisions that streamline operations and support business growth.

Key Components of Transportation and Logistics Analytics

1. **Data Collection:** Data collection is the foundation of transportation and logistics analytics. The types of data collected include:
   - **Operational Data:** Information related to shipping times, delivery performance, and transportation costs.
   - **Customer Data:** Insights into customer preferences, order patterns, and feedback.
   - **Environmental Data:** Factors such as weather conditions, traffic patterns, and regulatory changes that impact logistics operations.
   - **Financial Data:** Cost structures, revenue streams, and pricing models associated with transportation and logistics activities.
2. **Data Processing and Storage:** Once data is collected, it must be processed and stored in a manner that enables analysis. This typically involves:
   - **Data Integration:** Combining data from various sources, including Transportation Management Systems (TMS), Enterprise Resource Planning (ERP) systems, and Customer Relationship Management (CRM) systems.
   - **Data Cleaning:** Ensuring the accuracy and consistency of data by removing duplicates, correcting errors, and addressing missing values.
   - **Data Warehousing:** Storing processed data in a centralized repository that allows for easy access and retrieval.
3. **Data Analysis Techniques:** Several analytical techniques are employed in transportation and logistics analytics, including:
   - **Descriptive Analytics:** Provides insights into historical data to understand past performance and trends. Common metrics include delivery times, transportation costs, and service levels.
   - **Predictive Analytics:** Uses statistical models and machine learning algorithms to forecast future outcomes based on historical data. For instance, demand forecasting models can predict future shipping volumes, allowing companies to optimize inventory levels.
   - **Prescriptive Analytics:** Offers recommendations for optimal decision-making. For example, optimization algorithms can determine the best routes for delivery trucks based on factors like cost, distance, and time constraints.

4. **Visualization Tools:** Data visualization is crucial for interpreting complex data sets. Visualization tools, such as dashboards and interactive maps, help stakeholders understand key performance indicators (KPIs) and identify trends or anomalies at a glance.

Applications of Transportation and Logistics Analytics: Transportation and logistics analytics are applied in route optimization to enhance delivery efficiency, demand forecasting for accurate inventory management, performance measurement through key performance indicators, risk management by identifying potential disruptions, and inventory optimization to minimize carrying costs, ultimately improving operational efficiency and customer satisfaction. The application of transportation and logistics analytics are as:

1. **Route Optimization:** One of the most significant applications of analytics is route optimization. By analyzing traffic patterns, delivery schedules, and vehicle capacities, organizations can determine the most efficient routes for their fleets. This leads to reduced fuel costs, shorter delivery times, and improved customer satisfaction.
2. **Demand Forecasting:** Accurate demand forecasting is critical for effective inventory management and resource allocation. Analytics enables businesses to predict customer demand patterns, helping them adjust their supply chain strategies accordingly. This reduces the risk of stockouts or overstock situations.
3. **Inventory Management:** Analytics helps organizations manage inventory levels effectively by providing insights into turnover rates, lead times, and order quantities. By optimizing inventory levels, companies can minimize carrying costs while ensuring product availability.
4. **Performance Measurement:** Transportation and logistics analytics enable organizations to track and measure performance against established KPIs. Common KPIs include on-time delivery rates, transportation costs per unit, and order accuracy. Continuous monitoring of these metrics helps identify areas for improvement.
5. **Risk Management:** Analytics can also be employed for risk assessment and management. By analyzing historical data and identifying potential disruptions (such as natural disasters or supply chain interruptions), organizations can develop contingency plans and mitigate risks effectively.

Future Trends in Transportation and Logistics Analytics

1. **Increased Automation:** The future of transportation and logistics analytics will see greater automation in data collection, analysis, and decision-making processes. Automated systems will enhance efficiency and reduce the reliance on manual interventions.
2. **Real-time Analytics:** As technology evolves, organizations will increasingly rely on real-time analytics to make instantaneous decisions. This will enable faster responses to market changes and customer demands.

3. **Enhanced Predictive Capabilities:** Advancements in machine learning and AI will enhance predictive analytics, allowing organizations to anticipate trends and disruptions more accurately. This will facilitate proactive decision-making and risk mitigation.
4. **Sustainability Focus:** With growing concerns about environmental impact, analytics will play a vital role in developing sustainable logistics practices. Organizations will leverage data to minimize their carbon footprint and optimize resource usage.
5. **Integration of Blockchain Technology:** Blockchain technology can enhance transparency and traceability in the supply chain. By integrating blockchain with analytics, organizations can improve data accuracy and security, further optimizing logistics operations.

Conclusion

Transportation and logistics analytics are a critical component of modern supply chain management. By leveraging data effectively, organizations can optimize their operations, reduce costs, and enhance customer satisfaction. As technology continues to evolve, the potential for transportation and logistics analytics will only grow, enabling businesses to navigate complexities and drive innovation in an increasingly competitive landscape. Embracing these analytics strategies will be essential for organizations seeking to thrive in the future of logistics.

Real-world Examples and Applications

Supply chain and operations analytics have become integral to enhancing efficiency, reducing costs, and improving customer satisfaction in various industries. By leveraging data analytics, organizations can optimize their supply chains, streamline operations, and make informed decisions. This comprehensive exploration delves into real-world examples and applications of supply chain and operations analytics across different sectors.

1. Amazon: Demand Forecasting and Inventory Management

Overview: Amazon is a leader in e-commerce and logistics, employing advanced analytics for demand forecasting and inventory management. With millions of products and a vast customer base, the company must efficiently manage its inventory to meet varying customer demands.

Application of Analytics: Amazon utilizes machine learning algorithms to analyze historical sales data, customer behavior, seasonality, and external factors (like holidays and events) to predict future demand accurately. This predictive capability allows Amazon to:

- **Optimize Inventory Levels:** By anticipating which products will be in demand, Amazon can maintain optimal stock levels, reducing both stockouts and excess inventory.

- **Dynamic Pricing:** Amazon adjusts prices based on demand forecasts, competitor pricing, and customer behavior, maximizing revenue while remaining competitive.
- **Fulfilment Center Optimization:** Data analytics help determine the best locations for fulfilment centres, enabling faster delivery to customers and minimizing shipping costs.
- **Outcomes:** The implementation of these analytics strategies has resulted in improved inventory turnover rates and enhanced customer satisfaction due to quicker delivery times. Amazon's ability to predict demand accurately has solidified its position as a leader in the e-commerce space.

2. Walmart: Transportation Optimization

Overview: Walmart, one of the largest retailers globally, relies on an extensive transportation network to distribute products to its stores efficiently. With a commitment to low prices, optimizing transportation costs is crucial for maintaining profitability.

Application of Analytics: Walmart employs a sophisticated Transportation Management System (TMS) that utilizes analytics to optimize its logistics operations. Key applications include:

- **Route Optimization:** By analyzing traffic patterns, delivery schedules, and vehicle capacities, Walmart determines the most efficient routes for its delivery trucks.
- **Load Planning:** The analytics system assesses cargo loads to maximize space utilization in trucks, reducing transportation costs per unit.
- **Real-time Tracking:** Walmart uses IoT devices to monitor vehicle locations and conditions, enabling proactive adjustments to delivery routes and schedules based on real-time data.
- **Outcomes:** These analytics-driven strategies have led to significant cost savings and improved delivery efficiency. Walmart's ability to reduce transportation expenses while ensuring timely deliveries contributes to its competitive pricing model and customer satisfaction.

3. Coca-Cola: Supply Chain Visibility

Overview: Coca-Cola is a global beverage leader that relies on a complex supply chain to distribute its products worldwide. Maintaining visibility across this supply chain is critical for managing inventory levels and meeting customer demand.

Application of Analytics: Coca-Cola uses advanced analytics tools to enhance supply chain visibility. Key applications include:

- **Inventory Management:** Analytics allow Coca-Cola to monitor inventory levels in real time, ensuring that production aligns with demand.

- **Production Planning:** By analyzing sales data and market trends, Coca-Cola can adjust production schedules and quantities to meet changing consumer preferences.
- **Supplier Performance Tracking:** Analytics enable Coca-Cola to evaluate supplier performance based on metrics like lead times and quality, ensuring a reliable supply chain.
- **Outcomes:** The increased visibility provided by analytics has enabled Coca-Cola to respond quickly to fluctuations in demand, optimize production planning, and manage logistics effectively. This data-driven approach enhances operational efficiency and customer satisfaction.

4. Procter & Gamble (P&G): Sales and Operations Planning

Overview: Procter & Gamble, a multinational consumer goods company, relies on effective sales and operations planning (S&OP) to align its production and distribution with market demand. Accurate forecasting is crucial for minimizing excess inventory and ensuring product availability.

Application of Analytics: P&G employs a data-driven approach to S&OP, utilizing analytics to:

- **Demand Forecasting**: By analyzing historical sales data, market trends, and customer insights, P&G can predict future demand accurately.
- **Inventory Optimization:** Analytics help P&G maintain optimal inventory levels across its distribution centres, minimizing carrying costs while ensuring product availability.
- **Collaboration Across Functions:** P&G uses analytics to facilitate collaboration among sales, marketing, and supply chain teams, aligning their efforts to meet customer needs effectively.

Outcomes: P&G's use of analytics in S&OP has resulted in improved forecast accuracy, reduced excess inventory, and enhanced service levels. This integrated approach allows P&G to respond swiftly to market changes while maintaining cost efficiency.

5. FedEx: Predictive Analytics for Logistics

Overview: FedEx is a global leader in logistics and delivery services, known for its commitment to reliability and speed. To maintain its competitive edge, FedEx leverages predictive analytics to enhance its logistics operations.

Application of Analytics: FedEx employs predictive analytics to analyze historical shipment data, weather conditions, and traffic patterns. Key applications include:

- **Delay Prediction:** By analyzing past data and current conditions, FedEx can predict potential delays in delivery, allowing proactive measures to be taken.
- **Route Optimization:** Analytics help FedEx optimize delivery routes,

considering factors like traffic and weather to minimize delays and reduce fuel consumption.

- **Capacity Planning:** FedEx uses predictive analytics to assess capacity needs based on forecasted demand, ensuring that resources are allocated efficiently.

Outcomes: The application of predictive analytics has led to improve on-time delivery rates and enhanced customer trust. By anticipating delays and optimizing operations, FedEx maintains its reputation for reliability.

6. Zara: Agile Supply Chain Management

Overview: Zara, the fast-fashion retailer, is known for its ability to respond quickly to changing fashion trends. An agile supply chain is essential for maintaining this competitive advantage.

Application of Analytics: Zara leverages analytics to achieve agility in its supply chain. Key applications include:

- **Real-time Sales Data Analysis:** Zara continuously analyzes sales data and customer feedback to identify trends and preferences, allowing for rapid product development and inventory adjustments.
- **Production Planning:** By using analytics to forecast demand, Zara can adjust production schedules to meet changing consumer preferences, minimizing excess inventory.
- **Supply Chain Collaboration:** Analytics facilitate collaboration with suppliers, enabling Zara to respond quickly to market demands and produce limited-run collections.

Outcomes: Zara's analytics-driven approach to supply chain management has resulted in shorter lead times, reduced markdowns, and increased customer satisfaction. The ability to respond swiftly to trends gives Zara a significant advantage in the fast-paced fashion industry.

7. Nestle: Sustainability Analytics

Overview: Nestle, a global food and beverage company, is committed to sustainability in its supply chain. Analytics play a crucial role in tracking and optimizing resource consumption and waste management.

Application of Analytics: Nestle utilizes sustainability analytics to:

- **Monitor Resource Usage:** By analyzing data on water, energy, and raw material consumption, Nestlé can identify areas for improvement and implement sustainability initiatives.
- **Supply Chain Transparency:** Analytics enable Nestle to trace the origins of its ingredients, ensuring responsible sourcing and compliance with sustainability standards.
- **Waste Reduction:** By analyzing production data, Nestlé can implement

measures to reduce waste throughout its supply chain, contributing to its sustainability goals.

Outcomes: Nestles commitment to sustainability, supported by analytics, has led to significant reductions in resource consumption and waste. This approach not only benefits the environment but also enhances Nestle's brand reputation among consumers increasingly concerned about sustainability.

8. Tesla: Production Optimization

Overview: Tesla, known for its electric vehicles and innovative manufacturing processes, employs analytics to optimize its production operations.

Application of Analytics: Tesla leverages data analytics to:

- **Identify Production Inefficiencies:** By analyzing production line data, Tesla identifies bottlenecks and areas for improvement, streamlining operations.
- **Quality Control:** Analytics help Tesla monitor quality metrics in real time, enabling quick responses to defects or issues in the production process.
- **Supply Chain Optimization:** Tesla analyzes data related to supplier performance, inventory levels, and production schedules to ensure efficient resource allocation.

Outcomes: Tesla's data-driven approach to production optimization has led to improved efficiency, reduced production costs, and enhanced product quality. This focus on analytics contributes to Tesla's ability to scale production and meet growing demand for electric vehicles.

9. Intel: Supply Chain Resilience

Overview: Intel, a leader in semiconductor manufacturing, relies on a complex supply chain that spans the globe. Ensuring resilience in this supply chain is crucial for meeting demand and maintaining competitiveness.

Application of Analytics: Intel employs supply chain analytics to enhance resilience through:

- **Risk Assessment:** By analyzing data related to suppliers, geopolitical factors, and natural disasters, Intel can identify potential risks and develop contingency plans.
- **Supplier Performance Monitoring:** Analytics help Intel evaluate supplier performance, ensuring that quality and delivery standards are met consistently.
- **Demand Planning:** Intel uses analytics to forecast demand accurately, allowing for proactive adjustments in production and inventory management.

Outcomes: The application of analytics has enhanced Intel's supply chain resilience, enabling the company to respond swiftly to disruptions and maintain product availability. This proactive approach helps Intel stay competitive in a rapidly evolving market.

10. Nike: Customer-Centric Supply Chain

Overview: Nike is known for its innovative products and strong brand presence in the athletic footwear and apparel market. A customer-centric supply chain is vital for meeting consumer expectations.

Application of Analytics: Nike leverages analytics to enhance its customer-centric supply chain through:

- **Consumer Insights:** By analyzing data from various touchpoints, including online and in-store purchases, Nike gains valuable insights into consumer preferences and trends.
- **Inventory Management:** Analytics enable Nike to optimize inventory levels based on demand forecasts, ensuring that popular products are readily available.
- **Direct-to-consumer Strategies:** Nike uses analytics to inform its direct-to-consumer initiatives, allowing for personalized marketing and improved customer experiences.

Outcomes: Nike's analytics-driven approach to supply chain management has resulted in improved inventory turnover rates, enhanced customer satisfaction, and increased brand loyalty. By aligning operations with consumer preferences, Nike remains a leader in the competitive athletic market.

Conclusion

The application of supply chain and operations analytics is transforming how organizations manage their logistics, inventory, and overall operations. From Amazon's demand forecasting to Zara's agile supply chain, these real-world examples demonstrate the power of data-driven decision-making. By leveraging analytics, companies can optimize their operations, enhance customer satisfaction, and achieve sustainable growth. As technology continues to evolve, the potential for supply chain and operations analytics will only grow, enabling organizations to navigate complexities and drive innovation in an increasingly competitive landscape. Embracing these analytics strategies will be essential for organizations seeking to thrive in the future of supply chain management.

5. Human Resource Analytics

Human Resource Analytics (HRA), also known as People Analytics, refers to the systematic collection, analysis, and interpretation of data related to human resources. This data-driven approach empowers organizations to make informed decisions regarding workforce management, talent acquisition, employee engagement, and performance evaluation. As businesses increasingly recognize the strategic value of their human capital, HRA has emerged as a vital tool for optimizing workforce efficiency and enhancing overall organizational performance.

Human Resource Analytics (HRA) involves the systematic collection and analysis of workforce data to inform HR decision-making and improve organizational performance. By leveraging data from various sources such as employee records, recruitment metrics, and engagement surveys HR professionals can gain valuable insights into employee behavior, performance, and satisfaction. Key applications of HRA include talent acquisition, where data-driven approaches enhance recruitment processes; employee engagement, which helps identify factors affecting retention; and performance management, enabling organizations to recognize high performers and address areas for improvement. HRA also plays a crucial role in promoting diversity and inclusion by analyzing demographic data and identifying biases in hiring or promotion processes. However, challenges such as data privacy, data quality, and the need for skilled analytics professionals can hinder effective implementation. Successful examples, like Google and IBM, showcase how data analytics can lead to better management practices and improved employee outcomes. As organizations increasingly recognize the strategic value of their human capital, the role of HRA will continue to grow, driving more informed decisions and fostering a data-driven culture. Ultimately, HRA empowers organizations to optimize their workforce strategies, enhance employee experiences, and align HR practices with broader business goals, making it an essential component of modern human resource management.

Importance of HR Analytics: Human Resource Analytics (HRA) has emerged as a crucial component of strategic human resource management, transforming how organizations approach workforce management. The importance of HR analytics lies in its ability to leverage data to enhance decision-making, improve employee performance, and foster a more engaged workforce.

1. **Data-driven Decision Making:** One of the primary advantages of HR Analytics is its facilitation of data-driven decision-making. Traditional HR practices often rely on intuition or anecdotal evidence, which can lead to inconsistent results. HRA provides HR professionals with empirical data to identify trends and patterns, enabling informed decisions that align with organizational goals. This systematic approach minimizes biases and enhances the effectiveness of HR initiatives.

2. **Optimized Recruitment Processes:** Recruitment is one of the most critical functions in HR. HR Analytics can significantly streamline recruitment processes by analyzing data from various sourcing channels to determine which methods yield the best candidates. By assessing past hiring successes and failures, organizations can refine their selection criteria and improve their talent acquisition strategies. This not only saves time and resources but also enhances the quality of hires.

3. **Enhanced Employee Performance:** HR Analytics plays a vital role in assessing employee performance. By analyzing performance metrics, organizations can identify high-performing individuals and understand the underlying factors contributing to their success. This data-driven approach enables HR to implement tailored development programs, fostering a culture of continuous improvement and helping to replicate best practices across teams.

4. **Improved Employee Engagement and Retention:** Employee engagement is directly linked to organizational success. HR Analytics provides insights into factors influencing employee satisfaction and retention. By analyzing feedback from surveys and performance reviews, organizations can identify areas requiring attention. Proactive measures based on these insights can lead to increased engagement, reduced turnover, and a more motivated workforce.
5. **Effective Workforce Planning:** Strategic workforce planning is essential for aligning talent with business goals. HR Analytics enables organizations to forecast future hiring needs by analyzing data related to workforce demographics, turnover rates, and market conditions. This foresight allows HR to proactively address talent gaps, ensuring that the organization is equipped to meet future challenges.
6. **Targeted Learning and Development:** Investing in employee development is critical for retention and performance. HR Analytics allows organizations to evaluate the effectiveness of training programs by measuring performance improvements before and after interventions. This data-driven approach ensures that resources are allocated efficiently, enhancing the overall impact of learning and development initiatives.
7. **Diversity and Inclusion Metrics:** Diversity and inclusion are vital for fostering innovation and employee satisfaction. HR Analytics can track diversity metrics, assess the effectiveness of inclusion initiatives, and provide insights into organizational culture. By leveraging this data, organizations can implement targeted strategies to promote a more equitable workplace.
8. **Cost Efficiency:** Identifying inefficiencies through HR Analytics can lead to significant cost savings. For instance, understanding the reasons behind high turnover rates can help organizations implement retention strategies that minimize recruitment costs and ensure stability within teams.

Methodologies in HR Analytics:

1. **Descriptive Analytics**: Descriptive analytics focuses on historical data to understand past trends and behaviors. This involves analyzing employee turnover rates, engagement scores, and performance metrics to provide insights into organizational health. By identifying what has happened in the past, HR can make informed predictions about future trends.
2. **Predictive Analytics:** Predictive analytics uses statistical models and machine learning techniques to forecast future outcomes. For example, HR can predict employee turnover by analyzing factors such as job satisfaction, performance ratings, and engagement levels. This proactive approach allows organizations to implement strategies to mitigate potential turnover risks.
3. **Prescriptive Analytics:** Prescriptive analytics goes beyond predictions by recommending specific actions based on data insights. This methodology helps

HR professionals determine the best course of action to improve employee performance, enhance recruitment strategies, or increase engagement levels.

4. **Text Analytics**: Text analytics involves analyzing unstructured data, such as employee feedback from surveys or social media. By understanding sentiments and opinions, HR can gain insights into employee morale and organizational culture. This analysis is vital for addressing issues related to employee engagement and satisfaction.

Applications of HR Analytics: Human Resource Analytics (HRA) has become a cornerstone of strategic HR management, enabling organizations to harness data to optimize various HR functions. Here are key applications of HR Analytics that illustrate its transformative potential:

1. **Recruitment and Talent Acquisition:** HR Analytics enhances recruitment strategies by analyzing data from past hiring processes. Organizations can evaluate which sourcing channels yield the best candidates and understand the characteristics of successful hires. This insight allows HR teams to refine their selection criteria, improve job postings, and streamline interview processes, ultimately leading to faster and more effective recruitment.

2. **Performance Management:** Performance management is critical for employee development and organizational success. HRA provides a framework for assessing employee performance through data analysis. By tracking key performance indicators (KPIs), HR can identify high performers and those needing support. This allows for more personalized feedback, tailored development plans, and targeted training interventions, fostering a culture of continuous improvement.

3. **Employee Engagement:** Understanding employee engagement is essential for retention and productivity. HRA enables organizations to analyze engagement survey results, feedback, and performance data to identify factors that influence employee satisfaction. By pinpointing areas of concern, HR can implement targeted initiatives to enhance engagement, such as recognition programs, flexible work arrangements, or career development opportunities.

4. **Learning and Development:** HRA is instrumental in evaluating the effectiveness of training and development programs. By analyzing pre- and post-training performance metrics, organizations can determine which training initiatives yield the best results. This insight helps HR allocate resources effectively, ensuring that employees receive relevant training that enhances their skills and contributes to organizational goals.

5. **Retention and Turnover Analysis:** Employee turnover can be costly for organizations. HR Analytics helps identify patterns and predictors of turnover by analyzing employee demographics, engagement levels, and performance data. Understanding these factors enables HR to implement proactive retention

strategies, such as targeted career development paths or enhanced onboarding processes, ultimately reducing turnover rates.

6. **Workforce Planning:** Effective workforce planning is crucial for aligning talent with business objectives. HRA provides insights into workforce demographics, skills gaps, and future talent needs. By analyzing historical data and market trends, HR can forecast hiring requirements, develop succession plans, and ensure the organization has the right talent in place to meet strategic goals.
7. **Diversity and Inclusion Initiatives:** Diversity and inclusion are vital for fostering innovation and enhancing organizational culture. HR Analytics enables organizations to track diversity metrics, assess the effectiveness of inclusion initiatives, and identify areas for improvement. By understanding the impact of diversity on team dynamics and performance, organizations can implement targeted strategies to promote a more inclusive workplace.
8. **Compensation and Benefits Analysis:** HR Analytics helps organizations analyze compensation structures and benefits utilization. By examining data on employee performance, market benchmarks, and employee preferences, HR can ensure that compensation packages are competitive and equitable. This analysis supports effective talent management by aligning rewards with employee contributions and market standards.
9. **Legal Compliance and Risk Management:** Monitoring HR metrics can help organizations identify potential compliance issues and mitigate risks. By analyzing data related to employee relations, wage disparities, or harassment claims, HR can take proactive measures to address concerns before they escalate, ensuring a healthier workplace
10. e and compliance with labor regulations.

Employee Retention and Attrition Analysis

Employee retention and attrition are critical components of human resource management that significantly impact organizational performance, culture, and overall success. Understanding the factors influencing employee retention and the reasons behind attrition is essential for developing effective strategies that enhance workforce stability and engagement. This analysis explores the concepts of employee retention and attrition, the importance of data-driven insights, key factors' influencing both, and strategies to improve retention rates.

Employee retention and attrition are vital aspects of human resource management that directly impact organizational performance and culture. Employee retention refers to an organization's ability to keep its workforce over time, indicating employee satisfaction and commitment. High retention rates lead to increased stability, reduced recruitment costs, and a wealth of institutional knowledge. In contrast, employee attrition involves the gradual loss of employees, often through voluntary resignations, retirements, or layoffs. While some attrition can be natural and beneficial, high rates often signal underlying issues that need addressing.

Key factors influencing retention include job satisfaction, competitive compensation, career development opportunities, work-life balance, and organizational culture. Employees who find their roles fulfilling, feel valued, and see potential for growth are more likely to stay. Conversely, factors such as lack of advancement, poor management, job misalignment, and workplace conflict can drive employees to seek opportunities elsewhere. To enhance retention, organizations can implement strategies such as regular employee surveys, effective onboarding processes, ongoing training, and recognition programs. By focusing on these areas, organizations can foster a supportive environment that not only reduces attrition but also builds a committed and engaged workforce, ultimately contributing to long-term success.

Significance of Employee Retention and Attrition Analysis: Employee retention and attrition analysis is crucial for organizations aiming to enhance their workforce stability and overall performance. Here are key reasons highlighting its significance:

1. **Cost Reduction:** High attrition rates can lead to significant recruitment, onboarding, and training expenses. By analyzing retention data, organizations can identify the root causes of turnover and implement strategies to reduce these costs.
2. **Improved Employee Engagement:** Understanding why employees leave or stay helps organizations create a more engaging work environment. By addressing factors such as job satisfaction, management practices, and career development, companies can foster a more motivated workforce.
3. **Enhanced Organizational Culture:** Attrition analysis can reveal insights into the organizational culture. By identifying trends related to employee feedback, companies can make necessary adjustments to promote a positive workplace atmosphere that supports retention.
4. **Talent Management and Succession Planning:** Retention analysis helps organizations understand which employees are critical to their success and who might be at risk of leaving. This knowledge enables better talent management and effective succession planning, ensuring leadership continuity and stability.
5. **Informed Decision-making:** Data-driven insights from retention and attrition analysis empower HR leaders to make informed strategic decisions. This includes refining recruitment processes, improving employee engagement initiatives, and tailoring benefits and compensation packages.
6. **Competitive Advantage:** Organizations that effectively analyze and respond to retention and attrition data can create a strong employer brand. A reputation for high employee satisfaction can attract top talent, giving companies a competitive edge in the marketplace.
7. **Increased Productivity:** High retention rates contribute to a stable workforce with a wealth of institutional knowledge. Employees who are familiar with

their roles and the organization's processes tend to be more productive, leading to better overall performance.

8. **Predictive Insights:** By leveraging historical data, organizations can develop predictive models to foresee potential turnover trends. This proactive approach allows HR to implement interventions before attrition becomes a significant issue.

Step to Manage Attrition and Retention: Step-by-step process used to manage attrition and retention are as:

1. **Collect In-depth Data:** Collect data for a 360-degree attrition analysis. It must include much more than just employee profiles or demographic data. You must collect qualitative information from exit interviews, employee surveys, and social media. Besides, data about employees' roles and responsibilities, team structure, manager profiles, performance reviews, and career progression are also crucial.

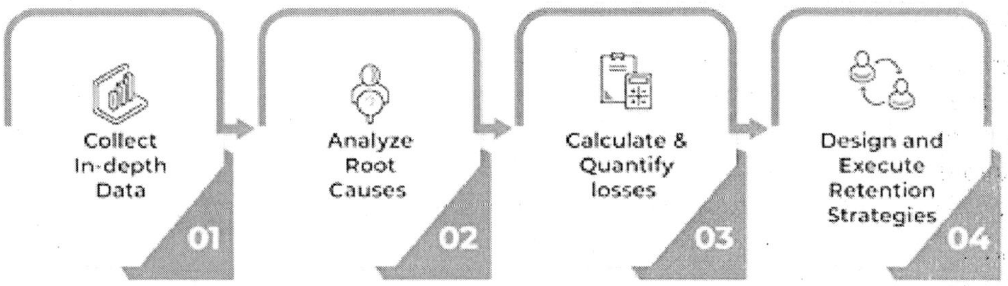

Fig.4.3

2. **Analyze Reasons:** Conduct a root cause analysis (RCA) for attrition and retention. Identify the components of your employee value proposition (EVP) that matter the most to your employees and those that need improvement. This analysis must also include benchmarking against competitor employee offerings.

3. **Calculate Costs:** Quantify the attrition losses in monetary terms to drive top management buy-in for strategic initiatives. Include the direct attrition costs such as recruiting, onboarding, and training replacements and indirect costs such as knowledge and productivity losses.

4. **Design and Execute Retention Strategies:** Based on the RCA and the cost-benefit analysis, create a roadmap for specific actions for improving the workplace environment and employee experience. Continuously measure retention and attrition metrics to track the effectiveness of your HR strategies.

Factors Influencing Employee Retention

Understanding the key factors that influence employee retention is crucial for developing effective strategies. Some significant factors:

1. **Job Satisfaction:** Job satisfaction is one of the most critical factors influencing retention. Employees who find their work meaningful, challenging, and rewarding are more likely to stay with the organization. Regular feedback, recognition, and opportunities for growth can enhance job satisfaction.
2. **Compensation and Benefits:** Competitive compensation and benefits packages are essential for retaining talent. Organizations that offer attractive salaries, bonuses, and benefits are better positioned to keep employees satisfied. Regular reviews of compensation structures can ensure they remain competitive within the industry.
3. **Career Development Opportunities:** Employees value opportunities for professional growth and advancement. Organizations that provide training, mentorship programs, and clear career paths are more likely to retain talent. Encouraging employees to pursue their career goals within the organization fosters loyalty.
4. **Work-life Balance:** A healthy work-life balance is increasingly important to employees. Organizations that promote flexible work arrangements, such as remote work or flexible hours, are more likely to retain employees. Supporting well-being initiatives can also enhance job satisfaction.
5. **Organizational Culture:** A positive organizational culture that promotes inclusivity, respect, and teamwork can significantly impact retention. Employees who feel valued and included in the workplace are more likely to remain committed to the organization.

Factors Influencing Employee Attrition: Understanding the reasons behind employee attrition can help organizations develop targeted interventions. Here are some common factors contributing to attrition:

1. **Lack of Career Advancement"** Employees who perceive limited opportunities for growth or advancement are more likely to seek opportunities elsewhere. Organizations should provide clear career paths and development opportunities to mitigate this issue.
2. **Poor Management Practices:** Ineffective leadership can lead to employee dissatisfaction and attrition. Managers who fail to communicate effectively, provide support, or recognize employee contributions can create a toxic work environment. Training programs for managers can enhance their leadership skills and positively impact retention.
3. **Workplace Conflict:** Conflicts among team members or between employees and management can lead to a negative work environment. Addressing interpersonal conflicts and promoting open communication can help reduce attrition.
4. **Job Misalignment:** Employees may leave if they feel their skills, values, or interests do not align with their roles. Ensuring proper job fit during the hiring

process and providing opportunities for skill development can help retain employees who might otherwise feel out of place.

5. **Personal Circumstances:** Sometimes, attrition occurs due to factors beyond an organization's control, such as relocation, family commitments, or health issues. While these situations cannot be entirely prevented, organizations can offer support through flexible work arrangements or leave options.

Factors Influencing Employee Retention: The key factors that influence employee retention is crucial for developing effective strategies. Here are some significant factors:

1. **Job Satisfaction**: Job satisfaction is one of the most critical factors influencing retention. Employees who find their work meaningful, challenging, and rewarding are more likely to stay with the organization. Regular feedback, recognition, and opportunities for growth can enhance job satisfaction.

2. **Compensation and Benefits:** Competitive compensation and benefits packages are essential for retaining talent. Organizations that offer attractive salaries, bonuses, and benefits are better positioned to keep employees satisfied. Regular reviews of compensation structures can ensure they remain competitive within the industry.

3. **Career Development Opportunities:** Employees value opportunities for professional growth and advancement. Organizations that provide training, mentorship programs, and clear career paths are more likely to retain talent. Encouraging employees to pursue their career goals within the organization fosters loyalty.

4. **Work-life Balance:** A healthy work-life balance is increasingly important to employees. Organizations that promote flexible work arrangements, such as remote work or flexible hours, are more likely to retain employees. Supporting well-being initiatives can also enhance job satisfaction.

5. **Organizational Culture:** A positive organizational culture that promotes inclusivity, respect, and teamwork can significantly impact retention. Employees who feel valued and included in the workplace are more likely to remain committed to the organization.

Conclusion

Employee retention and attrition are critical metrics that significantly impact an organization's success. By understanding the factors influencing both retention and attrition, organizations can develop data-driven strategies to enhance employee satisfaction, engagement, and loyalty. Investing in effective retention strategies not only reduces turnover costs but also fosters a positive workplace culture that contributes to overall organizational performance. In a competitive job market, organizations that prioritize employee retention will be better positioned to attract and retain top talent, ensuring long-term success.

Difference Between Employee Retention and Employee Attrition

Table 4.4

S.No.	Aspect	Employee Retention	Employee Attrition
1.	Definition	The ability of an organization to keep its employees.	The gradual reduction of employees through various means, often voluntary.
2.	Focus	Emphasizes strategies to maintain a stable workforce.	Concentrates on the loss of employees over time.
3.	Goal	Increase the number of employees staying with the organization.	Understand the reasons for employee departures.
4.	Impact on Costs	Reduces recruitment and training costs associated with new hires.	Can lead to increased costs due to the need for frequent hiring and training.
5.	Measurement Metrics	Measured through retention rates, employee satisfaction surveys, and engagement scores.	Measured through turnover rates and exit interview feedback.
6.	Organizational Implications	A high retention rate indicates employee satisfaction and loyalty.	High attrition rates may signal underlying issues that need to be addressed.

Workforce Planning and Talent Management

Workforce planning and talent management are essential components of effective human resource management, crucial for achieving organizational goals. Workforce planning involves forecasting an organization's future human resource needs, assessing current talent, identifying skill gaps, and aligning workforce capabilities with strategic objectives. This proactive approach ensures that the organization has the right people in place to meet its operational demands. Talent management, on the other hand, focuses on attracting, developing, and retaining skilled employees. It encompasses recruitment, onboarding, performance management, learning and development, and succession planning. By implementing robust talent management practices, organizations can enhance employee engagement, improve retention rates, and increase overall productivity.

Integrating workforce planning and talent management leads to a cohesive strategy that leverages data-driven insights to inform decision-making. Collaboration among HR, management, and department heads ensures that talent strategies align with business needs. Additionally, a continuous feedback loop allows organizations to adapt to changing market conditions and employee expectations. Despite the benefits, challenges such as data quality, rapid changes in the job market, and balancing short-term versus long-term needs persist. Organizations that prioritize both workforce planning and talent management can create a high-performing culture that drives success, fosters employee loyalty, and positions them effectively in a competitive landscape. Ultimately, a strategic approach to these processes is vital for sustaining growth and adaptability in an ever-evolving business environment.

Workforce Planning

Workforce planning is the systematic process of analyzing an organization's current and future workforce needs. It involves assessing current talent, predicting future demand for skills, and identifying gaps in talent that need to be filled. The primary purpose of workforce planning is to ensure that an organization can meet its operational and strategic goals efficiently. Key components of workforce planning are as:

1. **Demand Forecasting:** Estimating the number and types of employees required to meet future business goals. This involves analyzing factors such as market trends, organizational growth, and strategic initiatives.
2. **Supply Analysis:** Assessing the current workforce's skills, capabilities, and demographics to understand available talent.
3. **Gap Analysis:** Identifying discrepancies between current workforce capabilities and future needs. This includes recognizing skill shortages and planning for workforce changes.
4. **Action Planning:** Developing strategies to address identified gaps. This may involve recruitment, training, succession planning, or restructuring.

Importance of Workforce Planning: Effective workforce planning enables organizations to:

1. **Align Talent with Strategy:** Ensure that human resources align with organizational goals, facilitating better decision-making and operational efficiency.
2. **Improve Recruitment Efficiency:** Anticipate hiring needs, enabling proactive recruitment efforts that reduce time-to-fill positions.
3. **Enhance Employee Development:** Identify training and development needs, supporting employee growth and engagement.
4. **Increase Agility:** Respond swiftly to changes in the market or business environment, ensuring the organization can adapt to new challenges.

Talent Management

Talent management refers to the strategic approach to attracting, developing, and retaining skilled employees. It encompasses various HR practices, including recruitment, onboarding, performance management, learning and development, and succession planning. The ultimate goal of talent management is to create a high-performing workforce that drives organizational success. Key components of talent management are as :

1. **Attraction:** Developing employer branding and recruitment strategies to attract top talent. This includes creating a positive candidate experience and leveraging social media and job boards.

2. **Onboarding:** Implementing structured onboarding processes to help new hires acclimate to the organization. Effective onboarding improves retention and accelerates employee productivity.
3. **Performance Management:** Establishing a performance management system that sets clear expectations, provides regular feedback, and recognizes employee contributions. This helps employees understand their roles and align with organizational goals.
4. **Learning and Development:** Investing in employee training and development to enhance skills and knowledge. This includes offering workshops, mentoring programs, and e-learning opportunities.
5. **Succession Planning:** Identifying and developing internal talent to fill key leadership roles. Succession planning ensures continuity and prepares the organization for future challenges.

Importance of Talent Management: Effective talent management offers several benefits:

1. **Enhanced Employee Engagement**: Engaged employees are more productive and committed to their work. Talent management initiatives that support growth and recognition foster a positive work environment.
2. **Improved Retention Rates**: By providing development opportunities and a clear career path, organizations can retain top talent and reduce turnover costs.
3. **Increased Performance**: A focus on performance management ensures that employees understand their goals and receive feedback, leading to higher productivity.
4. **Stronger Employer Brand**: A reputation for effective talent management attracts high-quality candidates, enhancing the organization's ability to compete for top talent.

Integrating Workforce Planning and Talent Management: To maximize their effectiveness, workforce planning and talent management should be integrated into a cohesive strategy are as:

1. **Data-driven Insights:** Utilizing data analytics can enhance both workforce planning and talent management. By analyzing workforce data, organizations can identify trends, forecast future needs, and assess the effectiveness of talent management initiatives. This data-driven approach enables informed decision-making and resource allocation.
2. **Collaborative Approach:** HR, management, and department heads should collaborate on workforce planning and talent management initiatives. By

involving various stakeholders, organizations can gain insights into departmental needs and align talent strategies with overall business objectives.

3. **Continuous Feedback Loop:** Establishing a continuous feedback loop between workforce planning and talent management ensures that strategies remain relevant. Regularly assessing the effectiveness of talent initiatives helps organizations adapt to changing needs and emerging trends.

4. **Flexibility and Agility:** Organizations must remain flexible and agile in their workforce planning and talent management strategies. As market conditions and business objectives evolve, being able to pivot quickly ensures that the workforce is aligned with current demands.

Challenges in Workforce Planning and Talent Management: While workforce planning and talent management are essential, organizations may face several challenges:

1. **Data Quality and Availability:** Accurate data is critical for effective workforce planning and talent management. Organizations may struggle with incomplete or outdated data, hindering their ability to make informed decisions.

2. **Rapid Changes in the Job Market:** The job market is constantly evolving, with new skills and roles emerging. Keeping up with these changes and adapting workforce plans accordingly can be challenging.

3. **Retention of Top Talent:** Despite efforts in talent management, organizations may still face difficulties retaining top performers. Understanding the underlying causes of turnover is essential to address this issue effectively.

4. **Balancing Short-term and Long-term Needs:** Organizations must strike a balance between addressing immediate workforce needs and planning for long-term talent development. Focusing solely on short-term demands may compromise future organizational growth.

Conclusion

Workforce planning and talent management are integral to building a high-performing organization. By forecasting workforce needs and implementing strategic talent management initiatives, organizations can ensure they have the right people in the right roles to achieve their objectives. The synergy between these processes fosters a culture of engagement, development, and retention, ultimately driving organizational success. As the business landscape continues to evolve, organizations that prioritize workforce planning and talent management will be better equipped to navigate challenges and capitalize on opportunities.

Differences Between Workforce Planning and Talent Management

Table 4.5

S.No.	Aspect	Workforce Planning	Talent Management
1.	Definition	The process of forecasting and aligning workforce needs with organizational goals.	The strategic approach to attracting, developing, and retaining employees.
2.	Focus	Emphasizes future workforce needs and skill gaps.	Concentrates on the entire employee lifecycle, from recruitment to development.
3.	Primary Goal	Ensure the organization has the right number of employees with the right skills.	Maximize employee potential and engagement to enhance performance.
4.	Key Activities	Demand forecasting, supply analysis, gap analysis, and action planning.	Recruitment, onboarding, performance management, learning, and succession planning.
5.	Time Frame	Typically focuses on long-term needs and strategic objectives.	Involves both short-term and long-term employee development and engagement.
6.	Outcome Measurement	Success measured by workforce alignment with organizational goals and efficiency.	Success measured by employee engagement, retention rates, and performance outcomes.

Performance Measurement and KPIs

Performance measurement is the systematic evaluation of an organization's efficiency and effectiveness in achieving its strategic goals. It involves setting clear objectives, collecting relevant data, and analyzing performance metrics to inform decision-making and drive improvements. Key Performance Indicators (KPIs) are specific, quantifiable metrics that reflect how well an organization meets its objectives. Effective KPIs are specific, measurable, achievable, relevant, and time-bound (SMART), providing a clear framework for assessment.

There are several types of KPIs, including financial (e.g., revenue growth, profit margins), operational (e.g., cycle time, production costs), customer-related (e.g., customer satisfaction scores), and employee-focused (e.g., turnover rates, engagement levels). Developing KPIs involves defining strategic objectives, identifying relevant metrics, setting targets, collecting data, and regularly reviewing performance. Implementing performance measurement and KPIs requires a structured framework that includes leadership commitment, effective communication, and integration into daily operations. Organizations can leverage technology, such as performance management software and dashboards, to streamline data collection and enhance insights. Challenges may arise, such as ensuring data quality and maintaining employee buy-in. To mitigate these, organizations should focus on aligning KPIs with strategic goals, balancing quantitative and qualitative measures, and fostering a culture of continuous improvement. Ultimately, effective performance measurement and KPIs empower organizations to track progress, make informed decisions, and drive sustainable growth.

Performance Measurement

Performance measurement is a systematic approach to evaluating an organization's effectiveness in achieving its strategic objectives. It involves establishing clear goals, collecting relevant data, and analyzing performance metrics to provide insights into operational efficiency and effectiveness. By utilizing Key Performance Indicators (KPIs), which are specific and quantifiable metrics, organizations can track progress in various areas such as financial performance, customer satisfaction, operational efficiency, and employee engagement. The process includes defining objectives, selecting appropriate metrics, setting targets, and regularly reviewing outcomes to identify areas for improvement. Effective performance measurement fosters accountability by linking individual and team contributions to organizational goals, enabling data-driven decision-making. Additionally, it promotes a culture of continuous improvement, where feedback is used to adapt strategies and optimize processes. Challenges in performance measurement can include ensuring data accuracy, maintaining employee engagement, and aligning metrics with overarching strategic goals. However, when implemented effectively, performance measurement serves as a vital tool for organizations to enhance productivity, drive growth, and achieve long-term success.

Purpose: The primary purpose is to provide a framework for understanding how well an organization is performing and where improvements can be made. This process involves collecting data, analyzing it, and interpreting results to support decision-making and strategic planning.

Components of Performance Measurement: Performance measurement is a systematic process that helps organizations evaluate their effectiveness and efficiency in achieving strategic goals. It consists of several key components that work together to provide a comprehensive assessment of performance. Understanding these components is essential for developing an effective performance measurement system.

1. **Goal Setting:** The foundation of performance measurement lies in clear and measurable goal setting. Organizations must define specific objectives that align with their overall mission and vision. Goals should be:
   - **Specific:** Clearly articulated and focused on a particular outcome.
   - **Measurable:** Quantifiable to allow for objective evaluation.
   - **Achievable:** Realistic and attainable, considering available resources.
   - **Relevant:** Directly linked to the organization's strategic priorities.
   - **Time-bound:** Established within a specific timeframe for assessment.

   By setting well-defined goals, organizations can ensure that performance measurement efforts are aligned with their strategic direction.

2. **Data Collection:** Data collection is a crucial component of performance measurement, as it provides the necessary information to evaluate progress towards goals. This involves gathering both quantitative and qualitative data from various sources, including:
   - **Financial Reports:** Revenue, expenses, and profitability metrics.
   - **Operational Data:** Metrics related to production, efficiency, and process performance.
   - **Employee Feedback:** Surveys and performance appraisals to assess employee engagement and satisfaction.
   - **Customer Insights:** Feedback from customers regarding satisfaction and loyalty.

   Robust data collection methods are essential for ensuring the accuracy and reliability of the information used in performance assessments.
3. **Analysis:** Once data is collected, it must be analyzed to derive meaningful insights. Analysis involves evaluating performance data to identify trends, patterns, and areas for improvement. Key activities in this phase include:
   - **Comparative Analysis:** Assessing performance against benchmarks or industry standards to gauge competitiveness.
   - **Trend Analysis:** Examining historical data to identify patterns over time, helping to forecast future performance.
   - **Root Cause Analysis:** Investigating the underlying causes of performance gaps to inform action planning.

   Effective analysis enables organizations to make informed decisions based on evidence rather than intuition.
4. **Reporting:** Reporting is the process of communicating performance results to stakeholders. Clear and concise reporting ensures that relevant parties are informed about progress towards goals and areas needing attention. Key elements of effective reporting include:
   - **Clarity:** Presenting data in an easily understandable format.
   - **Visualization:** Utilizing charts, graphs, and dashboards to enhance comprehension of performance metrics.
   - **Timeliness:** Providing reports on a regular schedule to facilitate ongoing performance monitoring.

   Regular reporting fosters transparency and accountability within the organization, allowing stakeholders to track performance and make informed decisions.
5. **Action Planning:** The final component of performance measurement involves translating insights from analysis and reporting into actionable strategies for improvement. This includes:

Identifying Improvement: Using performance data to pinpoint areas that require enhancement.

- **Developing Action Plans:** Creating specific initiatives to address identified performance gaps, including resource allocation and timelines.
- **Monitoring:** Implementation Regularly assessing the effectiveness of implemented changes to ensure desired outcomes are achieved.

  Action planning is crucial for driving continuous improvement and ensuring that performance measurement leads to tangible organizational benefits.

Methodologies in Performance Measurement

1. **Balanced Scorecard:** The Balanced Scorecard is a strategic management framework that incorporates multiple perspectives (financial, customer, internal processes, and learning/growth) to provide a holistic view of organizational performance. By balancing these perspectives, organizations can align day-to-day operations with long-term strategic goals.
2. **Benchmarking:** Benchmarking involves comparing an organization's performance metrics against industry standards or best practices. This process helps identify performance gaps and opportunities for improvement. Organizations can learn from high-performing peers and adopt strategies that drive success.
3. **360-Degree Feedback:** 360-degree feedback is a performance appraisal method that collects feedback from multiple sources, including peers, subordinates, and supervisors. This comprehensive approach provides a well-rounded view of an employee's performance, fostering a culture of continuous improvement and development.

Challenges in Performance Measurement: Despite its importance, organizations may encounter challenges in performance measurement:

1. **Data Quality:** Ensuring the accuracy and reliability of data is crucial. Poor data quality can lead to misguided conclusions and ineffective strategies.
2. **Resistance to Change:** Employees may resist performance measurement initiatives, perceiving them as punitive. Effective communication and training can help mitigate this resistance.
3. **Overemphasis on Quantitative Metrics:** Focusing solely on quantitative metrics may overlook qualitative factors that contribute to performance, such as employee morale and innovation.
4. **Misalignment with Strategy:** KPIs must align with strategic goals; otherwise, they can lead to misguided efforts. Regular reviews are essential to maintain alignment.
5. **Balanced Scorecard:** The Balanced Scorecard is a strategic management

framework that incorporates multiple perspectives (financial, customer, internal processes, and learning/growth) to provide a holistic view of organizational performance. By balancing these perspectives, organizations can align day-to-day operations with long-term strategic goals.

6. **Benchmarking:** Benchmarking involves comparing an organization's performance metrics against industry standards or best practices. This process helps identify performance gaps and opportunities for improvement. Organizations can learn from high-performing peers and adopt strategies that drive success.360-Degree
7. **Feedback:** 360-degree feedback is a performance appraisal method that collects feedback from multiple sources, including peers, subordinates, and supervisors. This comprehensive approach provides a well-rounded view of an employee's performance, fostering a culture of continuous improvement and development.

Challenges in Performance Measurement: Despite its importance, organizations may encounter challenges in performance measurement:

1. **Data Quality**: Ensuring the accuracy and reliability of data is crucial. Poor data quality can lead to misguided conclusions and ineffective strategies.
2. **Resistance to Change:** Employees may resist performance measurement initiatives, perceiving them as punitive. Effective communication and training can help mitigate this resistance.
3. **Overemphasis on Quantitative Metrics:** Focusing solely on quantitative metrics may overlook qualitative factors that contribute to performance, such as employee morale and innovation.
4. **Misalignment with Strategy:** KPIs must align with strategic goals; otherwise, they can lead to misguided efforts. Regular reviews are essential to maintain alignment.

Regularly Review and Update Metrics: As business goals evolve, so should the metrics used to measure performance.

1. **Foster a Culture of Continuous Improvement:** Encourage employees to view performance measurement as a tool for growth.
2. **Leverage Technology:** Utilize performance management software and data analytics tools to streamline data collection and reporting.

Conclusion

Performance measurement is a vital component of organizational success. By establishing clear metrics, collecting relevant data, and analyzing performance, organizations can drive accountability, informed decision-making, and continuous improvement. Embracing effective performance measurement practices allows organizations to align operations with strategic goals, adapt to changes, and ultimately achieve sustainable growth.

Key Performance Indicators (KPIs)

Key Performance Indicators (KPIs) are critical metrics that organizations use to evaluate their success in achieving strategic objectives. These quantifiable measures help businesses track performance across various domains, such as financial health, operational efficiency, customer satisfaction, and employee engagement. By establishing clear, specific, and measurable KPIs, organizations can align their day-to-day operations with long-term goals, fostering accountability and facilitating informed decision-making.

Effective KPIs adhere to the SMART criteria Specific, Measurable, Achievable, Relevant, and Time-Bound. This ensures that each indicator provides meaningful insights into performance and drives the right behaviors within the organization. For example, a financial KPI like "Net Profit Margin" offers a clear view of profitability, while a customer-related KPI such as "Net Promoter Score" gauges customer loyalty. Regularly monitoring these KPIs allows organizations to identify trends, assess progress, and make data-driven adjustments as needed. By leveraging technology for data collection and analysis, businesses can enhance their ability to track performance and respond to changes effectively, ultimately fostering a culture of continuous improvement.

Purpose of KPIs: The primary purpose of KPIs is to provide a framework for performance measurement. They serve several key functions, including:

1. **Performance Measurement**: KPIs allow organizations to quantify and assess performance across various domains, such as finance, operations, customer satisfaction, and employee engagement.
2. **Strategic Alignment**: KPIs help align daily activities with long-term strategic objectives, ensuring that everyone in the organization is working towards common goals.
3. **Trend Identification**: By monitoring KPIs over time, organizations can identify trends and patterns, enabling them to respond proactively to changes in the market or internal operations.
4. **Accountability**: Assigning specific KPIs to teams or individuals fosters a culture of accountability and ownership over performance outcomes.

Characteristics of Effective KPIs: To be effective, KPIs must possess certain characteristics, often summarized by the SMART criteria:

1. **Specific:** KPIs should be clear and unambiguous, outlining precisely what is being measured. For example, instead of measuring "customer satisfaction," a more specific KPI might be "the percentage of customers who rate their experience as 4 or 5 on a 5-point scale."
2. **Measurable:** Effective KPIs must be quantifiable, allowing for objective assessment of performance. This requires reliable data collection methods to ensure accuracy.

3. **Achievable:** KPIs should be realistic and attainable, considering the organization's resources and capabilities. Setting overly ambitious targets can lead to frustration and disengagement among employees.
4. **Relevant:** KPIs must align with the organization's strategic objectives. They should reflect what is important to the business and drive behaviors that contribute to achieving those objectives.
5. **Bound:** Effective KPIs should be evaluated within a specific timeframe, such as quarterly or annually. This enables organizations to track progress and make timely adjustments as needed.

Types of KPIs: KPIs can be categorized into several types based on the aspects of performance they measure:

1. **Financial KPIs:** These KPIs assess an organization's financial health and performance. Common financial KPIs include:
   - **Revenue Growth Rate**: Measures the increase in revenue over a specific period, indicating the organization's growth trajectory.
   - **Gross Profit Margin**: Indicates the percentage of revenue that exceeds the cost of goods sold (COGS), providing insight into profitability.
   - **Return on Investment (ROI)**: Evaluates the profitability of an investment relative to its cost, helping organizations assess the effectiveness of their capital allocation.
2. **Operational KPIs:** Operational KPIs measure the efficiency and effectiveness of internal processes. Examples include:
   - **Cycle Time:** The total time taken to complete a process, from initiation to completion. Reducing cycle time can lead to increased efficiency.
   - **Inventory Turnover Ratio:** Measures how often inventory is sold and replaced over a specific period, indicating inventory management efficiency.
   - **Utilization Rate:** Indicates the percentage of available resources (like staff or equipment) actively in use, helping organizations optimize resource allocation:
3. **Customer KPIs:** Customer KPIs gauge customer satisfaction, loyalty, and engagement, which are crucial for long-term business success. Key examples include:
   - **Net Promoter Score (NPS):** Measures customer loyalty by asking how likely customers are to recommend the company to others.
   - **Customer Retention Rate:** The percentage of customers that continue to do business with the organization over a specific period, reflecting customer loyalty.
   - **Customer Acquisition Cost (CAC):** Calculates the cost associated with

acquiring a new customer, helping organizations assess the efficiency of their marketing efforts.

4. **Employee KPIs:** Employee KPIs evaluate workforce performance, engagement, and satisfaction. Important employee KPIs include:
   - **Employee Turnover Rate:** The percentage of employees who leave the organization within a specific timeframe, indicating workforce stability.
   - **Training Completion Rate:** The percentage of employees who have completed required training programs, reflecting investment in employee development.
   - **Employee Engagement Score:** KPIs can be categorized into several types based on the aspects of performance they measure:

Challenges in Implementing KPIs: Despite their importance, organizations often face challenges when implementing KPIs:

1. **Data Quality:** Ensuring the accuracy and reliability of data is crucial for effective KPI measurement. Poor data quality can lead to misguided conclusions and ineffective strategies.
2. **Overemphasis on Quantitative Metrics:** Focusing solely on quantitative metrics may overlook qualitative aspects that contribute to performance, such as employee morale and customer satisfaction.
3. **Resistance to Change:** Employees may resist KPI initiatives, viewing them as punitive rather than developmental. Effective communication and training can help mitigate this resistance.
4. **Misalignment with Strategy:** KPIs must align with the organization's strategic goals; otherwise, they can lead to misguided efforts. Regular reviews are essential to maintain alignment.

Case Studies in HR Analytics

Human Resource (HR) analytics has transformed the way organizations manage their workforce, driving data-driven decisions that enhance performance, retention, and overall employee satisfaction. Here, we explore several case studies that highlight the effective application of HR analytics across different industries.

1. IBM

Overview: IBM has been a pioneer in using HR analytics to enhance employee engagement and retention. Faced with high turnover rates, particularly among younger employees, IBM turned to data analytics to understand the factors influencing employee decisions.

Implementation: IBM collected data from various sources, including employee surveys, performance reviews, and social media interactions. They identified key metrics such as employee engagement scores, workload, and career advancement opportunities. By employing predictive analytics, IBM was able to develop a model that identified employees at risk of leaving the company.

Outcomes: The insights derived from the analytics enabled IBM to implement targeted retention strategies. For example, they introduced personalized career development plans and mentorship programs tailored to individual needs. As a result, IBM reported a significant reduction in turnover rates among high-potential employees, leading to enhanced productivity and organizational performance.

2. Google

Overview: Google is renowned for its innovative approach to HR analytics, particularly in understanding employee performance and satisfaction. The company uses data to enhance its workplace culture and foster employee engagement.

Implementation: Google's People Analytics team conducts rigorous data analysis on various employee metrics, including job satisfaction, performance evaluations, and team dynamics. One of their notable initiatives was Project Oxygen, which aimed to identify the key attributes of effective managers.

Outcomes: By analyzing employee feedback and performance data, Google identified eight key behaviors that distinguished high-performing managers. These included being a good coach, empowering the team, and expressing interest in employee success. The company then trained its managers to adopt these behaviors, resulting in a notable increase in employee satisfaction scores and productivity. This initiative has solidified Google's reputation as a top employer and has been instrumental in reducing turnover rates.

3. Unilever

Overview: Unilever, a multinational consumer goods company, leveraged HR analytics to enhance its recruitment processes and improve employee retention.

Implementation: Facing challenges in identifying the best candidates for specific roles, Unilever adopted a data-driven approach to recruitment. They analyzed historical hiring data, employee performance metrics, and employee feedback to identify patterns and traits that correlated with high performance within the company.

Outcomes: Unilever implemented an algorithmic selection process that utilized psychometric testing and machine learning to predict candidate success. This data-driven approach significantly reduced hiring times and improved the quality of hires. Additionally, by analyzing turnover data, Unilever identified key factors contributing to employee attrition, such as lack of career progression and insufficient training. The company responded by enhancing its onboarding and training programs, leading to improved employee retention and engagement.

4. Walmart

Overview: Walmart, one of the largest employers globally, faced challenges in employee turnover and engagement, particularly in its retail stores. To address these issues, Walmart turned to HR analytics.

Implementation: Walmart utilized data analytics to understand employee behavior, preferences, and satisfaction levels. By collecting data from employee surveys, performance evaluations, and operational metrics, Walmart could pinpoint areas for improvement in employee experience.

Outcomes: The analysis revealed that flexible scheduling and better communication with management were critical factors influencing employee satisfaction. Walmart implemented initiatives such as improved scheduling systems that allowed employees to have more control over their work hours and enhanced training programs for managers to improve communication. As a result, Walmart experienced a decrease in turnover rates and an increase in employee satisfaction scores, contributing to improved customer service and overall store performance.

5. Deloitte

Overview: Deloitte, a global consulting firm, faced a challenge in retaining top talent in a highly competitive industry. To combat this issue, they utilized HR analytics to gain insights into employee engagement and retention.

Implementation: Deloitte launched a comprehensive analytics program that analyzed employee engagement surveys, performance reviews, and exit interviews. They focused on identifying patterns that indicated potential turnover risks, such as job satisfaction levels and employee relationships with management.

Outcomes: The insights gained from the analytics led Deloitte to implement targeted interventions, such as mentorship programs and professional development opportunities tailored to employees' career aspirations. By fostering a supportive work environment and addressing specific employee concerns, Deloitte was able to reduce turnover rates significantly and improve overall employee engagement. The firm reported increased satisfaction scores and enhanced productivity, reinforcing the value of HR analytics in strategic decision-making.

6. Cisco

Overview: Cisco, a leading technology company, embraced HR analytics to enhance its workforce planning and improve employee engagement.

Implementation: Cisco collected data on employee performance, engagement surveys, and career development metrics. They utilized predictive analytics to identify trends in employee engagement and performance, which helped them anticipate future workforce needs.

Outcomes: The data-driven insights allowed Cisco to implement a more agile workforce planning strategy. They introduced initiatives to improve employee engagement, such as personalized career development plans and tailored training programs based on employee interests and skill gaps. As a result, Cisco experienced a notable increase in employee engagement levels and overall productivity, demonstrating the effectiveness of HR analytics in fostering a positive work environment.

Conclusion

These case studies illustrate the transformative power of HR analytics in addressing key challenges faced by organizations in managing their workforce. By leveraging data to understand employee behaviors, preferences, and performance, companies like IBM, Google, Unilever, Walmart, Deloitte, and Cisco have implemented targeted strategies that enhance employee engagement, improve retention rates, and drive overall organizational success. As the field of HR analytics continues to evolve, organizations that embrace data-driven decision-making will be better positioned to navigate the complexities of workforce management and achieve sustainable growth.

CASE STUDY OF APPLICATIONS AND CASE STUDIES

Case Study 1: Marketing Analytics at Netflix

Background

Netflix, a leader in the streaming industry, operates in a highly competitive market where understanding customer preferences is crucial. With over 230 million subscribers globally, Netflix leverages data to enhance user experience, optimize content delivery, and inform marketing strategies.

Challenge: As the competition in the streaming sector intensifies, Netflix faced the challenge of not only retaining existing subscribers but also attracting new ones. The company needed a more refined approach to content recommendations, user engagement, and marketing campaigns. Additionally, understanding the nuances of customer preferences across diverse demographics was essential for driving subscriptions.

Analytical Techniques Employed:

1. **Customer Segmentation and Targeting:** Netflix utilizes advanced segmentation techniques to categorize its users based on viewing habits, demographics, and preferences. Machine learning algorithms analyze vast datasets to identify distinct customer segments.
2. **Predictive Analytics:** By employing predictive modeling, Netflix can forecast which shows and movies will be popular among different segments. This is based on historical viewing data, trends, and consumer behavior.
3. **A/B Testing:** Netflix frequently conducts A/B tests to evaluate different marketing strategies and user interface changes. By presenting varied experiences to different user groups, Netflix can analyze engagement metrics to identify the most effective approaches.
4. **Recommendation Systems:** Netflix's sophisticated recommendation algorithm analyzes user data to suggest content tailored to individual preferences. This is crucial for keeping users engaged and reducing churn.

Implementation Process:

1. **Data Collection:** Netflix collects vast amounts of data, including user viewing

history, search queries, and ratings. This data is aggregated and stored in cloud-based solutions for real-time analysis.

2. **Algorithm Development:** Data scientists at Netflix develop algorithms that process user data to generate insights. These algorithms are continuously refined based on user feedback and new data.
3. **Testing and Iteration:** Through A/B testing, Netflix tests different approaches, such as new recommendation algorithms or marketing messages. This iterative process allows for continuous improvement based on real-world performance.
4. **Marketing Integration:** Insights from analytics inform marketing campaigns. For instance, targeted promotions are designed based on user segments identified through analytics, ensuring that the messaging resonates with specific audiences.

Outcomes Achieved:

1. **Enhanced Customer Experience:** The personalized recommendation engine significantly improved user satisfaction. Users reported higher engagement levels as they discovered content tailored to their tastes, leading to longer viewing times.
2. **Increased Subscriber Retention:** By understanding viewer preferences and viewing patterns, Netflix was able to reduce churn rates. Engaging content tailored to user interests kept subscribers satisfied and retained.
3. **Successful Content Strategy:** The predictive analytics models helped Netflix make informed decisions about which shows to produce or acquire. Content investments were aligned with viewer preferences, leading to successful launches of original programming like "Stranger Things" and "The Crown."
4. **Optimized Marketing Efforts:** Targeted marketing campaigns based on user data resulted in improved ROI. Netflix saw a significant increase in subscription rates from tailored advertising efforts, particularly in international markets.

Conclusion

Through its strategic use of marketing analytics, Netflix has transformed the way it engages with its subscribers, optimizing both content delivery and marketing strategies. The continuous refinement of its algorithms and reliance on data-driven decision-making has positioned Netflix as a leader in the streaming industry, driving sustained growth and customer loyalty.

Case Study 2: Healthcare Analytics at Mount Sinai Health System

Background

Mount Sinai Health System, based in New York City, is a prominent healthcare provider known for its commitment to innovative care and advanced research. With a diverse patient population, Mount Sinai aims to improve health outcomes while managing operational costs effectively.

Challenge: Mount Sinai faced several challenges, including managing patient data effectively, improving patient outcomes, and reducing hospital readmission rates. The healthcare system needed to leverage analytics to address these challenges, particularly in the face of increasing patient complexity and the demand for personalized care.

Analytical Techniques Employed:

1. **Predictive Modeling:** Mount Sinai employed predictive analytics to identify patients at high risk for readmission. By analyzing historical data, clinicians could predict which patients were most likely to return to the hospital within 30 days of discharge.
2. **Population Health Management:** The healthcare system utilized analytics to manage population health by segmenting patients based on chronic conditions, demographics, and healthcare needs. This approach allowed for targeted interventions.
3. **Electronic Health Records (EHR) Analytics:** Mount Sinai integrated data from EHRs to analyze patient outcomes, treatment effectiveness, and resource utilization. This comprehensive data integration was crucial for making informed clinical decisions.
4. **Real-time Monitoring:** By employing analytics tools, Mount Sinai monitored patient vitals and other health indicators in real-time. This facilitated timely interventions and improved patient management.

Implementation Process:

1. **Data Integration:** Mount Sinai centralized patient data from various sources, including EHRs, lab results, and patient surveys. This integration provided a comprehensive view of patient health and treatment history.
2. **Model Development:** Data scientists developed predictive models that analyzed patterns in patient data. These models were validated against historical outcomes to ensure accuracy and reliability.
3. **Interdisciplinary Collaboration:** Healthcare providers collaborated with data analysts to interpret the findings and translate them into actionable strategies for patient care.
4. **Pilot Programs:** Mount Sinai launched pilot programs targeting high-risk patients based on predictive analytics. These programs included personalized care plans and enhanced follow-up procedures.

Outcomes Achieved:

1. **Reduced Readmission Rates:** By identifying high-risk patients and implementing targeted interventions, Mount Sinai achieved a significant reduction in hospital readmissions. The healthcare system saw a 20% decrease in readmissions within 30 days post-discharge.

2. **Improved Patient Outcomes:** Predictive analytics enabled timely interventions, leading to better health outcomes for patients with chronic conditions. Enhanced management of these patients resulted in fewer complications and improved quality of life.
3. **Cost Savings:** The reduction in readmissions and improved patient outcomes translated into substantial cost savings for Mount Sinai. Fewer hospital stays reduced operational costs and enhanced resource allocation.
4. **Enhanced Care Coordination:** The use of analytics facilitated better communication and coordination among healthcare providers. Teams were able to work collaboratively, sharing insights and developing comprehensive care plans for patients.

Conclusion

Mount Sinai Health System's implementation of healthcare analytics has significantly transformed patient care and operational efficiency. By leveraging predictive modeling, EHR data, and population health management strategies, Mount Sinai has improved patient outcomes while reducing costs. This case study highlights the critical role of analytics in addressing the complex challenges faced by healthcare providers today.

SUMMARY OF APPLICATIONS AND CASE STUDIES

Analytics has emerged as a pivotal force across various industries, enabling organizations to leverage data for better decision-making and enhanced performance. This summary explores the applications and real-world case studies of analytics across five key domains: Marketing, Financial, Healthcare, Supply Chain and Operations, and Human Resource. Each section delves into specific analytical techniques and their practical implications, highlighting how organizations successfully implement these strategies.

1. Marketing Analytics

Marketing analytics involves the use of data to optimize marketing strategies, improve customer engagement, and increase ROI. It encompasses various techniques that help organizations understand their customers and evaluate the effectiveness of marketing efforts.

Customer Segmentation and Targeting

Customer segmentation is the process of dividing a customer base into distinct groups based on shared characteristics such as demographics, behaviors, and preferences. This targeted approach allows marketers to tailor their messages and offers to specific segments, leading to increased engagement and conversion rates.

For instance, a retail company may segment its customers into groups like "frequent buyers," "occasional shoppers," and "new customers." By understanding the unique needs and preferences of each segment, the company can design targeted marketing campaigns that resonate more effectively with each group.

Campaign Effectiveness Analysis

Campaign effectiveness analysis involves measuring the success of marketing campaigns by analyzing various metrics such as conversion rates, customer engagement, and return on investment (ROI). Organizations use this analysis to assess which campaigns perform well and which need adjustments. By employing A/B testing and multichannel attribution models, marketers can identify the most effective channels and messages. For example, a company might find that email marketing drives higher conversions than social media ads, prompting a shift in budget allocation.

Customer Lifetime Value Prediction

Customer Lifetime Value (CLV) prediction estimates the total revenue a customer will generate over their lifetime with the company. Understanding CLV helps organizations prioritize their marketing efforts and allocate resources effectively. Businesses can use predictive analytics to identify high-value customers and tailor their marketing strategies accordingly. For instance, a subscription service can analyze user behavior to identify patterns and predict which customers are likely to churn, allowing them to implement retention strategies.

Case Studies: Real-world Applications

Numerous companies successfully utilize marketing analytics. For example, Netflix employs sophisticated algorithms to analyze viewer data, enabling personalized content recommendations that enhance user satisfaction and retention. Similarly, Coca-Cola uses social media analytics to understand customer sentiment and adjust marketing strategies in real time, leading to improved brand loyalty and sales.

2. Financial Analytics

Financial analytics focuses on the use of data to inform financial decision-making, manage risk, and optimize investment strategies. It is crucial for organizations looking to improve their financial performance and mitigate potential risks.

Risk Management and Credit Scoring

Risk management in finance involves identifying, assessing, and prioritizing risks followed by coordinated efforts to minimize their impact. Credit scoring is a key aspect of this process, as it evaluates the creditworthiness of borrowers based on historical data. Financial institutions employ advanced analytics to develop predictive models that assess the likelihood of default. For instance, banks might analyze credit history, income levels, and economic indicators to generate accurate credit scores, allowing for better lending decisions.

Portfolio Optimization and Asset Valuation

Portfolio optimization aims to maximize returns while minimizing risk through careful asset allocation. Financial analytics plays a crucial role in analyzing historical performance and market conditions to inform investment strategies. Organizations utilize quantitative models to evaluate the potential performance of various asset combinations. For example, an investment firm might use optimization algorithms to determine the ideal mix of stocks, bonds, and other assets based on client risk tolerance and market forecasts.

Fraud Detection Techniques

Fraud detection relies on analytics to identify suspicious activities and prevent financial losses. Organizations use machine learning algorithms to analyze transaction data and detect anomalies that may indicate fraudulent behavior. For instance, credit card companies monitor transaction patterns in real-time, flagging unusual spending behavior for further investigation. This proactive approach helps mitigate losses and enhances security.

Financial Modeling Case Studies

Prominent financial institutions like Goldman Sachs utilize advanced financial modeling techniques to assess market risks and optimize trading strategies. By analyzing historical data and market trends, they can make informed investment decisions that maximize returns while managing risk.

3. Healthcare Analytics

Healthcare analytics involves analyzing data to improve patient care, optimize operations, and enhance health outcomes. It encompasses various applications that leverage patient data for better decision-making.

Patient Data Analysis and Predictive Modeling

Patient data analysis involves examining health records and demographic information to identify trends and improve patient outcomes. Predictive modeling enables healthcare providers to forecast patient needs and allocate resources effectively. For example, hospitals can analyze historical data to identify patterns in readmissions and develop targeted interventions to reduce them. Predictive analytics can also identify patients at risk of developing chronic conditions, allowing for proactive management.

Electronic Health Records (EHR) and Data Integration

EHR systems play a critical role in healthcare analytics by centralizing patient information from various sources. Integrating EHR data allows for comprehensive patient profiles, enabling healthcare providers to make informed clinical decisions. Analytics applied to EHR data can uncover trends in treatment effectiveness, patient outcomes, and resource utilization. This information can drive improvements in care delivery and operational efficiency.

Population Health Management

Population health management focuses on improving health outcomes for specific populations by analyzing data related to demographics, health behaviors, and outcomes. By identifying health trends within populations, healthcare organizations can design targeted interventions. For example, health systems can analyze data to identify communities with high rates of chronic diseases and implement preventive measures such as wellness programs and health education initiatives.

Case Studies in Healthcare Analytics

Cleveland Clinic utilizes predictive analytics to enhance patient care by identifying at-risk patients and tailoring interventions accordingly. Their data-driven approach has led to improved patient outcomes and reduced costs. Similarly, Mayo Clinic employs EHR analytics to streamline operations and enhance the quality of care delivered to patients.

4. Supply Chain and Operations Analytics

Supply chain and operations analytics focus on optimizing processes, improving efficiency, and reducing costs across the supply chain. By analyzing data, organizations can make informed decisions that enhance overall operational performance.

Demand Forecasting and Inventory Management

Demand forecasting is essential for effective inventory management. By analyzing historical sales data and market trends, organizations can predict future demand and optimize inventory levels accordingly. Accurate demand forecasts enable businesses to reduce excess inventory costs and minimize stockouts, leading to improved customer satisfaction. For instance, a manufacturer can use analytics to predict seasonal demand for products, ensuring sufficient stock is available.

Process Optimization and Simulation

Process optimization involves analyzing workflows to identify bottlenecks and inefficiencies. Simulation techniques allow organizations to model processes and test potential improvements before implementation.

For example, a logistics company might use simulation models to optimize delivery routes, reducing transportation costs and improving service levels. By analyzing different scenarios, organizations can make data-driven decisions that enhance operational efficiency.

Transportation and Logistics Analytics

Transportation analytics focuses on optimizing logistics and distribution networks. By analyzing transportation data, organizations can improve route planning, reduce fuel costs, and enhance delivery performance. For example, companies like FedEx utilize advanced analytics to optimize their logistics networks, ensuring timely deliveries while minimizing operational costs. By leveraging data, they can enhance customer satisfaction and maintain a competitive edge.

Real-world Examples and Applications

Amazon employs sophisticated analytics for demand forecasting and inventory management, enabling efficient supply chain operations and rapid fulfilments. Similarly, Walmart uses transportation analytics to optimize its logistics network, ensuring products are delivered on time while minimizing costs.

5. Human Resource Analytics

Human Resource Analytics (HRA) focuses on using data to optimize workforce management and enhance employee performance. By leveraging analytics, organizations can make informed decisions regarding talent acquisition, retention, and employee development.

Employee Retention and Attrition Analysis

HRA involves analyzing employee data to understand retention and attrition patterns. By identifying factors contributing to employee turnover, organizations can implement strategies to improve retention rates. For instance, HR departments can analyze exit interview data to identify common reasons for attrition and address issues such as workplace culture, career advancement opportunities, and compensation.

Workforce Planning and Talent Management

Workforce planning is essential for aligning human resources with organizational goals. Analytics helps organizations assess current employee skills, predict future workforce needs, and develop effective talent management strategies. For example, a tech company can analyze employee skill sets and project requirements to identify gaps, enabling them to invest in training programs that align with business objectives.

Performance Measurement and KPIs

HRA enables organizations to measure employee performance using key performance indicators (KPIs). By analyzing performance data, organizations can identify high performers and areas needing improvement.

For instance, organizations can implement 360-degree feedback mechanisms and performance reviews to gather insights and foster a culture of continuous improvement.

Case Studies in HR Analytics

Google is known for its data-driven approach to HR, using analytics to enhance employee engagement and performance. By analyzing employee feedback and performance metrics, Google implements effective management practices that contribute to its positive work culture. Similarly, IBM leverages HR analytics to predict employee turnover and identify at-risk employees, allowing for proactive retention strategies.

5

Future Trends and Challenges

The future of data analytics is marked by significant trends that promise to reshape how organizations harness data, while also presenting new challenges. One prominent trend is the integration of artificial intelligence (AI) and machine learning (ML) into analytics processes. These technologies allow for the automation of complex analyses, enabling organizations to uncover hidden patterns and generate predictive insights with remarkable speed and accuracy. Real-time analytics will become increasingly important, as businesses seek to make instantaneous decisions based on live data streams. Additionally, the advent of big data technologies like Apache Hadoop and Spark is empowering organizations to process vast datasets that were previously difficult to manage, unlocking new opportunities for insight generation. The democratization of data analytics is another vital trend; user-friendly tools are making data access possible for non-technical users, fostering a culture of data-driven decision-making across all levels of an organization. This shift not only increases accessibility but also encourages innovative uses of data as more employees engage with analytics.

However, these advancements are accompanied by significant challenges. Data privacy and security remain critical concerns, particularly with stringent regulations such as GDPR and CCPA. Organizations must implement robust data governance frameworks to safeguard sensitive information and ensure compliance with legal requirements. Furthermore, the growing complexity of data environments can lead to issues with data integration and interoperability among various tools and platforms, making it challenging to derive cohesive insights. As companies embrace advanced analytics, there's an urgent need for workforce upskilling to ensure that employees can effectively navigate and interpret these sophisticated tools. Balancing the adoption of cutting-edge technologies with ethical considerations and operational complexities will be essential for organizations aiming to thrive in this dynamic landscape. Ultimately, the future of data analytics holds immense potential, but success will depend on navigating these challenges while fully leveraging the opportunities presented by emerging technologies.

1. Artificial Intelligence in Data Analytics

Artificial Intelligence (AI) is fundamentally transforming data analytics by enhancing efficiency, accuracy, and the depth of insights derived from vast datasets. One of the most significant advancements is the automation of data processing, which reduces the time spent on tedious tasks like data cleaning and integration, allowing analysts to focus on interpretation and strategic decision-making. Predictive analytics powered by machine learning enables organizations to forecast trends by analyzing historical data, improving decision-making across sectors such as retail and finance. Additionally, Natural Language Processing (NLP) allows for the extraction of meaningful insights from unstructured data sources like customer reviews and social media, facilitating a deeper understanding of consumer sentiment and preferences. AI's capabilities extend to anomaly detection, where machine learning models can identify unusual patterns that signal fraud or operational issues, thereby enabling proactive risk management. Enhanced data visualization tools driven by AI create dynamic, interactive representations of complex information, making it easier for stakeholders to engage with and interpret data.

Real-time analytics powered by AI allows organizations to process and analyze data instantly, providing timely insights that are crucial in fast-paced environments. Furthermore, AI-driven recommendation systems analyze user behavior to deliver personalized experiences, significantly improving customer engagement and satisfaction. Despite these advancements, challenges remain, including ensuring data quality to prevent misleading insights, addressing potential biases in AI algorithms, and navigating the skill gap in the workforce. Organizations must also consider data privacy regulations when deploying AI technologies. As AI continues to evolve, its integration into data analytics will likely expand, unlocking new opportunities for innovation and driving competitive advantage across various industries. Ultimately, the synergy between AI and data analytics is poised to reshape how businesses operate, enabling them to harness the full potential of their data for informed decision-making and strategic growth.

Application of Artificial Intelligence in Data Analytics: Key applications of AI that enhance traditional data analytics methods are as:

1. **Automated Data Processing:** One of the most impactful contributions of AI is the automation of data processing tasks. Traditional data cleaning and integration can be time-consuming and prone to human error. AI algorithms can automate these processes, allowing analysts to spend less time on data preparation and more time on analysis. This efficiency accelerates the overall analytical workflow, enabling organizations to respond quickly to changing market conditions.

2. **Advanced Predictive Analytics:** AI excels in predictive analytics through machine learning (ML) techniques. By analyzing historical data, these algorithms identify patterns and trends, allowing businesses to make accurate forecasts about future events. For instance, retailers can predict customer

buying behaviors, while financial institutions can assess risk levels more effectively. The ability to anticipate trends helps organizations make proactive decisions, improving competitiveness.

3. **Natural Language Processing (NLP):** Natural Language Processing, a subset of AI, enables the analysis of unstructured data, such as text from customer reviews, emails, or social media posts. NLP tools can extract valuable insights from this data, helping organizations understand sentiment, identify emerging topics, and gauge customer satisfaction. This capability enhances customer relationship management and informs product development strategies.
4. **Anomaly Detection:** AI is particularly adept at identifying anomalies within data sets, a critical function for fraud detection, network security, and quality control. Machine learning models can flag unusual patterns that deviate from established norms, allowing organizations to address potential issues before they escalate. This proactive approach is essential in sectors such as finance and healthcare, where timely interventions can prevent significant losses or harm.
5. **Enhanced Visualization:** AI-driven data visualization tools provide dynamic, interactive representations of data, making complex information easier to interpret. These tools can adapt visualizations based on user inputs or changes in the data set, facilitating better understanding and quicker decision-making. Enhanced visualizations empower stakeholders to engage more deeply with data, fostering a data-driven culture within organizations.
6. **Real-time Analytics:** The integration of AI allows for real-time data processing and analysis, which is crucial in fast-paced environments like finance, retail, and logistics. Organizations can access immediate insights, enabling swift decision-making that responds to current trends or events. This capability is increasingly essential in today's fast-moving markets.
7. **Personalization and Recommendation Systems:** AI-driven recommendation systems analyze user behavior and preferences to deliver personalized experiences. E-commerce platforms utilize these systems to suggest products, while streaming services recommend content based on viewing history. This personalization enhances customer satisfaction and loyalty, ultimately driving sales.

AI is revolutionizing data analytics, making it more efficient, insightful, and accessible. As organizations increasingly adopt AI technologies, they can unlock new opportunities for innovation and growth, leading to more informed decision-making and enhanced competitiveness in their respective markets. The future of data analytics is undoubtedly intertwined with the advancements of AI, promising even greater capabilities on the horizon.

Role of AI and Machine Learning in Analytics

Artificial Intelligence (AI) and Machine Learning (ML) have become indispensable components of modern analytics, fundamentally transforming how organizations process, interpret, and leverage data. By integrating these technologies into their analytical frameworks, businesses can gain deeper insights, enhance decision-making, and drive operational efficiencies. This essay explores the multifaceted roles of AI and ML in analytics, detailing their applications, benefits, and the challenges they present.

1. **Automated Data Processing:** One of the most significant contributions of AI and ML to analytics is the automation of data processing tasks. Traditional data preparation involves time-consuming steps such as data cleaning, transformation, and integration. These tasks often require human intervention, making them susceptible to errors and inefficiencies. AI algorithms can automate these processes, significantly reducing the time analysts spend on repetitive tasks.

   For example, machine learning models can automatically identify and rectify inconsistencies in datasets, such as missing values or outliers. This automation accelerates the analytical workflow, allowing organizations to focus on extracting insights rather than getting bogged down in data preparation.

2. **Predictive Analytics:** Predictive analytics is one of the most powerful applications of AI and ML. By analyzing historical data, machine learning algorithms can identify patterns and trends that inform future outcomes. This capability allows organizations to make data-driven forecasts, improving decision-making in various sectors.

   In retail, for instance, predictive models can forecast customer purchasing behavior, enabling companies to optimize inventory levels and personalize marketing strategies. Similarly, in finance, machine learning can assess credit risk by evaluating historical loan performance data, helping institutions make informed lending decisions. Predictive analytics thus empowers organizations to anticipate trends and respond proactively to market changes.

3. **Anomaly Detection:** AI and ML excel in anomaly detection, a critical function for identifying unusual patterns in data that may indicate fraud or operational issues. By continuously monitoring data streams, machine learning algorithms can flag anomalies in real time, enabling organizations to take immediate action.

   For example, in the banking sector, AI can analyze transaction data to detect fraudulent activities, such as unauthorized credit card charges. In manufacturing, ML models can identify anomalies in production processes that could lead to defects or equipment failures. The ability to detect anomalies swiftly is essential for mitigating risks and ensuring operational integrity.

4. **Natural Language Processing (NLP):** Natural Language Processing, a branch of AI, facilitates the analysis of unstructured data, such as text from social media, customer feedback, and emails. By utilizing NLP techniques,

organizations can extract valuable insights from this data, helping them better understand customer sentiments and market dynamics.

For instance, businesses can analyze customer reviews to gauge satisfaction levels or identify common pain points. This information can inform product development, marketing strategies, and customer service improvements. NLP enhances the capability of analytics to derive insights from diverse data sources, fostering a more comprehensive understanding of consumer behavior.

5. **Enhanced Data Visualization:** AI-driven tools improve data visualization, making complex information easier to interpret. Traditional visualization techniques often fall short when dealing with large and intricate datasets. AI enhances this process by creating interactive and adaptive visual representations of data. These tools can dynamically adjust based on user inputs, allowing analysts to explore data in real time. Enhanced visualizations facilitate deeper exploratory analysis and improve communication of insights across teams. By making data more accessible and understandable, organizations can foster a data-driven culture that encourages informed decision-making at all levels.

6. **Real-Time Analytics:** The ability to analyze data in real time is increasingly important in today's fast-paced business environment. AI and ML enable organizations to process and analyze data as it is generated, providing immediate insights that can inform timely decisions.

   For example, in e-commerce, real-time analytics allows businesses to track customer interactions on their websites and adjust marketing strategies instantaneously. In healthcare, real-time data analysis can lead to quicker diagnoses and treatment decisions, ultimately improving patient outcomes. The capacity for real-time analytics ensures that organizations can remain agile and responsive to changing conditions.

7. **Personalization and Recommendation Systems:** AI and ML play a crucial role in powering personalization and recommendation systems that enhance customer experiences. By analyzing user behavior and preferences, these algorithms can deliver tailored product suggestions and content recommendations. For instance, streaming services like Netflix and Spotify use machine learning algorithms to analyze viewing and listening habits, suggesting content that aligns with individual tastes. E-commerce platforms leverage similar technologies to recommend products based on past purchases and browsing history. This level of personalization not only improves customer satisfaction but also drives sales and brand loyalty.

8. **Continuous Learning and Improvement:** One of the most compelling features of machine learning is its ability to learn and adapt over time. As models are exposed to new data, they can refine their algorithms and improve accuracy. This continuous learning process ensures that analytics remain relevant and

effective, enabling organizations to stay ahead of trends and respond to emerging challenges.

For example, a marketing campaign powered by machine learning can adjust its strategies in real time based on performance data, optimizing outreach efforts. Similarly, financial models can evolve as new economic data becomes available, ensuring that organizations make informed investment decisions.

Challenges and Considerations

Despite the numerous benefits of AI and ML in analytics, organizations face several challenges. Ensuring data quality is paramount; poor-quality data can lead to misleading insights, undermining the value of analytics. Organizations must invest in robust data governance practices to maintain the integrity of their datasets. Bias in AI algorithms is another significant concern. If training data contains biases, the models may perpetuate these biases, leading to unfair or discriminatory outcomes. Organizations need to implement fairness checks and continuously evaluate their models to mitigate these risks.

Moreover, the demand for skilled professionals who can effectively leverage AI and ML in analytics is growing. There is often a gap between the available talent pool and the expertise required, making it essential for organizations to invest in training and development. Lastly, navigating privacy regulations and ethical considerations surrounding data use is critical. Organizations must ensure compliance with regulations like GDPR while maintaining transparency with customers about how their data is used.

Conclusion

The roles of AI and Machine Learning in analytics are transformative, enabling organizations to harness data more effectively for strategic decision-making. By automating processes, enhancing predictive capabilities, and providing real-time insights, these technologies empower businesses to remain agile and competitive in an ever-changing landscape. As AI and ML continue to advance, their impact on analytics will deepen, unlocking new opportunities for innovation and growth while presenting challenges that organizations must navigate thoughtfully. Embracing these technologies with a focus on ethical considerations and data integrity will ultimately define success in the future of analytics.

Emerging Techniques: Reinforcement Learning, GANs

In the rapidly evolving field of artificial intelligence (AI), two of the most groundbreaking techniques gaining traction are Reinforcement Learning (RL) and Generative Adversarial Networks (GANs). These methodologies have transformed how we approach complex problems in various domains, from robotics and gaming to art and data synthesis. This article explores the fundamentals, applications, challenges, and future directions of both Reinforcement Learning and GANs.

Reinforcement Learning (RL)

Reinforcement Learning (RL) is a branch of machine learning focused on making decisions to maximize cumulative rewards in a given situation. Unlike supervised learning, which relies on a training dataset with predefined answers, RL involves learning through experience. In RL, an agent learns to achieve a goal in an uncertain, potentially complex environment by performing actions and receiving feedback through rewards or penalties.

Reinforcement Learning (RL) is a dynamic subset of machine learning focused on training agents to make decisions through interactions with their environment. The foundational principle of RL is based on trial and error, where an agent learns to choose actions that maximize cumulative rewards over time. Unlike supervised learning, which relies on labeled data, RL enables agents to explore various states and actions, receiving feedback in the form of rewards or penalties. Key components in this framework include the agent, which is the decision-maker; the environment, which provides context and feedback; states, representing the current situation; actions, which are the choices available to the agent; rewards, numerical signals indicating the success of actions; policies that guide the agent's behavior; and value functions that estimate expected cumulative rewards. Various algorithms underpin RL, such as Q-Learning, which focuses on learning the value of actions in different states; Deep Q-Networks (DQN), which apply deep learning to handle high-dimensional input data; policy gradient methods that optimize policies directly; and actor-critic methods that combine both value-based and policy-based strategies.

RL has a wide range of applications across diverse fields, showcasing its versatility and effectiveness. In robotics, RL is used to train robots to perform complex tasks such as navigating environments and manipulating objects, allowing them to adapt to dynamic scenarios. In gaming, RL has achieved significant milestones, notably through DeepMind's AlphaGo, which famously defeated a world champion in Go, demonstrating the ability of RL to excel in strategic decision-making. In finance, RL is employed to optimize trading strategies and portfolio management by learning from market dynamics to maximize returns. Furthermore, in healthcare, RL assists in personalized treatment planning by analyzing patient data to recommend optimal therapeutic pathways. Despite its potential, RL faces several challenges, including sample efficiency, as it often requires a substantial number of interactions with the environment; the exploration-exploitation dilemma, which necessitates balancing the discovery of new actions with the utilization of known rewarding ones; training stability, particularly with complex models that can lead to unpredictable outcomes; and transfer learning, which involves adapting learned strategies to new but related tasks. Overall, Reinforcement Learning represents a transformative approach in artificial intelligence, enabling autonomous and adaptive learning that paves the way for innovative applications across various domains. As research progresses, addressing these challenges will enhance RL's effectiveness and broaden its impact, ultimately contributing to the development of more intelligent and responsive systems.

How Reinforcement Learning Works

RL operates on the principle of learning optimal behavior through trial and error. The agent takes actions within the environment, receives rewards or penalties, and adjusts its behavior to maximize the cumulative reward. This learning process is characterized by the following elements:

1. **Policy:** A strategy used by the agent to determine the next action based on the current state.
2. **Reward Function:** A function that provides a scalar feedback signal based on the state and action.
3. **Value Function:** A function that estimates the expected cumulative reward from a given state.
4. **Model of the Environment:** A representation of the environment that helps in planning by predicting future states and rewards.

Reinforcement learning model can be represented by the fig.5.1.

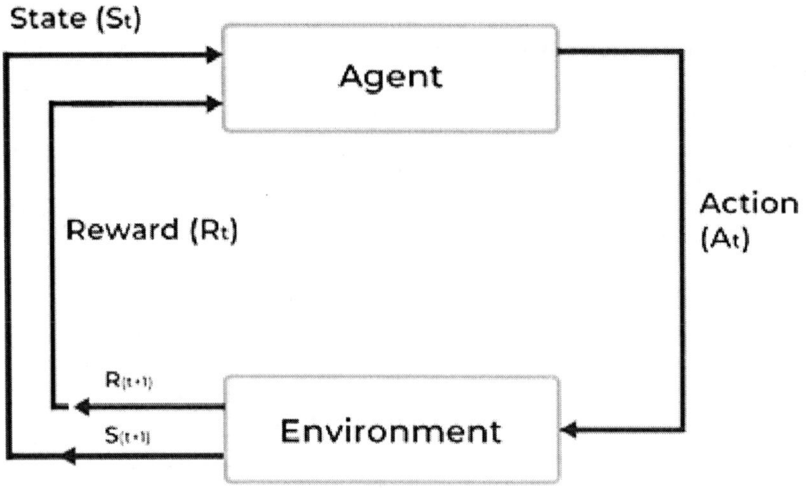

Fig.5.1

In the fig.5.1, a computer may represent an agent in a particular state (St). It takes action (At) in an environment to achieve a specific goal. As a result of the performed task, the agent receives feedback as a reward or punishment (R).

Algorithms and Techniques in Reinforcement Learning

Reinforcement Learning (RL) encompasses various algorithms and techniques that enable agents to learn optimal behaviors through interactions with their environment. Here's an overview of some of the key algorithms and methodologies used in RL:

1. **Q-Learning:** Q-Learning is a model-free algorithm that seeks to learn the value

of action choices in various states. The core idea is to update the Q-values, which represent the expected utility of taking a specific action in a given state. The agent iteratively refines its Q-values based on the rewards received and the maximum expected future rewards, using the Bellman equation for updates. This approach allows agents to learn optimal policies without needing a model of the environment.

2. **Deep Q-Networks (DQN):** DQN combines Q-Learning with deep learning to handle high-dimensional input data, such as images. Instead of maintaining a Q-table, a neural network approximates the Q-values. DQN introduces techniques like experience replay, where past experiences are stored and sampled randomly to break the correlation between consecutive samples, and target networks, which stabilize learning by using a separate network for generating target Q-values.
3. **Policy Gradient Methods:** Policy gradient methods directly optimize the policy instead of estimating value functions. These methods update the policy parameters based on the gradient of expected returns, enabling them to handle continuous action spaces effectively. Popular algorithms include REINFORCE and Proximal Policy Optimization (PPO), which aim to maximize the expected cumulative reward by adjusting policy parameters in the direction of increasing rewards.
4. **Actor-Critic Methods:** Actor-Critic methods combine the benefits of value-based and policy-based approaches. The "actor" is responsible for selecting actions based on the policy, while the "critic" evaluates those actions by estimating the value function. This dual approach stabilizes learning and can lead to more efficient training. Algorithms like A2C (Advantage Actor-Critic) and A3C (Asynchronous Advantage Actor-Critic) fall under this category, utilizing advantage functions to reduce variance in policy updates.
5. **Multi-agent Reinforcement Learning:** In scenarios where, multiple agents interact within an environment, multi-agent reinforcement learning (MARL) techniques are employed. These methods enable agents to learn cooperative or competitive behaviors based on their interactions with each other. Approaches can be centralized, where a shared policy is learned, or decentralized, where agents learn independently while considering the actions of others.
6. **Model-based Reinforcement Learning:** Model-based RL contrasts with model-free methods by incorporating a model of the environment. The agent learns a model that predicts the next state and reward based on the current state and action. This model can then be used to plan and make decisions more efficiently, allowing for faster learning and sample efficiency. Techniques such as Monte Carlo Tree Search (MCTS) are often integrated with model-based approaches.
7. **Hierarchical Reinforcement Learning:** Hierarchical RL involves decomposing

complex tasks into simpler subtasks, enabling agents to learn more efficiently. By structuring learning at different levels, agents can leverage knowledge gained from simpler tasks to solve more complicated ones. This approach reduces the complexity of learning and enhances the agent's ability to generalize across tasks.

8. **Transfer Learning in Reinforcement Learning:** Transfer learning focuses on leveraging knowledge gained from one task to improve learning in related tasks. This is particularly beneficial in environments where data is scarce or costly to obtain. Techniques include fine-tuning pre-trained policies or using knowledge distillation to transfer information between agents.

The algorithms and techniques in Reinforcement Learning offer diverse approaches to enable agents to learn from their environments effectively. From model-free methods like Q-Learning and policy gradients to more sophisticated frameworks like actor-critic and hierarchical learning, these methodologies empower RL to tackle complex decision-making problems across various domains. As research continues to evolve, advancements in these algorithms will enhance the efficiency, stability, and applicability of Reinforcement Learning in real-world scenarios.

Applications: Reinforcement Learning has diverse applications across various domains:

1. **Robotics:** RL is used to train robots to perform tasks such as grasping objects, navigating environments, and even playing sports. By learning through trial and error, robots can adapt to complex, dynamic tasks.
2. **Gaming:** RL has achieved remarkable success in gaming. Notably, DeepMind's AlphaGo defeated a world champion in the game of Go using deep reinforcement learning strategies, showcasing the potential of RL in complex strategic environments.
3. **Finance:** In finance, RL can optimize trading strategies, portfolio management, and risk assessment. Agents learn to make investment decisions based on market dynamics, maximizing returns over time.
4. **Healthcare:** RL can assist in treatment planning and personalized medicine. By learning from patient data, RL models can recommend optimal treatment pathways, improving patient outcomes.

Challenges of Reinforcement Learning: Reinforcement Learning (RL) presents a range of challenges that can complicate the learning process and limit its applicability. Here are some of the primary challenges faced in RL:

1. **Sample Efficiency:** RL often requires a significant amount of interaction with the environment to learn effective policies. This trial-and-error nature can be time-consuming and costly, particularly in real-world applications where obtaining data is expensive or impractical. Improving sample efficiency is crucial to make RL more viable in scenarios with limited data.

2. **Exploration vs. Exploitation:** Balancing exploration (trying new actions to discover their effects) and exploitation (selecting the best-known actions) is a fundamental dilemma in RL. Insufficient exploration can prevent the agent from discovering better strategies, while excessive exploration may lead to suboptimal performance and wasted resources. Finding the right balance is essential for effective learning.
3. **Stability and Convergence:** Training RL models can be unstable, especially when using function approximators like neural networks. The feedback loop between the policy and the value function can lead to oscillations or divergence, making it difficult to converge to optimal policies. Techniques to stabilize training, such as experience replay and target networks, are necessary but can add complexity.
4. **High Dimensionality**: Many real-world environments involve high-dimensional state and action spaces, making the learning problem more complex. As the dimensionality increases, the number of possible states and actions grows exponentially, leading to issues like the curse of dimensionality. This can hinder the agent's ability to generalize and learn effectively.
5. **Delayed Rewards:** In many environments, rewards are not immediately received after an action is taken, making it challenging for the agent to associate actions with their long-term consequences. This temporal credit assignment problem complicates learning, as the agent must figure out which actions contributed to the eventual reward, often requiring sophisticated strategies to manage credit assignment.
6. **Non-stationary Environments:** Many real-world environments are dynamic and non-stationary, meaning their conditions change over time. This variability can lead to outdated policies, as agents trained in a specific context may perform poorly when conditions shift. Adapting to changing environments while retaining learned knowledge poses a significant challenge.
7. Sparse Rewards: In some environments, rewards are infrequent or sparse, making it difficult for the agent to learn effective behaviors. When positive feedback is rare, the agent may struggle to understand which actions are beneficial, leading to slow learning and potential stagnation.
8. **Safety and Ethical Considerations:** When deploying RL in real-world scenarios, ensuring safety and ethical behavior becomes paramount. RL agents can take unpredictable actions that may cause harm or violate ethical guidelines. Developing frameworks that incorporate safety measures and ethical considerations into the learning process is a critical challenge.
9. **Transfer Learning:** Transferring learned knowledge from one task to another can be difficult in RL. While humans can often apply knowledge from previous experiences to new situations, RL agents may struggle to generalize across different tasks or environments. Enhancing the ability to transfer learning effectively is vital for improving RL applications.

10. **Reward Shaping:** Designing appropriate reward functions that guide the agent toward desired behaviors without leading to unintended consequences is complex. Poorly designed reward signals can result in suboptimal policies, known as reward hacking, where the agent finds ways to exploit the reward structure rather than achieve the intended goals.

Differences Between Reinforcement Learning Supervised Learning

Table 5.1

S.No.	Aspect	Reinforcement Learning (RL)	Supervised Learning (SL)
1.	Learning Approach	Learns from trial and error by interacting with an environment.	Learns from a labeled dataset where input-output pairs are provided.
2.	Feedback Type	Receives feedback in the form of rewards or penalties based on actions taken.	Receives explicit feedback through labeled examples (correct answers).
3.	Goal	Aims to maximize cumulative reward over time through a policy.	Aims to minimize prediction error by learning a mapping from inputs to outputs.
4.	Data Dependency	Requires exploration of the environment; data is generated through interactions.	Requires a fixed dataset; the model is trained on a pre-collected set of examples.
5.	Application Areas	Often used in areas like robotics, game playing, and autonomous systems.	Commonly used in classification, regression, and predictive modeling tasks.
6.	Model Structure	Involves complex structures such as value functions and policies, often requiring optimization over time.	Typically involves simpler structures (e.g., linear regression, decision trees) trained in a batch mode.

Generative Adversarial Networks (GANs)

Generative Adversarial Networks (GANs) are a revolutionary class of machine learning frameworks introduced by Ian Goodfellow and his colleagues in 2014, designed to generate new data samples that resemble a given dataset. GANs consist of two neural networks the generator and the discriminator that are trained simultaneously in a competitive setting. The generator creates synthetic data from random noise, aiming to produce samples that are indistinguishable from real data, while the discriminator evaluates the authenticity of these samples, distinguishing between genuine and generated data. This adversarial process drives both networks to improve: the generator enhances its ability to create realistic outputs, and the discriminator becomes better at detecting fakes. GANs have found diverse applications across various fields, including image synthesis, where they can generate photorealistic images, and video production, where they create realistic animations. Additionally, GANs are utilized for data augmentation in machine learning, helping to enhance datasets with synthetic samples, and in tasks like image-to-image translation, where they transform images from one domain to another. Despite their impressive capabilities, GANs face challenges such as training instability and mode collapse, where the generator produces limited varieties of outputs. Nonetheless, ongoing research continues to enhance their effectiveness, making GANs a powerful tool in the realm of artificial intelligence and creative applications.

GANs are made up of two neural networks, a discriminator and a generator. They use adversarial training to produce artificial data that is identical to actual data.

1. The Generator attempts to fool the Discriminator, which is tasked with accurately distinguishing between produced and genuine data, by producing random noise samples.
2. Realistic, high-quality samples are produced as a result of this competitive interaction, which drives both networks toward advancement.
3. GANs are proving to be highly versatile artificial intelligence tools, as evidenced by their extensive use in image synthesis, style transfer, and text-to-image synthesis.
4. They have also revolutionized generative modeling.

Through adversarial training, these models engage in a competitive interplay until the generator becomes adept at creating realistic samples, fooling the discriminator approximately half the time.

Architecture of GANs

A Generative Adversarial Network (GAN) is composed of two primary parts, are:

1. **Generator Model:** A key element responsible for creating fresh, accurate data in a Generative Adversarial Network (GAN) is the generator model. The generator takes random noise as input and converts it into complex data samples, such text or images. It is commonly depicted as a deep neural network.

   The training data's underlying distribution is captured by layers of learnable parameters in its design through training. The generator adjusts its output to produce samples that closely mimic real data as it is being trained by using backpropagation to fine-tune its parameters.

   The generator's ability to generate high-quality, varied samples that can fool the discriminator is what makes it successful.

   Generator Loss: The objective of the generator in a GAN is to produce synthetic samples that are realistic enough to fool the discriminator. The generator achieves this by minimizing its loss function JG*JG* The loss is minimized when the log probability is maximized, i.e., when the discriminator is highly likely to classify the generated samples as real. The following equation is given below:

$$J_G = -\frac{1}{m}\Sigma_{i=1}^{m} log D(G(z_i))$$

   where,

- J_G measure how well the generator is fooling the discriminator.
- *log* $D(G(z_i))$ represents log probability of the discriminator being correct for generated samples.
- The generator aims to minimize this loss, encouraging the production of samples that the discriminator classifies as real *(log* $D(G(z_i))$ close to 1.

2. **Discriminator Model:** An artificial neural network called a discriminator model is used in Generative Adversarial Networks (GANs) to differentiate between generated and actual input. By evaluating input samples and allocating probability of authenticity, the discriminator functions as a binary classifier.

   Over time, the discriminator learns to differentiate between genuine data from the dataset and artificial samples created by the generator. This allows it to progressively hone its parameters and increase its level of proficiency.

   Convolutional layers or pertinent structures for other modalities are usually used in its architecture when dealing with picture data. Maximizing the discriminator's capacity to accurately identify generated samples as fraudulent and real samples as authentic is the aim of the adversarial training procedure. The discriminator grows increasingly discriminating as a result of the generator and discriminator's interaction, which helps the GAN produce extremely realistic-looking synthetic data overall.

   Discriminator Loss: The discriminator reduces the negative log likelihood of correctly classifying both produced and real samples. This loss incentivizes the discriminator to accurately categorize generated samples as fake and real samples with the following equation:

$$J_D = -\frac{1}{m}\Sigma_{i=1}^{m} log\ D(x_i) - \frac{1}{m}\Sigma_{i=1}^{m} log(1 - D(G(z_i)))$$

   Where,

   - J_D assesses the discriminator's ability to discern between produced and actual samples.
   - The log likelihood that the discriminator will accurately categorize real data is represented by $logD(x_i)$.
   - The log chance that the discriminator would correctly categorize generated samples as fake is represented by $log(1\text{-}D(G(z_i)))$.
   - The discriminator aims to reduce this loss by accurately identifying artificial and real samples.

     MinMax Loss: In a Generative Adversarial Network (GAN), the minimax loss formula is provided by:

$$min_G\ max_D(G, D) = [\mathbb{E}_{x \sim p_{data}}[log\ D(x)] + \mathbb{E}_{z \sim p_z(z)}[log(1 - D(g(z)))]$$

     where,

- G is generator network and is D is the discriminator network
- Actual data samples obtained from the true data distribution $P_{data}(x)$ are represented by x.
- Random noise sampled from a previous distribution $p_z(z)$ usually a normal or uniform distribution) is represented by z.
- D(x) represents the discriminator's likelihood of correctly identifying actual data as real.
- D(G(z)) is the likelihood that the discriminator will identify generated data coming from the generator as authentic.

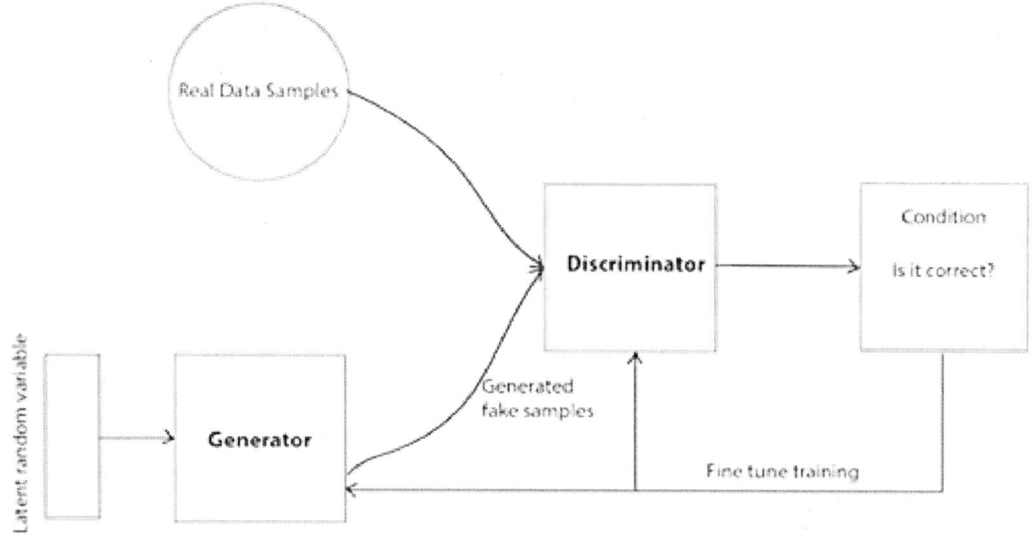

Fig.5.2

How does a GAN work?

The steps involved in how a GAN works:

1. **Initialization:** Two neural networks are created: a Generator (G) and a Discriminator (D).
   - G is tasked with creating new data, like images or text, that closely resembles real data.
   - D acts as a critic, trying to distinguish between real data (from a training dataset) and the data generated by G.
2. **Generator's First Move:** G takes a random noise vector as input. This noise vector contains random values and acts as the starting point for G's creation process. Using its internal layers and learned patterns, G transforms the noise vector into a new data sample, like a generated image.
3. **Discriminator's Turn:** D receives two kinds of inputs:

- Real data samples from the training dataset.
- The data samples generated by G in the previous step. D's job is to analyze each input and determine whether it's real data or something G cooked up. It outputs a probability score between 0 and 1. A score of 1 indicates the data is likely real, and 0 suggests it's fake.

4. **The Learning Process:** Now, the adversarial part comes in:
   - If D correctly identifies real data as real (score close to 1) and generated data as fake (score close to 0), both G and D are rewarded to a small degree. This is because they're both doing their jobs well.
   - However, the key is to continuously improve. If D consistently identifies everything correctly, it won't learn much. So, the goal is for G to eventually trick D.
5. **Generator's Improvement:**
   - When D mistakenly labels G's creation as real (score close to 1), it's a sign that G is on the right track. In this case, G receives a significant positive update, while D receives a penalty for being fooled.
   - This feedback helps G improve its generation process to create more realistic data.
6. **Discriminator's Adaptation:**
   - Conversely, if D correctly identifies G's fake data (score close to 0), but G receives no reward, D is further strengthened in its discrimination abilities.
   - This ongoing duel between G and D refines both networks over time.

As training progresses, G gets better at generating realistic data, making it harder for D to tell the difference. Ideally, G becomes so adept that D can't reliably distinguish real from fake data. At this point, G is considered well-trained and can be used to generate new, realistic data samples.

Future Directions

The future of GANs holds promising avenues for research and application. Some potential directions include:

1. **Improved Training Techniques:** Continued efforts to enhance training stability and address issues like mode collapse will be crucial for expanding the applicability of GANs. Research into novel loss functions, optimization strategies, and regularization techniques may yield better-performing models.
2. **Explainability and Interpretability:** As GANs become more integrated into critical applications, understanding their decision-making processes will be essential. Developing methods to interpret and explain GAN-generated outputs can help build trust and facilitate their adoption in sensitive fields like healthcare.

3. **Real-world Applications:** Further exploration of GANs in real-world applications, such as autonomous systems, robotics, and climate modeling, will be vital. Harnessing the power of GANs to address complex, real-world problems could lead to significant advancements across various industries.

4. **Ethical Considerations:** As GANs become increasingly powerful, ethical considerations regarding their use will come to the forefront. Issues related to deepfakes, misinformation, and data privacy must be addressed to ensure that GAN technology is applied responsibly and ethically.

Conclusion

Generative Adversarial Networks represent a groundbreaking advancement in the field of artificial intelligence and machine learning. By leveraging the adversarial training process between generators and discriminators, GANs can produce high-quality, realistic data across a multitude of domains. Despite facing challenges such as training instability and mode collapse, ongoing research continues to refine GAN methodologies and expand their applications. As the technology evolves, GANs are poised to play an integral role in shaping the future of generative modeling, impacting areas ranging from art and design to medicine and beyond. With careful consideration of ethical implications and a focus on interpretability, the potential of GANs can be harnessed for positive and transformative outcomes in society.

Differences Between Reinforcement Learning (RL) and Generative Adversarial Networks

Table 5.2

S.No.	Aspect	Reinforcement Learning (RL)	Generative Adversarial Networks (GAN)
1.	Purpose	Focuses on learning optimal policies for decision-making in dynamic environments.	Aims to generate new data samples that resemble a training dataset.
2.	Architecture	Consists of an agent, environment, policy, and value functions.	Comprises two neural networks: a generator and a discriminator.
3.	Training Method	Utilizes trial-and-error learning with feedback in the form of rewards or penalties.	Employs adversarial training where the generator and discriminator compete against each other.
4.	Feedback Type	Feedback is derived from the environment as rewards based on actions taken.	Feedback comes from the discriminator evaluating the authenticity of generated samples.
5.	Data Dependency	Learns from interactions with the environment; data is generated through these interactions.	Requires a fixed dataset to learn the distribution of real data for generating new samples.
6.	Common Applications	Robotics, game playing, autonomous systems, and sequential decision-making tasks.	Image synthesis, video generation, data augmentation, and artistic creation.

AI-Driven Analytics Platforms

In the era of big data, organizations are inundated with vast amounts of information. Traditional data analytics methods often fall short in providing the actionable insights needed to make informed decisions quickly. Enter AI-driven analytics platforms, which leverage artificial intelligence (AI) and machine learning (ML) to enhance data analysis, automate insights, and ultimately drive better business outcomes. This article explores the key features, benefits, technologies, applications, challenges, and future trends associated with AI-driven analytics platforms.

AI-driven analytics platforms are sophisticated tools designed to analyze data at scale, utilizing advanced algorithms and statistical methods. These platforms automate the data analysis process, allowing businesses to uncover patterns, trends, and correlations that might not be apparent through manual analysis. By integrating AI and ML, these platforms can adapt to new data, learn from historical trends, and continuously improve their analytical capabilities.

Key Components of AI-Driven Analytics Platforms: AI-driven analytics platforms integrate advanced technologies and methodologies to enhance data analysis and provide actionable insights. The key components of these platforms work together to automate data processing, leverage machine learning, and deliver user-friendly analytics. Here are the primary components that define AI-driven analytics platforms:

1. **Data Ingestion and Integration:** Data ingestion is the foundational step in any analytics platform. AI-driven platforms can seamlessly collect data from diverse sources, including databases, cloud storage, APIs, IoT devices, and social media. This integration capability ensures that organizations can consolidate structured and unstructured data into a single environment, facilitating comprehensive analysis. Advanced ETL (Extract, Transform, Load) processes automate data preparation, ensuring that data is cleansed, normalized, and ready for analysis without manual intervention.
2. **Data Preparation and Cleansing:** Quality data is crucial for accurate analytics. AI-driven platforms incorporate automated data preparation tools that streamline cleansing, transformation, and enrichment processes. These tools can identify and rectify inconsistencies, handle missing values, and remove duplicates, thereby improving data integrity. By automating these tasks, organizations save time and resources, allowing analysts to focus on deriving insights rather than getting bogged down in data wrangling.
3. **Machine Learning and Advanced Analytics:** At the heart of AI-driven analytics platforms are machine learning algorithms that perform predictive and prescriptive analytics. These algorithms analyze historical data to identify patterns, trends, and relationships, enabling businesses to forecast future outcomes. Predictive analytics helps organizations anticipate trends, while prescriptive analytics recommends optimal actions based on data insights. This combination enhances decision-making capabilities, allowing businesses to respond proactively to changing market conditions.

4. **Natural Language Processing (NLP):** NLP capabilities enable users to interact with analytics platforms using natural language queries, making data analysis more accessible to non-technical stakeholders. Users can pose questions in everyday language, and the platform translates these queries into structured data requests. This feature democratizes data access, fostering a data-driven culture within organizations by enabling more team members to engage with and understand analytics.
5. **Visualization and Reporting Tools:** Effective data visualization is essential for conveying complex insights in an understandable manner. AI-driven analytics platforms offer advanced visualization tools that allow users to create interactive dashboards, charts, and graphs. These visualizations help stakeholders quickly grasp trends and patterns, facilitating better communication of insights across teams. Customizable reporting tools enable users to generate and share reports that highlight key metrics and findings.
6. **Collaboration Features:** AI-driven analytics platforms often incorporate collaboration tools that enhance teamwork and information sharing. Users can comment on reports, share insights with colleagues, and work together on data analysis projects in real time. This collaborative environment promotes a shared understanding of data-driven strategies and encourages cross-functional teams to leverage insights effectively.
7. **Automated Insights and Recommendations:** Many AI-driven analytics platforms feature automated insight generation capabilities. Using machine learning models, these platforms can identify significant trends, anomalies, and opportunities without user input. Additionally, they can provide actionable recommendations based on analysis, helping organizations make data-informed decisions swiftly.
8. **Security and Governance:** Data security and governance are critical components of any analytics platform. AI-driven platforms implement robust security measures to protect sensitive data, including encryption, access controls, and compliance with regulations like GDPR. Governance frameworks ensure data quality and integrity, establishing policies for data usage and management.

Technologies Behind AI-Driven Analytics Platforms: AI-driven analytics platforms rely on a range of advanced technologies to automate data processing, enhance analysis capabilities, and deliver actionable insights. Understanding these underlying technologies is essential for appreciating how these platforms function and their potential to transform decision-making in organizations. Here are the key technologies that power AI-driven analytics platforms:

1. **Machine Learning Algorithms:** At the core of AI-driven analytics are various machine learning (ML) algorithms that enable predictive and prescriptive analytics. Common algorithms include:

- **Regression Models:** Used for forecasting and understanding relationships between variables.
- **Classification Algorithms:** Such as decision trees, support vector machines, and neural networks, which categorize data into predefined classes.
- **Clustering Algorithms:** Like k-means and hierarchical clustering, used to group similar data points for market segmentation or anomaly detection.
- **Deep Learning:** Leveraging neural networks, particularly for complex tasks like image recognition and natural language processing (NLP).

These algorithms allow platforms to learn from historical data, uncover patterns, and make data-driven predictions.

2. **Big Data Technologies:** Given the vast amounts of data organizations generate, big data technologies are crucial for processing and analyzing this information efficiently. Technologies such as:

- **Apache Hadoop:** A framework that allows for distributed storage and processing of large datasets across clusters of computers.
- **Apache Spark:** A fast, in-memory data processing engine that supports complex analytics and real-time data processing.
- **NoSQL Databases:** Such as MongoDB and Cassandra, which enable flexible data storage and retrieval for unstructured and semi-structured data.

These technologies facilitate the handling of large volumes of data while ensuring quick access and analysis.

3. **Cloud Computing:** Cloud computing has become a cornerstone of AI-driven analytics platforms, providing scalable infrastructure and services. Key benefits include:

- **On-demand Resources:** Organizations can scale their computing power and storage according to their needs, reducing costs associated with on-premises infrastructure.
- **Accessibility:** Cloud-based platforms allow teams to access data and insights from anywhere, promoting collaboration and flexibility.
- **Managed Services:** Many cloud providers offer managed analytics services that simplify deployment and maintenance, enabling organizations to focus on deriving insights rather than managing infrastructure.

4. **Natural Language Processing (NLP):** NLP technologies enhance user interaction with analytics platforms by enabling natural language queries. This allows users to ask questions and receive insights in plain language. Key NLP techniques include:

- **Sentiment Analysis:** Understanding user opinions and emotions from textual data.

- **Entity Recognition:** Identifying and classifying key information from text.
- **Chatbots and Virtual Assistants:** Facilitating data queries and providing insights interactively.

  These capabilities make analytics more accessible to non-technical users, fostering a data-driven culture within organizations.

5. **Data Visualization Tools:** Effective data visualization is critical for conveying insights clearly and engagingly. Technologies powering data visualization include:
   - **Visualization Libraries:** Such as D3.js and Plotly, which enable the creation of interactive and customizable visualizations.
   - **Business Intelligence (BI) Tools:** Tools like Tableau, Power BI, and Looker allow users to build dashboards and reports that provide real-time insights and facilitate data exploration.

   These tools help stakeholders easily interpret complex data, supporting better decision-making.

6. **Automation and Workflow Technologies:** Automation technologies streamline data processing and analysis workflows. These include:
   - **Robotic Process Automation (RPA):** Automating repetitive data tasks, such as data entry and report generation.
   - **Workflow Management Tools:** Enabling the orchestration of data pipelines and analytics processes, ensuring timely delivery of insights.

Future Trends in AI-Driven Analytics Platforms

1. **Increased Automation:** Future platforms are likely to feature even more automation in data preparation, analysis, and reporting, reducing the reliance on manual intervention.
2. **Enhanced NLP Capabilities:** As NLP technology advances, users will be able to interact with analytics platforms more intuitively, gaining insights through simple queries and conversations.
3. **Augmented Analytics:** Augmented analytics, which combines AI with traditional analytics, will empower users with automated insights, recommendations, and visualizations, making data exploration easier.
4. **Edge Analytics:** With the rise of IoT devices, edge analytics will enable data processing at the source, providing real-time insights and reducing latency.
5. **Explainable AI:** As organizations increasingly rely on AI for decision-making, the need for transparency and interpretability will drive the development of explainable AI methods.
6. **Ethical AI Practices:** There will be a growing emphasis on ethical AI practices, ensuring that algorithms are fair, transparent, and accountable in their decision-making processes.

Role of Technology in Ethical Data Analytics: The role of technology in ethical data analytics is pivotal, as it helps organizations navigate the complex landscape of data usage while adhering to ethical standards. Here are key ways in which technology facilitates ethical practices in data analytics:

1. **Automated Tools for Bias Detection:** Emerging technologies can aid in identifying and mitigating bias in data analytics. Automated tools can analyze algorithms and datasets for bias, ensuring fair outcomes.
2. **Privacy-Preserving Techniques:** Technologies such as differential privacy and federated learning enable organizations to analyze data without compromising individual privacy. These techniques allow for insights to be gained while protecting sensitive information.
3. **Blockchain for Transparency:** Blockchain technology can enhance transparency in data usage by providing an immutable record of data transactions. This can help organizations demonstrate accountability and build trust with stakeholders.

Conclusion

AI-driven analytics platforms are revolutionizing the way organizations analyze data and derive insights. By harnessing the power of artificial intelligence and machine learning, these platforms enhance decision-making, improve operational efficiency, and drive better business outcomes. Despite the challenges of implementation, the benefits and future trends indicate that AI-driven analytics will continue to play a pivotal role in the data-driven landscape. As technology evolves, organizations that adopt these platforms will be better positioned to navigate the complexities of big data and unlock valuable insights that propel their success.

Ethical Dilemmas in Data Analytics

Data analytics has transformed the way organizations make decisions, understand consumer behavior, and optimize operations. However, the power of data also brings significant ethical dilemmas that must be navigated carefully. These dilemmas arise from the nature of data collection, the use of algorithms, and the potential impact of analytics on individuals and society. This article explores the key ethical dilemmas in data analytics, examining their implications and offering insights on how organizations can address them responsibly.

1. **Data Privacy and Consent:** One of the most pressing ethical dilemmas in data analytics is the issue of data privacy. Organizations often collect vast amounts of personal data without fully informing individuals about how their data will be used. This raises several ethical concerns:
   - **Informed Consent:** Many users may not fully understand the implications of giving consent for data collection. Ethical data practices require transparency about what data is being collected, how it will be used, and who it will be shared with.

- **Surveillance and Intrusiveness:** The pervasive nature of data collection can feel intrusive, leading to a surveillance culture where individuals feel constantly monitored. This can erode trust between consumers and organizations.

  Organizations must establish clear consent processes and ensure that users have the option to opt-out of data collection practices. Providing users with control over their data fosters trust and aligns with ethical standards.

2. **Bias and Discrimination:** Data analytics can inadvertently perpetuate biases and discrimination, particularly when algorithms are trained on historical data that reflects existing inequalities. Ethical dilemmas related to bias include:

   - **Algorithmic Bias:** If the data used to train machine learning models is biased, the resulting algorithms can produce discriminatory outcomes. For example, biased hiring algorithms may favor certain demographic groups over others, reinforcing existing inequalities.

   - **Lack of Diversity in Data:** If datasets do not adequately represent diverse populations, the insights derived may not be applicable to all groups. This can lead to decisions that disproportionately affect marginalized communities.

   To combat bias, organizations should conduct regular audits of their data and algorithms, ensuring that they are fair and equitable. Involving diverse teams in the development of algorithms can also help identify and mitigate potential biases.

3. **Data Security and Breaches:** The ethical handling of data also encompasses security. Organizations must safeguard personal information to prevent unauthorized access and data breaches. Ethical dilemmas related to data security include:

   - **Responsibility for Data Breaches:** When a data breach occurs, organizations may face significant ethical scrutiny. They have a responsibility to protect user data, and failing to do so can have serious consequences for individuals, including identity theft and financial loss.

   - **Inadequate Security Measures:** Organizations that do not invest in adequate security measures may be seen as neglectful. Ethical practices demand that organizations prioritize data security and take proactive steps to protect sensitive information.

   Implementing robust security protocols, conducting regular security assessments, and developing response plans for potential breaches are critical steps for organizations to uphold ethical standards.

4. **Manipulation and Misuse of Data:** The potential for manipulating data to serve specific agendas poses another ethical dilemma in data analytics. Organizations may be tempted to present data selectively or misrepresent

findings to influence public opinion or decision-making. Key considerations include:

- **Data Integrity:** Maintaining the integrity of data is crucial. Ethical dilemmas arise when organizations selectively present data or omit relevant information to mislead stakeholders.
- **Public Trust:** Manipulating data can erode public trust in organizations, particularly if stakeholders perceive that they are being misled. This can have long-term reputational damage and affect relationships with customers and partners.

  Organizations should establish clear guidelines for data reporting and ensure that analyses are conducted transparently. Encouraging a culture of integrity within analytics teams is vital to preventing manipulation.

5. **Impact on Employment:** The rise of automated analytics and AI has implications for employment, raising ethical questions about job displacement and workforce changes. Ethical dilemmas related to employment include:
   - **Job Displacement:** As automation and data analytics become more prevalent, certain job roles may become obsolete. Organizations must consider the ethical implications of replacing human workers with machines and the potential social impact of job loss.
   - **Reskilling and Support:** Organizations have a responsibility to support their employees through transitions brought about by automation. This includes providing reskilling opportunities and assistance in finding new roles.

   Engaging in responsible workforce planning and developing strategies to support employees during transitions can help organizations navigate the ethical dilemmas associated with employment changes.

6. **Lack of Transparency in Algorithms:** As organizations increasingly rely on algorithms for decision-making, the lack of transparency in how these algorithms function poses ethical challenges. Considerations include:
   - **Black Box Algorithms:** Many machine learning models operate as "black boxes," making it difficult for stakeholders to understand how decisions are made. This lack of transparency can lead to distrust and scepticisms.
   - **Accountability:** When decisions are made by algorithms, it can be challenging to determine accountability for outcomes. If an algorithm makes a biased decision, who is responsible?

   Organizations should strive for transparency in their algorithms, providing explanations for how decisions are made. Implementing measures for algorithmic accountability is essential for ethical data practices.

7. **Ethical Use of Data for Social Good:** While data analytics has the potential to

drive positive social impact, ethical dilemmas arise when using data in ways that may inadvertently harm individuals or communities. Considerations include:

- **Social Justice:** Using data to address social issues must be done ethically. For example, predictive policing algorithms can perpetuate systemic biases if not designed and implemented carefully.
- **Beneficence vs. Maleficence:** Organizations must carefully weigh the potential benefits of using data for social good against the risks of harm. Ethical practices require a commitment to doing no harm while striving for positive outcomes.

  Engaging stakeholders and communities in discussions about data use for social good can help organizations navigate ethical dilemmas while ensuring that data serves the public interest.

The ethical dilemmas in data analytics are complex and multifaceted, requiring organizations to navigate a landscape fraught with challenges. By recognizing the importance of data privacy, addressing bias, ensuring data security, and maintaining transparency, organizations can cultivate ethical data practices that foster trust and integrity. Moreover, by considering the broader social implications of their data practices, organizations can use analytics responsibly and for the greater good. As data continues to play a central role in decision-making, prioritizing ethical considerations will be essential for sustainable success and positive societal impact.

Bias in Algorithms and Fairness Considerations

In the age of data-driven decision-making, algorithms play a pivotal role in shaping outcomes across various sectors, from healthcare to finance to criminal justice. However, the increasing reliance on algorithmic systems has brought to light significant concerns regarding bias and fairness. This article explores the nature of bias in algorithms, the implications for fairness, and strategies for mitigating these issues.

Algorithmic bias refers to systematic and unfair discrimination that arises when algorithms produce results that are prejudiced due to erroneous assumptions in the machine learning process. Bias can manifest in various ways, such as unequal treatment of individuals based on race, gender, socioeconomic status, or other characteristics. It can result from biased data, flawed algorithms, or biased interpretations of results.

Sources of Bias

Bias in algorithms can originate from several key sources, each contributing to the potential for unfair or discriminatory outcomes. Here's a detailed overview of the main sources of bias:

1. **Data Bias**
   - **Historical Bias:** Data reflecting past societal inequalities can perpetuate discrimination. For instance, if historical hiring data shows a preference

for certain demographics, an algorithm trained on this data may replicate those biases.

- **Sample Bias:** If the data used for training is not representative of the broader population, the algorithm may produce skewed results. For example, datasets that over-represent one demographic can lead to biased predictions for under-represented groups.
- **Label Bias:** When data labels (e.g., in supervised learning) reflect subjective judgments or societal prejudices, this can introduce bias. For example, biased human labeling can skew the training outcomes.

2. **Model Bias**
   - **Algorithmic Design:** Certain algorithms may inherently favor specific types of outcomes or relationships, which can introduce bias. For example, simpler models may fail to capture complex interactions, leading to inaccurate predictions for certain groups.
   - **Feature Selection:** The choice of features included in a model can also contribute to bias. If key variables that represent the complexity of a problem are omitted, the model may produce biased results.
3. **Feedback Loops**
   - **Reinforcement of Bias:** When users interact with algorithmic systems, their behaviors can influence future outcomes, creating feedback loops. For instance, biased content recommendations can lead to user engagement patterns that further entrench existing biases in the system.
4. **User Interaction Bias**
   - **Engagement Patterns:** The way users engage with an algorithm can introduce bias. For example, if an algorithm learns from user preferences that reflect biases, it may continue to recommend content that perpetuates those biases.
5. **Sociocultural Bias**
   - **Societal Norms:** Algorithms trained on data reflecting societal norms can carry forward the biases present in those norms. For example, cultural biases related to gender or race may influence how data is collected and interpreted.
6. **Environmental Bias**
   - **Contextual Influences:** Changes in the environment or context in which data is collected can introduce bias. For example, an algorithm trained during a specific economic condition may not perform fairly in different conditions.

Examples of Algorithmic Bias

1. **Criminal Justice:** Predictive policing algorithms have been criticized for disproportionately targeting minority communities, based on historical arrest data that reflects systemic biases in law enforcement practices.
2. **Healthcare:** Algorithms used to determine eligibility for healthcare programs may unintentionally discriminate against certain groups due to biased training data, leading to unequal access to essential services.
3. **Hiring Processes:** AI-driven recruitment tools have shown tendencies to favor male candidates over female candidates if trained on historical data from industries with gender imbalances.

Importance of Fairness

Fairness in algorithmic decision-making is crucial for several reasons. First and foremost, it promotes equity by ensuring that individuals are treated justly, regardless of their demographic characteristics such as race, gender, or socioeconomic status. In sectors like hiring, healthcare, and criminal justice, biased algorithms can reinforce systemic inequalities, leading to discriminatory outcomes that adversely affect marginalized groups.

Moreover, fairness fosters trust in technology and institutions. When people believe that algorithms are fair and transparent, they are more likely to accept and engage with these systems. Conversely, perceived unfairness can lead to scepticisms and resistance, undermining the potential benefits of data-driven decision-making.

In addition, ensuring fairness aligns with ethical and legal obligations. Many jurisdictions have laws and regulations aimed at preventing discrimination, and organizations must comply with these standards to avoid legal repercussions and reputational damage.

Finally, promoting fairness can lead to better overall outcomes. Diverse perspectives often lead to more robust solutions, and fair algorithms can enhance innovation by allowing all individuals the opportunity to succeed. By prioritizing fairness, organizations not only contribute to social justice but also enhance their credibility, stakeholder relationships, and long-term success in a data-driven world.

Mitigating Algorithmic Bias

Addressing algorithmic bias requires a multi-faceted approach that encompasses data collection, model development, and ongoing evaluation. Here are some strategies:

1. **Diverse and Representative Data:** Collecting diverse datasets that accurately reflect the population can help mitigate bias. Organizations should prioritize inclusivity in data collection, ensuring that marginalized groups are adequately represented. This includes:
   - **Data Augmentation:** Techniques such as oversampling underrepresented groups can help balance datasets.

- **Bias Audits of Training Data:** Regularly assessing datasets for bias can help identify and rectify potential issues before training algorithms.

2. **Transparent Algorithm Development:** Developing algorithms transparently fosters accountability. Involving diverse teams in the development process can provide multiple perspectives and reduce the risk of bias. Organizations should:
   - **Document Decision-Making:** Keeping detailed records of algorithm design choices, data sources, and model evaluations enhances transparency and facilitates scrutiny.
   - **Open-Source Models:** Sharing algorithms and models with the community can promote collaboration and collective efforts to identify and address biases.
3. **Bias Detection Tools:** Implementing tools to detect and measure bias in algorithms can help organizations identify issues early in the process. Techniques include:
   - **Fairness Testing:** Employing fairness testing frameworks that analyze model outputs for bias before deployment.
   - **Regular Audits:** Conducting periodic audits of algorithms in production to assess their fairness and effectiveness
4. **Stakeholder Engagement:** Engaging stakeholders, including affected communities, in discussions about algorithmic decision-making is crucial. Organizations should:
   - **Feedback Mechanisms**: Establish channels for stakeholders to provide feedback on algorithmic outcomes and report biases they encounter.
   - **Community Involvement**: Involve community representatives in the design and evaluation of algorithms to ensure their needs and perspectives are considered.
5. **Regulatory Frameworks:** Governments and regulatory bodies can play a role in promoting fairness in algorithms by establishing guidelines and standards. This may include:
   - **Legislation:** Implementing laws that require transparency and fairness in algorithmic decision-making, particularly in high-stakes areas like criminal justice and employment.
   - **Ethical Guidelines:** Developing ethical frameworks that guide organizations in their use of algorithms, emphasizing the importance of fairness and accountability.

Conclusion

Bias in algorithms presents significant ethical challenges that can undermine fairness and perpetuate existing inequalities. As organizations increasingly rely on algorithmic systems for decision-making, it is imperative to prioritize fairness considerations in their design and implementation. By acknowledging the sources of bias, evaluating fairness through appropriate metrics, and employing strategies to mitigate bias, organizations can work towards creating more equitable and just outcomes. Ultimately, fostering a culture of responsibility and accountability in algorithmic decision-making is essential for building trust and ensuring that technology serves the interests of all members of society.

Developing Ethical Guidelines for Analytics

As organizations increasingly rely on data analytics to drive decision-making, establishing ethical guidelines becomes imperative to ensure responsible practices. Ethical analytics can protect individual rights, promote fairness, and foster trust among stakeholders. This article outlines a comprehensive framework for developing ethical guidelines for analytics, covering key principles, implementation strategies, and ongoing evaluation.

Data analytics holds transformative potential for businesses and society, yet it also raises significant ethical concerns. The misuse of data can lead to privacy violations, discrimination, and erosion of trust. Therefore, organizations must proactively address these challenges by formulating clear ethical guidelines that govern their analytics practices.

Key Principles for Ethical Analytics

The key principles for ethical analytics, each designed to promote responsible practices in data usage and decision-making:

1. **Transparency:** Transparency is a cornerstone of ethical analytics, ensuring that stakeholders understand how data is collected, processed, and used.
    - **Clear Communication:** Clearly inform stakeholders about how data is collected, processed, and used.
    - **Algorithmic Explainability:** Ensure that algorithms and models are interpretable, allowing users to understand how decisions are made.
2. **Fairness:** Ensuring fairness in analytics is essential for promoting equity and preventing discrimination.
    - **Bias Mitigation:** Actively identify and reduce bias in datasets and algorithms to ensure equitable treatment across different demographic groups.
    - **Inclusive Practices:** Strive for diversity in data collection to ensure representation of all groups, minimizing the risk of discriminatory outcomes.
3. **Privacy and Data Protection:** Privacy and data protection are critical components of ethical analytics, ensuring that individuals' rights are respected and that sensitive information is handled responsibly.

- **Informed Consent:** Obtain clear consent from individuals regarding the collection and use of their data, ensuring they understand their rights.
- **Data Security:** Implement robust security measures to protect sensitive information from unauthorized access and breaches.

4. **Accountability:** Accountability is a fundamental aspect of ethical analytics, ensuring that organizations take responsibility for their data practices and the outcomes of their analytics efforts.
   - **Defined Roles:** Establish clear lines of responsibility for data practices, ensuring that individuals or teams are accountable for adherence to ethical guidelines.
   - **Redress Mechanisms:** Create processes for individuals to report concerns and seek redress if they believe their rights have been violated.
5. **Social Responsibility**: Social responsibility in analytics emphasizes the obligation of organizations to consider the broader societal implications of their data practices and to contribute positively to the community.
   - **Community Engagement:** Involve stakeholders in discussions about data usage, ensuring that diverse perspectives are considered.
   - **Impact Assessment:** Evaluate the potential societal impacts of analytics initiatives to ensure they align with ethical standards and promote the common good.
6. **Integrity:** Integrity in analytics ensures that organizations conduct their data practices honestly and ethically, fostering trust and accountability.
   - **Honesty in Reporting:** Ensure that analytics results are reported truthfully, without manipulation or selective presentation of data.
   - **Ethical Decision-making:** Encourage ethical considerations in all stages of the analytics process, from data collection to analysis and reporting.
7. **Sustainability:** Sustainability principles in ethical analytics ensure that data practices not only serve immediate organizational goals but also contribute to the long-term health of society and the environment.
   - **Long-term Consideration:** Assess the long-term implications of analytics practices on society and the environment, striving for solutions that promote sustainability.

By adhering to these principles, organizations can foster trust, promote fairness, and ensure that their analytics practices are ethical and responsible.

3. Future of Data Analytics

Data analytics has undergone a significant transformation over the past few years, driven by advancements in technology, the explosion of data generation, and the increasing importance of data-driven decision-making across industries. As we look to the future, several key trends and developments are poised to shape the landscape of data analytics.

1. **Integration of Artificial Intelligence and Machine Learning:** One of the most profound changes in data analytics is the integration of artificial intelligence (AI) and machine learning (ML). These technologies enhance analytical capabilities by enabling more sophisticated data processing, pattern recognition, and predictive modeling.
   - **Automated Insights:** Future analytics platforms will increasingly leverage AI to automate data analysis processes, allowing businesses to extract insights faster and more accurately. Automated systems can identify trends and anomalies in large datasets that would be challenging for human analysts to discern.
   - **Predictive Analytics:** Machine learning algorithms will continue to evolve, providing businesses with powerful tools for predictive analytics. Companies can anticipate customer behavior, optimize inventory management, and improve risk assessment, leading to more informed strategic decisions.
   - **Natural Language Processing (NLP):** The rise of NLP will facilitate more intuitive interactions with data analytics platforms. Users will be able to query data using natural language, making analytics accessible to non-technical users and democratizing data insights across organizations.
2. **Real-time Analytics:** The demand for real-time data insights is growing, driven by the need for immediate decision-making in fast-paced environments.
   - **Streaming Data Analytics:** Future analytics systems will be able to process and analyze streaming data in real-time, allowing businesses to respond swiftly to changing conditions. This capability will be crucial in sectors like finance, e-commerce, and healthcare, where timely insights can significantly impact outcomes.
   - **Enhanced Decision-making:** Real-time analytics will enable organizations to make decisions based on the most current data, improving operational efficiency and customer responsiveness. For example, retailers can adjust pricing and inventory in real-time based on customer demand patterns.
3. **Augmented Analytics:** Augmented analytics refers to the use of AI and ML to enhance data preparation, insight generation, and analysis.
   - **Self-Service Analytics:** The future of analytics will empower business users with self-service capabilities, enabling them to analyze data without relying heavily on IT or data science teams. Augmented analytics tools will simplify complex processes, allowing users to derive insights quickly and easily.
   - **Data Storytelling:** As data visualization techniques advance, augmented analytics will enable users to create compelling narratives around their

data. Enhanced storytelling capabilities will help stakeholders understand insights better and make data-driven decisions more effectively.

4. **Data Governance and Ethics:** As organizations increasingly rely on data analytics, the importance of data governance and ethical considerations will rise.
   - **Regulatory Compliance:** Future data analytics frameworks will need to prioritize compliance with evolving data privacy regulations, such as GDPR and CCPA. Organizations will require robust data governance policies to ensure responsible data handling and protect consumer rights.
   - **Ethical AI:** There will be a growing emphasis on ethical AI practices in analytics. Organizations must ensure that their algorithms are transparent, fair, and unbiased. This includes actively working to eliminate bias in training data and making algorithmic decisions explainable to users.
5. **Data Democratization:** Data democratization refers to the process of making data accessible to a broader range of users within an organization, irrespective of their technical expertise.
   - **User-Friendly Tools:** The development of user-friendly analytics tools will enable non-technical users to interact with data meaningfully. This democratization will foster a culture of data-driven decision-making across organizations, leading to better outcomes.
   - **Collaborative Analytics:** Future analytics will promote collaboration among teams by providing shared platforms for data analysis. Collaborative tools will enable stakeholders to work together, share insights, and make decisions collectively, enhancing organizational agility.
6. **Integration of Internet of Things (IoT) Data:** The proliferation of IoT devices will generate vast amounts of data, significantly influencing data analytics.
   - **IoT Analytics:** Future analytics platforms will increasingly incorporate IoT data, allowing organizations to analyze real-time information from connected devices. This integration will provide valuable insights into operational efficiency, customer behavior, and product performance.
   - **Predictive Maintenance:** In manufacturing and other sectors, analytics will leverage IoT data to predict equipment failures and optimize maintenance schedules. This capability will reduce downtime, save costs, and improve overall productivity.
7. **Cloud-Based Analytics:** The shift toward cloud computing will continue to reshape data analytics.
   - **Scalability and Flexibility:** Cloud-based analytics solutions offer scalability and flexibility, allowing organizations to process and analyze large datasets without investing heavily in on-premises infrastructure. This adaptability will support businesses in responding to changing demands.

- **Collaboration Across Borders:** Cloud technology facilitates collaboration among teams in different geographical locations. Analysts and decision-makers can access data and insights from anywhere, promoting global collaboration and innovation

8. **Data Quality and Integrity:** As the volume of data continues to grow, ensuring data quality and integrity will be paramount.

    - **Data Quality Management:** Future analytics will place a strong emphasis on data quality management practices to ensure accurate and reliable insights. Organizations will invest in technologies that automate data cleansing and validation processes.
    - **Data Provenance:** The ability to trace the origin and history of data will become increasingly important. Understanding data provenance helps organizations ensure data integrity and make informed decisions based on trustworthy information.

9. **Cross-Industry Applications:** The future of data analytics will see cross-industry applications, where insights from one sector can be applied to another.

    - **Knowledge Transfer**: Organizations will leverage analytics to transfer knowledge and best practices across industries. For instance, insights from healthcare analytics could inform practices in retail or finance, leading to innovative solutions and improved outcomes.
    - **Collaborative Innovations:** Partnerships among companies from different sectors will drive collaborative innovations, using data analytics to tackle complex challenges. This interdisciplinary approach can lead to groundbreaking advancements in areas such as smart cities, healthcare, and sustainability.

10. **Focus on User Experience**: The user experience will play a crucial role in the adoption of analytics tools.

    - **Intuitive Interfaces:** Future analytics platforms will prioritize user-friendly interfaces, enabling users to navigate and interact with data effortlessly. Intuitive design will enhance engagement and facilitate better decision-making.
    - **Personalization:** Analytics tools will increasingly incorporate personalization features, providing tailored insights and recommendations based on individual user preferences and behaviors. This customization will improve the overall user experience and drive greater adoption.

Conclusion

The future of data analytics is poised to be dynamic and transformative, driven by technological advancements and an increasing emphasis on ethical considerations. Organizations that embrace these trends such as AI integration, real-time analytics, and data democratization will gain a competitive edge in a data-driven world.

By prioritizing transparency, quality, and social responsibility, businesses can not only enhance their analytics capabilities but also contribute positively to society. As the landscape evolves, organizations must remain agile, adapting to new technologies and ethical challenges while leveraging data to drive innovation and growth. In doing so, they will create value not only for themselves but also for their customers and communities, shaping a sustainable future for data analytics.

Evolving Technologies: Quantum Computing, IoT

Evolving technologies like quantum computing and the Internet of Things (IoT) are reshaping the landscape of innovation and connectivity. Quantum computing harnesses the principles of quantum mechanics to perform complex calculations at unprecedented speeds, utilizing qubits that can represent multiple states simultaneously. This capability opens new frontiers in fields such as cryptography, drug discovery, and optimization problems, despite challenges like error rates and the need for stable systems.

Meanwhile, IoT connects a myriad of devices, allowing them to collect and share data in real time. From smart home gadgets to industrial sensors, IoT enhances operational efficiency and decision-making across various sectors. The integration of edge computing and the expansion of 5G networks further improve IoT performance, enabling faster data processing and reduced latency. Together, quantum computing and IoT can revolutionize data analysis, enhance security, and drive innovation. By leveraging the strengths of both technologies, industries can gain real-time insights from vast datasets and create more secure communication channels, paving the way for a smarter, more interconnected future.

Quantum Computing

Quantum computing leverages the principles of quantum mechanics to process information in fundamentally different ways than classical computers, utilizing quantum bits (qubits) that can exist in multiple states simultaneously due to superposition. This allows quantum computers to perform complex calculations at unprecedented speeds, making them potentially revolutionary for various fields. Key principles like entanglement enable qubits to be interconnected, allowing for enhanced processing capabilities. Current research is focused on overcoming significant challenges, such as decoherence and error rates, to create stable, scalable quantum systems. Prominent algorithms, such as Shor's and Grover's, demonstrate quantum computing's potential to disrupt traditional encryption methods and improve optimization tasks. Applications span industries, including cryptography, drug discovery, and machine learning, promising to transform how we solve complex problems. Additionally, the concept of a quantum internet, which would enable ultra-secure communication, is gaining traction. Despite the promise of quantum computing, technical hurdles and ethical considerations like data privacy remain significant. As research and collaboration between academia, industry, and government intensify, the future of quantum computing holds the potential for groundbreaking advancements, making it an exciting frontier in technology that could redefine our capabilities in computation and beyond.

Basic Principles of Quantum Computing: Quantum computing is grounded in several fundamental principles of quantum mechanics that distinguish it from classical computing. Here are the core concepts:

1. **Qubits:** The basic unit of quantum information is the quantum bit or qubit. Unlike classical bits, which can be either 0 or 1, qubits can exist in a state of 0, 1, or both simultaneously due to superposition. This allows quantum computers to process vast amounts of information concurrently.
2. **Superposition:** Superposition enables a qubit to be in multiple states at once. When a qubit is measured, it collapses to either 0 or 1, but until that point, it can represent both states. This property allows quantum computers to perform complex calculations more efficiently than classical computers.
3. **Entanglement:** Entanglement is a quantum phenomenon where the states of two or more qubits become linked, such that the state of one qubit directly influences the state of another, regardless of the distance between them. This correlation can be harnessed for powerful computations and secure communication.
4. **Quantum Gates:** Quantum gates are the building blocks of quantum circuits, similar to logic gates in classical computing. They manipulate qubits through operations that change their states, enabling the execution of quantum algorithms.
5. **Quantum Interference:** Quantum interference allows certain computational paths to reinforce each other, increasing the probability of desirable outcomes while canceling out less favorable ones. This principle is essential for optimizing quantum algorithms.
6. **Measurement:** The act of measuring a qubit affects its state, collapsing it into one of the possible outcomes. This characteristic is crucial in extracting results from quantum computations.

These principles collectively enable quantum computers to tackle complex problems, such as factoring large numbers and simulating quantum systems, more efficiently than classical computers.

Applications of Quantum Computing: Quantum computing is poised to revolutionize various fields by solving complex problems that classical computers struggle with. By leveraging the principles of quantum mechanics, such as superposition and entanglement, quantum computers can perform calculations at unprecedented speeds. This document explores some of the most promising applications of quantum computing across diverse domains.

1. **Cryptography:** Quantum computing threatens traditional encryption methods by enabling algorithms like Shor's to factor large numbers quickly, potentially

compromising data security. However, it also offers secure communication through Quantum Key Distribution (QKD), which uses quantum mechanics to ensure that intercepted keys can be detected, enhancing data protection.

- **Breaking Classical Encryption:** One of the most significant implications of quantum computing lies in its ability to break traditional cryptographic systems. Shor's algorithm can factor large integers exponentially faster than the best-known classical algorithms, which threatens widely used encryption methods like RSA and ECC (Elliptic Curve Cryptography). This capability necessitates the development of quantum-resistant cryptographic protocols to safeguard sensitive data against potential quantum attacks.
- **Quantum Key Distribution (QKD):** Conversely, quantum computing offers opportunities for enhancing security through Quantum Key Distribution (QKD). QKD uses the principles of quantum mechanics to create secure communication channels that are theoretically immune to eavesdropping. Protocols like BB84 allow two parties to exchange encryption keys with assurance that any attempt at interception can be detected.

2. **Drug Discovery and Pharmaceuticals:** Quantum computing accelerates drug discovery by simulating molecular interactions and chemical reactions more efficiently than classical computers. This capability allows researchers to identify potential drug candidates and optimize their properties, leading to faster development of new therapies and improved outcomes in biomedical research.
   - **Molecular Simulation:** In the pharmaceutical industry, the ability to simulate molecular interactions is critical for drug discovery. Quantum computers can model complex chemical reactions and molecular structures far more efficiently than classical computers. This capability enables researchers to identify potential drug candidates and optimize their properties, significantly accelerating the drug development process.
   - **Protein Folding:** Quantum computing can also contribute to understanding protein folding, a process vital for biochemistry and medicine. Accurately predicting how proteins fold into their functional shapes can lead to breakthroughs in treating diseases and designing new therapies. Quantum simulations can model these processes with greater precision, leading to enhanced biomedical research outcomes.
3. **Optimization Problems:** In industries like logistics and finance, quantum computing can solve complex optimization problems by evaluating numerous solutions simultaneously. This ability enables organizations to improve routes, schedules, and resource allocation, resulting in significant cost savings and increased operational efficiency across various sectors.
   - **Logistics and Supply Chain Management:** Many industries face complex optimization challenges, such as logistics and supply chain management.

Quantum algorithms can evaluate numerous potential solutions simultaneously, allowing companies to find optimal routes and schedules more quickly than classical methods. This capability can lead to significant cost savings and efficiency improvements in transportation and logistics.

- **Financial Modeling:** In finance, quantum computing can enhance portfolio optimization and risk analysis. Quantum algorithms can analyze vast datasets and optimize investment strategies by evaluating multiple scenarios at once. This potential for faster and more accurate financial modeling could lead to improved decision-making in asset management and trading.

4. **Machine Learning and Artificial Intelligence:** Quantum computing enhances machine learning by processing large datasets more efficiently and improving algorithm performance. Quantum algorithms facilitate faster data analysis, pattern recognition, and feature selection, leading to advancements in AI applications like natural language processing and image recognition.

   - **Quantum Machine Learning:** Quantum computing has the potential to transform machine learning by enabling faster data processing and improved algorithm performance. Quantum algorithms can efficiently search through large datasets, enhancing feature selection and pattern recognition. Techniques like quantum support vector machines (QSVMs) and quantum neural networks are being explored to improve AI applications in various fields.

   - **Natural Language Processing:** In natural language processing (NLP), quantum computing can facilitate advanced linguistic analysis and data modeling. By processing large volumes of text data more efficiently, quantum algorithms could enhance tasks such as sentiment analysis, translation, and information retrieval, leading to more sophisticated AI-driven applications.

5. **Climate Modeling and Environmental Science:** Quantum computing improves climate modeling by accurately simulating complex environmental systems and variables. This capability provides better predictions for climate change, helping policymakers make informed decisions about resource management and environmental protection to address global challenges.

   - **Climate Simulation:** Accurate climate modeling is essential for understanding climate change and its effects. Quantum computing can process complex climate models that involve numerous variables and interactions, providing more precise predictions. This capability can help policymakers make informed decisions regarding climate action and resource management.

   - **Energy Optimization:** Quantum computing can optimize energy consumption and improve the efficiency of renewable energy sources. By modeling energy grids and consumption patterns, quantum algorithms can help design more efficient energy systems, reducing waste and enhancing sustainability.

6. **Materials Science:** Quantum computing aids in discovering and understanding new materials by simulating atomic interactions at a quantum level. This ability can lead to breakthroughs in creating materials with tailored properties, impacting industries like electronics, aerospace, and renewable energy technologies.
   - **Discovering New Materials**: In materials science, quantum computing can aid in the discovery of new materials with desirable properties. By simulating atomic and molecular interactions, quantum computers can identify compounds that could lead to breakthroughs in areas like superconductors, catalysts, and nanomaterials.
   - **Understanding Material Properties:** Quantum computing can enhance our understanding of existing materials by accurately modeling their behavior at the quantum level. This understanding can lead to the development of materials with tailored properties, impacting industries such as electronics, aerospace, and construction.
7. **Telecommunications:** Quantum computing enhances telecommunications by enabling quantum networks that leverage entanglement for secure data transmission. Additionally, it optimizes signal processing, improving data rates and reducing latency, which benefits mobile networks and overall internet infrastructure performance.
   - **Quantum Networks:** Quantum computing can improve telecommunications by enabling quantum networks that leverage quantum entanglement for secure data transmission. These networks can facilitate ultra-secure communication methods, significantly enhancing data privacy and security.
   - **Signal Processing:** In telecommunications, quantum algorithms can optimize signal processing, improving data transmission rates and reducing latency. This enhancement can lead to better performance in mobile networks and internet infrastructure.
8. **Financial Services:** In financial services, quantum computing enhances risk assessment and fraud detection. By processing vast datasets and simulating market scenarios, it improves understanding of risks and helps institutions identify fraudulent activities, leading to better investment strategies and more secure transactions.
   - **Risk Assessment:** Quantum computing can revolutionize risk assessment in financial services by processing vast datasets and simulating various market scenarios. This capability can help financial institutions better understand risks and optimize their investment strategies.

- **Fraud Detection:** By leveraging quantum machine learning algorithms, financial institutions can enhance their fraud detection systems. Quantum computing can analyze patterns in transaction data more effectively, identifying anomalies and preventing fraudulent activities.

9. **National Security:** Quantum computing impacts national security through applications in defense and cybersecurity. It can optimize resource allocation and intelligence analysis while also developing advanced encryption methods that utilize quantum principles, ensuring secure communication and protecting sensitive data from potential threats.
   - **Defense Applications:** Quantum computing can significantly impact national security through its applications in defense. For example, it can optimize strategies for resource allocation, improve encryption methods for secure communications, and enhance intelligence analysis.
   - **Cybersecurity:** The potential to break existing encryption standards poses a threat to national security. However, quantum technologies can also develop advanced cybersecurity measures that utilize quantum principles to create secure communication channels, ensuring data integrity.

Features of Quantum Computing: Quantum computing represents a revolutionary approach to computation that leverages the principles of quantum mechanics. Here are the key features that distinguish quantum computing from classical computing:

1. **Qubits:** The fundamental unit of quantum information is the quantum bit, or qubit. Unlike classical bits that can only be in one of two states (0 or 1), qubits can exist in a superposition of states. This means a qubit can be both 0 and 1 simultaneously, allowing quantum computers to process a vast amount of information at once.
2. **Superposition:** Superposition enables qubits to perform multiple calculations simultaneously. When a quantum algorithm runs, qubits can represent numerous combinations of 0s and 1s at the same time. This property drastically increases computational power, especially for problems where many potential solutions must be evaluated.
3. **Entanglement:** Entanglement is a unique quantum phenomenon where qubits become interconnected such that the state of one qubit is dependent on the state of another, no matter how far apart they are. This correlation allows for the transmission of information with remarkable speed and efficiency, significantly enhancing computational capabilities and enabling complex problem-solving.
4. **Quantum Interference:** Quantum algorithms use interference to amplify the probability of correct outcomes and diminish the probability of incorrect ones. By cleverly orchestrating the phases of qubit states, quantum computers can

navigate the solution space of problems more efficiently than classical computers, leading to faster solution times for specific tasks.

5. **Quantum Gates:** Quantum gates are the building blocks of quantum circuits, analogous to classical logic gates. These gates manipulate qubits through quantum operations, transforming their states and enabling complex computations. Common quantum gates include the Hadamard gate, which creates superposition, and the CNOT gate, which introduces entanglement.
6. **Parallelism:** Due to superposition and entanglement, quantum computers can evaluate many potential solutions simultaneously. This parallelism allows them to tackle specific types of problems, such as optimization and factorization, far more efficiently than classical computers.
7. **Decoherence and Error Correction:** Quantum states are delicate and can be easily disrupted by environmental factors, leading to a phenomenon known as decoherence. To maintain reliable computation, quantum error correction techniques are vital. These methods detect and correct errors that occur during computation, ensuring that quantum systems can operate effectively.
8. **Quantum Algorithms:** Certain algorithms, like Shor's algorithm for factoring large integers and Grover's algorithm for searching unsorted databases, demonstrate quantum computing's potential advantages. Shor's algorithm, for example, can factor numbers exponentially faster than the best-known classical algorithms, which has profound implications for cryptography.
9. **Applications:** The potential applications of quantum computing are vast. Industries such as pharmaceuticals can utilize quantum simulations for drug discovery, while finance can employ quantum algorithms for risk analysis and optimization. Quantum computing also holds promise for machine learning and complex systems modeling, pushing the boundaries of what is computationally feasible.
10. **Hybrid Systems:** Researchers are increasingly exploring hybrid systems that combine classical and quantum computing. This integration leverages the strengths of both paradigms, enabling more practical solutions for a range of applications while waiting for fully scalable quantum systems to mature.

Conclusion

In summary, quantum computing is characterized by its use of qubits, superposition, entanglement, and quantum gates, among other features. Its unique properties enable unprecedented computational power, opening new frontiers in various fields and offering solutions to problems that are currently intractable for classical computers. As research progresses, the practical implications of quantum computing are poised to transform technology and society.

Internet of Things (IoT)

The Internet of Things (IoT) refers to the network of interconnected devices that communicate and exchange data over the internet, enhancing automation and efficiency across various sectors. IoT devices—ranging from smart home appliances to industrial sensors collect and share real-time data, enabling users to monitor and control their environments remotely. This connectivity fosters improved decision-making through data analytics, as insights derived from aggregated information can lead to optimized processes, energy savings, and predictive maintenance. In smart cities, IoT applications enhance urban management by improving traffic flow, waste management, and public safety. In healthcare, IoT devices enable remote patient monitoring and personalized treatment, improving patient outcomes. However, the proliferation of IoT also raises concerns about security and privacy, as increased connectivity can expose devices to cyber threats. As technology advances, the integration of artificial intelligence and machine learning with IoT is expected to drive further innovation, enabling smarter automation and enhanced user experiences. Overall, IoT has the potential to transform industries, improve quality of life, and create new business models, making it a pivotal element of the digital landscape.

IoT Architecture: Internet of things is based on four simple building blocks also called IoT architecture layers as shown in fig.5.3.

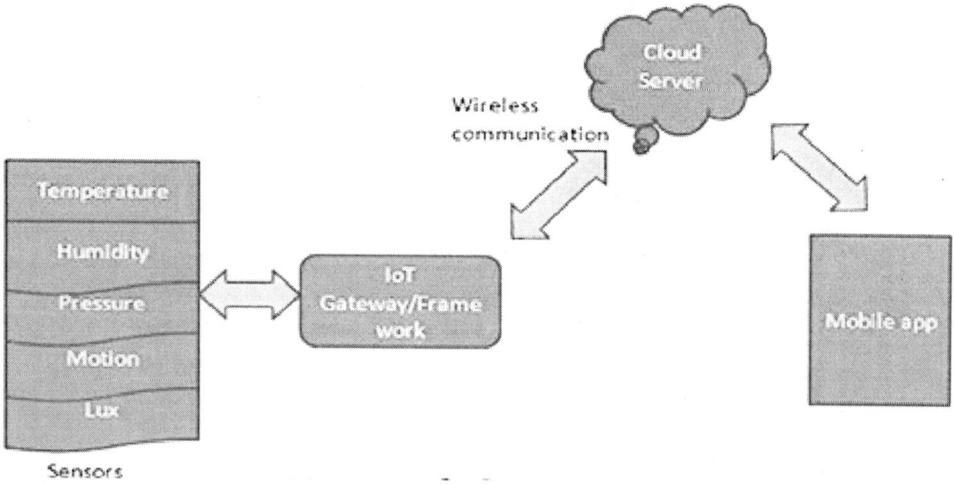

Fig.5.3

1. **Sensors:** Sensors are everywhere, sensors sense data from the atmosphere or place. The example, temperature sensor senses temperature from the room and shares it through IoT gateway.

   Sensors will sniff a wide variety of information ranging from Location, Weather/Environment conditions, running machine, from the human body, engine maintenance data to health essentials of a vehicle.

2. **IoT Gateways & Frameworks:** As the name rightly explains, it is a gateway to the internet for all the things/devices that we want to interact with. Gateways

act as a carrier between the internal network of sensor nodes with the external Internet or World Wide Web.

3. **Cloud server:** The data transmitted through the gateway is stored & processed securely within the cloud server i.e. in data centres. This processed data is then used to perform intelligent actions that make all our devices Smart Devices. In the cloud, all analytics and decision making happen considering user comfort.
4. **Mobile applications:** The intuitive mobile apps will help end-users to control & monitor their devices (ranging from the room thermostat to vehicle engines) from remote locations.

These apps push important information from the cloud on your smartphones, tablets. After analytics, Information is in the form of graphs, bars and in pi-diagram and display to the user in a user-friendly manner. From mobile application, we can send a command to sensors to change default values, like changing default temperature of air conditioner and many more.

Application of IoT: The Internet of Things (IoT) has rapidly transformed various sectors by connecting devices and enabling them to collect, share, and analyze data. This technological advancement enhances efficiency, improves decision-making, and creates new opportunities across diverse applications. Here's an in-depth look at the key applications of IoT across different domains as:

1. **Smart Homes:** IoT has significantly impacted residential life, leading to the emergence of smart homes. Devices such as smart thermostats, lights, and security systems can be controlled remotely through smartphones or voice-activated assistants. For example, smart thermostats like Nest learn user preferences and adjust heating or cooling automatically, resulting in energy savings. Smart locks and security cameras enhance home security by allowing homeowners to monitor their property in real-time and receive alerts on suspicious activities. IoT has revolutionized home automation, providing convenience, security, and energy efficiency. Key applications include:
   - **Smart Lighting and Appliances:** IoT technology allows homeowners to control lighting and appliances remotely. Smart bulbs can be programmed to adjust brightness or color based on the time of day, while smart plugs enable users to turn devices on or off from their smartphones.
   - **Home Security:** IoT-enabled security cameras and smart locks provide real-time monitoring and control. Users can receive alerts for unusual activities and manage access to their homes remotely, enhancing security.
   - **Climate Control:** Smart thermostats, such as Nest, learn user preferences and adjust heating and cooling automatically. This not only enhances comfort but also leads to significant energy savings.
2. **Healthcare:** IoT is revolutionizing healthcare through remote monitoring and

telemedicine. Connected devices, such as blood pressure monitors and glucose meters, allow patients to track their health metrics from home. Data is transmitted to healthcare providers, enabling real-time monitoring and reducing the need for frequent in-person visits. This is particularly beneficial for chronic disease management, where continuous data helps tailor treatment plans. In healthcare, IoT enhances patient care, monitoring, and operational efficiency. Notable applications include:

- **Remote Patient Monitoring:** IoT devices enable continuous monitoring of patients' health metrics, such as heart rate and glucose levels. Data collected is transmitted to healthcare providers, facilitating timely interventions and personalized care.
- **Wearable Devices:** Fitness trackers and smartwatches collect data on physical activity, sleep patterns, and vital signs, promoting healthier lifestyles and allowing users to track their health over time.
- **Telemedicine:** IoT technology supports remote consultations and diagnostics, enabling patients to receive care without needing to visit healthcare facilities.

3. **Smart Cities:** IoT plays a crucial role in the development of smart cities, enhancing urban management and improving the quality of life for residents. Applications include smart traffic management systems that analyze real-time traffic data to optimize signal timings, reducing congestion and emissions. IoT-enabled waste management systems utilize sensors in bins to monitor fill levels, optimizing collection routes and schedules. Additionally, smart street lighting adjusts brightness based on the presence of pedestrians, conserving energy. IoT applications in smart cities aim to improve urban living through enhanced efficiency and sustainability. Key areas include:
   - **Traffic Management:** IoT sensors installed in roads and traffic signals help optimize traffic flow by collecting real-time data on vehicle movement. This data can be used to adjust signal timings and reduce congestion.
   - **Waste Management:** Smart bins equipped with sensors can monitor fill levels and notify waste management services when they need to be emptied, optimizing collection routes and reducing operational costs.
   - **Public Safety:** IoT technology enhances public safety through smart surveillance systems that monitor public spaces and provide data analytics to law enforcement agencies.
4. **Industrial IoT (IIoT):** In manufacturing and industrial settings, IoT applications enhance operational efficiency and safety. IIoT involves connecting machines, sensors, and systems to collect data and improve processes. Predictive maintenance is a key application; by monitoring equipment conditions in real-time, companies can anticipate failures and perform maintenance before breakdowns occur, reducing downtime and costs.

Additionally, IoT-enabled supply chain management provides real-time visibility into inventory levels and logistics, optimizing the flow of goods. In industrial settings, IoT enhances productivity, safety, and operational efficiency. Key applications include:

- **Predictive Maintenance**: In manufacturing, IoT sensors monitor machinery performance and conditions. By analyzing this data, companies can predict when equipment is likely to fail and perform maintenance proactively, reducing downtime.
- **Supply Chain Optimization:** IoT enables real-time tracking of goods throughout the supply chain. This visibility helps companies manage inventory, optimize logistics, and improve overall efficiency.
- **Quality Control:** IoT devices can monitor product quality during the manufacturing process, ensuring that any defects are detected early and corrective actions are taken.

5. **Agriculture:** IoT applications in agriculture, often referred to as smart farming, have transformed traditional farming practices. Sensors placed in fields can monitor soil moisture, temperature, and nutrient levels, allowing farmers to make informed decisions about irrigation and fertilization. Drones equipped with IoT technology can survey crops and provide real-time data on plant health, enabling precise interventions and increasing yields. This data-driven approach enhances efficiency and sustainability in food production. IoT applications in agriculture focus on improving yield, sustainability, and resource management. Notable examples include:
   - **Precision Farming:** IoT sensors monitor soil moisture, temperature, and nutrient levels, allowing farmers to make data-driven decisions about irrigation and fertilization. This approach enhances crop yields and reduces resource wastage.
   - **Livestock Monitoring:** IoT devices can track the health and location of livestock, providing farmers with insights into animal behavior and well-being, thus improving productivity and reducing losses.
   - **Weather Monitoring:** IoT technology enables farmers to receive real-time weather updates, helping them make timely decisions regarding planting and harvesting.
6. **Transportation and Logistics:** IoT significantly impacts the transportation and logistics sectors by enhancing fleet management and improving safety. Connected vehicles can share data about their location, speed, and performance, allowing companies to optimize routes and reduce fuel consumption. Real-time tracking of shipments ensures transparency and accountability throughout the supply chain. In addition, IoT technology facilitates predictive maintenance in transportation fleets, enhancing safety

and reliability. IoT enhances efficiency and safety in transportation and logistics through various applications:

- **Fleet Management:** IoT devices installed in vehicles provide real-time tracking and diagnostics. Companies can monitor vehicle performance, optimize routes, and reduce fuel consumption.
- **Connected Vehicles:** Vehicles equipped with IoT technology can communicate with each other and with infrastructure, enhancing safety through features like collision avoidance and adaptive traffic signals.
- **Smart Parking:** IoT-enabled parking systems can guide drivers to available parking spaces, reducing congestion and improving urban mobility.

7. **Energy Management:** IoT applications in energy management contribute to more sustainable practices. Smart grids use IoT devices to monitor energy consumption and optimize distribution. Consumers can access real-time data about their energy usage through smart meters, allowing them to adjust consumption patterns and reduce costs. Additionally, IoT-enabled renewable energy systems, such as solar panels, can optimize energy production and consumption based on weather conditions and usage patterns. IoT applications in energy management promote efficiency and sustainability. Key areas include:

   - **Smart Grids:** IoT technology is integral to the development of smart grids, which optimize energy distribution based on real-time demand and supply data.
   - **Home Energy Management:** Smart meters provide homeowners with real-time insights into their energy consumption, enabling them to make informed decisions to reduce costs and improve efficiency.
   - **Renewable Energy Integration:** IoT devices help monitor and manage renewable energy sources, such as solar panels, ensuring optimal energy production and consumption.
   - **Demand Response Programs:** IoT allows utilities to manage energy demand during peak times by incentivizing consumers to reduce usage, balancing the load on the grid.

8. **Environmental Monitoring:** IoT technology is increasingly used for environmental monitoring and conservation efforts. Sensors can collect data on air and water quality, enabling authorities to respond promptly to pollution or contamination events. IoT-enabled wildlife tracking devices help researchers monitor animal movements and behaviors, aiding conservation efforts. Furthermore, smart irrigation systems can optimize water usage in agriculture, contributing to sustainable practices. IoT applications play a vital role in environmental protection and management. Key examples include:

   - **Pollution Monitoring:** IoT sensors can monitor air and water quality, providing valuable data for environmental protection and regulatory compliance.

- **Wildlife Conservation:** IoT technology supports wildlife tracking and monitoring, aiding conservation efforts by providing insights into animal movements and habitats.
- **Climate Change Research:** IoT devices collect data on weather patterns, enabling researchers to study climate change effects and develop mitigation strategies.

Conclusion

The applications of IoT span a wide range of sectors, each benefiting from enhanced connectivity and data-driven insights. As IoT technology continues to evolve, its integration into everyday life is expected to deepen, offering unprecedented opportunities for innovation and improvement. However, it is essential to address challenges such as security, privacy, and interoperability to maximize the benefits of IoT while ensuring a safe and reliable digital ecosystem. With continued advancements, IoT is poised to play a pivotal role in shaping the future of technology, economy, and society.

Differences Between Quantum Computing and IoT

Table 5.3

S.No.	Aspect	Quantum Computing	Internet of Things
1.	Nature of Technology	Leverages principles of quantum mechanics to process information.	Connects physical devices to the internet for data exchange and control.
2.	Purpose	Solving complex computational problems and simulations.	Enhancing automation, monitoring, and data collection in real-time.
3.	Data Processing	Operates on qubits, enabling parallel processing of multiple states.	Utilizes traditional binary data for processing and communication.
4.	Scalability	Currently in early stages, limited by hardware and error rates.	Highly scalable, with millions of devices already connected.
5.	Applications	Cryptography, drug discovery, optimization problems, and materials science.	Smart homes, industrial automation, healthcare monitoring, and smart cities.
6.	User Base	Primarily researchers and organizations in specialized fields.	Consumers, businesses, and municipalities across various sectors.

Predicting Trends in Data Analytics

Data analytics has become a cornerstone of modern decision-making across industries. As businesses and organizations increasingly rely on data to drive strategies, understanding the evolving trends in data analytics is crucial. This article explores the anticipated trends that will shape the landscape of data analytics in the coming years.

1. **Increased Adoption of Artificial Intelligence and Machine Learning:** One of the most significant trends in data analytics is the growing integration of artificial intelligence (AI) and machine learning (ML) technologies. As organizations generate massive amounts of data, traditional analytics methods are becoming insufficient. AI and ML enable more sophisticated analysis, uncovering patterns and insights that would be difficult to detect manually.
    - **Predictive Analytics:** AI-driven predictive models can forecast future trends based on historical data. For example, in retail, predictive analytics can help companies optimize inventory management by predicting customer demand.
    - **Natural Language Processing (NLP):** NLP allows organizations to analyze unstructured data, such as social media posts and customer reviews, enhancing sentiment analysis and market research.
2. **Rise of Self-Service Analytics:** The democratization of data analytics is another critical trend. Self-service analytics tools empower non-technical users to explore and analyze data without relying heavily on IT or data science teams.
    - **User-friendly Interfaces:** Modern analytics platforms offer intuitive dashboards and visualizations, making it easier for users to access and interpret data.
    - **Citizen Data Scientists:** As self-service analytics becomes more accessible, business users often referred to as "citizen data scientists" will emerge, driving insights within their departments without needing deep analytical skills.
3. **Real-time Analytics:** The demand for real-time data insights is on the rise. Organizations are increasingly recognizing the value of immediate data analysis for operational efficiency and strategic decision-making.
    - **Streaming Data:** With the advent of IoT and connected devices, data is generated continuously. Real-time analytics allows businesses to process this data instantly, enabling timely responses to changing conditions.
    - **Use Cases:** Real-time analytics can be pivotal in various sectors, such as finance for fraud detection, healthcare for patient monitoring, and e-commerce for personalized customer experiences.
4. **Data Privacy and Ethical Considerations:** As data analytics becomes more prevalent, concerns regarding data privacy and ethics are gaining prominence. Regulations like GDPR and CCPA emphasize the need for responsible data handling practices.
    - **Data Governance:** Organizations will need to invest in robust data governance frameworks to ensure compliance with legal standards and protect customer data.
    - **Ethical AI:** The ethical implications of AI and analytics will become a focal

point, leading to increased scrutiny of algorithmic bias and the need for transparency in data usage.

5. **Integration of Advanced Analytics with Business Intelligence (BI):** The convergence of advanced analytics and traditional BI tools will be a defining trend. While BI focuses on descriptive analytics, advanced analytics leverages complex techniques to gain deeper insights.
   - **Holistic Data Strategies:** Organizations will seek integrated platforms that combine BI capabilities with advanced analytics, enabling comprehensive data-driven decision-making.
   - **Predictive and Prescriptive Analytics:** This integration allows businesses to not only understand past performance (descriptive) but also predict future outcomes (predictive) and recommend actions (prescriptive).
6. **Data Visualization and Storytelling:** Effective data visualization and storytelling will continue to play a vital role in data analytics. As the volume of data increases, the ability to present insights clearly and compellingly becomes essential.
   - **Interactive Dashboards:** Advanced visualization tools allow users to create interactive dashboards that facilitate exploration and engagement with data.
   - **Data Storytelling:** Combining data visualization with narrative techniques helps communicate insights more effectively, making it easier for stakeholders to understand the implications of the data.
7. **Emphasis on Data Quality and Integrity:** As reliance on data grows, ensuring data quality and integrity will become paramount. Poor data quality can lead to incorrect insights and decision-making.
   - **Data Cleaning and Validation:** Organizations will invest in data cleaning processes and validation techniques to ensure the accuracy and reliability of their datasets.
   - **Data Lineage:** Understanding the data lineage where data comes from and how it transforms will help organizations maintain data integrity and trustworthiness.
8. **Edge Analytics:** With the rise of IoT devices and the increasing volume of data generated at the edge, edge analytics is emerging as a critical trend. Edge analytics involves processing data near the source of generation rather than relying solely on centralized data centers.
   - **Reduced Latency:** By analyzing data at the edge, organizations can reduce latency, enabling faster decision-making and response times.
   - **Bandwidth Optimization:** Edge analytics minimizes the need to transfer large volumes of data to centralized systems, optimizing bandwidth and reducing costs.

9. **Cloud-based Analytics Solutions:** The shift to cloud-based analytics solutions will continue to accelerate. Cloud platforms offer scalability, flexibility, and cost-effectiveness, making them ideal for organizations of all sizes.
   - **Scalability:** Cloud solutions allow businesses to scale their analytics capabilities according to demand, accommodating fluctuating data volumes.
   - **Collaboration:** Cloud-based analytics fosters collaboration across teams and departments, enabling seamless sharing of insights and promoting a data-driven culture.
10. **Augmented Analytics:** Augmented analytics, which leverages AI and ML to automate data preparation, insight generation, and data visualization, is set to transform the analytics landscape.
    - **Automation:** By automating routine tasks, augmented analytics frees up data professionals to focus on more strategic activities, enhancing productivity.
    - **Enhanced Decision-making:** Augmented analytics tools can generate insights based on user queries, making data analysis more accessible and efficient for business users.
11. **Data Democratization:** As organizations recognize the value of data-driven decision-making, data democratization will become increasingly important. This trend focuses on making data accessible to all employees, regardless of their technical skills.
    - **Training and Education:** Organizations will invest in training programs to help employees develop data literacy skills, empowering them to leverage data for decision-making.
    - **Collaborative Data Platforms:** Platforms that facilitate collaboration and knowledge sharing among teams will support data democratization efforts, fostering a culture of data-driven innovation.
12. **Collaborative Analytics:** The growing complexity of data environments necessitates collaborative analytics, where teams from different departments work together to analyze and interpret data.
    - **Cross-Functional Teams:** Organizations will establish cross-functional teams that bring together data scientists, business analysts, and domain experts to drive collaborative insights.
    - **Integrated Tools:** Collaborative analytics tools that enable seamless sharing and communication of insights will become essential for driving data-driven initiatives.

Conclusion

The landscape of data analytics is rapidly evolving, driven by technological advancements and changing business needs. As organizations increasingly rely on data to inform their strategies, staying abreast of these trends is essential for leveraging analytics effectively.

From the integration of AI and machine learning to the emphasis on data quality and privacy, the future of data analytics holds immense potential. By embracing these trends, organizations can unlock valuable insights, enhance decision-making, and foster a culture of data-driven innovation.

As we move forward, it is clear that data analytics will continue to be a key driver of success in an increasingly competitive landscape, shaping the way businesses operate and interact with their customers. Embracing these trends will empower organizations to harness the full potential of their data, leading to better outcomes and sustainable growth.

Preparing for the Future: Skills and Competencies

In an increasingly complex and fast-paced world, the skills and competencies required for success are evolving rapidly. As technological advancements reshape industries, and global challenges demand innovative solutions, individuals must equip themselves with a diverse set of skills to thrive in the future workforce. This article explores the essential skills and competencies needed to navigate the challenges ahead and prepare for the future.

1. **Technical Skills:** As technology continues to dominate various sectors, technical skills will be fundamental for many careers.
    - **Data Literacy:** In a data-driven world, the ability to read, interpret, and analyze data is crucial. Professionals must understand data sources, data visualization techniques, and statistical methods to make informed decisions. Data literacy empowers individuals to leverage insights from data analytics, fostering a culture of evidence-based decision-making.
    - **Programming and Software Development:** With the rise of automation and artificial intelligence, programming skills are increasingly valuable. Understanding programming languages such as Python, Java, or R enables individuals to create software solutions, automate tasks, and analyze data effectively.
    - **Cybersecurity Knowledge:** As digital threats grow, knowledge of cybersecurity practices is essential. Understanding how to protect data, recognize potential threats, and implement security measures will be vital across all sectors, particularly in finance, healthcare, and technology.
2. **Soft Skills:** While technical skills are important, soft skills are equally critical for long-term success.
    - **Adaptability and Flexibility:** The ability to adapt to change and remain flexible in the face of uncertainty is crucial. Industries are evolving rapidly, and workers must be open to learning new skills and adjusting to new

roles and technologies. Cultivating a growth mindset fosters resilience and encourages individuals to embrace change.

- **Communication Skills:** Effective communication is vital in any profession. Individuals must articulate their ideas clearly, collaborate with diverse teams, and convey information in a way that resonates with various audiences. Proficiency in both verbal and written communication enhances teamwork and drives engagement.
- **Emotional Intelligence:** Emotional intelligence (EI) refers to the ability to recognize and manage one's own emotions, as well as the emotions of others. High EI fosters better interpersonal relationships, enhances teamwork, and improves conflict resolution. It's a key competency in leadership roles, where understanding team dynamics is essential.

3. **Critical Thinking and Problem Solving:** In a world filled with complexity, the ability to think critically and solve problems creatively is paramount.
   - **Analytical Thinking:** Analytical thinking involves breaking down complex problems into manageable parts and evaluating the information critically. This skill enables individuals to identify patterns, make connections, and derive meaningful insights from data. Strong analytical skills are essential in decision-making processes across various fields.
   - **Creative Problem Solving:** Innovation often stems from creative problem-solving. Individuals must cultivate the ability to think outside the box and generate novel solutions to challenges. This skill encourages experimentation and embraces failure as a stepping stone to success.
4. **Collaboration and Teamwork:** As workplaces become more interconnected, collaboration skills are increasingly valuable.
   - **Interpersonal Skills:** Strong interpersonal skills foster effective collaboration within teams. The ability to build rapport, actively listen, and respect diverse perspectives enhances group dynamics and leads to better outcomes. Professionals should seek opportunities to engage with others, understand different viewpoints, and work towards common goals.
   - **Cultural Competence:** In a globalized world, cultural competence the ability to interact effectively with people from different backgrounds is essential. Understanding cultural differences and embracing diversity fosters inclusive environments, enhances creativity, and drives innovation.
5. **Lifelong Learning and Continuous Improvement:** The pace of change demands a commitment to lifelong learning.
   - **Self-directed Learning:** Individuals must take initiative in their learning journey. Self-directed learning involves identifying knowledge gaps, seeking resources, and pursuing opportunities for growth. Online courses,

workshops, and industry certifications are valuable tools for skill enhancement.

- **Networking and Knowledge Sharing:** Building a professional network is crucial for career development. Engaging with peers, mentors, and industry leaders provides access to valuable insights, resources, and opportunities. Knowledge sharing fosters collaboration and drives collective growth.

6. **Digital Literacy:** As digital technology permeates every aspect of life, digital literacy becomes essential.
   - **Understanding Digital Tools:** Familiarity with various digital tools and platforms enhances productivity and collaboration. Professionals should be proficient in using tools for project management, communication, and data analysis.
   - **Social Media and Online Presence:** An understanding of social media dynamics and online branding is vital in today's connected world. Individuals should cultivate a professional online presence that reflects their skills and values, enabling them to connect with potential employers and collaborators.
7. **Global Awareness and Sustainability:** In an interconnected world, awareness of global issues and sustainability is increasingly important.
   - **Global Perspective:** Understanding global trends, economic factors, and geopolitical dynamics enhances decision-making in a globalized economy. Professionals should stay informed about international developments and consider their implications for local and global contexts.
   - **Sustainability Practices:** As organizations prioritize sustainability, knowledge of sustainable practices and environmental stewardship will be essential. Professionals should understand the impact of their work on the environment and seek to implement sustainable solutions within their organizations.
8. **Innovation and Entrepreneurship:** The ability to innovate and think entrepreneurially is crucial in today's dynamic landscape.
   - **Entrepreneurial Mindset:** Cultivating an entrepreneurial mindset involves embracing risk-taking, creativity, and resilience. Professionals should be open to exploring new ideas, challenging the status quo, and identifying opportunities for growth and improvement.
   - **Innovation Management:** Understanding how to manage innovation processes is essential for driving change within organizations. This includes fostering a culture of innovation, encouraging collaboration, and implementing strategies to bring new ideas to fruition.

Conclusion

Preparing for the future requires a multifaceted approach to skill development.

As technology continues to evolve and global challenges intensify, individuals must equip themselves with a diverse set of skills and competencies. Technical skills, soft skills, critical thinking, collaboration, and a commitment to lifelong learning will be essential for navigating the complexities of the modern workforce.

By embracing these skills and competencies, individuals can position themselves for success in an ever-changing landscape. Organizations, too, play a vital role in fostering a culture of continuous learning and development, ensuring that their workforce is equipped to meet the demands of the future. Ultimately, the key to thriving in the future lies in adaptability, resilience, and a proactive approach to skill enhancement.

CASE STUDIES OF FUTURE TRENDS AND CHALLENGES

Case Study 1: Healthcare Transformation through Telemedicine

Overview

The healthcare sector has experienced a significant transformation in recent years, particularly accelerated by the COVID-19 pandemic. Telemedicine emerged as a critical solution, reshaping how healthcare services are delivered and consumed. This case study explores the future trends and challenges in telemedicine and digital health.

Future Trends

1. Widespread Adoption of Telehealth Services: Telemedicine has become more mainstream, with a marked increase in both provider and patient adoption. A report from McKinsey & Company indicates that telehealth usage stabilized at levels 38 times higher than pre-pandemic rates.
    - **Patient Preference:** Patients favor telehealth for convenience and reduced travel times, leading to a more patient-centered approach to care.
    - **Policy Changes:** Governments and insurers are revising regulations to support telehealth reimbursement, facilitating broader access.
2. **Integration of Artificial Intelligence:** AI is poised to play a transformative role in telemedicine by enhancing diagnostic accuracy and operational efficiency.
    - **Chatbots and Virtual Assistants:** These tools can manage patient inquiries, schedule appointments, and even conduct preliminary assessments, allowing healthcare providers to focus on more complex tasks.
    - **Predictive Analytics:** AI algorithms can analyze patient data to predict outcomes and recommend personalized treatment plans, thereby improving care quality.
3. **Wearable Health Technology:** Wearables are becoming integral to telemedicine, allowing for continuous monitoring of health metrics such as heart rate, glucose levels, and physical activity.

- **Remote Patient Monitoring:** Devices that monitor chronic conditions can alert healthcare providers to potential issues before they escalate, facilitating timely interventions.
- **Data-driven Insights:** Wearable data can enhance telehealth consultations, providing clinicians with real-time health information during virtual visits.

4. **Expanded Access to Specialists:** Telemedicine allows patients in remote areas to access specialized care that may not be available locally.
   - **Cross-state Licensure:** Initiatives to streamline licensing for telehealth providers will facilitate interstate consultations, increasing access to specialized services.
   - **Teleconsultations:** Virtual specialist consultations will become standard practice, improving patient outcomes and reducing referral delays.

Challenges

1. **Data Privacy and Security Concerns:** As telemedicine grows, so do concerns about data privacy and cybersecurity.
   - **Regulatory Compliance:** Organizations must navigate complex regulations like HIPAA to ensure patient data is protected, increasing administrative burdens.
   - **Cyber Threats:** The rise in cyberattacks on healthcare systems poses risks to patient confidentiality and system integrity.
2. **Digital Divide:** Not all populations have equal access to telemedicine, leading to disparities in healthcare.
   - **Access to Technology:** Individuals without reliable internet or smartphones are at risk of being excluded from telehealth services, particularly in rural areas.
   - **Health Literacy:** Patients must possess a certain level of digital literacy to utilize telehealth effectively, which can be a barrier for older adults or marginalized communities.
3. **Integration with Traditional Care Models:** Integrating telemedicine into existing healthcare systems can be challenging.
   - **Operational Complexities:** Healthcare providers may face difficulties in merging telehealth with traditional in-person care models, leading to inefficiencies.
   - **Training and Adoption:** Clinicians need training to adapt to telemedicine technologies and workflows, which can be time-consuming and costly.
4. **Insurance and Reimbursement Issues:** While policy changes are favorable, reimbursement for telehealth services remains inconsistent.

- **Insurance Coverage:** Not all insurers cover telehealth visits equally, which can lead to confusion for patients regarding out-of-pocket costs.
- **Reimbursement Rates:** Variability in reimbursement rates for telehealth services compared to in-person visits may discourage providers from fully embracing telemedicine.

Conclusion

Telemedicine is poised to reshape the future of healthcare, offering increased access and improved patient outcomes. However, challenges related to data privacy, the digital divide, integration with traditional care models, and reimbursement must be addressed to realize its full potential. As the landscape continues to evolve, a collaborative approach involving stakeholders, policymakers, and healthcare providers will be essential for overcoming these hurdles.

Case Study 2: Retail Evolution in the Age of E-Commerce

Overview

The retail industry is undergoing a dramatic transformation as e-commerce gains prominence. The pandemic accelerated shifts in consumer behavior, forcing retailers to adapt to an increasingly digital marketplace. This case study explores the future trends and challenges facing the retail sector as it embraces e-commerce and omnichannel strategies.

Future Trends

1. **Growth of E-Commerce:** E-commerce has witnessed unprecedented growth, with estimates indicating that online sales will continue to rise significantly.
   - **Mobile Commerce:** The increasing use of smartphones for shopping will drive the need for mobile-optimized websites and apps.
   - **Subscription Models:** Retailers are adopting subscription-based services to foster customer loyalty and create steady revenue streams.
2. **Omnichannel Retailing:** Consumers expect a seamless shopping experience across multiple channels, leading to the rise of omnichannel retailing.
   - **Integrated Experiences:** Retailers are focusing on creating cohesive experiences that allow customers to transition between online and offline environments effortlessly.
   - **Click-and-Collect Services:** The popularity of buying online and picking up in-store is growing, combining the convenience of e-commerce with the immediacy of physical stores.
3. **Personalization through Data Analytics:** Retailers are leveraging data analytics to offer personalized shopping experiences, enhancing customer engagement.

- **Targeted Marketing:** AI algorithms analyze consumer behavior to deliver personalized recommendations and marketing messages.
- **Customer Segmentation:** Retailers are employing advanced segmentation techniques to tailor offers and promotions to specific customer groups.

4. **Sustainability and Ethical Practices:** As consumers become more environmentally conscious, sustainability is increasingly influencing retail strategies.
    - **Eco-friendly Products:** Retailers are expanding their offerings of sustainable products, appealing to environmentally aware consumers.
    - **Transparent Supply Chains:** Brands are emphasizing transparency in their supply chains, providing consumers with information about sourcing and production practices.

Challenges

1. **Supply Chain Disruptions:** The pandemic exposed vulnerabilities in global supply chains, affecting inventory management and fulfilment.
    - **Inventory Shortages:** Retailers faced significant challenges in maintaining adequate stock levels, leading to lost sales and dissatisfied customers.
    - **Logistics Complexity:** Increased demand for e-commerce has put pressure on logistics networks, necessitating investments in infrastructure and technology.
2. **Increased Competition:** The low barrier to entry in e-commerce has intensified competition, with traditional retailers competing against agile startups and direct-to-consumer brands.
    - **Price Wars:** Retailers are engaging in aggressive pricing strategies to capture market share, impacting profit margins.
    - **Brand Loyalty:** Building brand loyalty has become more challenging as consumers have access to numerous alternatives online.
3. **Customer Expectations:** With the rise of e-commerce, consumer expectations regarding service speed, convenience, and personalization have skyrocketed.
    - **Fast Delivery:** The demand for quick shipping options is pushing retailers to enhance their logistics capabilities and streamline operations.
    - **Customer Support:** Providing effective customer support across multiple channels is essential for maintaining customer satisfaction.
4. **Cybersecurity Risks:** As retailers expand their online presence, they become more susceptible to cyber threats.
    - **Data Breaches:** Protecting customer data is paramount; breaches can damage brand reputation and lead to legal repercussions.

- **Fraud Prevention:** Retailers must implement robust fraud prevention measures to safeguard transactions and protect customers.

Conclusion

The retail industry is evolving rapidly in response to the growth of e-commerce and changing consumer expectations. While the future holds significant opportunities for innovation and growth, challenges such as supply chain disruptions, increased competition, customer expectations, and cybersecurity risks must be addressed. Retailers that embrace digital transformation and focus on creating exceptional customer experiences will be better positioned to thrive in the competitive landscape of tomorrow.

These case studies illustrate how two different sectors healthcare and retail are adapting to future trends while facing distinct challenges. By understanding these dynamics, stakeholders can better navigate the complexities of their respective industries and leverage opportunities for growth and improvement.

SUMMARY OF FUTURE TRENDS AND CHALLENGES IN DATA ANALYTICS

1. Artificial Intelligence in Data Analytics

Artificial Intelligence (AI) enhances data analytics by automating complex tasks, uncovering patterns, and providing predictive insights. Techniques like machine learning, reinforcement learning, and generative adversarial networks (GANs) improve accuracy and efficiency, while AI-driven platforms democratize data access, enabling users across organizations to make informed, data-driven decisions.

Role of AI and Machine Learning in Analytics: Artificial Intelligence (AI) and Machine Learning (ML) have become integral to data analytics, enhancing the ability to process vast amounts of information and derive actionable insights. These technologies automate complex analytical tasks, enabling organizations to make data-driven decisions more quickly and accurately. AI algorithms can uncover hidden patterns in data, predict outcomes, and provide recommendations, significantly improving operational efficiency and strategic planning.

Emerging Techniques: Reinforcement Learning and GANs: As the field evolves, new techniques like Reinforcement Learning (RL) and Generative Adversarial Networks (GANs) are gaining prominence. RL focuses on training models through a system of rewards and penalties, making it particularly useful for decision-making processes in dynamic environments, such as real-time bidding in advertising or robotics. GANs, on the other hand, involve two neural networks contesting with each other, enabling the generation of new, synthetic data that closely resembles real data. This technique has vast applications in image generation, data augmentation, and even drug discovery.

AI-driven Analytics Platform

The rise of AI-driven analytics platforms is revolutionizing how organizations approach data analytics. These platforms integrate various AI capabilities, providing user-friendly interfaces for non-technical users to perform complex analyses. With natural language processing and intuitive dashboards, these tools democratize access to data insights, allowing organizations to harness the power of data analytics across all levels of the business.

2. Ethics and Responsible Data Analytics

Ethics in data analytics addresses privacy, bias, and transparency. Organizations must navigate ethical dilemmas by implementing guidelines that ensure responsible data use. This includes addressing algorithmic bias, ensuring fairness, and fostering accountability, ultimately building public trust and promoting ethical standards in data-driven decision-making and practices.

Ethical Dilemmas in Data Analytics

As data analytics continues to expand, ethical dilemmas surrounding data usage are becoming increasingly complex. Issues related to data privacy, consent, and transparency are paramount. Organizations must navigate the fine line between leveraging data for insights and respecting individual rights. The ethical use of data is not just a regulatory requirement but also a fundamental aspect of maintaining public trust.

Bias in Algorithms and Fairness Considerations

Bias in algorithms poses significant challenges for responsible data analytics. Machine learning models can inadvertently perpetuate existing biases present in training data, leading to unfair treatment of individuals or groups. Addressing these biases requires organizations to implement fairness considerations in model development, testing for biases, and ensuring diverse representation in training datasets. Continuous monitoring and auditing of algorithms are essential to mitigate these risks.

Developing Ethical Guidelines for Analytics

To foster responsible data analytics, the development of ethical guidelines is crucial. Organizations should establish clear policies regarding data collection, usage, and sharing practices. These guidelines should include principles such as accountability, transparency, and respect for privacy. Engaging stakeholders. such as data scientists, ethicists, and legal experts in the formulation of these guidelines can ensure a balanced approach to ethical considerations in data analytics.

3. Future of Data Analytics

The future of data analytics will be shaped by advancements in quantum computing and IoT, enabling real-time insights and complex problem-solving. Emerging trends include self-service analytics, enhanced data integration, and a focus on data literacy, equipping professionals with the skills needed to navigate a data-driven landscape.

Evolving Technologies - Quantum Computing and IoT

The future of data analytics will be significantly influenced by emerging technologies like Quantum Computing and the Internet of Things (IoT). Quantum computing promises to revolutionize data processing capabilities, enabling the analysis of vast datasets at unprecedented speeds. This technology can address complex problems that are currently intractable for classical computers, particularly in fields such as drug discovery and optimization.

IoT, on the other hand, will generate an enormous amount of real-time data from interconnected devices. This influx of data presents both opportunities and challenges for analytics, requiring robust frameworks for data integration, processing, and analysis. The synergy between IoT and advanced analytics can lead to enhanced decision-making in various sectors, from healthcare to smart cities.

Predicting Trends in Data Analytics

The landscape of data analytics is continually evolving, driven by technological advancements and shifting business needs. Key trends include the rise of self-service analytics tools, enabling non-technical users to explore and analyze data independently. Real-time analytics will become standard practice as organizations seek to make timely, data-driven decisions. Additionally, the integration of advanced analytics with traditional business intelligence tools will provide a more holistic approach to data analysis, combining descriptive, predictive, and prescriptive insights.

Preparing for the Future - Skills and Competencies

As the field of data analytics grows, so too does the need for a diverse skill set among professionals. Future competencies will encompass not only technical skills in AI and machine learning but also soft skills like critical thinking, communication, and collaboration. Data literacy will be essential for employees across all sectors, empowering them to engage with data meaningfully. Organizations must invest in training and development programs to cultivate these skills, ensuring their workforce is prepared to navigate the complexities of future data analytics landscapes.

Conclusion

The future of data analytics is characterized by rapid advancements in technology, increasing ethical considerations, and the evolving needs of businesses. Embracing AI and machine learning, addressing ethical dilemmas, and preparing for technological disruptions will be critical for organizations aiming to harness the power of data effectively. By focusing on responsible analytics practices and cultivating a skilled workforce, organizations can navigate the challenges and opportunities that lie ahead in the data-driven future.

About The Authors

Dr. Ramesh Kait is a distinguished academician and dedicated researcher, currently serving as an Assistant Professor in the Department of Computer Science and Applications at Kurukshetra University, Kurukshetra. Since joining the department in 2002, he has played a pivotal role in shaping the academic landscape through his unwavering commitment to teaching, research, and innovation.

With a profound passion for knowledge dissemination and scholarly inquiry, Dr. Kait has successfully guided numerous research scholars, fostering a culture of critical thinking and academic excellence. His prolific contributions to the field are reflected in the publication of over one hundred research papers in esteemed international journals. In addition, he has actively participated in more than fifty national and international conferences and seminars, sharing his insights and engaging with scholars worldwide.

An accomplished author, Dr. Kait has also contributed to academia through the publication of 8 books, earning recognition for his depth of knowledge and scholarly rigor. His enduring dedication continues to inspire students and researchers alike, marking him as a respected figure in the academic community.

Dr. Pooja Mittal, currently working as Associate Professor, Department of Computer Science & Applications, Maharshi Dayanand University (NAAC A+ State University), Haryana. She has approx. 23 years of total teaching experience. She did her Ph.D in Computer Science from Maharshi Dayanand University (NAAC A+ State University), Haryana under supervision of Prof. Nasib Singh Gill in 2017. She is SLET (Haryana) and TOEFL qualified. She did her MCA from IGNOU, B.Sc (Computer Science) from Kurukshetra University. Before joining the teaching domain, she had worked as Corporate Trainer with Tata Infotech Ltd. Convened various important committees like AICTE, Women Cell, Anti Ragging Squad and many more at University level. She has more than 65 research papers to her credits published in renowned SCI, SCIE, ESCI, SCOPUS and Web of Science indexed journals. More than 50 papers presented in different International and National Conferences/ Seminars/Webinars at different platforms. Also acting as reviewer in different reputed journals. She has authored chapters with renowned publishers and seven patents (published) to her credentials. She has guided four research scholars and currently guiding 02 research scholars working in Data Analytics, Smart Technology (IoT) and Machine Learning/ Deep Learning areas.

Dr. Supreet Thapar is a researcher and academic specializing in Artificial Intelligence and Machine Learning. She holds a Ph.D. in Computer Science, with research focused on recommender systems using machine learning. She also holds an M.Tech in Computer Science and Engineering and an MCA.

Dr. Thapar has published several research papers on machine learning and continues to explore innovative AI applications. Her motivation for writing this book stems from a desire to simplify complex AI concepts and bridge the gap between academic research and practical implementation, empowering readers to apply AI effectively in real-world contexts.